HTML

Your visual blueprint™ for designing Web pages with HTML, CSS, and XHTML

P9-DEE-081

by Paul Whitehead and James H. Russell

WILEY

Wiley Publishing, Inc.

HTML: Your visual blueprint™ for designing Web pages with HTML, CSS, and XHTML

Published by
Wiley Publishing, Inc.
111 River Street
Hoboken, NJ 07030-5774

Published simultaneously in Canada

Library of Congress Control Number: 2005921027

ISBN-13: 978-0-7645-8331-5

ISBN-10: 0-7645-8331-X

Manufactured in the United States of America

10 9 8 7 6 5 4 3 2 1

1K/SQ/QU/QV/IN

Trademark Acknowledgments

Contact Us

For general information on our other products and services please contact our Customer Care Department within the U.S. at 800-762-2974, outside the U.S. at 317-572-3993 or fax 317-572-4002.

For technical support please visit www.wiley.com/techsupport.

Ayasofya, or Hagia Sophia, Istanbul

In its various incarnations as a cathedral, a mosque, and finally a museum, this magnificent landmark has inspired awe for nearly 1500 years. Designed by preeminent sixth century architects Anthemius of Tralles and Isidorus of Miletus, this feat of engineering was completed in A.D. 537 under the Emperor Justinian. Wars, occupations, and earthquakes have altered its appearance through the centuries, but its mystique shines on as brightly as the thirty million tiny gold tiles gracing the dome's interior.

Learn more about this and other treasures of Istanbul in *Frommer's Turkey*, available wherever books are sold or at www.frommers.com.

WILEY

PRAISE FOR VISUAL BOOKS...

"This is absolutely the best computer-related book I have ever bought. Thank you so much for this fantastic text. Simply the best computer book series I have ever seen. I will look for, recommend, and purchase more of the same."

–David E. Prince (NeoNome.com)

"I have several of your Visual books and they are the best I have ever used."

–Stanley Clark (Crawfordville, FL)

"I just want to let you know that I really enjoy all your books. I'm a strong visual learner. You really know how to get people addicted to learning! I'm a very satisfied Visual customer. Keep up the excellent work!"

–Helen Lee (Calgary, Alberta, Canada)

"I have several books from the Visual series and have always found them to be valuable resources."

–Stephen P. Miller (Ballston Spa, NY)

"This book is PERFECT for me - it's highly visual and gets right to the point. What I like most about it is that each page presents a new task that you can try verbatim or, alternatively, take the ideas and build your own examples. Also, this book isn't bogged down with trying to 'tell all' – it gets right to the point. This is an EXCELLENT, EXCELLENT, EXCELLENT book and I look forward purchasing other books in the series."

–Tom Dierickx (Malta, IL)

"I have quite a few of your Visual books and have been very pleased with all of them. I love the way the lessons are presented!"

–Mary Jane Newman (Yorba Linda, CA)

"I am an avid fan of your Visual books. If I need to learn anything, I just buy one of your books and learn the topic in no time. Wonders! I have even trained my friends to give me Visual books as gifts."

–Illona Bergstrom (Aventura, FL)

"I just had to let you and your company know how great I think your books are. I just purchased my third Visual book (my first two are dog-eared now!) and, once again, your product has surpassed my expectations. The expertise, thought, and effort that go into each book are obvious, and I sincerely appreciate your efforts."

–Tracey Moore (Memphis, TN)

"Compliments to the chef!! Your books are extraordinary! Or, simply put, extra-ordinary, meaning way above the rest! THANK YOU THANK YOU THANK YOU! I buy them for friends, family, and colleagues."

–Christine J. Manfrin (Castle Rock, CO)

"I write to extend my thanks and appreciation for your books. They are clear, easy to follow, and straight to the point. Keep up the good work! I bought several of your books and they are just right! No regrets! I will always buy your books because they are the best."

–Seward Kollie (Dakar, Senegal)

"I am an avid purchaser and reader of the Visual series, and they are the greatest computer books I've seen. Thank you very much for the hard work, effort, and dedication that you put into this series."

–Alex Diaz (Las Vegas, NV)

Credits

Project Editor
Jade L. Williams

Acquisitions Editor
Jody Lefevere

Product Development Manager
Lindsay Sandman

Copy Editor
Scott Tullis

Technical Editor
Wendy V. Williams

Editorial Manager
Robyn Siesky

Permissions Editor
Laura Moss

Media Development Specialist
Angela Denny

Manufacturing
Allan Conley
Linda Cook
Paul Gilchrist
Jennifer Guynn

Production Coordinator
Maridee Ennis

Book Design
Kathryn Rickard

Layout
Sean Decker
Jennifer Heleine
Amanda Spagnuolo

Screen Artist
Jill A. Proll

Cover Illustration
David E. Gregory

Proofreader
Mildred Rosenzweig

Quality Control
Amanda Briggs
Susan Moritz
Brian H. Walls

Indexer
Richard T. Evans

Special Help
John Moss

**Vice President and Executive
Group Publisher**
Richard Swadley

Vice President and Publisher
Barry Pruett

Composition Director
Debbie Stailey

About the Authors

Paul Whitehead is a computer consultant specializing in I.T. support and administrative services for the medical and pharmaceutical industries. Based in Toronto, Canada, Paul is the author of many books.

James H. Russell became acquainted with the Internet in 1997 while he was a student at Indiana University in Indianapolis. He quickly became engulfed in the Internet, becoming editor in chief at Amiga.org and later a member of the Mozilla community, where he worked with Mozilla.org staff and contributors to rewrite the release notes and README file for the Mozilla .6 and 1.0 releases. James has also created and co-designed Web pages; most recently he co-designed www.indybahai.org for the Indianapolis Bahá'í community. He also maintains his own blog at http://weblogs.mozillazine.org/kovu/.

TABLE OF CONTENTS

HOW TO USE THIS BOOK XII

1 INTRODUCING HTML AND XHTML 2

Introduction to HTML 2
Introduction to XHTML..4
Introduction to Cascading Style Sheets (CSS) 6
Web Browsers 8
Creation Tools 9

2 USING WEB PAGE BASICS .10

Create and Save a Web Page 10
Display a Local Web Page in a Browser 12
Create a Paragraph 14
Insert New Lines and Spaces 16
Create a Heading 18
Add Comments to the Code 20
Add an Image to a Web Page 22
View Web Page Source Code 24
Publish Your Web Page 26
Organize Your Files 30
Save and Open a Web Page 32

3 FORMATTING AND ALIGNING TEXT 34

Make Text Bold and Italic 34
Adjust the Font Size 36
Use Preformatted Text 38
Use Quoted Text 40
Add Superscript and Subscript 42
Use Descriptive Tags 44
Change the Font Color and Type 46

4 LINKING WEB PAGES 48

Create a Link 48
Develop and Link to Anchors 50
Target Links 52
Set Tab Order for Links 54
Show Tooltips for Links 56

Use Mailto Links 58
Link to a File 60
Define Link Colors 62

5 WORKING WITH IMAGES 64

Display Images with Other Elements 64
Change the Image Size 66
Display Text Descriptions 68
Make Images into Links 70
Develop an Image Map 72
Preload Images 74

6 WORKING WITH STYLE SHEETS 76

Develop a Global Style Sheet 76
Construct a Rule 78
Use an Internal Style Sheet 80
Apply a Rule to a Single Element 82
Use a Class to Style Similar Elements 84
Insert Local Styles 86
Apply Styles to Web Page Sections 88
Apply Rules to Multiple Elements 90
Add Comments to Style Sheet 92
Insert Page Breaks for Printing 94
Apply Styles to Links 96
Add Alternative Style Sheets 98

7 APPLYING STYLE PROPERTIES 100

Apply Style Sheets to Fonts 100
Select a Typeface for Your Site Text 102
Set Font Size 104
Set Font and Background Color 106
Create Borders Around Your Text 108
Apply Italics and Bold Face 110
Insert White Space and Control Indent 112
Align Text to Fit Your Layout 114
Change the First Letter and Line of Text 116
Add a Background Image to Text 118

TABLE OF CONTENTS

8 SETTING PAGE LAYOUT 120

Position Elements Absolutely 120
Specify Width and Height of Elements 122
Position an Element Relatively 124
Overlap Elements 126
Adjust Padding and Margins 128
Float an Element 130
Show or Hide Elements 132
Change the Mouse Pointer 134
Draw an Outline 136
Work with Element Overflow 138
Use System Fonts and Colors 140

9 DISPLAYING TABULAR DATA IN TABLES AND LISTS 142

Create a Basic Table 142
Define the Table Border 144
Set Width and Height Properties 146
Create Cells Spanning Multiple Columns and Rows 148
Adjust Cell Properties 150
Combine Tables 152
Display a Bulleted List 154
Display a Numeric List 156
Nest a List 158
Create a Definition List 160

10 ADDING FORMS 162

Create a Form 162
Add a Text Box 164
Insert a Text Area 166
Build a Drop-Down Box 168
Hide Data in a Form 170
Include Check Boxes and Radio Buttons 172
Configure Submit and Reset Buttons 174
Allow File Uploads to Your Site 176

Arrange Tab Order 178
Disable and Lock Form Elements 180
Group Related Form Elements 182
Send Form Data Using E-mail 184

11 WORKING WITH FRAMES 186

Create a Frame-Based Web Page 186
Create Rows and Columns of Frames 188
Show or Hide Scroll Bars 190
Work with Frame Borders 192
Force the Frame Size 194
Target Links to a Frame 196
Use a Hidden Frame to Preload Images 198
Display a Message for Non-Frame-Enabled Browsers 200
Create a Floating Frame 202

12 PERFORMING BASIC HTML TASKS 204

Center Elements on a Web Page 204
Apply Background Color and Images 206
Align Elements 208
Lay Out a Web Page Using Tables 210
Insert Spacer Images 212
Add an XHTML Declaration 214
Verify Your XHTML Code 216
Enhance Site Promotion with HTML Tags 218

13 ADDING MULTIMEDIA TO YOUR PAGE 220

Add a Welcome Message 220
Embed a Background Sound 222
Include a Media Player in a Web Page 224
Add a QuickTime Video to a Web Page 226
Enable Users to Download a Media Player 228
Add a Flash Presentation 230
Create Moving Text 232
Stream Video Using RealPlayer 234

TABLE OF CONTENTS

14 WORKING WITH JAVASCRIPT 236

Add JavaScript to a Page 236
Get Up to Speed with JavaScript Basics 238
Utilize if Statements 240
Create for Loops 242
Use Event Handlers 244
Generate Dynamic Content 246
Display a Message 248
Create a Pop-Up Window 250

15 WORKING WITH XML 252

Create an XML Declaration 252
Add XML Elements 254
Verify an XML Document 256
View an XML Document 258
Apply a Style Sheet 260
Create and Validate Document Type Definitions 262

16 TESTING AND VALIDATING WEB PAGES 266

Watch for Common HTML Mistakes 266
Check for Common XHTML Mistakes 268
Look at Common CSS Problems 270
Avoid Common Design Mistakes 272
Check for Image Problems 274
Search for Linking Problems 276
Consider Browser Differences 278
Employ Debugging Resources 280

APPENDIX A HTML SUMMARY 282

HTML Tag Summary 282
Core HTML Attributes 291
HTML Colors 292
Event Handlers 293

APPENDIX B CASCADING STYLE SHEETS
SUMMARY 294

Cascading Style Sheets Property Summary 294

INDEX 298

HOW TO USE THIS BOOK

HTML: Your visual blueprint™ for designing Web pages with HTML, CSS, and XHTML uses clear, descriptive examples to show you how to create powerful, dynamic Web pages. HTML is the official language for creating multimedia documents for publishing on the World Wide Web.

To get the most out of this book, you should read each chapter in order, from beginning to end. Each chapter introduces new ideas and builds on the knowledge learned in previous chapters. When you become familiar with *HTML*, you can use this book as an informative desktop reference.

Who Needs This Book

This book is for the beginner programmer who wants to find out more about creating effective Web pages with HTML. No prior experience with programming Web designing is required.

Book Organization

HTML: Your visual blueprint™ for designing Web pages with HTML, CSS, and XHTML has 16 chapters and 2 appendixes.

Chapter 1, "Introducing HTML and XHTML," gives you a brief introduction to HTML, XHTML, style sheets, and some tools you will need to get up and running.

Chapter 2, "Using Web Page Basics," demonstrates how to create and publishing a basic Web page using HTML.

Chapter 3, "Formatting and Aligning Text," shows how to make your Web page stand out by adjusting the font size, applying color, and more.

Chapter 4, "Linking Web Pages," provides instruction on creating, anchoring, and formatting hyperlinks.

Chapter 5, "Working with Images," walks you through the steps of adding multiple images, creating image links, and adding animation to your Web page.

Chapter 6, "Working with Style Sheets," demonstrates developing style sheets, inserting styles, and applying rules, using class within a style sheet, and more.

Chapter 7, "Applying Style Properties," walks you through working with fonts, size, spacing, and color.

Chapter 8, "Setting Page Layout," enables you to use your computer to position and adjust elements for a vibrant look.

Chapter 9, "Displaying Tabular Data in Tables and Lists," shows you how to present information in tables, rows, columns, and list to catch the readers' attention.

Chapter 10, "Adding Forms," directs you on making your Web page interactive by adding menus, list boxes, interactive forms, and buttons.

Chapters 11, "Working with Frames," walks you through the steps of placing your content and images in frame-based web pages for impact.

Chapter 12, "Performing Basic HTML Tasks," demonstrates some of the key steps you will need to enhance your Web site.

Chapter 13, "Adding Multimedia to Your Page," assist you in adding audio and visual messages through presentations and other means.

Chapter 14, "Working with JavaScript," shows you how to add dynamic content o your Web page using JavaScript statements, loops, handlers, and added features.

Chapter 15, "Working with XML" enables you to store data in your Web page.

Chapter 16, "Testing and Validating Web Pages," gives you the tools you need to troubleshoot your Web page by looking for mistakes.

Appendixes A lists brief summary of HTML element tags, attributes, and handlers.

Appendix B lists a brief summary of Cascading Style Sheets Properties.

What You Need to Use This Book

To perform tasks in t his book, you need a computer with a text editor, for example Notepad, and a Web browser, such as Microsoft Internet Explorer or Netscape.

The Conventions in This Book

A number of styles have been used throughout *HTML: Your visual blueprint™ for designing Web pages with HTML, CSS, and XHTML* to designate different types of information.

Courier Font

Indicates the use of code such as tags or attributes, scripting language code such as statements, operators, or functions, and code such as objects, methods, or properties.

Bold

Indicates information that you must type.

Italics

Indicates a new term.

Apply It

An Apply It section takes the code from the preceding task one step further. Apply It sections allow you to take full advantage of the code examples.

Extra

An Extra section provides additional information about the preceding task. Extra sections contain the inside information to make working with HTML easier and more efficient.

What Is on the Web Site

The accompanying Web site contains the sample files for each of the two-page lessons. This code saves you from having to type the code by helping you get started quickly creating your Web pages with HTML.

Moving Forward

Visual blueprint books are modular. The modular format results in a more active, living text that a reader can refer to again and again.

You can read this Visual book from cover to cover. On the other hand, you can look over the table of contents and find a task or topic that interests you, go directly to the task spread you need, and learn how to perform the task by walking through a set of illustrated steps. Either way you choose to use this Visual book, it is made to suit you.

If related information occurs elsewhere in the book, you will find a cross-reference in the text or task steps, directing you to the appropriate section. Alternatively, if you are faced with a problem or have a concern, you can look in the Index or Table of Contents of the Visual book and then turn to the section to learn more. You will have the answer and be back on track designing your Web site in short order.

Chapters 1 and 16 give you good information about Web programming in general whereas all the chapters in between give you the specifics of how to design your pages. The appendixes give you some useful specific syntax that you can use with your Web pages. So, if you are ready to start designing Web pages, turn the page and get started!

Introduction to HTML

Hypertext Markup Language, or HTML, is a markup language that enables you to structure and display content such as text, images, and links in Web pages. HTML is a very fast and efficient method of describing and formatting information that can be easily exchanged with other people. Because HTML was created to be a human-readable programming language, it is relatively easy to learn and does not require any special applications to create: you can design HTML pages in simple text editors, such as Notepad in Windows.

Web Servers and Clients

The World Wide Web consists of computers called Web servers that store Web pages, making them available to other Web servers as well as Web clients. *Web client* is a term used to describe an application, such as a Web browser, that is capable of viewing Web pages. The Web pages are made of plain-text files that contain HTML code and links to other content, such as images, music, and movies. Web pages are stored (or *hosted*) on Web servers. When a user enters the address of a page into his or her browser, the HTML file stored at that address transfers the content of the Web page over the Internet to the user's computer. The user's Web browser processes the HTML code and displays the Web page according to instructions found within the HTML code.

Standards

Although HTML was initially created by a few select organizations, the increasing popularity of the World Wide Web and HTML made it necessary to create an additional organization to ensure that HTML was written according to a standard; this would make HTML easier to implement, and help guarantee that a Web page would look much the same in all Web browsers. The World Wide Web Consortium (referred to as the *W3C* for short) is the organization that today oversees the development and standards of many Web-related technologies, including HTML: essentially the W3C decides what code will comprise the HTML specification. You can find more information about the W3C, and HTML, at the World Wide Web Consortium's Web site at www.w3c.com.

Elements

Web pages created using HTML consist of elements. Elements are the content items such as text, images, and movies that make up a Web page. The job of HTML is to tell Web browsers how to display these elements to the user. Text headings, a table containing lists of information, and an image banner are all examples of elements. Elements can contain other elements; for example, a table may contain elements such as text headings or images.

HTML Tags

HTML tags create the elements that comprise a Web page. For example, the `<p>` tag denotes text as a paragraph and the `<img>` tag indicates an image. Most HTML tags consist of two parts: an opening tag and a closing tag. You create both opening and closing tags in the same way: Each tag starts with the symbol for less than (`<`) and ends with the symbol for greater than (`>`). The name of the tag goes between the two brackets. In the closing tag, you precede the name of the tag with a forward slash (`/`). To create an HTML tag, then, you simply place the name of the tag in both the start and the end

tag, and then specify the content of the element between the tags. For example, the name of the paragraph tag is simply `p`. Therefore, the opening tag of the paragraph tag is `<p>` and the closing tag is `</p>`. The text that will comprise the paragraph must be placed within the opening and starting HTML tags, as in `<p>This is some text</p>`. Some HTML tags do not require a closing tag. For example, the horizontal rule tag `<hr>` does not require a closing tag because it does not enclose any information: it simply generates a horizontal line on the Web page.

Tag Attributes

You can enhance HTML tags with the use of attributes. Attributes define additional parameters and characteristics for the HTML element. Although an HTML tag can create a paragraph of text, you can add attributes to the paragraph tag instructing the Web browser how to display that text. For example, an attribute can indicate how to align the text within that paragraph. Apart from straightforward characteristics such as setting the alignment and the color of an element, you can also use attributes to apply programming code such as

JavaScript, or formatting information using Cascading Style Sheets, to the element. Insert attributes into the opening tag of the element; the attribute name is followed by the equal sign (`=`) and then the value of the attribute, which is enclosed in quotation marks. For example, to instruct the browser to center a paragraph on a Web page, add the `align` attribute with the value `center` to the `<p>` tag, as in `<p align="center">`. You do not need to make any other changes to the content of the element or the closing tag.

The Future of HTML

The latest version of HTML (HTML 4.01) is also the last version of the language. XHTML and Cascading Style Sheets (CSS) are intended to replace HTML. XHTML and CSS separate Web page content from any formatting instructions, making that content easier to manage. Although HTML contains code that describes and formats information, XHTML describes the structure of the content, and Cascading Style Sheets formats the information.

This creates smaller XHTML documents that are easier for people to read, and faster for clients such as Web browsers to load and interpret (or parse). Although HTML will be replaced eventually by XHTML and CSS, HTML is still available and likely to remain on the World Wide Web for many years to come.

Introduction to XHTML

Extensible Hypertext Markup Language, or XHTML, is similar to HTML. If you know how to create Web pages using HTML, then you already know most of what you need to know about creating Web pages using XHTML. Although HTML can define both the structure and the appearance of a Web page, XHTML defines the structure of a Web page while relying on other technologies, such as Cascading Style Sheets (CSS), to specify the formatting information. XHTML is a markup language like HTML, but was made to conform to the XML standard.

XML

Extensible Markup Language, or XML, is a markup language that, like HTML, is used to create documents. Many applications and devices use the XML standard to exchange information, and sometimes between quite dissimilar objects — such as a database application and an application running on a mobile phone. XML is a widely used industry standard. XHTML was an attempt to create a language for constructing Web pages that conforms to the standards and principles of XML. You can think of XHTML as an attempt to rewrite the HTML language using XML.

Differences Between HTML and XHTML

There are a number of differences between HTML and XHTML, the most notable being that, unlike HTML, XHTML requires all tags to have a closing tag. Although most HTML tags have a closing tag, some do not, such as the break tag `<br>`. In XHTML these tags must have a closing tag. If the tag does not enclose any content, such as the `<br>` tag, you can add a forward slash (/) preceded by a space to the opening tag instead of using two tags, as in `<br />`. The tag `<br />` is the correct XHTML version of the HTML `<br>` tag. Although a number of major differences exist between HTML and XHTML, somebody learning XHTML who is already familiar with HTML would immediately notice only a small number of differences. One example is that all tag names are lowercase in XHTML. So, the HTML tag `<BODY>` is only valid in XHTML as `<body>`. All attribute names in XHTML must also be lowercase, and all of the values within tags must be enclosed in quotation marks.

XHTML Standards

Although XHTML is a single language, it consists of two major standards: XHTML Strict and XHTML Transitional. XHTML Strict is just that: it requires XHTML code to strictly follow the rules of the XML standard. XHTML Transitional is not as strict as XHTML Strict; XHTML Transitional was deliberately made to be less strict to help bridge the gap between the loose, more forgiving HTML standard of yesterday and the stricter, less forgiving XHTML standard of today. XHTML Transitional was made to be just that — transitory — so it is not a good idea to standardize on XHTML Transitional. XHTML Transitional is more like a short-term solution for quickly re-creating existing HTML pages in XHTML until an XHTML Strict version can be made.

Benefits of XHTML

XHTML allows developers who are specialized in creating content to focus solely on what they are good at: creating and compiling content. By using another technology, such as Cascading Style Sheets (CSS), to format the information, experts such as graphic designers and layout artists can focus solely on the appearance of information without getting bogged down in the content and meaning of the information. Separating information from its formatting also allows that information to be more easily accessed on dissimilar devices such as handheld computers, mobile phones, and television set top boxes. For example, you can create a Web page containing a company directory of personnel, and display the same Web page on a computer monitor, a handheld computer, or mobile phone, completely formatted for printing, without having to create multiple Web pages. Although the formatting instructions for the computers and the printer would be different, the underlying information would remain the same.

XHTML is far stricter in its syntax that HTML, which leads to less errors in your code and makes your Web pages accessible to different Web browsers and other Web-based tools, such as search engines. This strictness is necessary to standardize Web pages across the Internet, but it can result in a learning curve for people used to the more forgiving HTML standard.

XHTML retains the best ideas and features of HTML, but has been created so that XHTML can be improved in the future with minimal impact on existing Web pages. Unlike HTML, XHTML is extensible, meaning that it can easily be added to, and that changes to XHTML will not have to wait for Web browser manufacturers to implement the new features of XHTML before the benefits of these features are realized.

Disadvantages of XHTML

Because XHTML is stricter than HTML and requires the use of other technologies such as Cascading Style Sheets (CSS) to create Web pages, creating Web pages using XHTML will initially take more time. XHTML is also less forgiving than HTML when a Web page's code contains errors.

Many of today's Web developers use specialized tools to create Web pages. Any of the tools that are more than a couple of years old may not be able to create valid XHTML Web pages without upgrading or replacing the software.

Because XHTML uses CSS to format Web page elements, users must also learn how to implement CSS if they want their Web pages to resemble those created with just HTML.

When to Use XHTML

Generally, if you are creating Web pages that will exist on the Internet for a long period, you should use XHTML to ensure that your Web pages will be compatible with Web browsers of the future. If you are simply creating a list of this week's

fixtures for your local sporting club's Web page and do not need the information to be accessible for very long, you can safely use HTML instead of XHTML to structure and format your Web page.

Introduction to Cascading Style Sheets (CSS)

Cascading Style Sheets, or CSS, is a markup language used to specify instructions for displaying XHTML and HTML elements. Unlike HTML and XHTML, CSS is used exclusively for the formatting and display of information. Page background colors, font colors, and colors of hyperlinks on a Web page are the kinds of formatting that CSS controls. For example, you can use CSS to change the color of a paragraph of text and to describe where on the Web page that text is to be placed.

Style Sheet Properties

Style sheets are comprised of style sheet *rules* that apply to the elements of a Web page. Each style sheet rule consists of a *selector* and a *declaration block*. The selector indicates to which part of the Web page the style sheet will apply. For example, if the selector name in the style sheet rules is p, the style sheet rule will apply to all <p> tags found within the Web page. The declaration block consists of one or more *declarations* enclosed in curly brackets ({}). The declaration consists of a style sheet *property* and its value. A colon (:) separates the style sheet property name and the value of the style sheet property. Semicolons (;) separate declarations from each other. You must become familiar with only a few essential properties to effectively use style sheets. For example, the color property defines the color of an element. A simple style sheet rule that defines the color property of a paragraph of text is p {color: blue}.

Internal, External, and Local Style Sheets

There are a number of places where you can define the style sheets for your Web pages. The code for *internal* (or *embedded*) style sheets is stored within the code of the Web page that uses the style sheet. The Web browser does not display the style sheet itself; it applies the style sheet information to any elements within the Web page that have been instructed to use that information. *External* style sheets are style sheets that are saved in a file separate from the Web page code. The Web browser processes the Web page code first, sees from instructions in the Web page code that it needs to access the external style sheet file, and then retrieves and processes the information in the style sheet file. The major benefit of external style sheets is that you can use a single external style sheet to format multiple pages on your Web site. *Local* (or *inline*) style sheets consist of style sheet code that is applied to single elements within a Web page. Local style code is actually embedded within the individual tags of the Web page elements to which they apply.

Cascading Style Sheets

Because there are multiple ways of applying style sheet information to an element, a single element within a Web page can use style sheet information from external, internal, and local style sheets. If all of the style sheet properties being applied are different, then all the style sheet properties will be *cascaded* into one set of style sheet instructions and applied to the single element. This allows the Web developer great flexibility when creating style sheets for Web pages that have many different formatting requirements. For example, if a certain paragraph on a Web page sees a conflicting rule in external, internal, and local style sheets, the three style sheets are applied in a cascading fashion — one after the other. The local style sheet, which is applied last, prevails over the external and internal style sheets and determines the formatting of the element in question. So, if an external style sheet specifies that text on the Web page should be black, an internal style sheet specifies that text should be dark blue, and the local style sheet specifies that text should be white, the text will be white. This cascading effectively enables you to set one global style sheet for the entire Web page and then specify individual exceptions to this rule using internal or local style sheets.

Advantages of CSS

There are many benefits to using CSS to format the information on your Web pages. Style sheets give you enormous control over the appearance of information on your Web pages. You can use style sheets to precisely position elements on a Web page and to apply characteristics such as borders, colors, and backgrounds to individual elements. Using CSS to format the information on your Web pages can save you a large amount of work. You can create one style sheet that will determine the type of formatting used on all the Web pages in a Web site. For

example, if you have a Web site that contains hundreds or even thousands of Web pages, you can use a single style sheet to define the background color of all those Web pages instead of coding those formatting instructions into each individual page. Using a single CSS file also saves time when you want to make changes to Web pages that use the CSS file; for example, by changing a few lines of code within a single external style sheet, you can change the background color of all Web pages that use that style sheet.

Disadvantages of CSS

There are some disadvantages to CSS. When using style sheets, you have to be more organized and keep up-to-date information about your Web site. Because style sheets often involve the creation of separate files, you must be more careful when modifying, adding, or removing files from your Web server. You must also keep track of what styles are applied to which Web pages so that you do not inadvertently create style sheet rules that conflict, which can result in Web pages that do not appear as intended. Using external style sheets requires a Web browser to download an additional file from the Web server before a Web page displays, which can add precious seconds to loading times. Using local style sheet rules, while

quick and easy to implement, are more difficult to maintain, particularly if you have a large number of them. Many older Web browsers do not support CSS; and even if they do, they often support only a portion of the available CSS properties, which can lead to inconsistent results when your Web pages are viewed on these older browsers.

The benefits of using style sheets far outweigh the disadvantages. If you are contemplating creating a large amount of Web pages or intend to create Web pages in the future, you should take the time to learn the benefits that style sheets offer in creating Web pages.

Web Browsers

Web browsers are applications that display Web pages you create with HTML, XHTML, and CSS. Many different browsers are available, and most are free of charge. Almost all PC operating systems include a Web browser by default, and most people use the browser that came with their PC.

Compatibility

One of the major reasons to create standards for HTML, XHTML, and CSS is so that different Web browsers will display Web pages in the same way. As long as a Web browser can identify and render a Web page using the version of HTML, XHTML, and CSS that the Web page utilizes, the Web page will display to the user as the page's author intended.

Current Standards

XHTML, XHTML, and CSS use numbering schemes to identify their versions to Web browsers. Although new versions of these technologies will be available in the future as the technologies are improved and enhanced, any Web pages created with these versions should be compatible with current Web browsers.

Major Web Browsers

Starting with Netscape Navigator in the early- to mid-1990s, many Web browsers have come and gone. Today, only a few browsers remain viable. This section names and briefly discusses three of the more popular browsers.

Firefox

Firefox is a new, free Web browser that was designed to be fast, secure, and simple to use. Firefox includes powerful features such as tabbed browsing, multiple home pages, and an integrated search feature that lets you search major Web search engines such as Google, Amazon.com, and eBay. You can download Firefox from www.getfirefox.com.

Internet Explorer

Because of the popularity of the Microsoft Windows operating system, it should be no surprise that the most popular Web browser is currently Microsoft's Internet Explorer. Although IE is included with Windows, you can also download it from www.microsoft.com/ie.

Netscape Navigator

Netscape Navigator was one of the first commercial Web browsers available. Earlier versions of Netscape (versions 4 and prior), though still used by some people, do not support many modern Web standards. It is therefore a good idea to test all Web pages you design in both newer versions of Netscape (such as Netscape 7.2) and older versions (such as Netscape Communicator 4.8). Netscape is available free at www.netscape.com.

Versions

A few years ago, Web browser manufacturers would introduce new versions of their browsers on a frequent basis. Because of the standardization in HTML, XHTML, and CSS, Web browsers today typically offer a major upgrade once every year or two. You should always make sure that your Web pages are viewable with the most popular Web browsers at the current time.

Enhancements

In the early days of the Web, browser manufacturers would introduce enhancements to their Web browsers that only applied to Web pages viewed with that manufacturer's browser. This practice made writing Web pages difficult because designers had to figure out how to handle users who did not have the browser for which a certain Web site was optimized. In many cases, the users would receive a message saying the site was not supported by their browser. This was more of a concern in the past, before the standardization of HTML, XHTML, and CSS. This should not happen in the future, as most Web browser manufacturers now support most of the latest Web standards.

Creation Tools

Before you can create Web pages using HTML, XHTML, and CSS, you will need some sort of creation tools. Because these Web-based technologies store their information in plain-text files, it is possible to create Web pages and many related files with a simple text editor. Most of the coding examples in this book were created with a simple text editor that comes with the operating system. If you will be creating complex Web pages or need to create and maintain a large amount of Web pages, you may want to consider using an application made specifically for creating Web pages and style sheets. Using dedicated creation tools will reduce the amount of errors in your code and speed up the time required to create Web pages. Most Web page creation tools include not just the features required to create Web pages, but also other features such as spell checkers, file transfer utilities, and code formatting features that make it easier to maintain, manage, and deploy Web pages.

Types of Creation Tools

Text Editors

There are many different types of text editors available, ranging in features from the very sophisticated to the very simple. Almost all operating systems include their own text editor that you can use to create Web pages (Windows comes with Notepad, for example). Many experienced Web development professionals use text editors to create some or all of their Web pages. Most Web servers also have text editors available, enabling you to quickly update your Web pages from where they reside on the server.

HTML Editors

HTML editors make it easier for you to create Web pages using HTML and XHTML. Standard features include quick insertion of popular tags, automatic checking that you are using the appropriate tags, and utilities that format your code with spaces and indents for easier readability. If you intend to create a large number of Web pages, you should consider using an HTML editor.

WYSIWYG Editors

WYSIWYG is an abbreviation for "what you see is what you get." WYSIWYG editors are Web page creation tools that enable you to create Web pages without having to learn any of the underlying language (such as HTML). Information is placed on a Web page in the same manner that you would place information in a word processing document. You can type text and paste images right into the Web page; the application will then generate the required HTML, XHTML, and style sheet code. WYSIWYG editors are quite suitable for users who do not want to learn HTML, XHTML, and CSS coding and only need to create a small number of Web pages.

Creation Tools

1st Page 2000

1st Page 2000 is a professional HTML editing application that works just as well for people learning to create Web pages as it does for experienced professionals. It is available on the World Wide Web at www.eversoft.com.

HomeSite

HomeSite is a comprehensive HTML, XHTML, and style sheet editor available from Macromedia. HomeSite has been widely used by Web development professionals for many years. More information about HomeSite is available on the World Wide Web at www.macromedia.com.

TopStyle

TopStyle is a robust Web page editor that excels in the creation and maintenance of style sheets. You can use TopStyle by itself to create Web pages, or integrate it with your other Web page development applications to create and maintain style sheets. For more information about TopStyle, visit www.bradsoft.com.

UltraEdit

UltraEdit is a superb text editor used by many Web developers who prefer working with raw HTML, XHTML, and style sheet code. Although it is a text editor, UltraEdit includes many features that make working with Web pages easier. For more information about UltraEdit, visit www.ultraedit.com.

Create and Save a Web Page

You create a Web page using HTML code before viewing the Web page in a Web browser. A text editor is used to create HTML code. Most operating systems include a simple text editor that can create Web pages. The Microsoft Windows operating system includes the text editor Notepad that can create Web pages.

Web pages consist of HTML code. Each element of a Web page is enclosed in tags. A tag consists of a start and end tag. The start tag is the name of the tag enclosed by a less than symbol and the greater than symbol. For example, the body start tag is specified using `<body>`. The end tag is similar to the start tag, except that the text in the end tag is preceded by a forward slash as in `</body>`.

A simple Web page consists of an `<html>` tag, a `<body>` tag, and some text that will be displayed by the Web browser. The `<body>` tag encloses the text of the Web page, and the `<html>` tag encloses all elements of the Web page.

A document created within the text editor must be saved before the Web browser can display it. You can save Web pages that you create to your hard drive and then view them in your Web browser. You do not need to be connected to the Internet in order to view Web pages that are stored on your own computer.

You must save the document with a file extension that Web browsers recognize as a Web page. Web browsers interpret documents that use the .html file extension as Web pages.

Create a Web Page

① Click Start.

② Click All Programs.

③ Click Accessories.

④ Click Notepad.

The Notepad text editor starts.

⑤ Type the **<html>** tag.

⑥ Type the **<body>** tag.

⑦ Type the text you want to display in the Web page.

⑧ Type **</body></html>**.

1 Click File.

2 Click Save As.

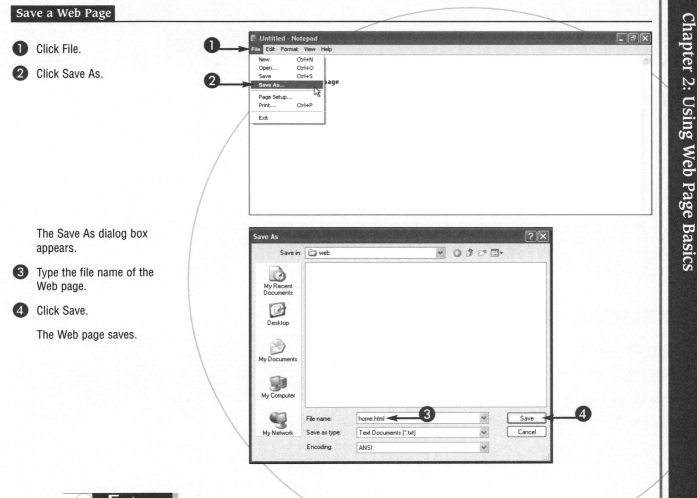

The Save As dialog box appears.

3 Type the file name of the Web page.

4 Click Save.

The Web page saves.

Extra

Web browsers typically interpret any files that have a .html extension as a Web page and display them correctly; therefore, you can create a Web page without using the <html> and <body> tags. Even so, it is not considered proper form to create Web pages without them and including all the required tags will ensure that the Web page remains compatible with future Web browsers.

Web page documents must be saved with a file extension that is recognized by a Web browser to enable the browser to identify the document as a Web page. Most Web browsers recognize any Web page that uses the .html or .htm file extension. Your Web server administrator can tell you which file extensions you can use for your Web pages.

To display your Web pages on the World Wide Web where others can view your Web pages, you must publish your Web pages from your PC to a Web server so that they are publicly accessible. Your users' Web browsers will access your Web page from this server. For more information about publishing Web pages, see the section "Publish Your Web Page" in this chapter.

Display a Local
Web Page in a Browser

When displaying Web pages you used HTML or XHTML to create, the Web browser examines the contents of the HTML file and displays the contents of the Web page as directed by the HTML tags in the Web page. The HTML tags used in the creation of the Web page do not display.

Although Web browsers are used primarily to view Web pages over the World Wide Web, Web browsers can also be used to view Web pages that are stored locally on your computer. This is a good method for making sure your Web page displays properly before you post it to a Web server. It is always prudent to ensure that your Web page is working properly before you make it available over the Web.

The Web browser that you use depends on which Web browser is installed on your computer. Most operating systems have a Web browser included with the operating system. Computers that use the Microsoft Windows operating system almost always have Microsoft Internet Explorer installed as the default Web browser.

Web pages that are stored on your computer display faster than those on the World Wide Web; the Web browser does not have to transfer any information from the Internet to your computer prior to displaying the Web page.

You can view your Web pages with many different types of Web browsers. Each Web browser may display the same Web page in a slightly different way. Most Web developers test their Web pages in several browsers to ensure that the pages appear as intended in different Web browsers.

Display a Local Web Page in a Browser

① Click Start.

② Click All Programs.

③ Click Internet Explorer.

The Web browser starts.

④ Click File.

⑤ Click Open.

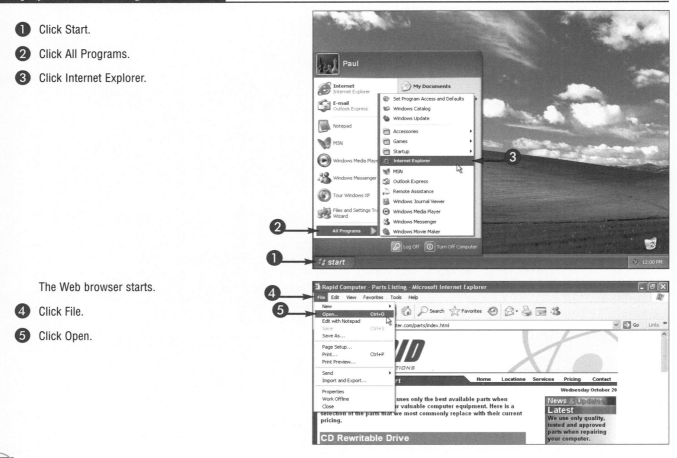

The Open dialog box appears.

6 Type the name and location of your Web page.

7 Click OK.

● The Web browser displays your Web page.

Open

Type the Internet address of a document or folder, and Internet Explorer will open it for you.

Open: C:\web\home.html

☐ Open as Web Folder

OK   Cancel   Browse...

C:\web\home.html - Microsoft Internet Explorer

File Edit View Favorites Tools Help

Back   Search Favorites

Address C:\web\home.html   Go Links »

Welcome to my Web page

Extra

If you do not know the precise location or name of your Web page, you can browse your computer's storage locations to attempt to locate the Web page. When the Open dialog box appears, click Browse. A dialog box appears allowing you to browse to the Web page on your computer. When you locate the file, click the Web page file name, click Open, and then click OK.

Web pages can be stored on media other than your computer hard drive. For example, Web pages can be stored on (and displayed using a Web browser from) floppy disk, USB storage drives, network locations, or compact discs. Even if you use your PC hard drive as your main storage location, it is a good idea to back up the files for your Web page to one of these other media.

If you do not know where you saved your Web page, you can use the search function of your operating system to locate the Web page. If you are using the Microsoft Windows XP operating system, click Start and select Search. Select Documents in the task pane, type the name of your Web page, and then click Search.

Create a Paragraph

A Web browser displays unformatted text as one large paragraph, ignoring any blank lines contained in the text. This causes the separate paragraphs within the HTML code to run together when viewed in the Web browser, making reading large amounts of text on a Web page very difficult. Most Web surfers will not bother to try to read unformatted text and will simply leave your page and read one that is properly formatted.

You cannot use multiple spaces to divide sections of HTML code, as Web browsers reduce all multiple spaces to one space when displaying the page. For example, if you separate two sentences using two or more lines of spaces, the Web browser displays only one space between the sentences when displaying the Web page.

Text on a Web page can be divided into separate paragraphs for easier reading, or simply for aesthetic reasons. Using paragraphs helps to format text in an easily readable format regardless of the font size of the text, the computer's screen resolution, or the size of your display. You will want all of your Web page's visible text to be formatted so that visitors to your Web site can easily read the text on your page.

To achieve properly formatted paragraphs you use the <p> and </p> tags to format your paragraph text. The <p> tag consists of a start tag <p>, which you insert before a given paragraph, and the end tag </p>, which you insert after the text of the same paragraph. Any text enclosed by the start and end tags is preceded and followed by a blank line. The <p> tag also inserts some additional space before the start of the paragraph.

The following task walks you through creating one or more paragraphs of text and formatting them for proper viewing on a Web page.

Create a Paragraph

① Open or create a Web page in a text editor.

② Type the text of the Web page.

③ Type **<p>** before the text of your paragraph.

④ Type **</p>** after the text of your paragraph.

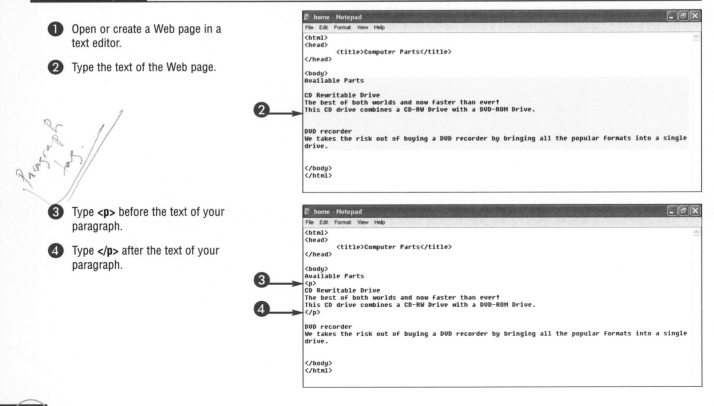

5 Repeat steps **3** to **4** to set off each paragraph of text in the Web page.

6 Save your Web page.

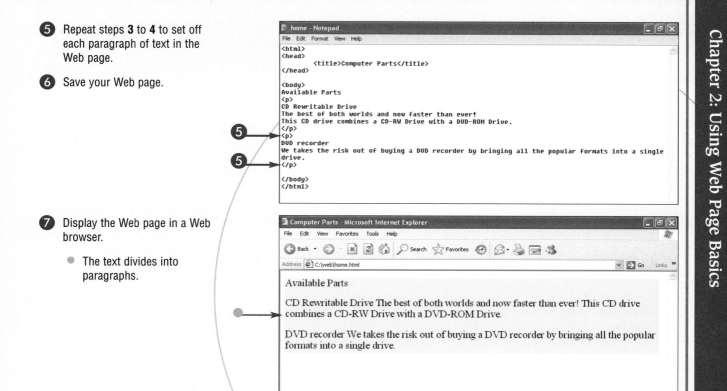

7 Display the Web page in a Web browser.

● The text divides into paragraphs.

Extra

The <p> tag is a *block-level element*. A block-level element creates a separate area on a Web page that can contain multiple elements such as text and images. For example, the information contained within the start and end <p> tags can include tags such as <img> within them to include an image with a text caption with your paragraph.

HTML specifications before XHTML allowed the use of presentation attributes (such as <font> tags, for example) with the <p> tag to assist in laying out a Web page. To ensure that your code is truly XHTML compliant, you should use style sheets instead of presentation attributes in your page's code. For more information about style sheets, see Chapter 6.

Many browsers correctly display paragraphs that include the start <p> tag but not the end tag, as in

```
<p>Paragraph One
<p>Paragraph Two
```

While omitting the end tag works in most browsers, to ensure compatibility with future Web browsers and to comply with XHTML standards you should include the ending </p> tag.

Insert New Lines and Spaces

You can insert new lines and spaces into your HTML code to make your Web pages look more appealing to look at. Lines and spaces can also help separate distinct sections of information on your Web pages, making it easier for the reader to quickly find the information they are looking for.

The following task shows you how to add blank spaces and new lines into your Web page to help format it for easier, more intuitive reading. You can do this by using the `<br>` tag for new lines and ` ` for new spaces.

Use the `<br>` tag to insert a blank line into your Web page. A blank line is inserted anywhere you put the `<br>` tag in your HTML code. When processing the code, a Web browser moves any text following a `<br>` tag down one line, aligning the paragraph to the left side of the Web page. In HTML the

`<br>` tag has no end tag, and it is still very common to see Web developers using the `<br>` tag this way. Although most Web browsers render the `<br>` tag correctly, you can always use the full `<br />` tag to ensure compliance with the XHTML standard, and to ensure that your Web pages will be compatible with Web browsers in the future.

When you include multiple spaces in the text of the Web page, the Web browser combines all the spaces into one single space. This makes it impossible to use regular spaces to indent or align the information on your Web page. To force a Web browser to insert a space where you want, you must use the characters ` ` instead of a space. The ` ` characters are referred to as a *nonbreaking space*. You can insert as many nonbreaking spaces into your Web page as needed.

Insert New Lines and Spaces

1 Open or create an XHTML Web page in a text editor.

2 Type **
**.

```
parts - Notepad
File  Edit  Format  View  Help
<html>
<head>
        <title>Computer Parts</title>
</head>

<body>
<p>
CD Rewritable Drive:<br>          2
The best of both worlds and now faster than ever!
This CD drive combines a CD-RW Drive with a DVD-ROM Drive.
</p>

<p>
DVD recorder:
We takes the risk out of buying a DVD recorder by including all the popular
formats into a single drive.  This drive comes with an impressive, industry
standard software bundle.
</p>

</body>
</html>
```

3 Type ** **.

4 Repeat step **3** for each space.

```
parts - Notepad
File  Edit  Format  View  Help
<html>
<head>
        <title>Computer Parts</title>
</head>               4

<body>
<p>
CD Rewritable Drive:<br>
   The best of both worlds and now faster than ever!
This CD drive combines a CD-RW Drive with a DVD-ROM Drive.
</p>

<p>
DVD recorder:
We takes the risk out of buying a DVD recorder by including all the popular
formats into a single drive.  This drive comes with an impressive, industry
standard software bundle.
</p>

</body>
</html>
```

5 Repeat steps **2** to **4** for each new line or group of spaces you want to add.

6 Save your Web page.

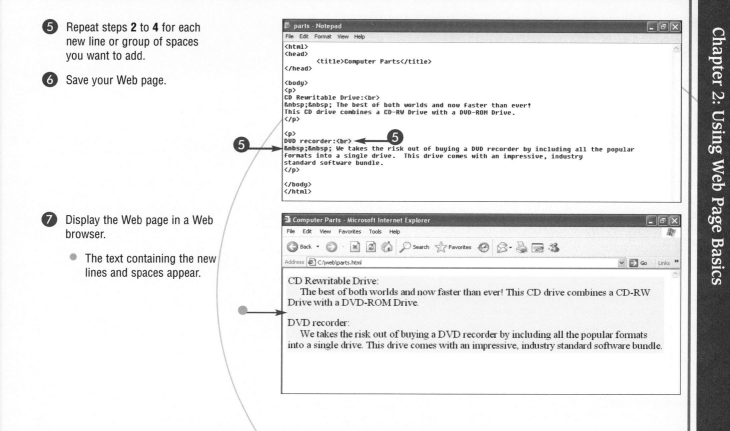

7 Display the Web page in a Web browser.

- The text containing the new lines and spaces appear.

Apply It

You may come across Web pages that use methods other than using `<p>` tags, which is the standard method, to indicate where new paragraphs begin. For example, some developers use the `<br>` tag for this purpose. Although you can use the `<br>` tag to indicate the start of a new paragraph of text, you should use the `<p>` tag instead. Not only does the `<p>` tag start a new line, it also adds some additional space before the paragraph to better define the start of a new paragraph.

You can use multiple `<br>` tags to insert many blank lines into a Web page. You can also use this technique to add white space to your page where you think it is necessary and/or helpful to displaying your information in the most readable form possible.

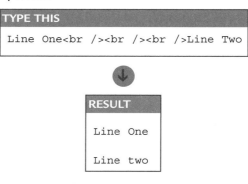

TYPE THIS

```
Line One<br /><br /><br />Line Two
```

RESULT

```
Line One

Line two
```

Create a Heading

Headings enable you to visually divide the content and identify the separate sections of the Web page. You can use headings to change the format of text within your Web pages, making important words or phrases more prominent. Headings not only make your Web pages easier to read but assist users in quickly locating important information within your Web page.

The headers that you can use in your Web page come in different sizes. Each header has a slightly different tag consisting of the letter *h* followed by a number from 1 to 6 that indicates the level of the header tag. The `<h1>` tag creates the biggest and boldest header, and the `<h6>` tag creates the smallest header.

Headers are preceded and followed by a line break, so any header text automatically separates from any text that it follows or precedes.

Each header tag consists of a start tag and the corresponding end tag. Any text enclosed in the header tag is formatted according to the header tag used. You should only include plain text within the header tag and not other tags such as paragraph or line break tags.

In older versions of HTML, the header tag allowed the `align` attribute to be used. To ensure your code is XHTML compliant, do not use the `align` attribute with the header tags.

Headers should be used to define the structure of Web pages. For example, the `<h1>` tag is used for section titles, the `<h2>` tag for subsections, and the `<h3>` tag for table captions. Web page cataloging tools, such as search engines, can use headers to catalog your Web page. The consistent, proper use of headers enables these tools to better categorize your Web page. The following task walks you through creating a level 1 heading and level 2 headings after it.

Create a Heading

① Open or create an XHTML Web page in a text editor.

② Type **<h1>** at the start of the main header text.

③ Type **</h1>** at the end of the main header text.

④ Type **<h2>** at the start of the subsection header text.

⑤ Type **</h2>** at the end of the subsection header text.

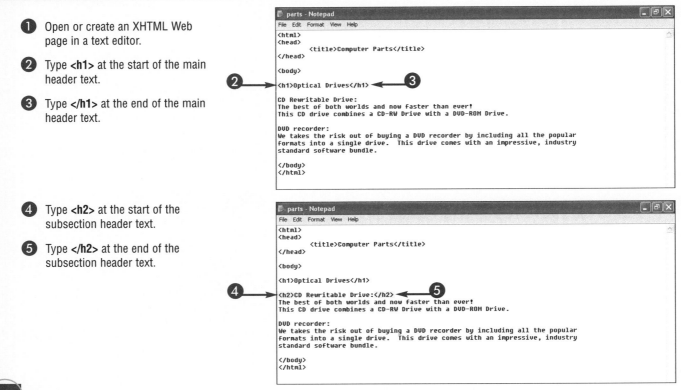

6 Repeat steps **4** to **5** for each subsection header you want to add.

7 Save your Web page.

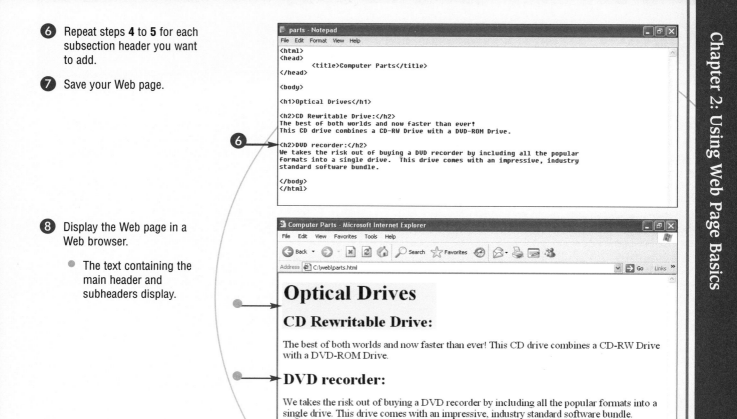

8 Display the Web page in a Web browser.

- The text containing the main header and subheaders display.

You should never use heading tags to format the main body text (text that isn't a heading) in your Web page. If you want your text to resemble the size and appearance of a heading, format the text with the appropriate tags. See Chapter 3 for more information about formatting text using HTML formatting or Chapter 6 for more information about using style sheets (the XHTML-compatible method of formatting text).

The Web browser that is used to view a particular Web page determines the font size of that page's headers. Different Web browsers use different standards for which font sizes to use for Web page elements such as headings. Therefore, because one browser may display the same header using fonts of different sizes than a competing browser, you should not use header tags to specifically define font size.

Headings should all be followed by text: two headings without text between them are called *bumping heads* and are considered bad form in publishing. Also, make sure that each subheading has at least one other subheading to balance it: You don't subdivide something into one, and thus if you subdivide a topic using subheadings you should have two or more subheadings or none at all.

Add Comments to the Code

You can make your Web page code easier to edit in the future by adding comments. Comments are like little notes inserted into the code of a Web page that explain why you used a particular piece of code. Not only can comments help you to better understand your code in the future, when you may have forgotten how or why you used some particular code, but they can be of great assistance if someone else, such as a co-worker, has to edit Web pages that you have created.

A comment can be any plain text. Comment text is preceded by the characters < ! – and followed by –>. Comments can also be used to insert purely informational data into a Web page. You should always use comments to insert the name and purpose of a Web page into the code. Comments should be used to store the Web site author's contact information in case a user has a query or comment about the Web page.

If a Web page is continually being modified, you can use comments to instruct the Web developer where changes have to be made. This can greatly increase the speed with which Web pages can be updated, as locating the relevant parts of the code is faster and easier. Short, brief comments are best. A large amount of text embedded in the HTML code reduces the speed at which a Web page transfers to a user's computer even though the user doesn't see the text unless they look at the code.

The Web browser does not display the comments themselves. The only way that comments can be read is by viewing the source code of the Web page. For more information about how to view the source code of a Web page, see the section "View Web Page Source Code" in this chapter.

Add Comments to the Code

① Open or create an XHTML Web page in a text editor.

② Type **<!--**.

③ Type **-->**.

④ Position the mouse pointer between the comment start and end delimiters, and then type the comment text.

5 Repeat steps **2** to **4** for each comment you want to add.

6 Save your Web page.

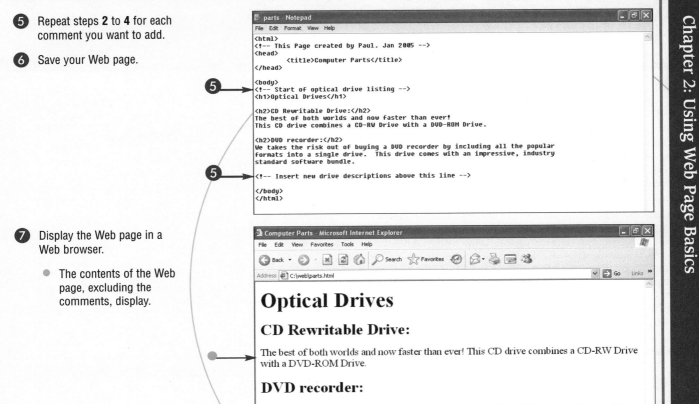

7 Display the Web page in a Web browser.

- The contents of the Web page, excluding the comments, display.

Extra

You can use a block of text as a comment by placing the start and end comment tags on separate lines. The browser considers any text between the lines containing the tags to be a comment.

Example
```
<!—
Author: Paul
Date: Jan 2005
—>
```

While initially time consuming, you should always get into the habit of adding comments to your code. You may be surprised at how fast you can forget your own work. A simple comment can save you many hours of research in the future when you need to update a Web page.

Naturally, code whose purpose is obvious requires no comments: Adding comments to explain items such as headings and paragraphs of text is unnecessary, but you will always want to comment on more complex parts of code that may refer to elements such as forms.

Add an Image to a Web Page

You can make your Web page much more aesthetically pleasing by using images for logos, buttons, or other visual elements on the page. You can also use images such as maps or graphs, charts, and diagrams to assist you in explaining things such as driving directions or complex mathematical concepts that would be more difficult to explain using text alone.

Images are available in different formats. Each format is slightly different from the other. The three most common image formats used on the World Wide Web are Graphics Interchange Format (GIF) images, Portable Network Graphics Specification (PNG) images, and Joint Photographic Experts Group (JPEG) images. GIF and JPEG images are the most popular image formats used. The format of an image can be determined by the extension of the file. GIF images use the .gif file extension, and JPEG images use either the .jpeg or .jpg file extension.

Use the `<img>` tag to add an image to a Web page. The `<img>` tag can include one attribute, `src`, which indicates the location and name of the image file. The value of the `src` attribute must be enclosed in quotation marks.

In HTML the `<img>` tag had no end tag, but XHTML requires the `<img>` tag to be properly closed. The `<img>` tag can be properly closed by inserting a forward slash before the greater than symbol that indicates the end of the tag.

The `<img>` tag can be placed anywhere on a Web page, including right in the middle of text.

As with any content you have not created yourself, you must make sure that you have permission to display any images for which you do not own a copyright. Many images have licensing restrictions preventing them from being displayed on unauthorized Web sites.

Add an Image to a Web Page

① Open or create a Web page.

② Type **<img src="" />**.

③ Type the name of the image.

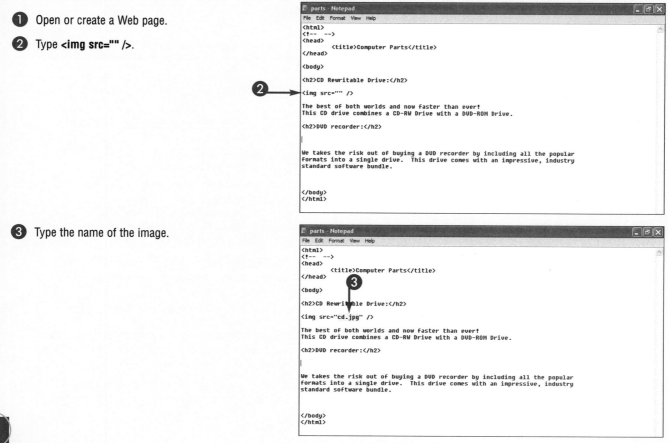

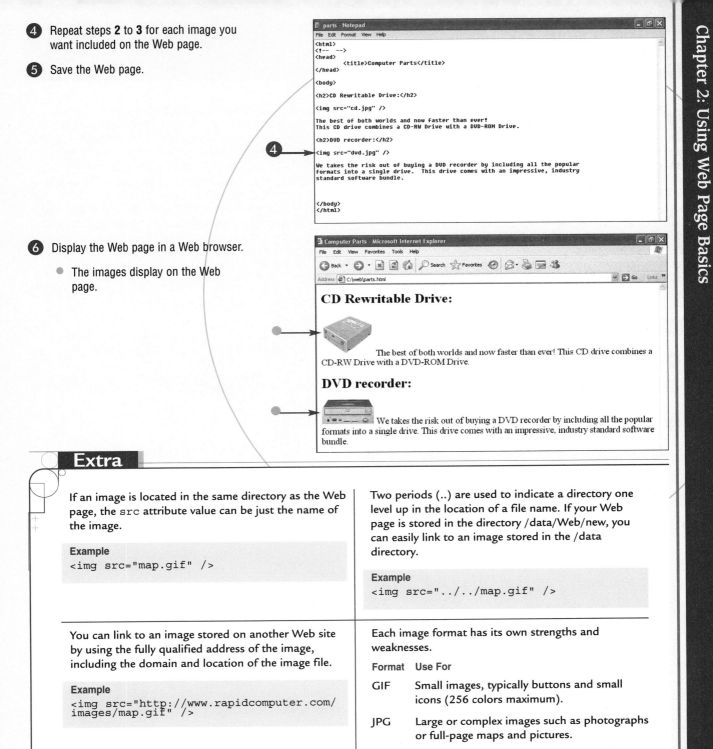

④ Repeat steps **2** to **3** for each image you want included on the Web page.

⑤ Save the Web page.

⑥ Display the Web page in a Web browser.

● The images display on the Web page.

Extra

If an image is located in the same directory as the Web page, the src attribute value can be just the name of the image.

Example
`<img src="map.gif" />`

You can link to an image stored on another Web site by using the fully qualified address of the image, including the domain and location of the image file.

Example
`<img src="http://www.rapidcomputer.com/images/map.gif" />`

Two periods (..) are used to indicate a directory one level up in the location of a file name. If your Web page is stored in the directory /data/Web/new, you can easily link to an image stored in the /data directory.

Example
`<img src="../../map.gif" />`

Each image format has its own strengths and weaknesses.

Format	Use For
GIF	Small images, typically buttons and small icons (256 colors maximum).
JPG	Large or complex images such as photographs or full-page maps and pictures.
PNG	More complex smaller images (intended to replace the GIF format).

View Web Page Source Code

You can view the source code of Web pages that you create to help troubleshoot problems when they occur. You may also view the source code of Web pages that others have created to determine what code was used to create a Web page. Examining the HTML code created by others, and the resulting Web pages, is an excellent method for increasing your skill at creating Web pages. You can even copy and paste code from other Web pages and modify it to use for your own Web pages, as long as you ensure that you are not using someone else's copyrighted material.

Your Web browser opens a window displaying the source code of a Web page. The window that opens depends upon your Web browser and operating system. Users browsing with Microsoft's Internet Explorer browser will see a

text-editing program called Notepad will appear to display source code. Users of other browsers, such as Firefox, may see only a window showing the source of the page. Viewing the source of the Web page enables you to see any comments the Web page author included in the code.

Every Web browser allows you to view the source code of a Web page, although the exact steps to view the source code differ depending on the type of Web browser and operating system you use. For more information about displaying the source code of Web pages in your Web browser, you should consult your Web browser's documentation, but the typical location for viewing the source code to a Web page is under the browser's View menu, where you may see a Source (Internet Explorer) or Page Source (Firefox) item that you can choose to view the page's source code.

View Web Page Source Code

1. Start a Web browser.

2. In the address bar, type the address of a Web page.

3. Click Go.

- The Web page displays.

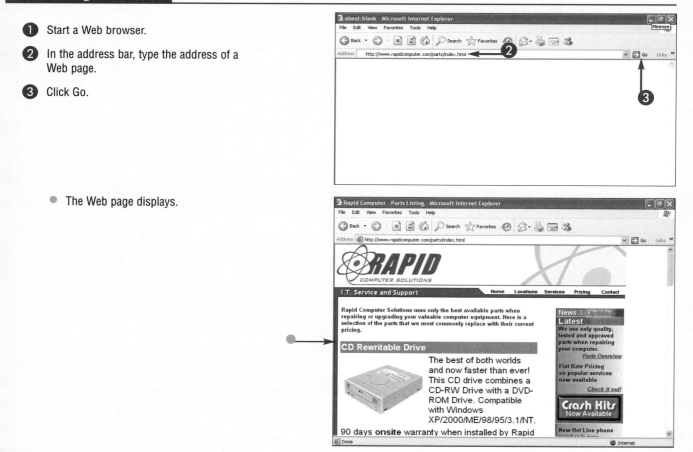

④ Click View.

⑤ Click Source (or Page Source).

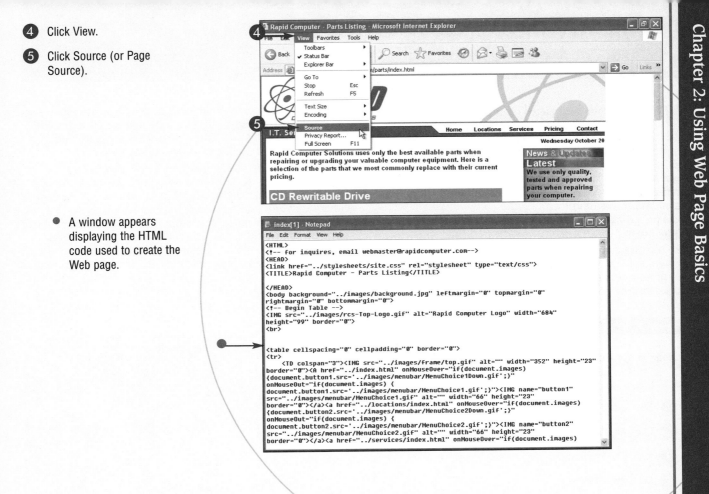

● A window appears displaying the HTML code used to create the Web page.

Extra

When the source code of a Web page is displayed in a text editor, you can save that code to your own computer. To later display the page, you may need to copy any images or other page elements to your computer. You can also do this by clicking File, clicking Save As, and then saving the page as a complete Web page.

Even though the source code of the Web page is displayed in a text-editing program, you cannot change the Web page by editing the code unless you save the code to your computer and then publish the Web page. For more information about publishing Web pages, see the section "Publish Your Web Page" in this chapter.

In Internet Explorer, the source code of a Web page is in plain text format and thus contains no text formatting such as bolding or underlines, which can make reading source code difficult. You may want to view the source code in Firefox or Netscape, which use color-coding and other formatting to make the code more readable.

Publish Your Web Page

To view your Web pages on the World Wide Web, you must first publish them to a Web server. The Web server that you use must be connected to the Internet. Many Internet service providers give their users access to a Web server to store their Web pages and make them accessible from the Web. Often, universities allow their students Web server space for a student Web page or for an online portfolio.

If your Internet service provider does not allow you to publish Web pages to their server, you can use a dedicated Web hosting company instead. Many of these companies are available, with most charging only a few dollars per month to access their servers, and others even granting you access for free. Typically, free services insert some form of

advertising on your Web site; but free Web hosting services are ideal if your Internet service provider does not provide Web hosting, and you want to learn how to create and publish a Web site without incurring any cost.

When transferring Web pages to a Web server, you must not only transfer the Web page, but you must also transfer any elements, such as images, that the Web page requires. Otherwise your Web page may not display correctly. Furthermore, you must make sure that if you have the files for your page set up in a certain folder structure on your computer (for example, if all of your images are in an /images folder) that you upload all of the files to the Web server using the exact same folder structure. Failure to do so may result in your Web page not displaying correctly.

Publish Your Web Page

Note: In this example, we are using WS_FTP Pro available at www.ipswitch.com.

1 Click Start.

2 Click All Programs.

3 Click FTP Program.

4 Click WS_FTP Pro.

The WS_FTP Pro: Connect to Remote Host dialog box appears.

5 Click Create Site.

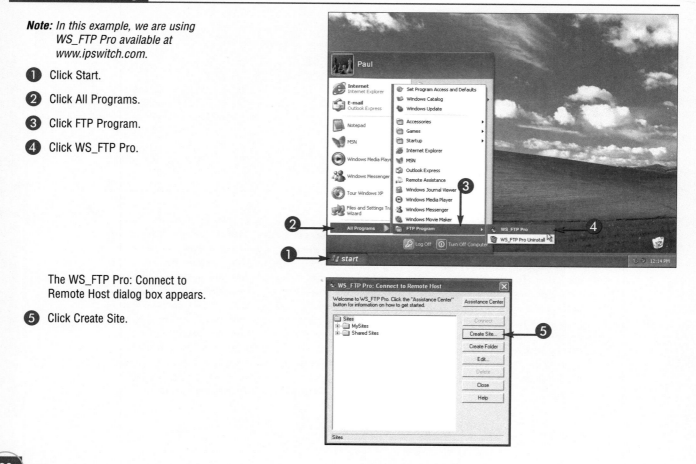

The WS_FTP Pro Site Profile Wizard dialog box appears.

6 Type a name for your site.

7 Click Next to continue.

WS_FTP Pro Site Profile Wizard

Profile Name

In this step you choose a name for your new site profile, and decide where in the site list to save it. You may always rename it or move it later.

Name:
My Web Site

Where do you want to save the new site profile?

Browse ...

< Back | Next > | Finish | Cancel | Help

8 Type the name of the Web server.

9 Click Next to continue.

WS_FTP Pro Site Profile Wizard

Host Address

Enter the Host Address of the server you want to connect to.   Usually these addresses start with ftp and continue with the domain where they belong, like ftp.ipswitch.com.   Or they may be a sequence of numbers like 192.168.100.1

Host Address:
gamma.pair.com

< Back | Next > | Finish | Cancel | Help

Extra

Many operating systems include file transfer capabilities that enable you to transfer Web pages to a Web server. However, the file transfer process is not very straightforward. If you anticipate creating many Web pages, or updating Web pages on an ongoing basis, you should consider using a dedicated FTP application for transferring your Web page files. For more information about the file transfer capabilities of your operating system, please refer to your operating system's documentation.

If you anticipate creating complex Web pages (for instance, Web sites that use databases), you will probably need to use a dedicated Web hosting company to publish your Web pages. Unlike Web hosting companies, most Internet service providers do not provide the tools necessary to create complex Web sites. When choosing a Web hosting company, evaluate whether the company not only meets your needs now, but also in the future. Transferring Web domains and Web sites from one hosting provider to another typically results in disruption of your Web site availability, so changing hosts should be avoided.

continued →

To transfer your Web pages from your computer to the Web server, you may need a *file transfer protocol* (FTP) application. Other types of Web hosting services may not require an FTP application; some of these services have other means of uploading your files, such as a Web interface for doing so, others might allow you to use either FTP or a Web interface. You may also be able to use your Web browser as an FTP application; see your browser's documentation for details.

An FTP application enables you to securely connect to and exchange files with a Web server. To use an FTP application, you need a few items of information: a user name to identify your account on the Web server, and a password to prevent unauthorized access to the Web server.

After you connect to a Web server, the FTP application needs to know the location on the Web server where your files will be placed. Consult with your Web hosting provider to find out where on the Web server they allow you to publish Web pages.

When you transfer your Web pages to a Web server, any changes you have made to your Web pages become immediately effective. As soon as your Web page has finished transferring, any user who views that Web page accesses the latest version of that page. Also, any existing Web pages in the folder to which you are transferring the files that have the same name as the file being transferred will be overwritten. Always make sure that you have a current backup of any Web pages that you are working on, in case you overwrite a Web page by mistake.

Publishing Your Web Page *(continued)*

⑩ Type your user name.

⑪ Type your password.

⑫ Click Next to continue.

The Connect to Remote Host dialog box appears, displaying your Web site entry.

⑬ Double click the name of your Web site.

A connection to the Web server is established.

⑭ Type the location on the Web server to store your files.

⑮ Double-click the file you want to transfer to the Web server.

● The Web page is transferred to the Web server.

Extra

Some Web hosting providers may require that you use specific file extensions on your Web pages. For example, one Web hosting provider may require that all your Web pages end with the file extension .html, while another provider may require that you use the file extension .htm instead. If you have problems viewing Web pages that you publish after you upload them to the Web server and you have double-checked everything else that could possibly be causing the problem, check with your Web hosting provider to find out which file extension you should use for your pages.

If you are publishing a Web site, you may want to use a domain name to identify your Web site on the Internet. The domain name is the address of your Web site, such as www.domain.com, that people type into the address bar of their Web browser to access your page. In order to register a domain name and have it assigned to your Web site, you need to consult with your Web hosting provider. Many Web hosting providers register domain names and assign them to members' sites for a fee.

Organize
Your Files

You can make updating and transferring your Web pages easier if you learn earlier rather than later how to properly organize your files when you first start to create your Web pages. Although a Web page can consist of a single file, many pages require multiple files, such as images and video files, to display properly. You will find that a single Web page can grow into a complex Web site in a very short time. Reorganizing files and folders after the Web site has been created is a tedious and time-consuming process, and one that can easily be avoided by properly organizing your files from the moment you start creating Web pages. Keeping your Web site files organized is a good habit to get into.

With your files organized, transferring specific portions of a Web site becomes easier. If all your files are in a single

folder, selecting which files to transfer to a Web server can be quite daunting. Properly organizing your files into distinct folders makes selecting and transferring only the required files much easier.

The process of organizing files consists mainly of placing files that are related into separate folders. For example, all the images of a single Web page can be contained in one folder, and the actual Web page that displays the images can reside in a different folder.

The file and folder structure that you use when creating your Web pages remains the same when transferred to the server. For example, if you create two folders on your computer, one for images and one for Web pages, that same folder structure is duplicated on the Web server.

Organize Your Files

① Open Windows Explorer and navigate to the folder that stores your Web files.

② Click Make a new folder.

③ Type the name of the new folder.

④ Repeat steps **2** to **3** for each folder you want to create.

⑤ Press the Control key and click the file you want to move.

⑥ Drag the files selected in step **5** to the folder created in step **3**.

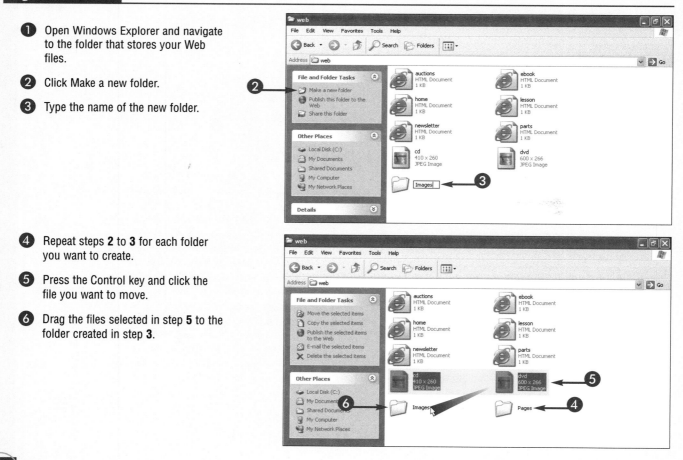

7 Repeat steps **5** to **6** to move the remaining files to the folder created in step **4**.

8 Drag the files selected in step **7** to the second folder you created.

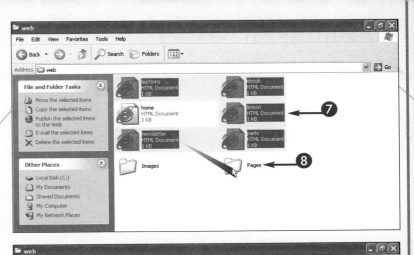

The files within your Web folder are now organized.

Extra

Although the principles of organizing files are the same regardless of the operating system your computer uses, the actual process of creating folders and moving and copying files is different for each operating system. For example, the previous task specified Windows Explorer, which only applies to PCs running Microsoft's Windows operating system. For more information about creating folders and copying files on your computer, please refer to your operating system's documentation.

A *Subfolder* is a folder created within another folder. When using subfolders, simply include the location of the file, including the subfolders, in the links and addresses in the Web page. For example, if you put your images in an /images folder, make sure that the addresses in your Web page that call those images look for the images in that folder.

The words *folder* and *directory* are often used interchangeably. Both refer to the same thing: a location where files are stored. The original term was directories, but when the graphical user interface was later added to operating systems (Unix, which predates Windows, originally had no graphical user interface) directories were represented visually by folders, hence the new term.

Save and Open a Web Page

You can save a Web page, including all the images and text, to your computer so that you can view the page at a later time. You do not need to be connected to the Internet to view the saved Web page after you have saved it to your computer. Usually you can do this by clicking File and then clicking Save As (or Save Page As) and choosing Web Page, Complete in the Save as type field of the Windows Save dialog box.

Saving Web pages enables you to easily backup or archive any pages that you have created and published to the Internet. You can also save any Web pages of interest to you for future reference. One example of how this can be useful is in research: If you are looking for information on a topic and decide that you want to save certain pages for

future reference (say to quote from them and/or cite them as a reference) you can save all the pages you find of interest on the topic to your hard drive so that you can later go back and sort through the information later.

When you save a Web page that contains elements such as images or Java applets, the Web browser automatically organizes the files into folders on your computer and updates the saved Web page accordingly. The file and folder structure on the Web server is not duplicated, so you cannot publish a saved Web page to the Web server.

Be sure to make a note of the location on your computer where you saved the Web page. To open the saved Web page in your Web browser, simply enter the name and location of the saved Web page in your Web browser's address bar.

Save and Open a Web Page

SAVE A WEB PAGE

1. Open a Web page in the Web browser.

2. Click File.

3. Click Save As.

4. Select the folder that stores your Web files.

5. Type the name of the Web page.

6. Click Save.

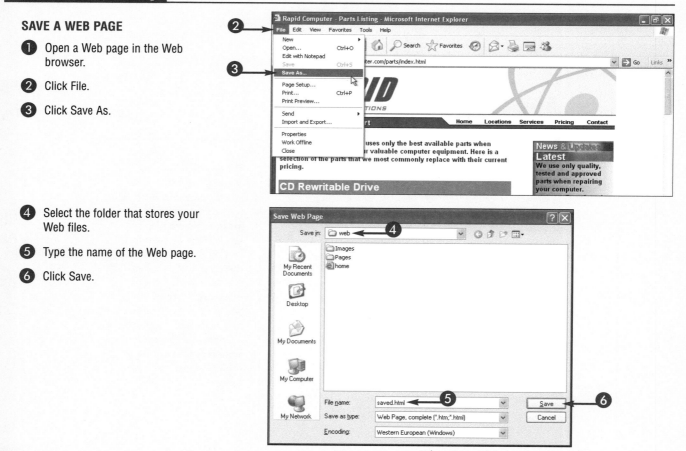

OPEN A WEB PAGE

① Open a Web browser.

② Type the name and location of the Web page saved on your computer.

③ Click Go.

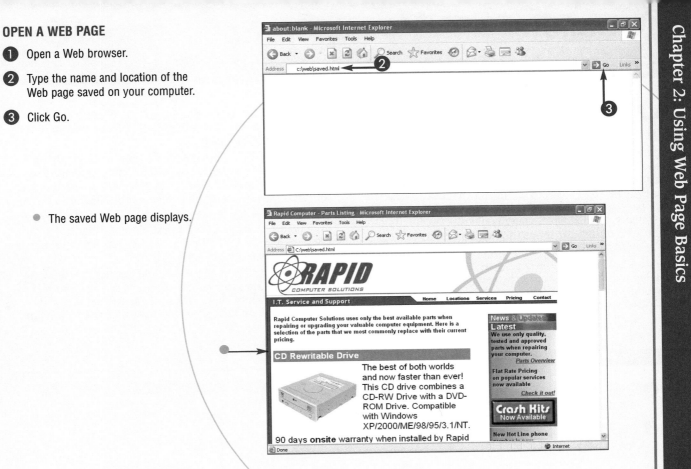

● The saved Web page displays.

Extra

The process used for saving Web pages differs depending on what Web browser you use. Most Web browsers — including Internet Explorer 6 and Firefox 1.0 — save everything including images. You can also save only the HTML or save the page as a text file. For information about saving Web pages in your browser, refer to your Web browser's documentation.

You can use the Offline Favorite Wizard in Internet Explorer to archive Web pages without saving them manually every time. To do so in Internet Explorer, click Favorites, right-click the name of the page you want to make available offline, and then click Make available offline from the drop-down menu. The Offline Favorite Wizard appears with instructions for making the Web page available offline.

Some Web pages use elements such as clocks or databases to generate the content of the page. When you save a page, only the information contained in that page at the time it was saved gets stored. Dynamic information will not be updated the next time you view the saved page. You have to view the original Web page on the Web to update the dynamic content.

Make Text Bold and Italic

You can use different tags to change the appearance of text on your Web pages. Changing the appearance of text on a Web page enables you to emphasize important information or to make specific portions of text stand out from the surrounding Web page. The typical use for bold and italic text is to highlight key words that you want the person viewing your document (in this case a Web page) to pay especially close attention to or to commit to memory. For example, many books use bold and/or italic texts to indicate terms that are important enough to be on tests.

You can bold text on a Web page in a similar manner to bolding text within a word processing document. Bold text displays in a heavier, darker font than normal, and is indicated with the `<b>` tag. The starting `<b>` tag must be accompanied by the closing `</b>` tag. All text enclosed within the starting and ending tags is rendered bold when displayed in a Web page.

You can also italicize text to add emphasis to words on a Web page. Italicized text has a slant, and is specified with the `<i>` tag. Similar to the `<b>` tag, `<i>` is the opening tag and must always be accompanied by the closing `</i>` tag.

You should try not to overuse bold and italic text in your Web pages. Overuse of the physical formatting styles can cause them to lose their purpose of emphasizing or drawing attention to specific sections of text.

The bold and italic tags are suitable for quickly changing the physical appearance of text on a Web page, but text appearance can be more effectively controlled using style sheets. For more information about using style sheets to control the appearance of text, see Chapter 6.

Make Text Bold and Italic

① Open or create a Web page in a text editor.

② Place the insertion point before text you want to bold and type `<b>`.

③ Place the insertion point after the text you want to bold and type `</b>`.

④ Repeat steps **2** to **3** for each section of text that will appear bolded.

⑤ Place the mouse pointer before text you want to italicize and type `<i>`.

⑥ Place the insertion point after the text you want to italicized and type `</i>`.

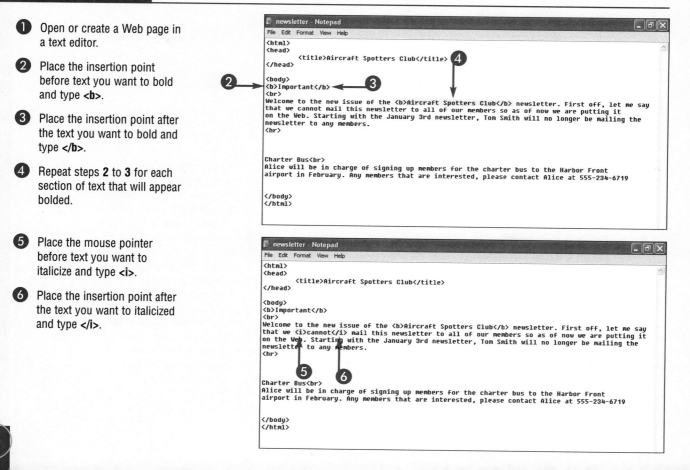

7 Repeat steps **2** to **6** for all text that you want to format with bold or italics.

8 Save the Web page.

```
newsletter - Notepad
File  Edit  Format  View  Help
<html>
<head>
        <title>Aircraft Spotters Club</title>
</head>

<body>
<b>Important</b>
<br>
Welcome to the new issue of the <b>Aircraft Spotters Club</b> newsletter. First off, let me say
that we <i>cannot</i> mail this newsletter to all of our members so as of now we are putting it
on the Web. Starting with the January 3rd newsletter, Tom Smith will no longer be mailing the
newsletter to any members.
<hr>


Charter Bus<br>
<b>Alice</b> will be in charge of signing up members for the charter bus to the Harbor Front
airport in February. Any members that are interested, please <i>contact Alice at 555-234-6719</i>


</body>
</html>
```

7

9 Display the Web page in a Web browser.

The bolded and italicized text appears with the specified formatting.

```
Aircraft Spotters Club - Microsoft Internet Explorer
File  Edit  View  Favorites  Tools  Help
Back   •          Search   Favorites
Address  C:\web\newsletter.html                              Go   Links

Important
Welcome to the new issue of the Aircraft Spotters Club newsletter. First off, let me say
that we cannot mail this newsletter to all of our members so as of now we are putting it on
the Web. Starting with the January 3rd newsletter, Tom Smith will no longer be mailing the
newsletter to any members.

Charter Bus
Alice will be in charge of signing up members for the charter bus to the Harbor Front
airport in February. Any members that are interested, please contact Alice at 555-234-6719
```

Extra

When you apply physical styles to text on a Web page, the browser ultimately decides how the text will display when users view the Web page. Although you can use tags to instruct the Web browser to either bold or italicize text, beyond that you have no control over how the text appears in the Web browser. In many cases, users can alter the appearance of bold or italicized text even further by adjusting the settings in the Preferences or Options settings in their own Web browsers.

You can use tags to make your text stand out. For example, you can use the <u> tag to underline any text that you want to emphasize on your Web page. You must be careful about using the underline tag, however, in order to prevent confusion between emphasized text and links.

Example
```
please contact <u>Alice</u> at
555-234-6719
```

You can also use the <strong> tag and the <em> emphasis tags wherever you would use <b> or <i> tag, respectively. Both the <strong> and emphasis tags produce the same results as the bold and italic tags, although they are a bit more descriptive than <b> or <i>.

Adjust the Font Size

You can change the font size of the text that appears on a Web page to make the text easier to read, add emphasis, or simply allow your text to fit better within the Web browser window. For example, you could make the first paragraph of text on a page bigger to indicate its greater importance, as news sites sometimes do for the first paragraph of a news story (news stories more often bold the first paragraph, but the intent to increase the prominence of the first paragraph is the same).

You can use the HTML tag `<font>` with the `size` attribute to specify a size for text. The `<font>` tag has a corresponding end tag: `</font>`. The value of the `size` attribute is a number from 1 to 7 representing a text size from small to large. The font that is used to display the text will not change, only the size changes.

Using the `<font>` tag restricts you to only seven different font sizes, but you can use style sheets to change your text to almost any size. Keep in mind that XHTML does not support the `<font>` tag; it is an HTML-only tag, and so you should only use it if you are comfortable being non-compliant with the XHTML standard. Although most Web browsers will continue to support the `<font>` tag for the near future, you should use style sheets instead if you anticipate a long life for your Web pages. For more information about how to use style sheets to change the size of text, see Chapter 6.

The following task will show you how to adjust the font size on your Web page using `<font>` tags.

Adjust the Font Size

① Open or create a Web page that contains text.

② Place the insertion point before the text you want to resize and type **<font size="">**.

③ Place the insertion point between the quotation marks and type the size of the text.

④ Type **</font>**.

⑤ Repeat steps **2** to **4** for each section of text you want to resize.

⑥ Save the Web page.

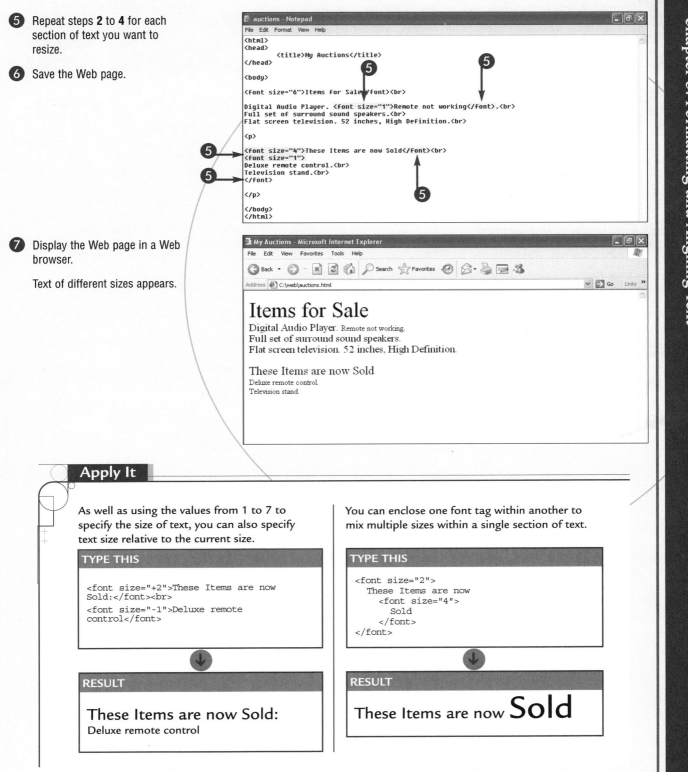

⑦ Display the Web page in a Web browser.

Text of different sizes appears.

Apply It

As well as using the values from 1 to 7 to specify the size of text, you can also specify text size relative to the current size.

TYPE THIS

```
<font size="+2">These Items are now
Sold:</font><br>
<font size="-1">Deluxe remote
control</font>
```

RESULT

These Items are now Sold:
Deluxe remote control

You can enclose one font tag within another to mix multiple sizes within a single section of text.

TYPE THIS

```
<font size="2">
   These Items are now
     <font size="4">
       Sold
     </font>
</font>
```

RESULT

These Items are now Sold

Use Preformatted Text

Yy ou can preformat text on a Web page to help you align columns of text data. Ordinarily, Web browsers automatically format the Web page text to fit on the screen and condense multiple spaces placed side-by-side into a single space. This can make it impossible to correctly align text information into columns.

Regardless of any hard returns or blank lines within the text of the HTML code, the Web browser displays text as a long continuous segment. For example, if your HTML code contains two sentences separated by three blank lines and any number of spaces, the text displayed on a Web page will contain only a single space placed between the two sentences.

Preformatted text appears the same on the Web page as it does in your HTML code, complete with any spaces or new lines you may have used. The <pre> tag (together with the closing </pre> tag) indicates the preformatting of text when presented on a Web page.

Preformatted text is usually presented in a different font from the other text on the Web page. The Web browser typically displays preformatted text using a monospaced font, where each character is the same width as every other character in the font. The equal size of each character ensures that the text aligns correctly when formatted into columns.

Note that the font used to display preformatted text may differ from one operating system to another; most operating systems, including Microsoft Windows, use the Courier font. Remember that any user can override the font specified by the Web browser, so you cannot be sure how your preformatted text will appear.

Also note that, while preformatting is a quick method of lining up small amounts of text, tables are much more efficient. For more information about tables, see Chapter 9.

Use Preformatted Text

① Open or create a Web page that contains text.

② Type a column of text in the Web page.

```
auctions - Notepad
File  Edit  Format  View  Help
<html>
<head>
        <title>My Auctions</title>
</head>

<body>

<h3>Items for Sale</h3><br>


Digital Audio Player. Remote not working
Full set of surround sound speakers.
Flat screen television. 32 inches, High Definition.



<p>
<h3>These Items are now Sold</h3>
Deluxe remote control.<br>
Television stand.
</p>

</body>
</html>
```

③ Type an aligned column of text.

```
auctions - Notepad
File  Edit  Format  View  Help
<html>
<head>
        <title>My Auctions</title>
</head>

<body>

<h3>Items for Sale</h3><br>

|
Digital Audio Player. Remote not working               $145
Full set of surround sound speakers.                   $399
Flat screen television. 32 inches, High Definition.    $950



<p>
<h3>These Items are now Sold</h3>
Deluxe remote control.<br>
Television stand.
</p>

</body>
</html>
```

④ Type **<pre>** before the text you want to display as preformatted.

⑤ Type **</pre>** after the text you want to display as preformatted.

⑥ Save the Web page.

```
auctions - Notepad
File  Edit  Format  View  Help
<html>
<head>
        <title>My Auctions</title>
</head>

<body>

<h3>Items for Sale</h3><br>

<pre>
Digital Audio Player. Remote not working                        $145
Full set of surround sound speakers.                            $399
Flat screen television. 32 inches, High Definition.             $950
</pre>


<p>
<h3>These Items are now Sold</h3>
Deluxe remote control.<br>
Television stand.
</p>

</body>
</html>
```

④ ⑤ (pointing to the <pre> and </pre> lines)

⑦ Display the Web page in a Web browser.

● The text appears preformatted.

```
My Auctions - Microsoft Internet Explorer
File  Edit  View  Favorites  Tools  Help
Back        Search  Favorites
Address  C:\web\auctions.html                          Go   Links

Items for Sale


Digital Audio Player. Remote not working                        $145
Full set of surround sound speakers.                            $399
Flat screen television. 32 inches, High Definition.             $950

These Items are now Sold

Deluxe remote control.
Television stand.
```

Extra

Because the Web browser displays preformatted text as it appears in the code, make sure that your text does not exceed the width of the Web browser window. It is impossible to know what size window or what size font a person will use to display a Web page. A good rule of thumb is to keep the maximum number of characters per line in your preformatted text to 80 characters. You can limit the amount of characters on a line by inserting a new line at the end of a sentence.

Example
```
<pre>
Welcome to the new issue of the
Aircraft Spotters Club newsletter.
First off, let me say that we cannot
mail this newsletter to all of our
members so as of now we are putting
it on the Web.
</pre>
```

Use Quoted Text

Quoted text enables you to use material that comes from outside sources, such as speeches, books, or other Web pages, on your own Web page. The `<blockquote>` tag indicates text (or other elements such as images) from another source that is being used on your Web page.

The material placed within the `<blockquote>` tag is set apart visually from the material surrounding it. The quoted material is preceded and followed by a blank line, similar to a paragraph of text. The material is also indented slightly from both the left and right side margins. Surrounding the material with space helps to differentiate it from other items on the Web page.

Although the most common material found in the `<blockquote>` tag is text, other elements, such as images, may also be included. For short pieces of text, you should

just use quotation marks instead of the `<blockquote>` tag to indicate that the information is a quotation. If images are used, their appearance will not change, but they will be subject to the same margin restrictions as text; that is, they will be indented slightly from both the left and right side margins.

Text contained within the `<blockquote>` tag may also be rendered in a different font from other text on the Web page. The text may even appear in italic, depending on the Web browser. For this reason it is a good idea for you to test your page in various Web browsers to see how they display the quoted text and ensure that you are happy with the presentation. If you are not happy with the presentation in a certain browser, you can take steps such as indicating a certain font style, size, or other specification using style sheets and `<font>` tags to correct the problem.

Use Quoted Text

1 Open or create a Web page.

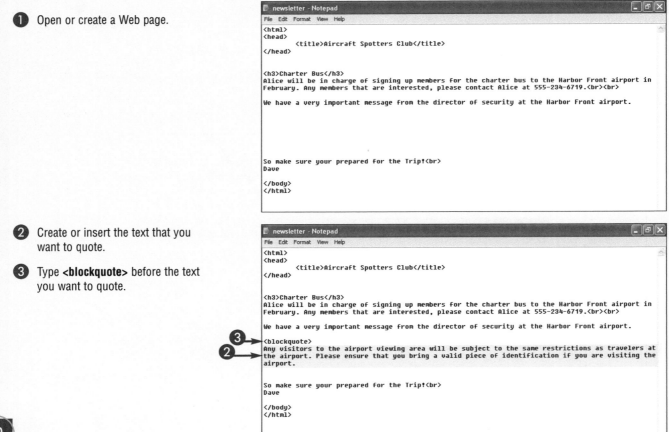

2 Create or insert the text that you want to quote.

3 Type **\<blockquote\>** before the text you want to quote.

④ Type **</blockquote>** after the text you want quoted.

⑤ Save the Web page.

newsletter - Notepad
File Edit Format View Help

```
<html>
<head>
        <title>Aircraft Spotters Club</title>
</head>


<h3>Charter Bus</h3>
Alice will be in charge of signing up members for the charter bus to the Harbor Front airport in
February. Any members that are interested, please contact Alice at 555-234-6719.<br><br>

We have a very important message from the director of security at the Harbor Front airport.

<blockquote>
Any visitors to the airport viewing area will be subject to the same restrictions as travelers at
the airport. Please ensure that you bring a valid piece of identification if you are visiting the
airport.
</blockquote>

So make sure your prepared for the Trip!<br>
Dave

</body>
</html>
```

④

⑥ Display the Web page in a Web browser.

● The text appears indented from both margins.

Aircraft Spotters Club - Microsoft Internet Explorer
File Edit View Favorites Tools Help

Back ● Search ☆ Favorites

Address C:\web\newsletter.html   Go   Links

Charter Bus

Alice will be in charge of signing up members for the charter bus to the Harbor Front airport in February. Any members that are interested, please contact Alice at 555-234-6719.

We have a very important message from the director of security at the Harbor Front airport.

> Any visitors to the airport viewing area will be subject to the same restrictions as travelers at the airport. Please ensure that you bring a valid piece of identification if you are visiting the airport.

So make sure your prepared for the Trip!
Dave

Apply It

You can use other formatting tags within the <blockquote> tag to change the appearance of the text you are quoting by adding italics or bold, changing text color, and so on.

TYPE THIS

```
<blockquote>
Any visitors to the airport viewing area
<b><i>will</i></b> be searched.
</blockquote>
```

⬇

RESULT

Any visitors to the airport viewing area

will be searched.

Block quotes are typically used to indicate that information has come from another source. Because most countries have laws governing the proper use of other people's materials, you should secure permissions from the owner of the work before placing it on your Web page to avoid possible consequences, such as litigation, later on. You should also indicate the source of the material within your own Web site, ideally on the same page where the material is used, to ensure that the author of the work is given proper credit.

Add Superscript and Subscript

You can change the position of characters within a line of text, which enables you to add items such as footnotes to your Web page. The superscript and subscript tags are used to change position of text within a line. The superscript tag positions text half a character higher than the surrounding text. The subscript tag positions the text half a character below the surrounding text. Both tags render any enclosed text with the same formatting as the preceding text.

Superscripts and subscripts are often used on a Web page to represent mathematical material, information that uses scientific notation, or text used to represent chemical formulas. If you have ever dealt with numbers put to the nth power (for example, nine to the fourth power), you should already be able to identify superscript.

Web page developers often use the superscript tag to reference footnotes on a Web page. Footnotes can include additional information about the original sources of the text that appears on a Web site. Footnotes are often used in research articles to expand on information that is tangential to the main article. The superscript tag consists of an opening `<sup>` tag and a corresponding ending `</sup>` tag. The subscript tag is comprised of a start `<sub>` tag and an ending `</sub>` tag.

When using superscript or subscript text within your Web pages, particularly for long sections of text, you must be careful that the superscript or subscript text does not change the line spacing within your paragraphs. In some cases, extra line space appears above a line of text that contains a superscript, or below a line of text that contains a subscript. While not catastrophic, the extra line certainly looks tacky.

Add Superscript and Subscript

1 Open or create a Web page that contains text.

2 Locate text that will be superscript and type **<sup>**.

3 Type **</sup>** after the text that you want to appear in superscript.

4 Locate text that will appear in subscript and type **<sub>**.

5 Type **</sub>** after the text that you want to appear in subscript.

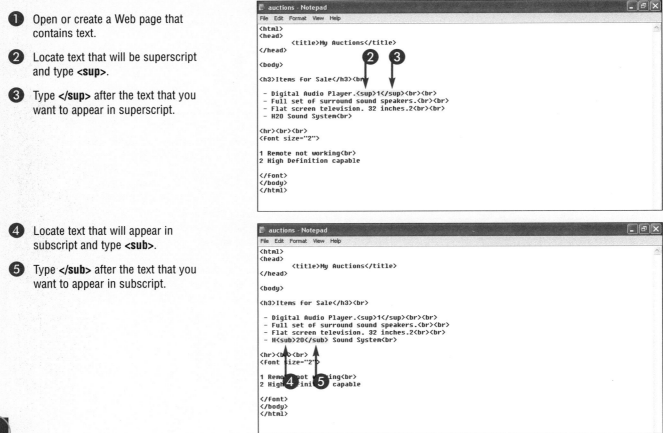

⑥ Repeat steps **2** to **5** for any text you want to superscript or subscript.

⑦ Save the Web page.

⑧ Display the Web page in a Web browser.

The superscript and subscript text appears.

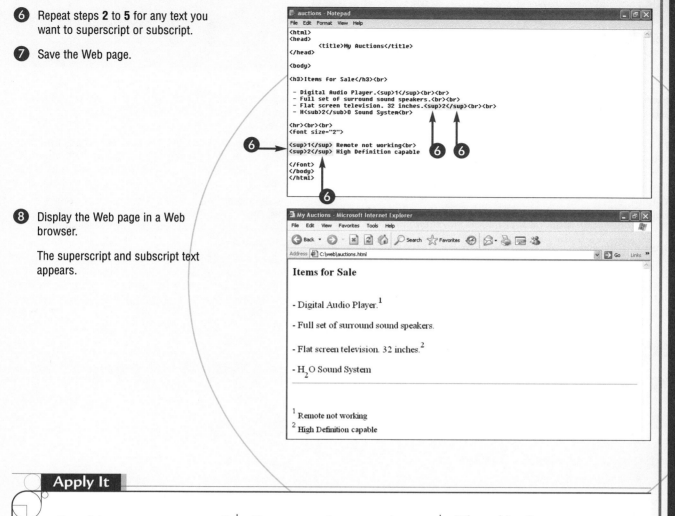

Apply It

One of the most common uses of the superscript tag is to place the initials TM next to a word or a phrase to indicate that the word or phrase is a trademark.

TYPE THIS

```
RAPID COMPUTER
SOLUTIONS<sup>TM</sup>
```

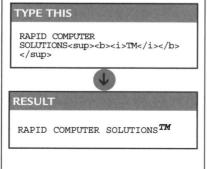

RESULT

RAPID COMPUTER SOLUTIONS^{TM}

You can use other tags to change the appearance of text within the superscript or subscript tags.

TYPE THIS

```
RAPID COMPUTER
SOLUTIONS<sup><b><i>TM</i></b>
</sup>
```

RESULT

RAPID COMPUTER SOLUTIONS$^{\textit{\textbf{TM}}}$

When adding footnotes to your Web page, you can make the text within the superscript tag a link to the actual footnotes on your Web page, enabling users to quickly access the related footnotes.

Example

```
Flat screen television.
32 inches.<sup><a href=
"#details">2</a></sup>
```

Use Descriptive Tags

Formatting text on a Web page typically consists of using tags such as <b> that definitively describe the format of the text. Formatting tags instruct the browser to render the text in a certain typeface, with no consideration about the meaning of the text. HTML enables you to use descriptive tags to better describe the information in your Web page. For example, instead of using the italicize tag <i> to indicate that a word has a special meaning, you can use the emphasis tag <em> to describe the text as material that should be emphasized on the Web page. Web browsers display emphasized text in italics, so, although the results are the same as using the <i> tag, you have used the tag to describe as well as format the content of your Web page.

Using descriptive tags as opposed to physical formatting tags such as <b> or <i> to describe text in your Web pages

is a good habit to get into. Descriptive tags make it easier for some cataloging tools to correctly categorize the information on your Web page.

There are a number of tags that you can use to describe the text on your Web page. Each tag consists of a starting and ending tag. The emphasis tag <em> describes text that is of some importance.

The <code> tag describes information that is typically programming code. Text described with the <code> tag is generally displayed in a monospaced font. Naturally the ending tag is </code>.

The <address> tag specifies text that forms part of a mailing address. The <address> tag is generally rendered in an italicized font; but unlike the other descriptive tags, a line break will appear before the information. The ending tag is, of course, </address>.

Use Descriptive Tags

① Open or create a Web page that contains text.

② Type **<em>** before text you want to emphasize.

③ Type **</em>** after the text you want to emphasize.

④ Repeat steps **2** to **3** for each section of emphasized text.

⑤ Type **<code>** before a block of code.

⑥ Type **</code>** after a block of code.

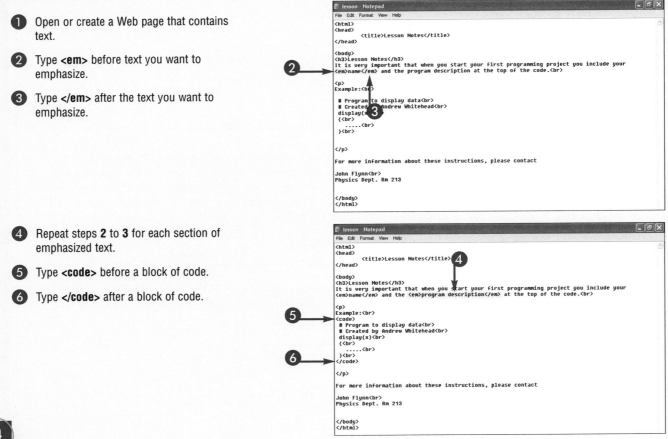

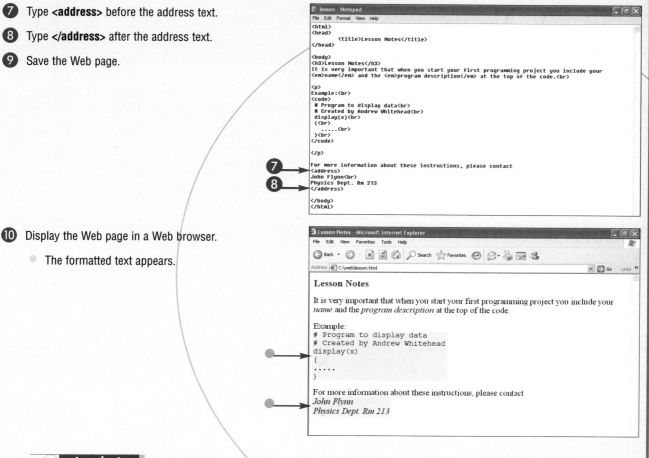

⑦ Type **<address>** before the address text.

⑧ Type **</address>** after the address text.

⑨ Save the Web page.

⑩ Display the Web page in a Web browser.

● The formatted text appears.

Apply It

Many Web pages display computer programming code and the resultant output of that code. There are a number of descriptive tags used specifically for describing this type of information. The `<kbd>` tag describes text that one may type on a keyboard, and the `<samp>` tag describes the results of a program.

TYPE THIS

```
Type <kbd>time</kbd> and press Enter<br>
<samp>The current time is: 14:42:36.96</samp>
```

RESULT

Type time and press Enter
The current time is: 14:42:36.96

Some descriptive tags do not have any effect on the text of your Web page or its presentation. For example, the `<acronym>` and `<abbr>` tags are used to describe text that may be an acronym or an abbreviation. Most browsers do not currently render this type of information any differently from the surrounding text; therefore, unless you analyze the source code you will not know if either of these tags has been used. Of course, you can still use the tags for proper categorization of the elements in your text.

Change the Font Color and Type

Y ou can specify the color and the font of the text displayed on your Web page. Changing the color and font enables you to emphasize important information or to make your Web pages more aesthetically pleasing or more readability. For example, say you want your page's background to be black. The default color for text is black, so you will need to change the text color (to white or gray, for example) so that the text of your page is not invisible against the black background.

The `<font>` tag has different attributes that change the color of the font as well as the actual typeface that is displayed on your Web page. The `color` attribute of the font tag specifies the color that the font will be rendered in. You can use the name of common colors, such as `red`, `yellow`, `green`, `magenta`, and so on.

The `face` attribute defines the font type that that Web browser will use to display the text. Commonly used font types are Arial and Times New Roman. The font that you use must be available on the computer that is viewing the Web page. For this reason you should only specify commonly used font types. You can specify multiple font types with the `face` attribute, separating each font name by a comma. The Web browser will try each font specified in turn until it finds one that is installed on the computer. If the font type you specify is not available on the computer viewing the Web page, the Web browser typically uses the default font to render the text.

The `<font>` tag consists of the opening `<font>` tag and a closing `</font>` tag. The `face` and `color` attributes are specified in the opening tag. As with all HTML tag attributes, the values of the `face` and `color` attributes should be enclosed in quotations.

Change the Font Color and Type

① Open or create a Web page that contains text.

② Locate the text to change and type **<font face="" color="">**.

```
auctions - Notepad
File  Edit  Format  View  Help
<html>
<head>
          <title>My Auctions</title>
</head>

<body>

<font face="" color="">Items for Sale
<hr>

Digital Audio Player. Remote not working.<br>
Full set of surround sound speakers.<br>
Flat screen television. 52 inches, High Definition.<br>

<p>
These Items are now Sold<br>

Deluxe remote control.<br>
Television stand.<br>

</p>

</body>
</html>
```

③ Type the name of a font face.

④ Type the name of a common color.

⑤ Type **</font>**.

```
auctions - Notepad
File  Edit  Format  View  Help
<html>
<head>
          <title>My Auctions</title>
</head>

<body>

<font face="arial" color="blue">Items for Sale</font>
<hr>

Digital Audio Player. Remote not working.<br>
Full set of surround sound speakers.<br>
Flat screen television. 52 inches, High Definition.<br>

<p>
These Items are now Sold<br>

Deluxe remote control.<br>
Television stand.<br>

</p>

</body>
</html>
```

6 Repeat steps **2** to **5** for each section of text you want to change.

7 Save the Web page.

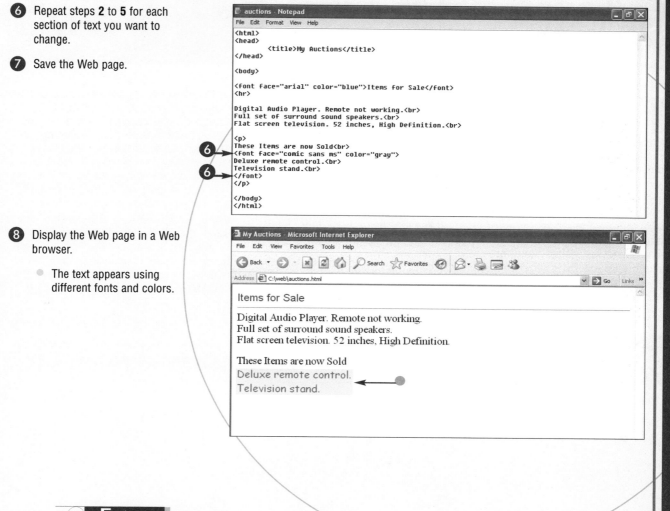

8 Display the Web page in a Web browser.

● The text appears using different fonts and colors.

Extra

As mentioned elsewhere in this book, the `<font>` tag is deprecated in HTML. It is not a tag that is supported by the XHTML standard. Web browsers will continue to support the `<font>` tag for many years into the future. Ideally you should use style sheets to change the appearance of the text on your Web pages, but you are of course able to use your own discretion in deciding whether you want your code fully XHTML-compliant or not. For more information about using style sheets, see Chapter 6.

Instead of typing the actual name of the color in the `<font>` tag, you can also use hexadecimal values to represent the color of the font. A two digit hexadecimal number from 00 to FF preceded by the pound symbol (#) allows you to define the amount of each red, green, and blue color that makes up the font. For example, the value #000000 represent white, and the value #00FF00 produces a green font. The RGB color chart in Appendix A offers a few colors that you can specify with hexadecimal values.

Create a Link

The ability to link to other Web pages is arguably one of the most useful features of the World Wide Web. You can create a link on your Web page that links to another document from your own Web site or from any Web site on the Internet. The text that comprises a link is called *hypertext*.

When a user clicks on a link, the page being linked to replaces the page that contains the link. The anchor tag `<a>` is used to create links. This tag consists of an opening and closing tag, and any text contained within these tags forms the link. Link text on a Web page is typically underlined and colored blue, helping to differentiate it from the surrounding text.

The `href` attribute of the opening `<a>` tag is used to specify the name of the Web page to which the user is linking. `href` is an abbreviation for hypertext reference. If you are linking to a Web page on another Web site, you must use the full address of the Web page and the Web site in your code. When linking to Web pages on your own Web site, you do not need to specify the domain name within the Web page address, just the location and name of the Web page being linked to.

When you view a Web page containing text links that you have clicked and visited, the color of the links change to magenta. However, regardless of whether the link has been visited or not, the link will usually appear underlined. The user can change this behavior by altering the Web browser settings, so you cannot depend on this being the case all the time.

Create a Link

1 Open or create a Web page.

2 Locate the text to be made into a link and type **<a href="">**.

3 Type **</a>**.

4 Type the location and name of the Web page to link to.

5 Save the Web page.

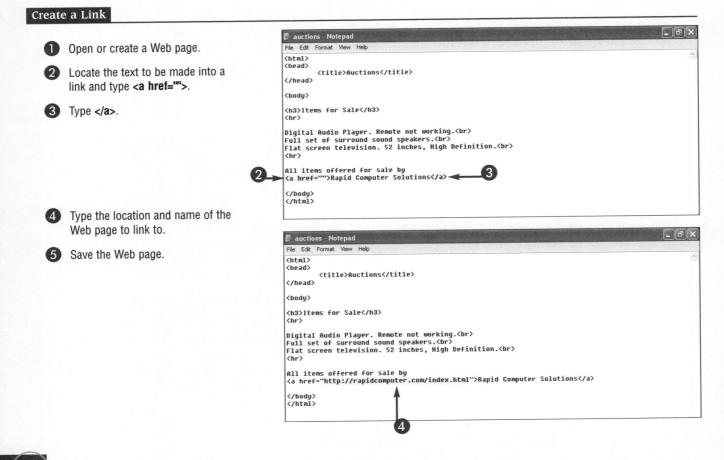

6 Open the Web page in a Web browser.

7 Click the link text.

Auctions - Microsoft Internet Explorer

File Edit View Favorites Tools Help

Back · Search Favorites

Address C:\web\auctions.html Go Links

Items for Sale

Digital Audio Player. Remote not working.
Full set of surround sound speakers.
Flat screen television. 52 inches, High Definition.

All items offered for sale by Rapid Computer Solutions ◄── **7**

The page that was linked appears in the Web browser.

Rapid Computer Solutions - Computer Repair - Microsoft Internet Explorer

File Edit View Favorites Tools Help

Back · Search Favorites

Address http://rapidcomputer.com/index.html Go Links

RAPID
COMPUTER SOLUTIONS

I.T. Service and Support   Home   Locations   Services   Pricing   Contact

Rapid Computer Solutions Inc. provides
fast, accurate support for your business computer hardware and software environments.

905 609-3223

Check out the **customised** support section available to all our customers ➡ Go

Your Computer Repair Source   Request a Service Call

News & Updates
Latest
We use only quality, tested and approved parts when repairing your computer.
Parts Overview
Flat Rate Pricing on popular services now available
Check it out!

Crash Kits
Now Available

New Hot Line phone number is now

Done   Internet

Extra

When specifying the address of a local Web page, you can use two periods (. .) to indicate that the page being linked to is located in the parent directory of the Web page containing the link. File systems have historically specified two periods as referring to the parent directory.

Example
```
<a href="..\MasterIndexhtml">Back
to the table of contents</A>
```

The text you choose for your link should be as descriptive as possible, though not too long. Extra long text links can be difficult to read; ideally, a user should be able to scan your Web pages and quickly locate links. For example, instead of specifying "click here to go to the news page," simply use "news page" as the link text.

When you create links to Web pages that you do not control, there is always the chance that the Web page may not be available in the future. You should periodically review any links on your Web site to ensure that they are still valid. See Chapter 16 for more information on validating links on your page.

Develop and Link to Anchors

Not only can you link to Web pages within your own Web site and beyond, but you can actually link to different areas within a single Web page. This is extremely useful for Web pages that are very long and contain large amounts of text. For example, you can have a glossary or an index on your Web page. You can put the words in a list at the top of the page and link each word to its entry in the page below. Designers often do this, and typically, they put a Back to Top link in the headers of the entries themselves to allow users to quickly move back and forth between the list at the top of the page and the entries themselves.

The first step in creating a link within a document is to use the anchor tag to identify the location you want to link to; the anchor tag `<a>` is used with the `name` attribute to

identify this location. The `href` attribute does not need to be used when the anchor tag identifies an area of a Web page as being linked to.

Any text within an anchor tag that uses just the `name` attribute is not treated as a link; that is, the text does not change color or become underlined. An anchor tag used to identify an area of a Web page being linked is called a *named anchor*.

When creating the link to the location you defined in the Web page, the `href` attribute is used, but its value is the same as the name attribute in the target location. The value of the `href` attribute is preceded by the pound symbol (#).

Develop and Link to Anchors

① Open or create a Web page.

② Type **<a href="#">**.

③ Type **</a>**.

④ Type **<a name="">**.

⑤ Type **</a>**.

⑥ Type the name of the link in the linked anchor.

⑦ Type the name of the link in the anchor tag.

⑧ Save the Web page.

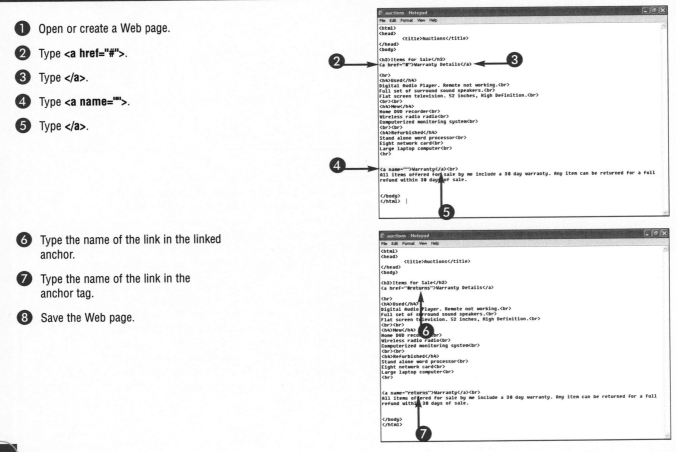

⑨ Open the Web page in a Web browser.

⑩ Click the link.

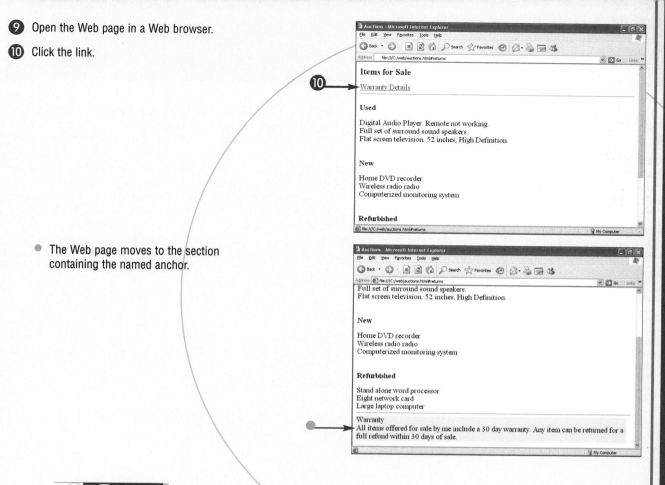

● The Web page moves to the section containing the named anchor.

Extra

Not only can you create links to areas within the same Web page that contains the link, but you can also create links to specific areas within other Web pages. To create a link to an area within another Web page, simply append the name of the target link preceding the pound symbol to the value of the `href` attribute. For example, to link to the area named `parts` of a Web page with the file name inventory.html, use the following code.

Link to File Name

```
<a
href="inventory.html#parts">Part
Ordering</a>
```

You can use both the `href` and `name` attributes within the same anchor tag. This enables you to use the name of an anchor as the target of another link. For example, say you created the following link:

```
<a href="#chapter1"
name="contents">Go to Chapter
One</a>
```

You can then use the name of the link *as* the link by simply appending a hash symbol (#) to the specified name; so, the `href` could be specified in another link as follows:

```
<a href="#contents">Back to Table
of Contents</a>
```

Target Links

You can create a link that opens a Web page in a new browser window. This is useful if you have links to outside Web pages; however, you want to prevent users from leaving your Web site entirely. Otherwise, it is possible that users could spend an extended period exploring those outside Web pages only to forget which Web site they were originally viewing.

The `target` attribute of the anchor tag is used to open a Web page in a new browser window. The value of the `target` attribute should be `_blank` to ensure that the new Web browser window appears before displaying the page being linked to.

You should only open a new browser window to display Web pages that provide secondary or supporting information for your own Web site. Opening pages that contain many links may annoy some users. All Web pages of importance or Web pages hosted on the same site should be opened within the same Web browser window.

When opening a Web page in a new browser window, some Web browsers will actually start a new instance of the Web browser, and others simply open a new tab within the same Web browser. Each Web browser determines exactly how it handles the command to open a new window.

Note that you cannot use the target attribute of the anchor tag to open new browser windows in the background. Any Web page that is directed to open in a new Web browser window opens in front of the Web page currently being viewed. In some cases, this may not be desirable.

Target Links

1. Open or create a Web page.

2. Type the code that creates a link.

3. Type **target="_blank"**.

4. Save the Web page.

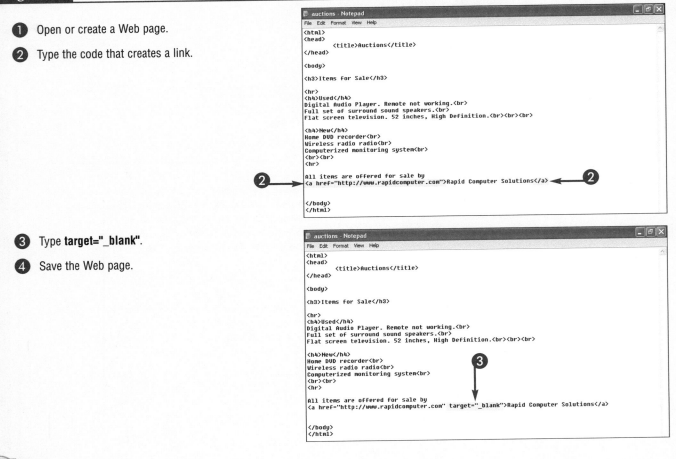

⑤ Open the Web page in a Web browser.

⑥ Click the link.

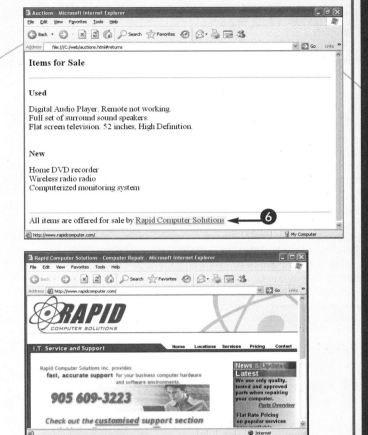

The new Web browser window appears and displays the Web page.

You can force all pages you want opened in a new browser window to open in the same window, greatly reducing clutter on your screen. Instead of using the `_blank` value for the target attribute, simply specify a unique name for the window. Each subsequent link that you use to target that window name will open in the same browser window.

Example
```
<a href="contents.html"
target="mywindow">Table of
Contents</a>

<a href="reference.html"
target="mywindow">Reference Guide
</a>

<a href="privacy.html"
target="mywindow">Privacy
Policy</a>
```

If you need every link of a Web page to open in a new browser window, you can use the `<base>` tag with the `target` attribute. The `<base>` tag should be placed within the header section of the HTML document. Any link in the page will then open in a new browser window.

Example
```
<head>
    <title>Table of
Contents</title>
<base target="_blank">
</head>
```

Set Tab Order for Links

Many people still use the keyboard as much or more than they use the mouse to navigate through a Web page. Even users who primarily use a mouse may do so in conjunction with the keyboard. You can customize the links on your Web page to make navigation easier for people who use a keyboard to assist them as they surf the Web.

When a Web page is first opened and displayed in a Web browser, when the user presses the Tab key on the keyboard the first link on the Web page is highlighted automatically. Each subsequent press of the Tab key highlights the next link on the Web page, and so on. Pressing Enter displays the Web page whose link is currently highlighted.

You can specify which links will be highlighted when the Tab key is pressed, and in which order. The `tabindex` attribute of the anchor tag `<a>` is used to specify in which order the links are to be selected when the Tab key is pressed. The value of the `tabindex` attribute is a number that represents the placement of the link in the highlighting sequence; it is this number that determines which link the Tab key highlights when pressed. Typically the first link has a `tabindex` value of 1, the second link has a `tabindex` value of 2, and so on.

The `tabindex` attribute may also be used with other elements such as text boxes and other form elements. When using the `tabindex` attribute with the anchor tab, you must ensure that the values you use do not conflict with the `tabindex` values of any other elements.

Set Tab Order for Links

1 Open or create a Web page that contains links.

2 Type **tabindex=""**.

3 Type a number that represents the selection sequence of the link.

4 Repeat steps **2** to **3** for each link that you want to be accessible in sequence.

5 Save the Web page.

```
ebook - Notepad
File  Edit  Format  View  Help
<html>
<head>
        <title>Sales Repor 2 ook</title>
</head>

<body>
<h2>Directors Marketinging Book</h2>

<a href="sales.html" tabindex=""><h3>Sales</h3></a>

<a href="sales.html#1">Chapter 1</a><br>
<a href="sales.html#2">Chapter 2</a><br>
<a href="sales.html#3">Chapter 3</a><br>

<a href="reports.html"><h3>Reporting</h3></a>

<a href="reports.html#4">Chapter 4</a><br>
<a href="reports.html#5">Chapter 5</a><br>


</body>
</html>
```

```
ebook - Notepad
File  Edit  Format  View  Help
<html>
<head>
        <title>Sales Report eBo 3 title>
</head>

<body>
<h2>Directors Marketinging Book h2>

<a href="sales.html" tabindex="1"><h3>Sales</h3></a>

<a href="sales.html#1">Chapter 1</a><br>
<a href="sales.html#2">Chapter 2</a><br>
<a href="sales.html#3">Chapter 3</a><br>

<a href="reports.html" tabindex="2"><h3>Reporting</h3></a>

<a href="reports.html#4">Chapter 4</a><br>
<a href="reports.html#5">Chapter 5</a><br>


</body>
</html>
```

6 Open the Web page in a Web browser and press the Tab key.

- The first link in the sequence is highlighted.

7 Press the Tab key.

- The second link in the sequence is highlighted.

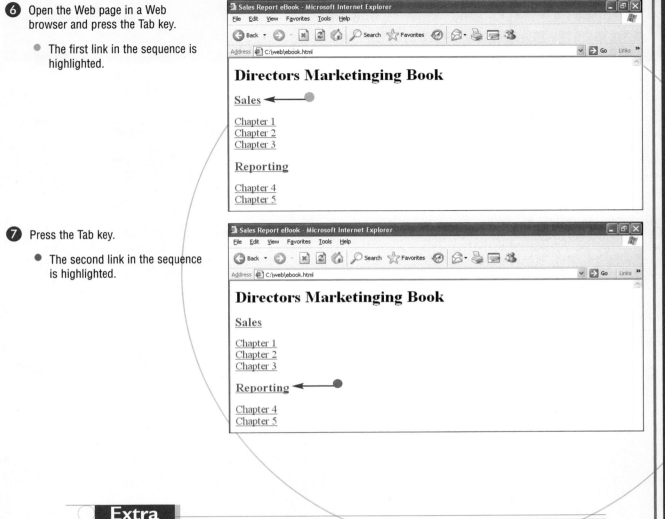

Y ou can create a tooltip that provides more
information to users about a link without requiring
them to click the link. This can be very useful for
providing information about the destination of the link, or
any unexpected behavior the user should be aware of
before clicking on the link. For example, you can use a
tooltip to inform a user that a link will open in a new Web
browser window.

A *tooltip* is a small text box of information that appears
beside the mouse pointer when the user positions the
pointer over the link. Typically, a tooltip is comprised of
black text on a yellow background that is slightly taller and
wider than the text of the tooltip. The user is not required
to click the link for the tooltip to appear.

The `title` attribute of the anchor tag is used to define the
text that will be used as a tooltip. You should strive to keep
the tooltips you create for your Web pages concise and to

the point. Users are more likely to read the information that
you include in a tooltip if you do not inundate them with
information. Try to include only information that the user
needs to decide whether or not one wants to click a link
rather than the entire text of the page to which the link
leads.

Tooltips are also very useful for explaining cryptic links. For
example, a text link that simply reads "News" may display
a tooltip with the text "Click to view today's latest news
headlines."

Some Web browsers may display additional information
about a link in the tooltip. For example, the Opera Web
browser will not only display the value you define in the
`title` attribute, but also the address referred to by the link.

Show Tooltip for Links

1 Open or create a Web page.

2 Type the code that creates a number of
links.

```
ebook - Notepad
File  Edit  Format  View  Help
<html>
<head>
        <title>Sales Report eBook</title>
</head>

<body>
<h2>Directors Marketinging Book</h2>

<a href="sales.html"><h3>Sales</h3></a>

<a href="sales.html#1">Chapter 1</a><br>
<a href="sales.html#2">Chapter 2</a><br>
<a href="sales.html#3">Chapter 3</a><br>

<a href="reports.html"><h3>Reporting</h3></a>

<a href="reports.html#4">Chapter 4</a><br>
<a href="reports.html#5">Chapter 5</a><br>


</body>
</html>
```

3 In the link with the tooltip, type **title=""**.

```
ebook - Notepad
File  Edit  Format  View  Help
<html>
<head>
        <title>Sales Rep  eBook</title>
</head>

<body>
<h2>Directors Marketinging Book</h2>

<a href="sales.html" title=""><h3>Sales</h3></a>

<a href="sales.html#1">Chapter 1</a><br>
<a href="sales.html#2">Chapter 2</a><br>
<a href="sales.html#3">Chapter 3</a><br>

<a href="reports.html"><h3>Reporting</h3></a>

<a href="reports.html#4">Chapter 4</a><br>
<a href="reports.html#5">Chapter 5</a><br>


</body>
</html>
```

4 Type the text of the tooltip.

5 Save the Web page.

```
ebook - Notepad
File  Edit  Format  View  Help
<html>
<head>
        <title>Sales Report eBook</title>   4
</head>

<body>
<h2>Directors Marketinging Book</h2>

<a href="sales.html" title="Overview of sales procedures"><h3>Sales</h3></a>

<a href="sales.html#1">Chapter 1</a><br>
<a href="sales.html#2">Chapter 2</a><br>
<a href="sales.html#3">Chapter 3</a><br>

<a href="reports.html"><h3>Reporting</h3></a>

<a href="reports.html#4">Chapter 4</a><br>
<a href="reports.html#5">Chapter 5</a><br>


</body>
</html>
```

6 Open the Web page in a Web browser.

7 Position the mouse pointer over the link.

● The tooltip displays.

```
Sales Report eBook - Microsoft Internet Explorer
File  Edit  View  Favorites  Tools  Help
Back    ⬛  🔄  🏠   🔍 Search  ⭐ Favorites  ✉  🔄  📄  📧  🗑
Address  C:\web\ebook.html                                      Go   Links

Directors Marketinging Book

Sales   7

Chapte [Overview of sales procedures]   ●
Chapter 2
Chapter 3

Reporting

Chapter 4
Chapter 5
```

Extra

The title attribute can be used with all the Web page elements to provide tooltips for different parts of a Web page. For example, you could use a tooltip to provide a description of an image.

Example
```
<a href="go.html" title="Large
view of map"><img
src="map.gif"></a>

<a href="now.html" title="Current
Temperature"><img
src="now.jpg"></a>

<a href="manual.html"
title="Caution: Large File"><img
src="man.jpg"></a>
```

The actual format of the tooltip depends on the Web browser. Most Web browsers display the tool tip in a small pop-up window with a rectangular border.

Some Web browsers, particularly older ones, do not understand the title attribute and will therefore simply ignore it. Therefore, you are safe using tooltips on any Web page, but make sure that you do not rely on tooltips for the user to be able to successfully navigate your Web page. When designing your page, always keep in mind that the user may not be able to see the tooltips or they may simply not bother to check them; you and the people viewing your page should be fine.

Use Mailto Links

ou can create a link that enables users to quickly send you e-mail by using the mailto value in URLs similarly to the way you use HTTP:// in URLs that point to Web pages. When the anchor tag is used to create a link, the href attribute specifies the target of the link. The href value, when referring to a Web site, typically starts with HTTP://. HTTP represents the protocol used to transfer information from a Web server to a Web browser. The protocol can be thought of as the language your Web browser uses to communicate with the Web server.

You can replace HTTP:// with mailto: to force the link to use the mailto protocol. Clicking a link for which the mailto protocol is specified causes a user's e-mail program to open and prepare a new blank e-mail message. You can specify

to whom the message should be sent by defining an e-mail address after the mailto:. This saves the user time by not having to type in the e-mail address. The e-mail address is already filled in the To: field for the user.

Some Web browsers, particularly very old ones, may not support the use of a mailto link. Other Web browsers can be configured to not utilize mailto links. When creating pages for the World Wide Web, you should display an e-mail address that a user can copy and paste to their own e-mail program in addition to a mailto link in case their browser does not allow them to use or simply does not support mailto links. In order for the mailto link to work, users must have an e-mail program installed on their computer.

Use Mailto Links

① Open or create a Web page.

② Type **<a href="mailto:">**.

③ Type **</a>**.

④ Type the e-mail address after the colon.

⑤ Save the Web page.

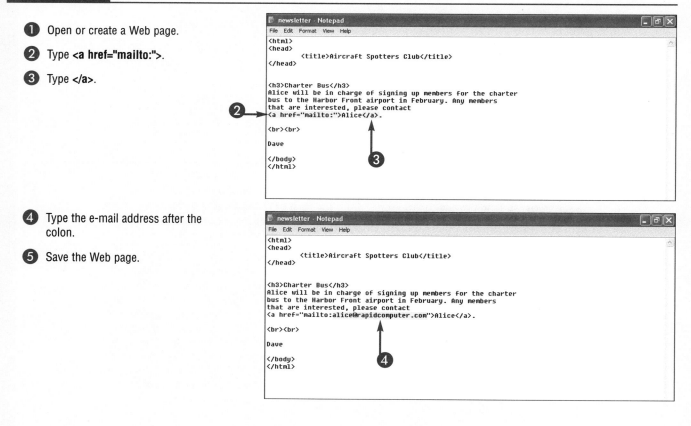

6 Open the Web page in a Web browser.

7 Click the link created in steps **2** to **4**.

Aircraft Spotters Club - Microsoft Internet Explorer

File   Edit   View   Favorites   Tools   Help

Back ▼   Search   Favorites

Address C:\web\newsletter.html   Go   Links

Charter Bus

Alice will be in charge of signing up members for the charter bus to the Harbor Front airport in February. Any members that are interested, please contact Alice.

Dave

7

The e-mail program opens a blank e-mail displaying the e-mail address specified in step **4**.

New Message

File   Edit   View   Insert   Format   Tools   Message   Help

Send   Cut   Copy   Paste   Undo   Check

To: alice@rapidcomputer.com
Cc:
Subject:

B I U A

Apply It

You can specify the subject or even the text of the e-mail message that will open when the user clicks a `mailto` link. To do so, append a question mark to the `href` value, followed by the field names, =, and then the field's value.

To fill out a subject line
```
<a
href="mailto:WM@rapidcomputer.com
?subject=Question">Send me a
question</a>
```

To CC an e-mail message to another e-mail address
```
<a
href="mailto:WM@rapidcomputer.com
?cc=archive@rapidcomputer.com">
Send me a question</a>
```

You can specify information for more than one field to be automatically filled in (or *populated*) by typing an ampersand (&) after the `href` attribute value for one field and then typing in the second field name and its information. In this way, you can stack information for populating multiple fields within a single hyperlink.

Example
```
<a href="mailto:info@rapidcomputer
.com?subject=Request&cc=backup@
rapidcomputer.com">Send me a
question</a>
```

Link to
a File

You can create a link that enables users to access files stored on an FTP server. An FTP server is a computer connected to the Internet that stores files such as documents, images, or archives of multiple files. By definition, the FTP protocol is specifically for transferring files: FTP stands for *file transfer protocol*.

As with all links, the anchor tag is used to create a link to the file. The `href` value contains the information necessary to locate and access the file on the FTP server. The `href` value must start with `ftp://` to indicate that the FTP protocol will be used when the user clicks on the link.

Retrieving a file from an FTP site requires a user name and password, the name of the FTP server, and the name and location of the file to be retrieved. All of this information is

defined in the value of the `href` attribute. The username and password feature allow you to control who views and downloads files from your FTP server, although you can allow users to log in anonymously if you are not concerned about controlling access to your files.

The user name and password, separated from each other with a colon, are specified after the protocol. These are followed by the `@` symbol and then the name of the FTP server. The name of the file and the location of the file on the server are then appended after a forward slash.

What happens to a file depends on how the Web browser is configured. In most cases, the Web browser asks the user if he or she wants to download the file, and then gives the user the opportunity to specify where on the computer to save the file.

Link to a File

1 Open or create a Web page.

2 Type **<a href="ftp://">**.

3 Type the FTP site user name and password.

4 Type **</a>**.

```
newsletter - Notepad
File  Edit  Format  View  Help
<html>
<head>
        <title>Aircraft Spotters Club</title>
</head>


<h3>Charter Bus</h3>
Alice will be in charge of signing up members for the charter bus to the Harbor Front airport in
February. Any members that are interested, please contact Alice.
<hr>

You can <a href="ftp://dave:all">download a archive</a> of all
last years newsletters from our ftp site.

<br><br>
Dave

</body>
</html>
```

5 Type @ followed by the name of the FTP site.

6 Type / followed by the name and location of the file.

7 Save the Web page.

```
newsletter - Notepad
File  Edit  Format  View  Help
<html>
<head>
        <title>Aircraft Spotters Club</title>
</head>


<h3>Charter Bus</h3>
Alice will be in charge of signing up members for the charter bus to the Harbor Front airport in
February. Any members that are interested, please contact Alice.
<hr>

You can <a href="ftp://dave:all@ftp.rapidcomputer.com/archive.zip">download a archive</a> of all
last years newsletters from our ftp site.

<br><br>
Dave

</body>
</html>
```

8 Open the Web page in a Web browser.

9 Click the link.

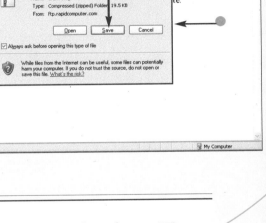

- A dialog box appears asking the user what action to take.

10 Click Save to save the file to your computer.

Apply It

Instead of linking to a file on an FTP server, you can specify the name of the directory containing the file instead. When the user clicks the link, the Web browser displays a listing of files and folders in the directory and enables the user to browse or retrieve the files that they want.

Example
```
<a
href="ftp://dave:all@
ftp.rapidcomputer.com
/">Browse</a>
```

If you do not specify the password in the `href` attribute, the user will be asked to enter a password upon connecting to the FTP site, before downloading any files specified in the link.

Example
```
<a href="ftp://dave@
ftp.rapidcomputer.
com/manual.pdf">
Instructions</a>
```

If you do not have an FTP site, you can store the files on your own Web server and link to them using standard hyperlinks. You will not be able to assign a user name or password to the file access, so anyone viewing your Web site can download the file.

Example
```
<a href="archive.zip">
Download the archive
</a>
```

Define
Link Colors

You can change the color of the link text so that the links stand out better from the Web page, making them easier to use. By default, text links are blue in color; after a user clicks on a link, the link appears magenta in color.

As an example of when you might want to change these colors, say you decide that your site would look best with a blue background. Depending on the color blue that you choose for your site's background color, you will likely render the color blue that is used by default by Web browsers to display your links as invisible or so difficult to see that they may as well be. In such a case, you would likely want to change the color of the unvisited links on your Web page to a color other than blue (such as white,

for example) that would better contrast with your page's background color.

You can change the colors of visited and unvisited links to a color of your own choice by using the link and vlink attributes of the <body> tag. The link attribute is used to define the color of a visited link, and the vlink attribute is used to define the color of an unvisited link. As with the color attribute of other tags, you can either specify the full color name if the color is common, or use hexadecimal notation to specify the red, green, and blue components to manually define the color you wish to use. Please refer to Appendix A for a description of common colors and their corresponding hexadecimal notation equivalents. After you specify the link and vlink attributes in the body tag, all links on your Web page will be affected.

Define Link Colors

1 Open or create a Web page.

2 In the body tag, type **link=""**.

```
ebook - Notepad
File  Edit  Format  View  Help
<html>
<head>
          <title>Sales Report eBook</title>
</head>

<body bgcolor="black" link="">

<h2>Directors Marketinging Book</h2>
<font face="Arial">
<a href="sales.html" title="Overview of sales procedures"><h3>Sales</h3></a>

<a href="sales.html#1">Chapter 1</a><br>
<a href="sales.html#2">Chapter 2</a><br>
<a href="sales.html#3">Chapter 3</a><br>

<a href="reports.html" title="Overview of reporting procedures"><h3>Reporting</h3></a>

<a href="reports.html#4">Chapter 4</a><br>
<a href="reports.html#5">Chapter 5</a><br>
</font>

</body>
</html>
```

3 Type the name of a common color.

4 Type **vlink=""**.

```
ebook - Notepad
File  Edit  Format  View  Help
<html>
<head>
          <title>Sales Report eBook</title>
</head>

<body bgcolor="black" link="white" vlink="">

<h2>Directors Marketinging Book</h2>
<font face="Arial">
<a href="sales.html" title="Overview of sales procedures"><h3>Sales</h3></a>

<a href="sales.html#1">Chapter 1</a><br>
<a href="sales.html#2">Chapter 2</a><br>
<a href="sales.html#3">Chapter 3</a><br>

<a href="reports.html" title="Overview of reporting procedures"><h3>Reporting</h3></a>

<a href="reports.html#4">Chapter 4</a><br>
<a href="reports.html#5">Chapter 5</a><br>
</font>

</body>
</html>
```

⑤ Type the name of a common color.

⑥ Save the Web page.

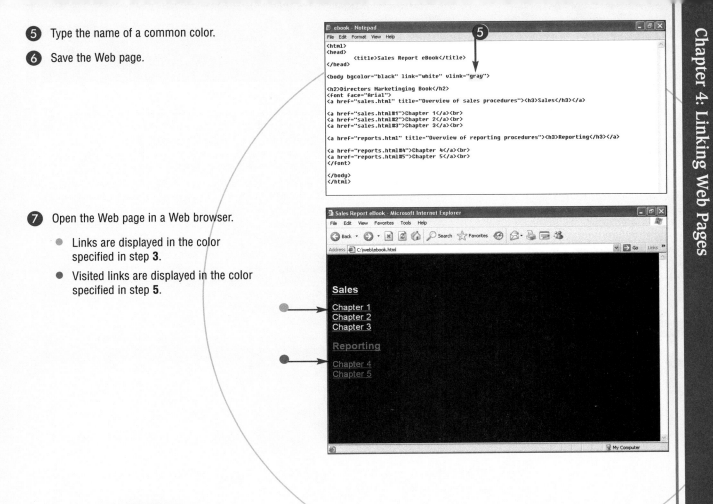

⑦ Open the Web page in a Web browser.

● Links are displayed in the color specified in step **3**.

● Visited links are displayed in the color specified in step **5**.

In addition to visited and unvisited links, a third state that a link can be is active. An active link is currently being clicked on by a user, and the state lasts only momentarily. Choosing the color of an active link can give more feedback to any user who selects links on your Web page. The `alink` attribute of the body tag is used to define the color of the active link.

Example
```
<body link="green" vlink="black"
alink="red">
```

You do not have to specify a color for all the link types. For example, if you want to change only the color of unvisited links, just use the `link` attribute to specify the color. The colors that visited and active links are displayed as will remain unchanged.

Example
```
<body link="green">
<body bgcolor="black"
link="yellow">
```

Display Images with Other Elements

You can display images on a Web page and position the images at various locations in a line of text. It can be hard to predict how images will look on a Web page when positioned alongside other images or text. By default, only one image may appear next to a single line of text. This can adversely affect the flow of text around an image. You can control the flow of text better by using the align attribute of the `<img>` tag. The align attribute changes the position of the image on the Web page. Text flows around any image that is aligned to the left or to the right. For example, you can align an image on the right-hand side of the Web page, and any text adjacent to the image will flow down the left-hand side of the image.

The values for the align attribute are left and right, depending on which side you want to position the image. If an image is contained within another element, such as a table cell, the image is aligned within that containing element, not with the margins of the Web page.

Use a `<br>` tag, with the clear attribute set to a value of all, to insert a line break into a Web page after an image and its adjacent text. You can then add text, images, or other elements.

Aligning multiple images properly on a Web page can be quite confusing. Always test your Web pages with various Web browsers to ensure the page elements display the way you intended. You may need to make adjustments several times before you get the images to display as you intended in multiple Web browsers.

Display Images with Other Elements

① Open or create a Web page.

② Position the mouse pointer where you want the image to appear and type **<img src="" />**.

```
index - Notepad
File  Edit  Format  View  Help
<html>
<head>
<title>Auctions</title>
</head>

<body>

<img src="" />   ← 2
We have a fine selection of oil on canvas nature themed paintings up for auction this month.


All artwork will be available for viewing in the main gallery hall on Saturday afternoon.


Opening bids will be accepted at 5 pm. Please seal all bids in the envelopes provided.


</body>
</html>
```

③ Position the mouse pointer between the quotes and type the name of the image.

④ Position the mouse pointer in the image tag and type **align=""**.

```
index - Notepad
File  Edit  Format  View  Help
<html>
<head>
<title>Auctions 3 title>  4
</head>

<body>

<img src="bigcat.jpg" align="" />
We have a fine selection of oil on canvas nature themed paintings up for auction this month.


All artwork will be available for viewing in the main gallery hall on Saturday afternoon.


Opening bids will be accepted at 5 pm. Please seal all bids in the envelopes provided.


</body>
</html>
```

5️⃣ Position the mouse pointer between the quotes and type the kind of alignment to apply to the image.

6️⃣ Repeat steps **2** to **5** for each image you want to add to the Web page.

7️⃣ Position the mouse pointer where you want breaks to appear and type **<br clear="all" />**.

8️⃣ Save the Web page.

9️⃣ Open the Web page in a Web browser.

The aligned images appear on the Web page.

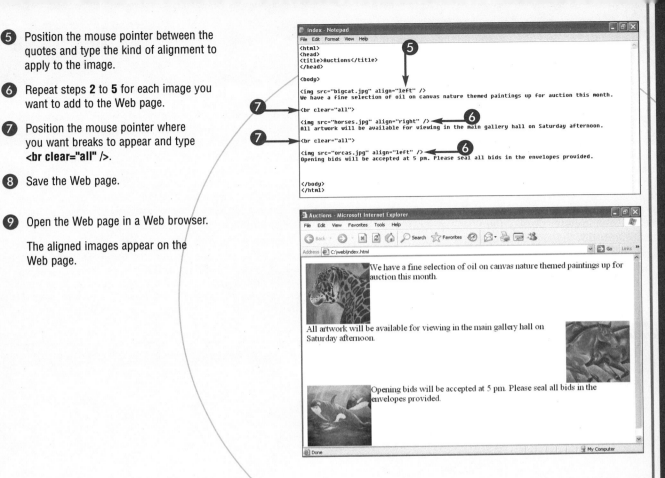

Apply It

Keep in mind that style sheets allow you much greater control over the presentation of your Web page than just using align attributes and HTML tags. For example, you can position images more accurately on a Web page by using style sheet properties. The style sheet properties top and left enable you to specify in pixels how far the image should be from the top and left-hand margins of the Web page.

Example
```
<img src="horses.jpg"
style="left: 15px; top: 20px;"
border="2" />
```

You can use the clear attribute with the <br> tag to specify that you want the image clear of content on one side or both sides of the image. For example, if you want the <br> tag to keep the image clear of text and other Web page elements to the right or left of the image you would use the right or left values; if you want the image clear of Web page content on both sides, use the all value instead.

Example
```
<br clear="right" />
```

Change the Image Size

Y ou can quickly change the displayed size of an image on a Web page. Every image has a specific size. Images for which you do not specify a size display at their full size. For many images, this is perfectly normal; but if you are trying to position elements on a Web page more accurately, you will want to specify the actual size of the images. If you are using an image on the Web that you cannot resize yourself, you also may decide to have the Web browser display the image at a different height and width than that of the actual image.

Specify the height of an image using the `height` attribute of the `<img>` tag. Likewise, the `width` attribute of the `<img>` tag determines the width of an image. Image size is typically expressed in pixels. For example, a width value of

`100` will displays an image 100 pixels wide. You can also specify a percentage for the size of an image. When you specify a percentage value, the size of the image is determined in relation to the current size of the Web browser window. For example, a value of `50%` for the `width` attribute displays an image that is half as wide as the Web browser window. Resizing the Web browser window also resizes the image. Not all Web browsers support the use of percentage values to specify image size.

You can display multiple versions of the same image on a Web page, using different values for the `width` and `height` attribute of each `<img>` tag, and the Web browser will retrieve the image from the Web server only once so that people viewing your page do not have to wait for more than one image to load.

Change the Image Size

① Open or create a Web page that contains an image.

② Position the mouse pointer within the image tag and type **width="".**

③ Position the mouse pointer between the quotes and type the width of the image.

④ Position the mouse pointer within the `<img>` tag and type **height ="".**

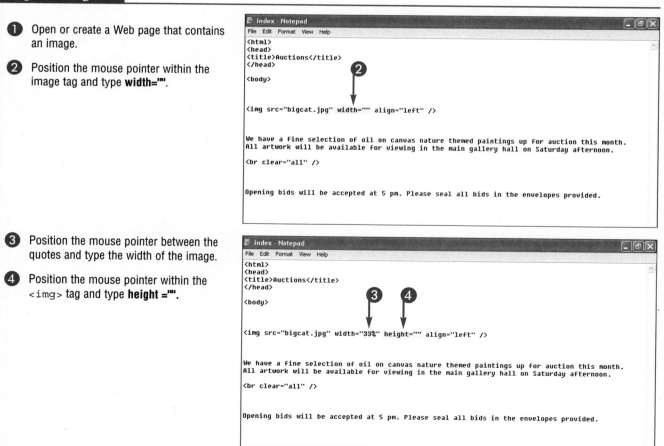

5 Position the mouse pointer between the quotes and type the height of the image.

6 Repeat steps **2** to **5** for each image you want to add to the Web page.

7 Save the Web page.

8 Open the Web page in a Web browser.

The images of differing sizes display.

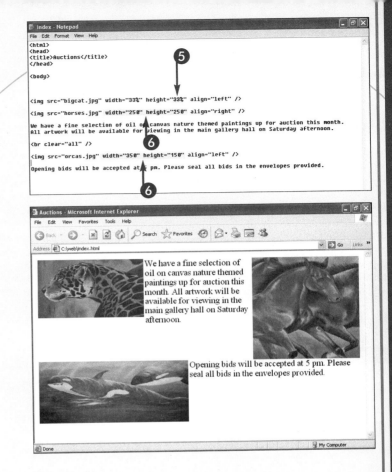

Extra

When you open a Web page in a browser, the textual information displays first while the images continue to download. Specifying the height and width of the images on your Web page decreases the time it takes for a Web browser to display them; the Web browser does not have to load an image before determining its size, and therefore its position on the Web page. This will allow your Web page to appear visually in its true layout faster than if you did not specify the height and width.

You can use the width and height attributes of the <img> tag to specify a size that is smaller than the actual image, but the complete image is always loaded despite the size specified within the <img> tag. This enables you to create thumbnails of larger images, but because the complete image must load the thumbnails are not true thumbnail images. True thumbnail images are smaller versions of images that are used on many Web pages. Thumbnail images usually link from the thumbnail image to the larger image so that users can choose to view larger versions of the thumbnails.

Display Text Descriptions

Alternative text displays when an image is not available, or when you position the mouse pointer over an image. Alternative text can provide more information about the images on your Web page, or display error messages when an image is not available. Alternative text is also used when viewing Web pages in a text-based Web browser, or when utilizing accessibility devices or Web readers for the visually impaired.

Use the alt attribute of the `<img>` tag to display alternative text when an image is unavailable. The Web browser typically draws an outline of the missing image, and places the text specified by the alt attribute within the outline. Usually some sort of icon indicating that the image is unavailable accompanies the alternative text.

Sometimes users disable the display of images in their Web browsers, usually to decrease the time it takes to view Web pages. Any alternative text you specify with the alt attribute will display for these users in place of the image on the Web page.

The text specified as a value of the alt attribute should be brief and to the point. The alt attribute is not meant to display paragraphs of text. The text you choose should ideally contain a description of the image, enabling people who cannot view the image to have an idea of what the image looks like. Furthermore, if your images contain links to other pages, your alternative text should indicate that the image is a link and to where it links. For example, if you use an arrow image to indicate a link to the next page, the alternative text should be something like "Click to advance to next page" rather than just "arrow."

Display Text Descriptions

① Open or create a Web page that contains an image.

② Position the mouse pointer within the `<img>` tag and type **alt=""**.

③ Position the mouse pointer between the quotes and type the alternative text.

④ Save the Web page.

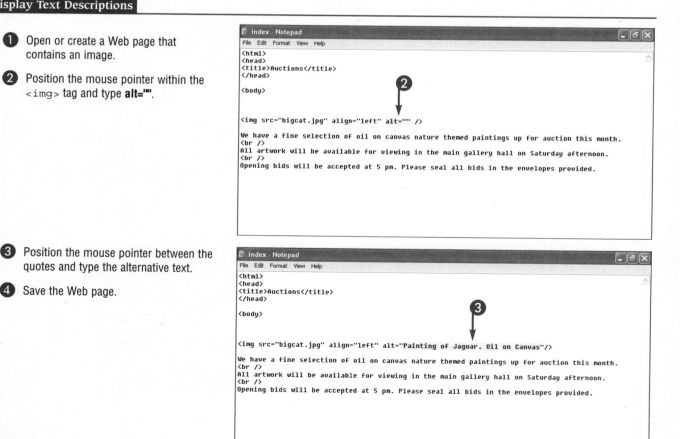

⑤ Open the Web page in a Web browser.

⑥ Position the mouse pointer over the image.

● The alternative text appears.

● If the image is unavailable, the alternative text appears.

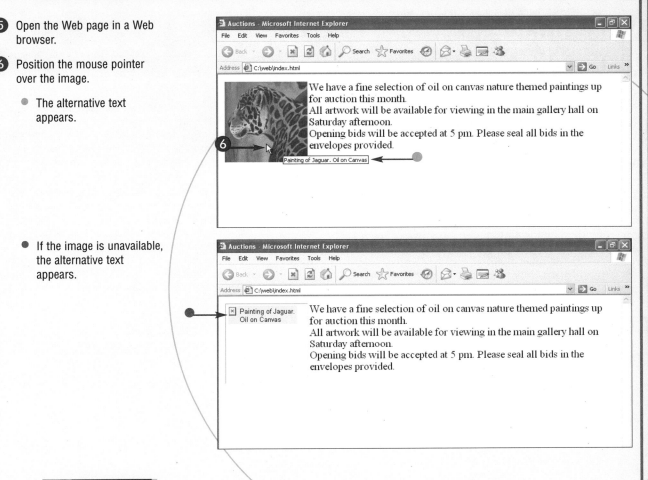

You should always use the `alt` attribute for people who have turned off images as well as for visually impaired people who are using Web readers or accessibility devices. However, if you are simply providing textual information for a tooltip, then you should use the `title` attribute of the `<img>` tag to provide small amounts of information. You can use the `alt` and `title` attributes within the same `<img>` tag.

Example
```
<img src="horses.jpg" alt="Horse
painting" title="Bidding starts
at $500" />
```

As with most attribute values, you must always use quotation marks around the `alt` attribute value to ensure that your code functions properly. Missing quotation marks can cause total havoc with your code and render your Web page unreadable. If quotes are required with the value, use single quotes to prevent the attribute from being interpreted incorrectly.

Right
```
<img src="anthem.jpg" alt="Tony
singing 'God Save The Queen' "
/>
```

Wrong
```
<img src="anthem.jpg" alt="Tony
singing "God Save The Queen" "
/>
```

Make Images into Links

Instead of text links, you can use images as links to enhance the appearance of your Web page. The <a> tag, which creates the link to another Web page, is made up of a starting and ending tag. These tags usually encompass the text that creates the link. You can just as easily enclose an image within the start and end <a> tags to create a link.

You can use links with images for many things. For example, you can use small images, referred to as *thumbnail images*, to link to larger versions of the same image. Using thumbnails allows users to preview images before they commit to clicking the thumbnail to view the entire image. On the other hand, you can add links to images that are specifically created to act as links, such as an image of an envelope that links to a Web page where a

user can compose an e-mail message or an image of an arrow that links to another Web page. Many commercial Web sites even use large, complex images with image maps as the main navigation for the site. See the "Develop an Image Map" section in this chapter for more information on image maps.

When using images as links, make sure that the purpose of the image is immediately apparent to the person viewing the page. If the image by itself is not obvious as a link, place text adjacent to the image indicating that a user may click the image to access another Web page. To be safe, though, you should always use images such as buttons or icons that are easily interpreted as links; doing so will help ensure that navigating your site is as intuitive as possible.

Make Images into Links

① Open or create a Web page that contains an image.

② Position the mouse pointer before the image and type **<a href="">**.

③ Position the mouse pointer between the quotes and type the location of the Web page to which you want to link.

④ Position the mouse pointer after the image and type **</a>**.

⑤ Save the Web page.

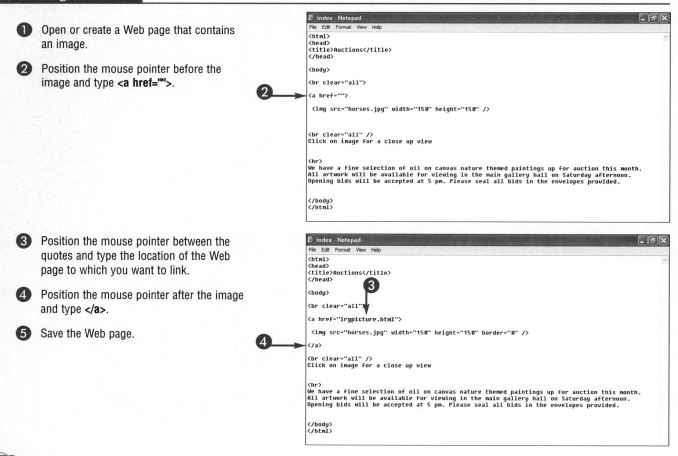

6 Open the Web page in a Web browser.

7 Click the image.

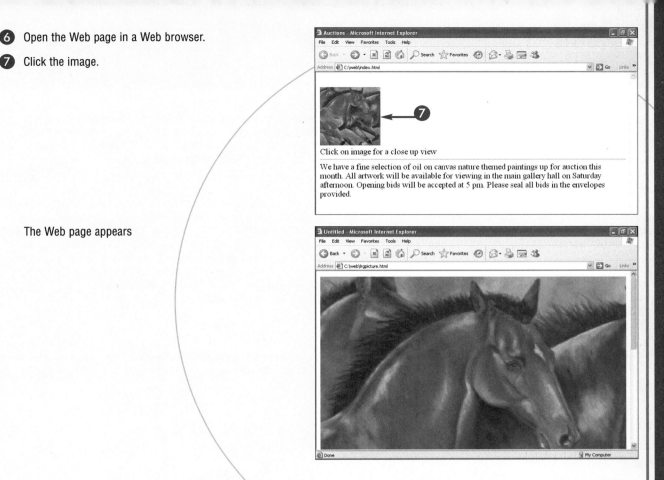

The Web page appears

You can create a border around an image link by setting the `border` attribute of the `<img>` tag to a value greater than `0`. For example, to place a 5-pixel-wide border around an image, use the following code.

Example
```
<a href="dollar.html">
<img src="sales.jpg" border="5" />
</a>
```

Conversely, many Web designers consider the border link around an image to be ugly and set the border as 0 deliberately to avoid it.

The same color rules that apply to text links apply to borders placed around image links. For example, an image link to a Web page that has already been viewed will by default have a purple border. An image link to a Web page that has not been visited will have a blue border. You can change the color of the border surrounding an image link by defining `link` and `vlink` attributes of the `<body>` tag.

```
<body link="red" vlink="green">
```

Develop an Image Map

You can develop more sophisticated links to your documents using an image map. An image map is essentially an image that contains multiple links to different Web pages. People viewing your site access the various links depending on what region of the image they hover their mouse pointer over. The result to the user is that the image is itself a navigational tool; the image map is invisible so as far as the user is concerned they are working directly with the image to interface with your site.

Image maps work by creating hot spots on an image. A *hot spot* (called a *hot region* by some) is an area that acts as a link; clicking on the area loads a new Web page.

You must define the coordinates for the area that will act as the hot spot on an image. Define a rectangular area by specifying the coordinates of the top-left corner and the bottom-right corner of the hot spot. For example, the coordinates 0,0,10,10 create a 10-x-10-pixel hot spot in the top left-hand corner of an image.

The usemap attribute of the <img> tag specifies the name of the image map. The actual coordinates of the hot spots, along with the href attribute that specifies the name of the linked Web page, are placed in the cords attribute of an <area> tag. The <area> tags are then enclosed by the start and end <map> tags. The name attribute of the <map> tag identifies the image to use with the hot-spot coordinates. The <map> tag, although placed in the body of the Web page, does not display in the Web browser.

Develop an Image Map

① Open or create a Web page that contains an image.

② Position the mouse pointer within the <img> tag and type **usemap=""**.

③ Position the mouse pointer on a new line and type **<map name="">**.

④ Position the mouse pointer between the quotes and type the name of the map preceded by **#**.

⑤ Position the mouse pointer between the quotation marks and type the name of the map specified in step **4**.

⑥ Position the mouse pointer on a new line and type **<area cords="" href="">**.

⑦ Position the mouse pointer on the following line and type **</map>**.

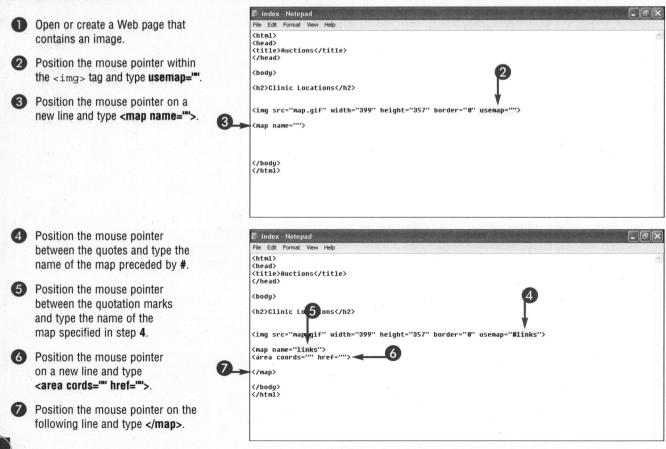

8 Position the mouse pointer between the quotes and type the coordinates of the hot spot.

9 Position the mouse pointer between the quotes and type name of the Web page to link to.

10 Repeat steps **6** to **9** for each hot spot on the image map.

11 Save the Web page.

12 Open the Web page in a Web browser.

● The image map displays. You can click a hot spot to display a Web page.

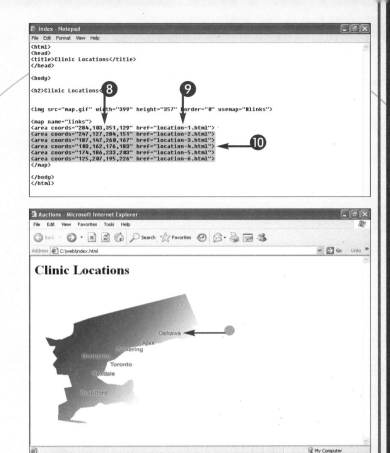

Apply It

Image maps allow you to use the image as the navigational "dashboard" for your Web site. Ideally, the hot spots on an image map should complement the links on the image map so that people viewing your page find it intuitive and obvious where to click for the information they are looking for. For example, if part of your image shows buttons that say News, Home, and About, the hot spots on the corresponding image map should link to News, Home, and About pages, respectively.

The area allocated to hot spots is rectangular by default. If you want a different shape for your hot spots (to accommodate circular buttons, for example), you can use the shape attribute of the <area> tag, along with the necessary coordinates, to define different area types for your hot spots. The following examples show you how to create hot spots that are circular and triangular.

Circle
```
<area shape="circle" coords"120,
70,  30" href="location.htmL" />
```

Triangle
```
<area shape="poly" coords=
"120,134,  225,290,  230,325,"
href=" location.htmL " />
```

Preload Images

You can preload the images that appear throughout your Web site to decrease download time and, thereby, enable your site to appear that much more quickly in a user's Web browser. Download time is a very important factor for a Web site; quick versus long download time can mean the difference between a user viewing your Web page or surfing to another page that does not take so long to load.

Web browsers must download images from a server before displaying the images on your Web page. Images retrieved from a Web server are placed in an area called the *cache*, which is simply a folder that stores images the Web browser downloads to your computer. If your Web page contains multiple copies of the same image, or if the image is already present in the computer's cache because it is displayed on another Web page that was visited by a user,

the Web browser simply uses the image stored in the cache instead of repeatedly downloading the same image from the Web server.

The trick to preloading is to set the `height` and `width` of your images to `0`. That way, the images are placed into the computer's cache without displaying on the Web page. Any occurrences of the images on subsequent Web pages display instantly, without the usual delay as the images download from the Web server.

Preloading images makes your Web site faster to navigate and more responsive to user input. Preloading typically takes place on the first page of a Web site. If you are preloading a large number of images, you may want to display a message indicating that images are preloading in the background.

Preload Images

1 Open or create a Web page.

2 Position the mouse pointer within the body of the Web page and type the code that creates an `<img>` tag.

3 Position the mouse pointer within the `<img>` tag and type **width="" height=""**.

4 Position the mouse pointer between the width quotes and type **0**.

5 Position the mouse pointer between the height quotes and type **0**.

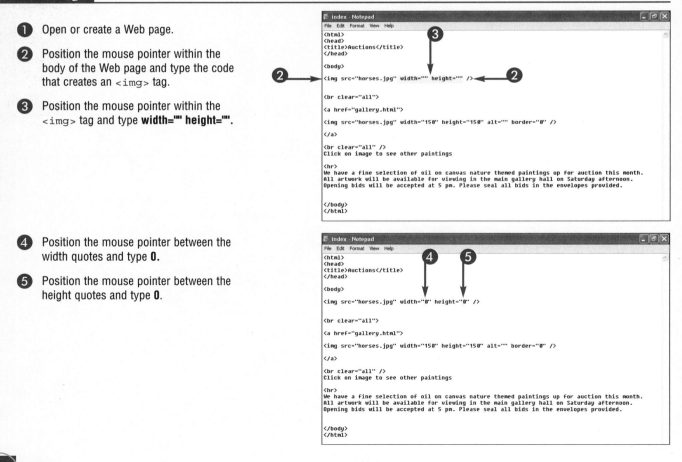

6 Repeat steps **2** to **5** for each image on your Web site that you want to preload on the current Web page.

7 Save the Web page.

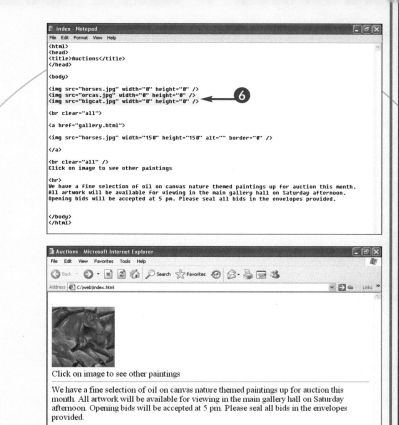

8 Open the Web page in a Web browser.

The Web page appears; however, the preloading images do not display.

Next step

Develop a Global Style Sheet

You can use a style sheet to change the appearance of your Web pages. A *style sheet* is a text document that instructs the browser to change the appearance of Web page elements according to directions you specify. Style sheets specify items such as text color, text alignment, and the background color of the Web page.

A style sheet that changes the background color of a Web page can be specified in any `<body>` tag within the page. The attribute used to set the background color is called `background-color`. When specifying style sheet attributes, follow the attribute name with a colon, the value of the attribute, and then a semicolon. A set of brackets (preceded by the tag name, in capital letters, to which the attributes pertain) encloses all of the style sheet attributes.

A global style sheet is a style sheet that can be utilized by many different Web pages on your site. The style information is saved in a separate text file with the file extension .css.

The `<link>` tag included within your HTML code instructs the Web browser to use the style sheet. The `<link>` tag must contain the `rel` attribute with a value of `stylesheet`. The `type` attribute must be set to `text/css`. The `href` attribute of the `<link>` tag specifies the file name of the style sheet. The `<link>` tag must be enclosed within the `<head>` element of your HTML code.

Note that when using external style sheets, the Web browser must not only retrieve the Web page from the server, but it must also retrieve the separate style sheet file. This may cause the Web browser to take slightly longer to display the Web page.

Develop a Global Style Sheet

SET A BACKGROUND COLOR

1 Open a text editor.

2 Type **BODY { }**.

3 Inside the brackets, type **background-color: black;**.

4 Save the style sheet file.

SET THE STYLESHEET TYPE

1 Open or create a Web page.

2 Type **<link rel=stylesheet >**.

3 Type **type="text/css"**.

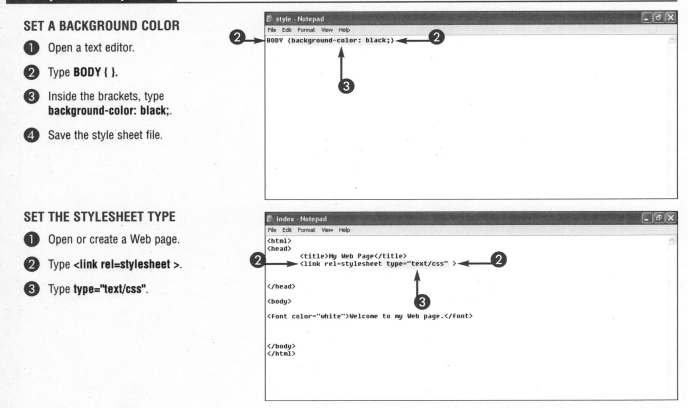

76

④ Type **href=""**.

⑤ Type the name of the style sheet.

⑥ Save the Web page.

```
index - Notepad
File  Edit  Format  View  Help
<html>
<head>
        <title>My Web Page</title>
        <link rel=stylesheet type="text/css" href="style.css">     ← 4

</head>

<body>

<font color="white">Welcome to my Web page.</font>


</body>
</html>
```

⑦ Open or create a Web page.

The style sheet is applied and the Web page displays.

```
My Web Page - Microsoft Internet Explorer
File  Edit  View  Favorites  Tools  Help
Back          Search  Favorites
Address  C:\web\index.html                              Go   Links

Welcome to my Web page.
```

Construct a Rule

You can create a rule that will apply different style sheet properties to an element of a Web page. Rules can create quite complex instructions for the Web browser to use to display elements such as text or images. Most style sheets include multiple rules for styling Web page elements such as text color, link color, background color, table formatting, and so on. Rules are located in style sheet files and can therefore be used by any Web page.

A rule consists of a *selector*, which is typically the name of the HTML tag that will use the style instructions of the rule, and then a list of properties and values which are all enclosed in a set of curly brackets { }. Properties and their values are separated by a colon (:), and property and value pairs are separated from each other by a semicolon (;). Typically, each property and value pair will be on its own line to make reading and understanding the style sheet easier.

There are many different properties whose values affect the appearance of elements on your Web page. The background-color property specifies the color to place behind elements such as text or images. The value of background-color can be any valid color. The text-decoration property defines effects that are applied to any text on a Web page. The values for the text-decoration property are underline, overline, and line-through. These values cause a line to display underneath, on top of, or through the center of a portion of text.

The font-variant property defines a specific variant of the font being used on the Web page. For example, the value small-caps of the font-variant property replaces all the lowercase letters in a section of text with small capital letters.

Construct a Rule

1 Open or create a style sheet file.

2 Type the name of the HTML tag to which the rule will apply, followed by { }.

3 Type **background-color:**.

4 Type the name of a color followed by ;.

5 Type **text-decoration: underline;**.

6 Type **font-variant: small-caps;**.

7 Save the style sheet.

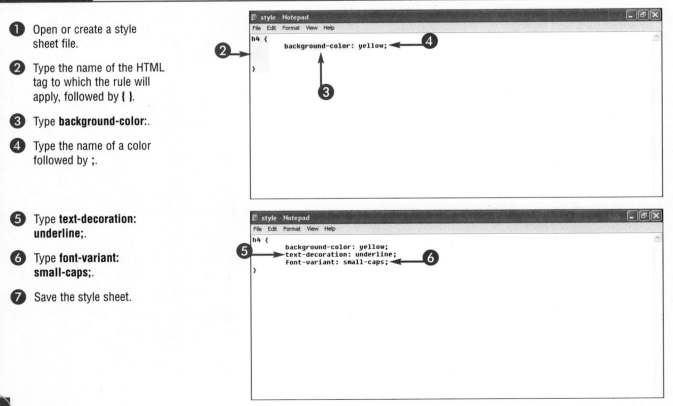

8 Open or create a Web page.

9 Type the code that links to the style sheet saved in step **7**.

10 Insert the HTML tags specified in step **2**.

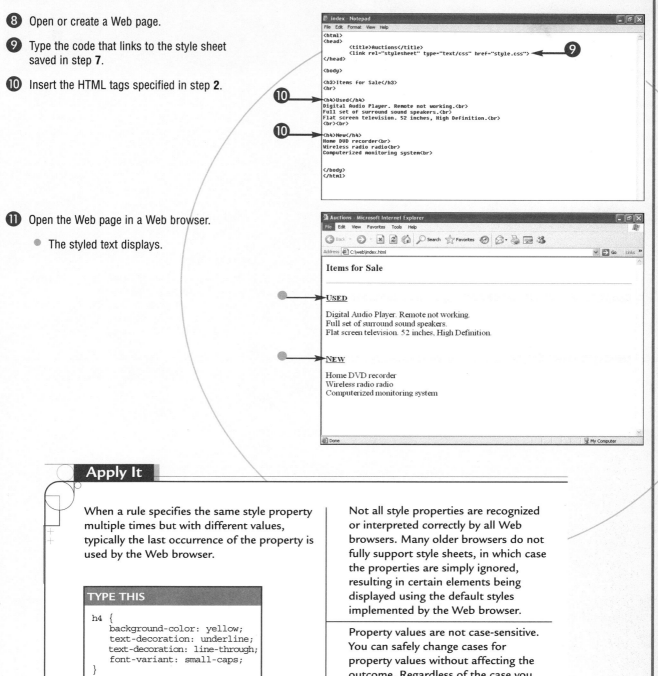

11 Open the Web page in a Web browser.

● The styled text displays.

Apply It

When a rule specifies the same style property multiple times but with different values, typically the last occurrence of the property is used by the Web browser.

TYPE THIS

```
h4 {
    background-color: yellow;
    text-decoration: underline;
    text-decoration: line-through;
    font-variant: small-caps;
}
```

RESULT

~~Latest News~~

Not all style properties are recognized or interpreted correctly by all Web browsers. Many older browsers do not fully support style sheets, in which case the properties are simply ignored, resulting in certain elements being displayed using the default styles implemented by the Web browser.

Property values are not case-sensitive. You can safely change cases for property values without affecting the outcome. Regardless of the case you use when specifying property values, it is good programming practice to remain consistent. This will make your code easier to read and understand.

Use an Internal Style Sheet

External style sheets are not the only way that Web pages can access style sheet rules. You can embed style sheet rules directly into your HTML code. Style sheet information embedded directly into the HTML page is called an *internal style sheet*.

Internal style sheets are useful if you want to use style sheet properties within a single Web page. Unlike external style sheets, which can be used by multiple Web pages, an internal style sheet can only format the Web page into which the style sheet is embedded.

Style sheets are considered cascading because the external style sheet applies first, internal style sheets are applied second, and local style sheets (also called *in-line style sheets*) are applied last. This cascading effect allows you to set global style sheet rules and then override them on a case-by-case basis by using internal and/or inline

style sheets. Internal style sheets, therefore, will override external style sheets if there are any contradictory rules in place. Similarly, local style sheets will overrule your internal style sheet rules.

You define rules for the internal style sheet the same way you do for an external style sheet, but the rules are placed between opening and closing <style> tags instead of in a separate file. The <style> tag is placed within the <head> section of the HTML code.

When you define a rule for an HTML tag using internal style sheets, the rule applies any time that tag appears in the HTML code of the Web page.

In many cases, the style sheet rules can be used to replace some of the functions of HTML tag attributes. You should always use style sheet rules whenever possible, as in the future many Web browsers will only use style sheet information to format Web page elements.

Use an Internal Style Sheet

① Open or create a Web page.

② Type **<style>**.

③ Type **</style>**.

④ Type the HTML tag name to which the rule will apply.

⑤ Type **{ }**.

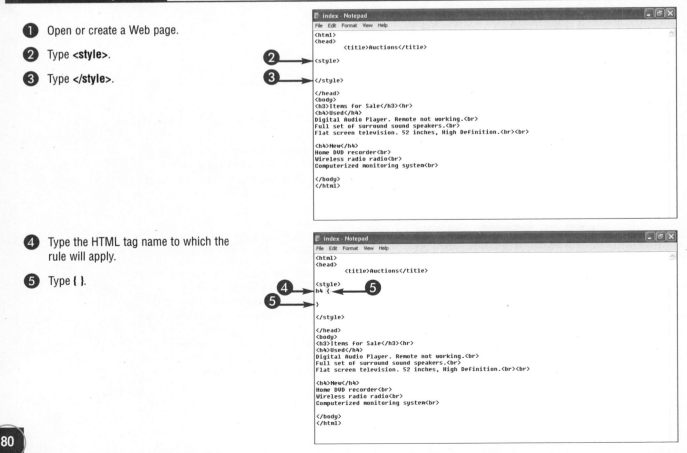

6 Type the style sheet property and values to be applied to the HTML tag.

7 Repeat steps **4** to **6** for each HTML tag.

8 Save the Web page.

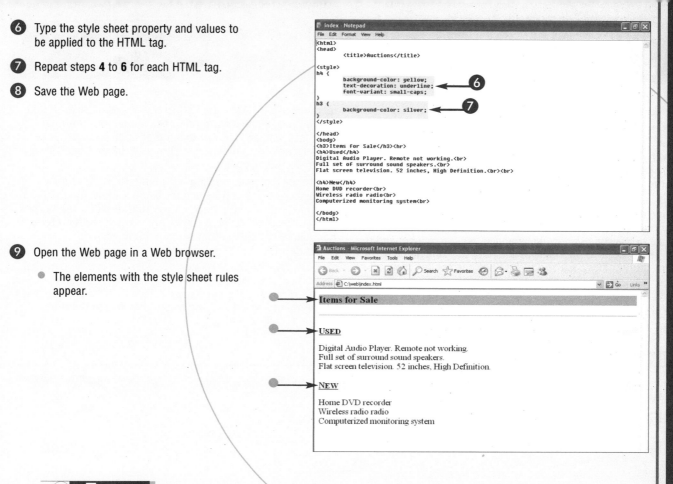

9 Open the Web page in a Web browser.

● The elements with the style sheet rules appear.

Some older Web browsers do not recognize the `<style>` tag. If the internal style sheet is correctly placed within the `<head>` section of the HTML code, any Web browser that does not recognize the `<style>` tag simply ignores the style sheet information.

Although internal style sheets can be used for large amounts of rules, updating and maintaining large amounts of style sheet information is easier in an external style sheet. You should use internal style sheets for defining lesser amounts of style sheet rules.

Style sheet rules can become quite complex and quite lengthy. As with most programming languages, the consistent and correct use of white space and indentations can make complex code easier to understand.

Non-Formatted Code
```
h4{background-color: yellow;text-
decoration: underline;font-variant:
small-caps;}
```

Code Formatted and Indented
```
h4 {
    background-color: yellow;
    text-decoration: underline;
    font-variant: small-caps;
    }
```

Apply a Rule to a Single Element

style sheet rules can be applied to different elements even if there are multiple elements of the same type within the Web page. For example, if you are using seven instances of the <h1> header tag within the same Web page, you can apply a style to just the first occurrence of the <h1> tag.

Styles are applied to an individual HTML tag using a reference name defined with the ID attribute. The value of the ID attribute will be the reference name. Specify the reference name in the style sheet rule by appending a # symbol and the reference name to the name of the rule. The rule name is the name of the HTML tag to which the rule is applied. For example, if you have named an anchor tag as anchor1 in the ID of the tag, your reference name would be #anchor1.

Reference names defined within the style section of the Web page must be unique. Use reference names with a single instance of an HTML tag within a Web page. Be sure that you do not use the same reference name with multiple elements. For an efficient method of applying style sheet rules to multiple similar elements, see the section "Use a Class" in this chapter.

Reference names can begin with either a letter or an underscore (_), but they cannot begin with a number. You should try to use reference names that describe the purpose or the effects of the style sheet rules to which the reference name applies. This will make your code easier to understand.

You can use reference names in either internal or external style sheets. However, you should use reference names only within internal style sheets, as it may be hard to keep track of reference names and the pages that utilize them in external style sheets.

Apply a Rule to a Single Element

① Open or create a Web page.

② Type the opening and closing style tags.

③ Type the HTML tag name to which the rule will apply followed by { }.

④ Type # followed by the reference name of the tag.

⑤ Type the style sheet property and values to be applied to the HTML tag.

⑥ Repeat steps 3 to 5 for each style sheet rule.

⑦ Type id ="" in the tag to which the style sheet rule will apply.

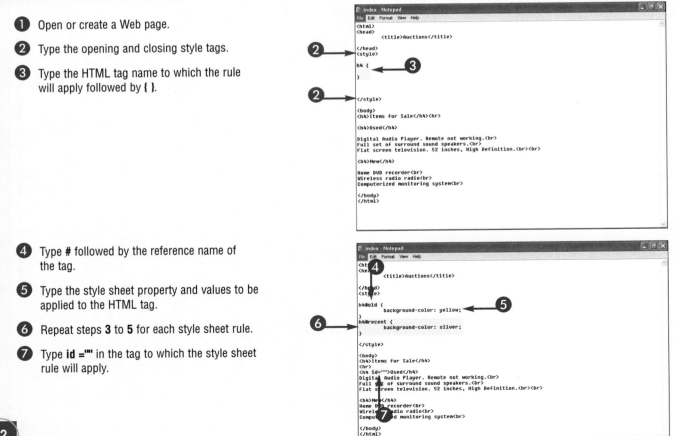

8 Type the reference name defined in step **4**.

9 Repeat steps **7** to **8** for each reference name created in step **6**.

10 Save the Web page.

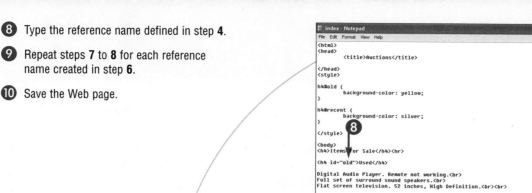

11 Open the Web page in a Web browser.

● The elements with the style sheet rules are displayed.

Extra

Using reference names to apply style sheet information to HTML tags makes for easier Web page maintenance. Although initially it takes longer to create the code, using reference names saves you time because you will not have to scan through your Web pages to locate formatting information that is already contained in the style sheet section at the beginning of your code.

You can use the ID attribute with most HTML tags. Simply **type id=""** and add the identifying term in between the quotation marks.

Example
```
<hr id="start">
<body id="master">
<strong id="headline">My News</strong>
```

The reference name specified with the ID attribute of an HTML tag may also be used as an identifier when creating a link to an area within a Web page, in which case the ID attribute replaces the name attribute. For more information about creating links, see Chapter 4.

Attribute Replacement
```
<a href="#used">Go to used good for sale</a>
```

Use a Class to Style Similar Elements

You can use a class to apply style rules to multiple similar elements within a Web page. For example, you can use a class to highlight specific paragraphs of text within a Web page, with the highlighting being applied only to the paragraphs that you specify.

Create a class the same way as any other style sheet rule. The name of the rule is the class name preceded by a period. Apply a class to a Web page element using the class attribute within the starting tag of the element. For example, if you want to use a class with an <h1> header element, the class attribute is inserted into the opening <h1> header tag. As with all attribute values of HTML tags, the value, which is the class name, must be enclosed in quotations.

A class can be applied to multiple similar Web page elements. Typically, the rules in a class all relate to the type of element in which the class will be used. For example, a class that is used primarily with text may contain rules governing font families and type sizes.

You can define classes within either an external or internal style sheet. The class attribute can be used with almost all HTML and XHTML elements.

Note that if you have already defined a style sheet rule for a tag with which you are using the class attribute, both style rules will be applied to the Web page element. For example, if you have defined a rule that applies an underline to all paragraphs, and in one paragraph tag, you are using a class attribute that defines a gray background, that paragraph will have both an underline and a gray background.

Create a Class

① Open or create a Web page.

② Type the opening and closing style tags.

③ Type . followed by the class name and then { }.

④ Type the style sheet rules.

⑤ Repeat steps **3** to **4** for each class.

⑥ Type **class=""**.

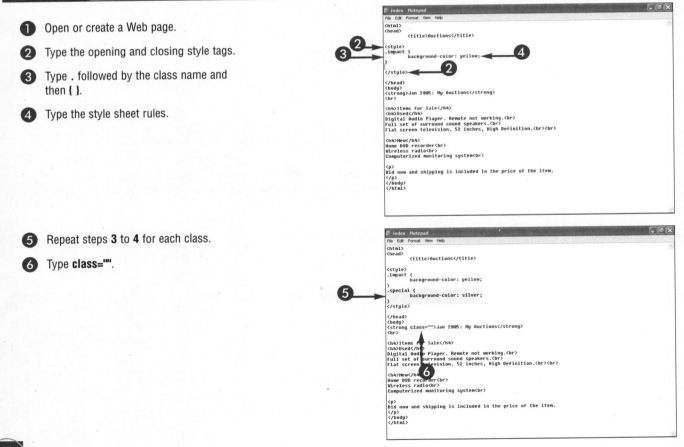

7 Type the name of the class to apply to the tag.

8 Repeat steps **6** to **7** for each class to be used.

9 Save the Web page.

10 Open the Web page in a Web browser.

● The elements with the style sheet rules appear.

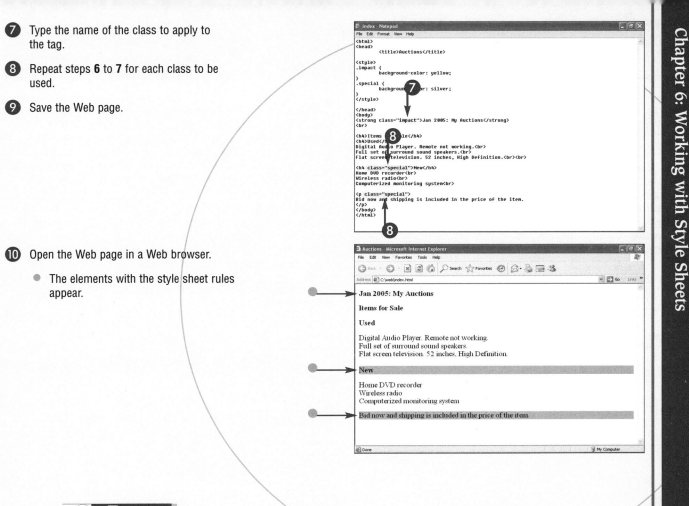

You can use multiple classes with a single instance of an element by defining multiple class names as the value of the `class` attribute. You must separate individual class names with a space.

Example
```
<p class="important
highlight">THE FOLLOWING IS A
VERY IMPORTENT MESSAGE</p>
<h1 class="visible dark
large">Welcome"</h1>
```

You can create a class that can only be used with specific tags, preventing the incorrect application of styles to an element. To define to which tags a class may be applied, simply append the tag names to the class name when creating the style rule. For example, to restrict a class that changes the background color to only the paragraph tag `<p>`, use the following rule:

Example
```
p.impact {
    background-color: yellow;
}
```

Insert
Local Styles

A style rule can be applied directly to a single HTML tag without having to define the rule in either an internal or external style sheet. For example, you can apply a style sheet rule to the first `<h1>` tag on a Web page to make the header stand out more. Because local styles (also called in-line styles) are applied after external and internal style sheets are, they overrule contradictory external and internal rules. In this example, therefore, only the first `<h1>` tag is affected by the style; all other `<h1>` will function normally unless you specify the same local style to them manually.

A style rule consists of a style sheet property and a value for that property. You can specify the property and value pair in an HTML tag using the `style` attribute. The starting tag always contains the `style` attribute. The value of the

`style` attribute is the property and value that specifies the style sheet rule to be applied to the tag. As with all rules that are defined in external or internal style sheets, the property name is followed by a colon (:), the value of the property, and then a semicolon (;). In addition, as with all HTML tag attributes, the value of the `style` attribute must be enclosed in quotations.

Applying styles locally to each tag is a fast way to use style sheets, as long as the Web page uses a limited amount of elements that require styles. When applying styles to a large number of elements, using an external or internal style sheet is much more efficient. Maintaining and updating locally applied styles can be time consuming, so they should only be used if you do not think you will be changing the styles in the future.

Insert Local Styles

① Open or create a Web page.

② Type **style=""**.

```
index - Notepad
File  Edit  Format  View  Help
<html>
<head>
        <title>Auctions</title>
</head>
<body>

<strong style="">Jan 2005: My Auctions</strong>

<br>

<h4>Items For Sale</h4>

<h4>Used</h4>
Digital Audio Player. Remote not working.<br>
Full set of surround sound speakers.<br>
Flat screen television. 52 inches, High Definition.<br><br>

<h4>New</h4>

Home DVD recorder<br>
Wireless radio<br>
Computerized monitoring system<br>

<p>

  Bid now and shipping is included in the price of the item.

</p>

</body>
</html>
```

③ Type the property name followed by **: ;**.

```
index - Notepad
File  Edit  Format  View  Help
<html>
<head>
        <title>Auctions</title>
</head>
<body>

<strong style="background-color: ;">Jan 2005: My Auctions</strong>

<br>

<h4>Items For Sale</h4>

<h4>Used</h4>
Digital Audio Player. Remote not working.<br>
Full set of surround sound speakers.<br>
Flat screen television. 52 inches, High Definition.<br><br>

<h4>New</h4>

Home DVD recorder<br>
Wireless radio<br>
Computerized monitoring system<br>

<p>

  Bid now and shipping is included in the price of the item.

</p>

</body>
</html>
```

④ Type the value of the property between the colon(:) and the semicolon(;).

⑤ Repeat steps **2** to **4** for each tag that has a style applied.

⑥ Save the Web page.

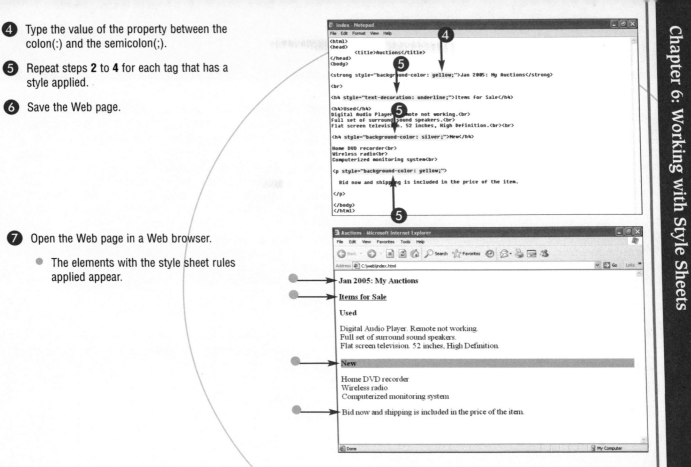

⑦ Open the Web page in a Web browser.

● The elements with the style sheet rules applied appear.

Apply It

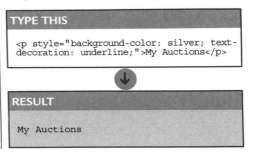

You can use the `style` attribute to apply a style directly to a tag, even if the HTML tag has styles applied to it using internal or external style sheets. As mentioned elsewhere in this book, the "cascading" in Cascading Style Sheets means that style sheets are applied in cascading order: external style sheets are applied first, internal style sheets are applied second, and local style sheets are applied last. Therefore, styles applied using the `style` attribute override any other styles that have previously been defined for that tag in another style sheet.

You can use the `style` attribute to apply more than one style characteristic to an element. To apply additional styles, simply make sure that your property and value pairs within the value of the `style` attribute are separated from each other by a colon (:).

TYPE THIS

```
<p style="background-color: silver; text-decoration: underline;">My Auctions</p>
```

RESULT

```
My Auctions
```

Apply Styles to Web Page Sections

You can use style sheet rules in any section of a Web page. When a tag such as a header or a paragraph tag encloses a section of a Web page, you can apply styles to the HTML tag to change the appearance of the element. However, you can also use the `<div>` and `<span>` tags to apply style sheets to elements that may not be enclosed in a HTML tag, such as a word or phrase in the middle of a sentence.

The `<div>` tag defines specific, distinct areas on the Web page. Any part of a Web page contained within `<div>` tags will be separated from the other elements on the page by white space, although not as much white space as the `<p>` tag produces. The `<div>` tag is used to define paragraphs of text or closely related items such as an image and its

caption. The `<div>` tag enables you to quickly apply styles to large areas of your Web page. Like other HTML tags, `<div>` has the corresponding `</div>` closing tag.

The `<span>` tag is used to apply styles to a span of items such as individual words or phrases. No white space appears before or after elements enclosed by the `<span>` tags, so only the changes defined by the styles affects the appearance of those elements. Close the span of text you wish to set apart with the `</span>` tag.

Although you can apply styles locally to the `<div>` and `<span>` tags, applying the styles using a class defined in an internal or external style sheet is much more efficient if you intend to use the styles in more than one location on your page.

Apply Styles to Web Page Sections

1. Open or create a Web page.

2. Type the opening and closing style tags.

3. Type a class name followed by **{ }**.

4. Type the style sheet rule.

5. Type **<div class="">**.

6. Type **</div>**.

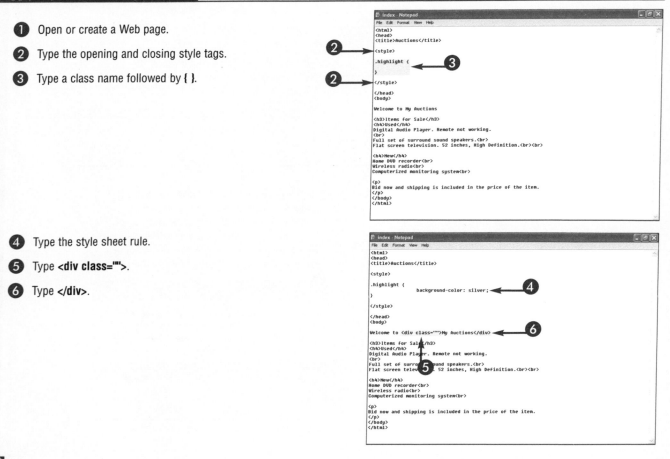

7 Type **<span="">**.

8 Type **</span>**.

9 Type the class name specified in step **3**.

10 Save the Web page.

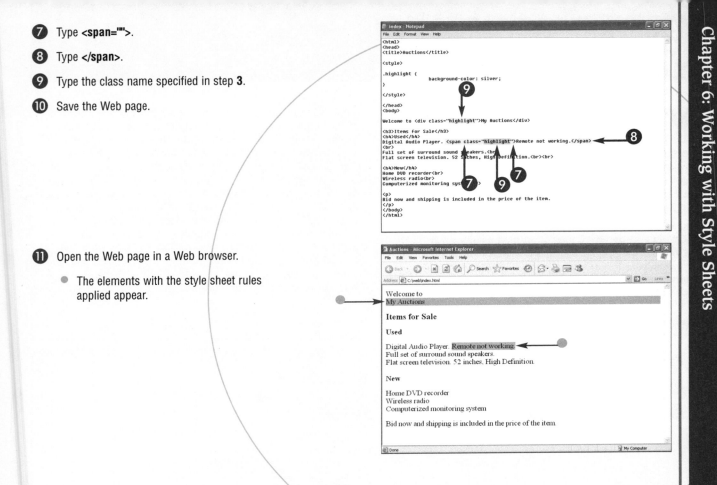

11 Open the Web page in a Web browser.

● The elements with the style sheet rules applied appear.

Extra

HTML tags may be *nested*, which means that one tag may enclose another start and end tag. For example, a paragraph of text, defined using the <p> tag, may contain individual words emphasized using the <b> tag. Any style applied to the paragraph also affects the text defined with the <b> tag. This process is known as *inheritance*: the <b> tag inherits the styles from the <p> tag. Any Web page elements enclosed by the <div> tags will inherit any styles associated with those tags.

Because the <span> tag applies styles to items within an HTML element, it is called an *in-line* element. The <div> tag is called a *block level* element because it defines distinct areas of a Web page that will appear separated from the surrounding elements.

If you need to quickly apply a style to a word or phrase within your text, you can apply styles locally using the <span> tag with the style attribute.

Example
```
Digital Audio Player. <span
style="background-color:
yellow;">Remote not working.</span>
```

Apply Rules to Multiple Elements

Y ou can apply a rule to many different HTML tags. For example, you can apply a rule that changes the appearance of text in multiple HTML tags that share the same display characteristics. Creating one rule that can be applied to multiple elements eliminates the need to specify a separate style sheet rule for each tag on your Web page that requires the same formatting.

To define a rule for different HTML tags, create a rule as you would for a single HTML tag, but use multiple HTML tag names in the selector section of the rule. Each HTML tag name that you specify in the selector must be separated by a comma (,). It is very important that you do not inadvertently leave out the comma, as this may cause the Web browser to interpret the rule incorrectly.

You must be cautious when creating one rule for different HTML tags. The effects of the style rule that you choose should be applicable to the content of the tags. For example, you do not want to create a rule that specifies the type of font that should be used by a tag and then apply that rule to an image tag. Rules should generally specify properties that are related. For example, you could have one rule that specifies multiple characteristics of text, and another rule that specifies the positioning of elements on the Web page. Failure to follow these guidelines can result in your Web page behaving in unexpected (and likely unwanted) ways. In addition to specifying tag names, you can also associate rules with multiple classes. To do so, simply specify class names separated by commas within the selector.

Apply Rules to Multiple Elements

1. Open or create a Web page.

2. Type the opening and closing style tags.

3. Type the name of an HTML tag followed by { }.

4. Type a comma and a space.

5. Type the name of another HTML tag.

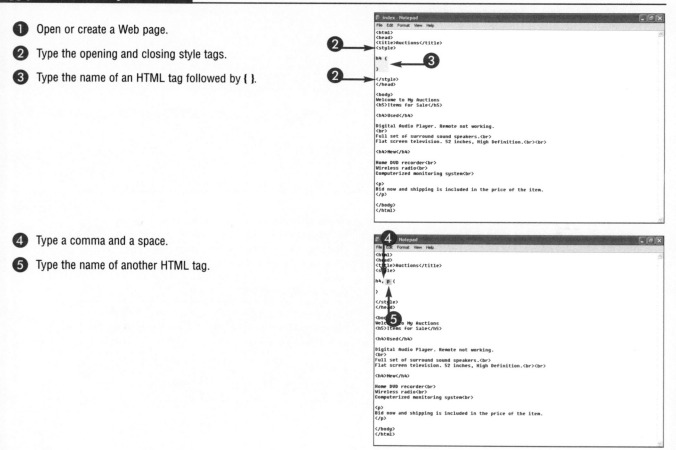

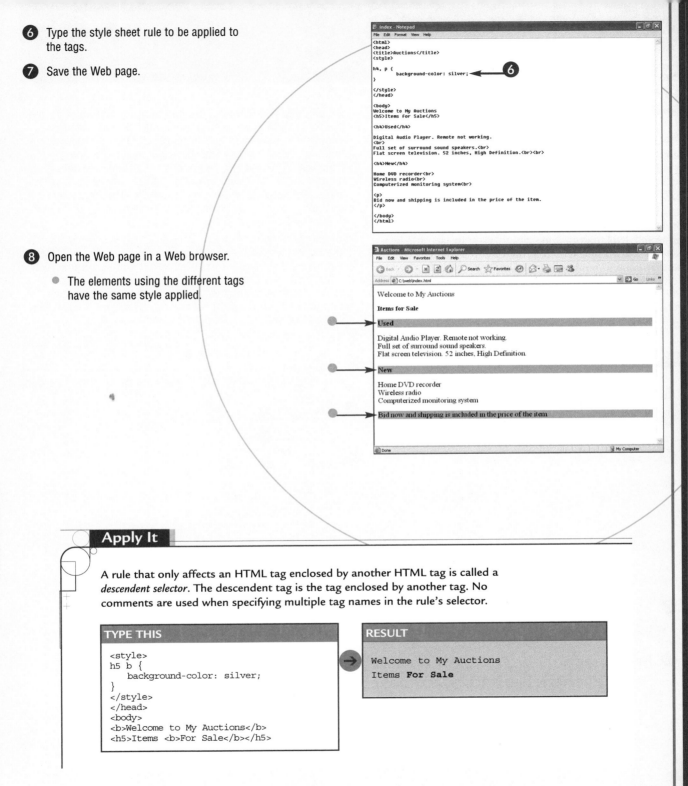

⑥ Type the style sheet rule to be applied to the tags.

⑦ Save the Web page.

⑧ Open the Web page in a Web browser.

● The elements using the different tags have the same style applied.

Apply It

A rule that only affects an HTML tag enclosed by another HTML tag is called a *descendent selector*. The descendent tag is the tag enclosed by another tag. No comments are used when specifying multiple tag names in the rule's selector.

TYPE THIS

```
<style>
h5 b {
    background-color: silver;
}
</style>
</head>
<body>
<b>Welcome to My Auctions</b>
<h5>Items <b>For Sale</b></h5>
```

RESULT

Welcome to My Auctions

Items **For Sale**

Add Comments to Style Sheet

Comments make your style sheets easier to understand and therefore easier to maintain and upgrade. Comments are very useful for explaining the purpose of the style sheet code within your Web page. Trying to understand style sheet rules without the help of comments can be a very time-consuming process.

Comments can consist of entire paragraphs of text, enabling you to write very detailed descriptions of your code. You do not need to add a comment to explain the purpose of code that is self-explanatory and easy to read. In fact, the best code should be concise and structured in a manner that makes it easy to read and understand without the need for additional comments. Comments should be reserved for code that is somewhat ambiguous, or be used to explain the overall purpose of the code.

You can add comments to the end of a line within your style sheets, enabling you to explain specific line of code and what conventions you had in mind when you created them. Comments are denoted within a style sheets by using delimiters. The starting delimiter is /* and the closing delimiter is */. The Web browser ignores any code, text, or characters between these two delimiters. The only way to view these comments within the Web browser is to view the source code of the Web page.

Comments may be added to internal or external style sheets. To add comments to your HTML code, you must use HTML comments. For more information about adding comments to HTML code, see Chapter 2. You can also use comments when adding inline styles, as long as the comments are contained within the value of the `style` attribute and follow the semicolon (;) that denotes the end of the rule.

Add Comments to Style Sheet

① Open or create a Web page.

② Type the opening and closing style tags and the style sheet rules.

③ Type /*.

④ Type */.

⑤ Type the text of the comment that describes the purpose of the style sheet rules.

⑥ Type /* */.

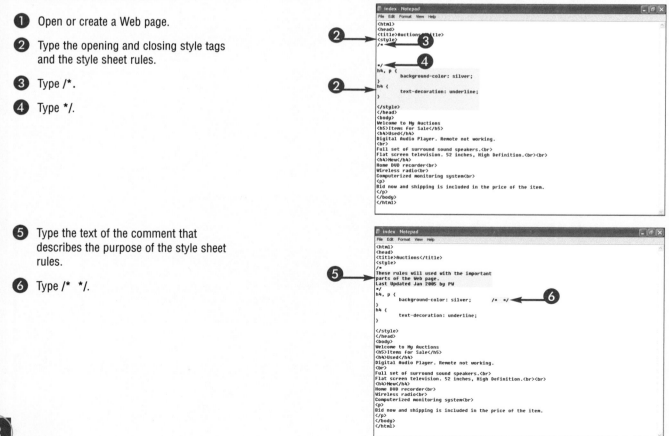

7 Type the text of the comment that describes the purpose of the rule.

8 Repeat steps **6** to **7** for each comment in your style sheets.

9 Save the Web page.

10 Open the Web page in a Web browser.

The Web page appears, but the comments do not display.

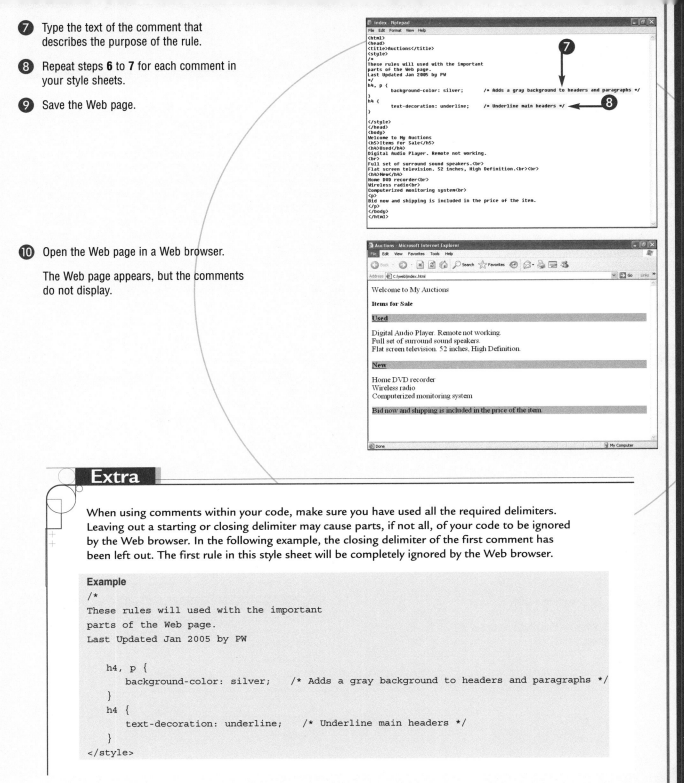

Extra

When using comments within your code, make sure you have used all the required delimiters. Leaving out a starting or closing delimiter may cause parts, if not all, of your code to be ignored by the Web browser. In the following example, the closing delimiter of the first comment has been left out. The first rule in this style sheet will be completely ignored by the Web browser.

Example

```
/*
These rules will used with the important
parts of the Web page.
Last Updated Jan 2005 by PW

    h4, p {
        background-color: silver;    /* Adds a gray background to headers and paragraphs */
    }
    h4 {
        text-decoration: underline;    /* Underline main headers */
    }
</style>
```

Insert Page Breaks for Printing

You can use a style sheet to better format the data on your Web pages for printing. Just because a Web page looks good in a Web browser does not necessarily mean it will print in the most readable form on a printer. You can see how your Web page will appear when printed by using your Web browser's Print Preview feature. The Print Preview feature displays your Web page in your browser just as it will appear on the printed page.

The biggest problem with printing Web pages is that the Web browser does not know when to start a new page. This can cause elements such as links, images, tables of contents, paragraphs of text, and headings to split across multiple pages. This can be quite inconvenient in many cases; for example, if you are printing a page that includes a map, having the map image split across two pages can

make the map much harder to follow. You can use style sheets to control where the page breaks occur on your Web page when the page is printed.

The style sheet property `page-break-before` can be used to indicate where the printer should start a new page. The `page-break-before` style sheet property, when applied to an HTML tag, inserts the page break when the opening HTML tag is encountered. When used with the value `always`, regardless of how much data has already been printed, the printer will start to print the information following the `page-break-before` property on a new page. The easiest way to apply the `page-break-before` style sheet property is to use the `<div>` tag to enclose the information that you want printed on the start of a new page.

Insert Page Breaks for Printing

① Open or create a Web page that contains an internal style sheet.

② Type **div { }**.

③ Type **page-break-before: always**.

④ Create a `<div>` tag enclosing the elements to be printed at the start of a new page.

⑤ Save the Web page.

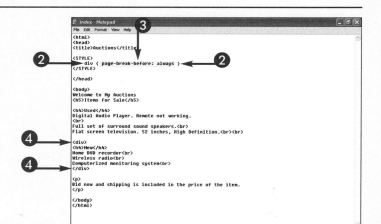

⑥ Open the Web page in a Web browser.

The content of the Web page appears with no page breaks.

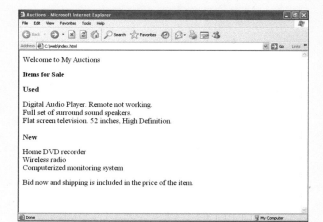

7 Click File.

8 Click Print Preview.

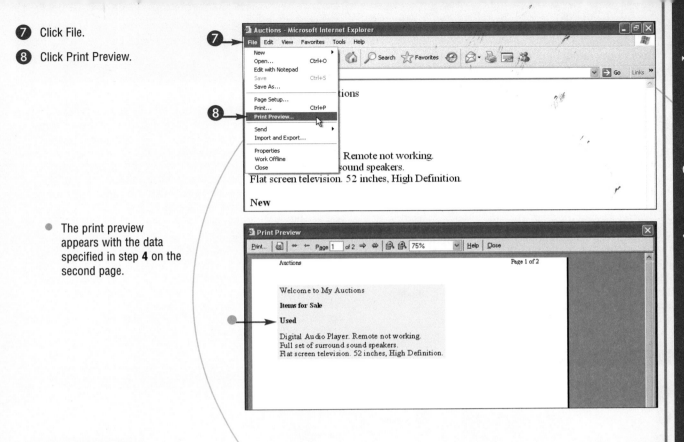

● The print preview appears with the data specified in step **4** on the second page.

Where the page breaks appear in a Web browser is no indication of where they will appear when the Web page is printed. For the users to see where page breaks are, they will have to either print the Web page or view the Web page using the Print Preview feature of the Web browser.

You can also use locally applied styles to insert page breaks in printed material. The page break instructions would refer only to the tag for which the locally applied style is used. The following code illustrates how to apply a page break before a paragraph of text:

Example
```
<p STYLE="page-break-
before: always"> This is
a very important message
</p>
```

The `page-break-after` property enables you to insert a page break after the closing HTML tag. For example, if the `page-break-after` property is applied to a `<div>` tag, the page break is applied where the closing `</div>` tag occurs within the HTML code. You can specify that the page break appears after the element by using the `always` value with the `page-break-after` property.

Example
```
<style>
div { page-break-after:
always }
</style>
```

Apply Styles to Links

You can use style sheet rules to change the colors of links on your Web page, making the links easier to locate or simply fit in with a color scheme of your Web page. Links typically occur in two different states: visited or unvisited. A visited link is one that you have previously viewed. By default, most Web browsers display visited links in purple and unvisited links in blue.

Sometimes it is even necessary to change the color of your links. For example, if your background color is blue, depending on the color blue of your background the default link color of blue is likely to be either extremely difficult to see or downright invisible against the page background. Similarly, if the page background color is purple, the default visited link color of purple might be impossible to see against the page background.

You can define a rule that uses the selector A: followed by either visited or unvisited to indicate for which link type you are specifying the color. The style sheet property used to set the color of the link is color. Although it is not mandatory to use different colors for the visited and unvisited links, most users expect the links to be in different colors. Some designers use the same color for both visited and unvisited links; whether you decide to do so or not is obviously up to you.

A Web browser examines its cache to determine whether a link is visited or unvisited. If the Web page that is being linked to is found in a Web browser's cache, then the link will be treated as a visited link. To change a link from visited to unvisited, you can simply empty the Web browser's cache. Emptying the Web browser's cache is a very simple procedure; for more information, see your Web browser's documentation.

Apply Styles to Links

① Open or create a Web page.

② Type the opening and closing style tags.

③ Type **A:link { }**.

④ Type **color: black;**.

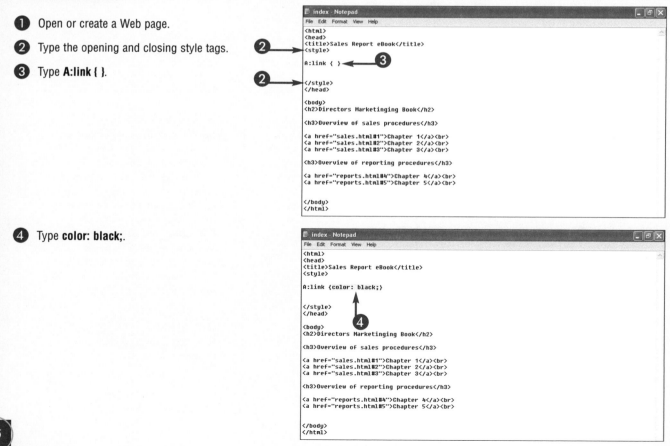

⑤ Type **A:visited { }**.

⑥ Type **color: silver;**.

⑦ Save the Web page.

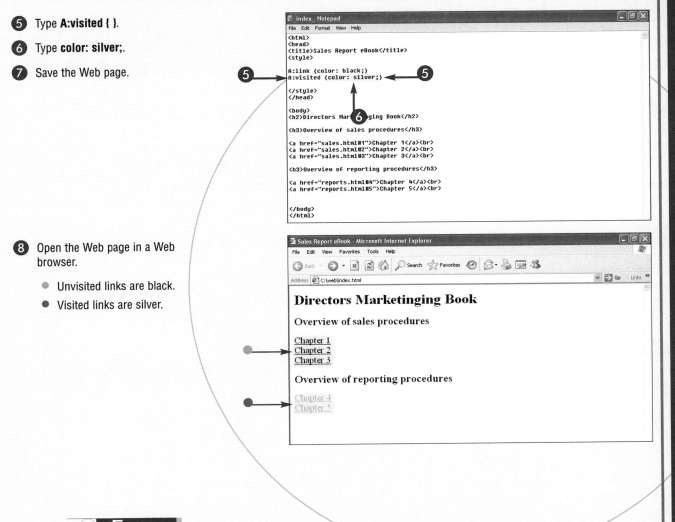

⑧ Open the Web page in a Web browser.

● Unvisited links are black.

● Visited links are silver.

Add Alternative Style Sheets

You can create multiple style sheets and let the user select which style sheet to use to display your Web page. You can create multiple internal style sheets within your Web page, with each style sheet specifying different characteristics. For example, you could define a style sheet that renders text in black-and-white to make it easier to read by people who are visually impaired or you could create alternate color schemes or layouts simply so that users can view your site in a manner that is most aesthetically pleasing to them.

Multiple style sheets on a Web page are differentiated from each other by each style tag's `title` attribute. The `title` attribute of the style tag must have a unique value.

Many Web browsers do not currently support the use of alternative style sheets, though Netscape Navigator is an exception. In Netscape, simply click View and then click

Page Style to choose from available styles for a Web page. You can obtain Netscape Navigator free at www.netscape.com.

A rule specified in one style sheet does not have to be duplicated in all the alternative style sheets. You may have one style sheet that addresses positioning of elements, and another style sheet that deals specifically with text formatting. Web browsers that support alternative style sheets typically use the first style sheet to render the Web page. As a result, calling the first style sheet `default`, via the `title` attribute, is usually a good practice.

Note that most Web browsers do not indicate to the user that alternative style sheets are available; so if you have multiple style sheets to choose from, you should indicate the fact on your Web page.

Add Alternative Style Sheets

① Open or create a Web page that contains an internal style sheet.

② In the `<style>` tag, type **title=""**.

③ Type **Default**.

④ Create any other internal style sheets you want to use to display the Web page.

⑤ Save the Web page.

6 Open the Web page in a Web browser.

The Web page is displayed using the default style sheet.

Note: In this example we are using the Netscape Navigator Web browser.

7 Click View.

8 Click Use Style.

9 Click the name of the alternative style sheet.

The Web page is displayed using the alternative style sheet.

Extra

Although most Web browsers do not currently support alternative style sheets, they are still useful if you are creating Web pages in an environment where you know that the majority of users are using a Web browser that supports alternative style sheets. While this is not yet true of the Internet, if you are creating web pages for an intranet or other type of corporate or organizational network, you can safely assume that the users you are writing the page for have Web browsers that allow them to use alternative style sheets.

You can also provide alternative external style sheets. External style sheets are style sheets contained in separate files, which are accessed using the `<link>` tag. As with the `<style>` tag, the `<link>` tag uses the `title` attribute to differentiate between different style sheets.

Example
```
<LINK REL="stylesheet"
TYPE="text/css" HREF="gray.css"
TITLE="Default">

<LINK REL="alternate stylesheet"
TYPE="text/css" HREF="yellow.css"
TITLE="Highlight">
```

Apply Style Sheets to Fonts

You can apply style sheet rules to fonts to change the appearance of the text on your Web page. Changing the appearance of fonts is one of the most popular reasons to use style sheets. Using style sheets can result in significantly less complex HTML files than when using `<font>` tags. For example, using `<font>` tags you would have to use them on any text that you did not want to be styled as the browser's default font and font color. Just a few lines of style sheet code can have the same effect.

One of the easiest and most efficient ways of applying style sheet rules to text is to create an external style sheet or an inline style sheet that changes the appearance of the tags that display text in your Web page. An external style sheet is a separate file from your HTML code. An inline style sheet is placed in the `<head>` section of the HTML code that makes up the Web page. You can also apply style sheet rules locally by using the `style` attribute of the tag used to generate the text. Regardless of the method you use to apply style sheets to your Web pages, the style sheet properties and values will be the same.

The `color` style sheet property is used to define the foreground color of text. The color value of the `color` property can be any valid color name, including the hexadecimal representation of the color code.

The `text-transform` property is used to change the case of text. Text often uses a mixed case, but in some instances you may want your text to be in all uppercase or in all lowercase. To change text to either uppercase or lowercase, simply specify the case as the value of the `text-transform` property.

Apply Style Sheets to Fonts

1. Open or create a Web page.

2. Type the opening and closing **<style>** tags.

3. Type the name of a text tag used in the Web page.

4. Type **{ }**.

5. Type the text property to apply.

6. Type the value of the property followed by **;**.

7. Type the opening and closing **<span>** tags.

8. Type **style=""**.

9 Type the local style to apply to the text.

10 Repeat steps **3** to **6** for each additional style block in the inline style sheet.

11 Save the Web page.

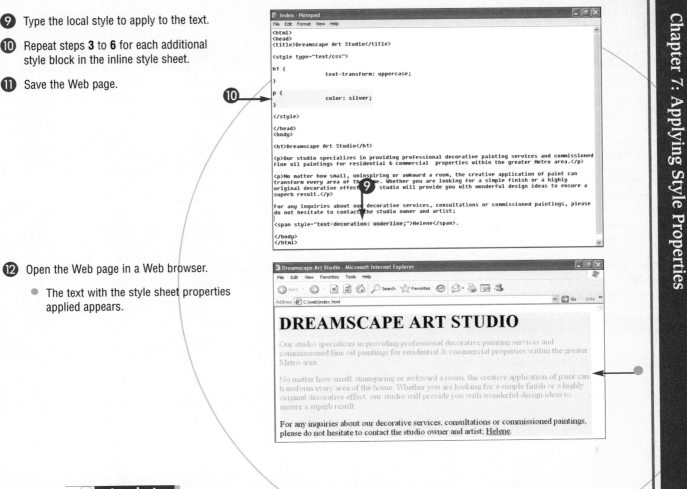

12 Open the Web page in a Web browser.

● The text with the style sheet properties applied appears.

Apply It

The `capitalize` value used with the `text-transform` property formats text so that the first letter of each word is capitalized. Regardless of the preexisting case of any of the letters within the text, only the first letter of each word is capitalized and the remaining characters are lowercase. This is sometimes referred to as title case.

TYPE THIS

```
<h1 style="text-transform: capitalize;">
   dreamscape ART studio
</h1>
```

RESULT

```
Dreamscape Art Studio
```

Current Web browsers usually support all style sheet properties such as `color` and `text-transform`. However, many older browsers do not support style sheets at all, and others offer only partial support. When Web pages designed using style sheets are viewed with a browser that does not support the style sheet property, the text displays according to the Web browser's default text settings. When designing Web pages for the Web, however, it is safe to assume that most people will be using Web browsers that fully support style sheets.

Select a Typeface for Your Site Text

You can select the font in which you want your text to display. Most Web browsers display fonts in Times New Roman or some similar font; but you can specify the exact name of any font you want. You can even use different fonts for different parts of your Web page. When specifying the exact font to use, however, remember that the font must exist on the user's computer in order for the Web browser to render the font as you intended. If the font you specified using a style sheet rule is not available on the computer that is viewing your Web page, then the Web browser displays the font using the default font of the Web browser, or attempts to substitute the font with one similar to the one you have specified.

In addition to specifying the exact font you want to use, you can also specify a group of related fonts. If you specify

multiple fonts, the Web browser tries each one in turn until it finds the first available font. Instead of specifying a single font name, simply specify multiple font names separated by a commas. You can also specify a font family. For example, if you specify the font family as serif, the Web browser attempts to use one of the serif fonts available on the computer.

Not only can you specify an exact font or font family, you can also select the font that your system uses to display messages. For example, if you specify the font as status-bar, your text will be displayed with the same font that your computer uses to display messages in the status bar of applications. This means that the font will change depending on the user's personal preference settings for the computer fonts.

Select a Typeface for Your Site Text

① Open or create a Web page that contains an inline style sheet.

② Type **font:;**.

③ Type **status-bar**.

④ Type **font-family:;**.

5 Type the font style or font name.

6 Repeat steps **4** to **5** for each font style or type to be applied.

7 Save the Web page.

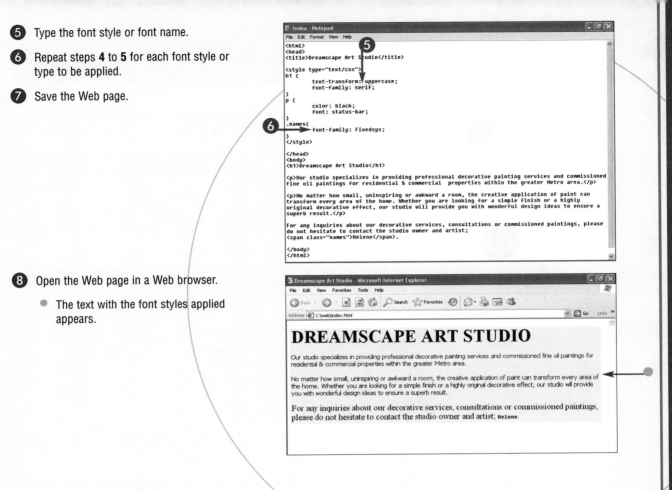

8 Open the Web page in a Web browser.

● The text with the font styles applied appears.

Extra

Some font names consist of multiple words separated by spaces. When specifying a font name that contains a space, you should enclose a font name in quotations.

Example
```
p{
font-family: "Microsoft
Sans Serif";
}
```

Font names are often more than one word; for example, Times New Roman or Microsoft Sans Serif. When using a font with a name that includes multiple words in the `style` attribute of an HTML tag, you should enclose the font name within single quotes to avoid confusing the Web browser.

Example
```
<p style="font-family:
'Microsoft Sans
Serif'";">
```

As mentioned earlier in this section, you can specify that fonts match font settings for certain operating system settings so that your site can match the user's preferences. There are other system fonts besides `status-bar` that you can specify with the `font` style sheet property. For example, you can also choose the fonts used for displaying `caption`, `icon`, `menu`, `message-box`, and `small-caption`.

Set Font Size

You can specify the font size of the type on your Web page with the `font-size` property. This allows you to have greater control over the layout and aesthetics of the text on your page on a word-by-word or line-by-line basis. While you can use heading tags to do this to some degree, you can use font sizes to have much greater control.

Specify the font size absolutely by using the pixel size of the font as the value. To indicate that the value of the `font-size` property is a pixel size, `px` is appended to the numeric value of the property. For example, to specify a text size of 10 pixels, use the value `10px`. You can also specify the size of the font as a percentage of the preceding font. To make the font twice the height, simply use the value of `200%` for the `font-size` property. If you are more familiar

with using points to specify the size of a font, simply specify the point size followed by the characters `pt`, as in `12pt`.

Use the `line-height` property to specify the line height with which to display the text. Regardless of the font size, the distance between the top of one line and the top of the next line is the distance specified with the `line-height` property. You should be careful when specifying the `line-height` property; if it is too small, text will be rendered on top of existing text, while setting the distance too far apart will make your text hard to read.

You can also specify either font size in general terms, such as `small`, `medium`, or `large`. The font size will typically be in relation to the size of the preceding font.

Set Font Size

① Open or create a Web page that contains an inline style sheet.

② Type **line-height: ;**.

③ Type the height of the line.

④ Type **font-size: ;**.

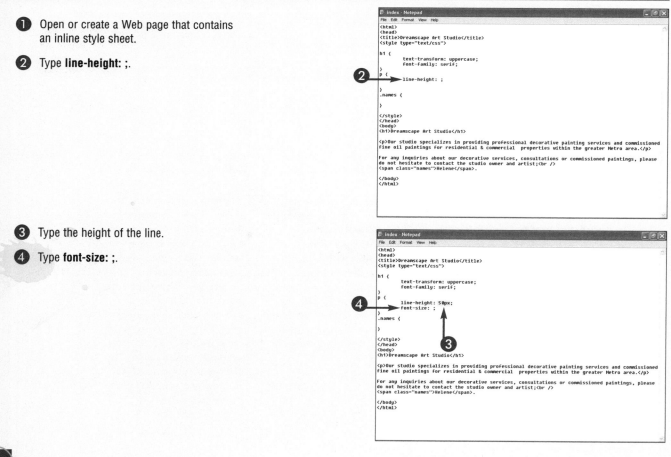

5 Type the size of the font.

6 Repeat steps **4** to **5** for each font size you want to apply.

7 Save the Web page.

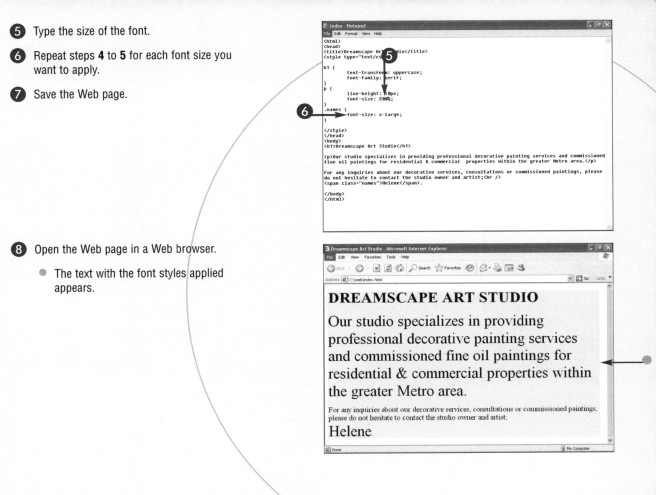

8 Open the Web page in a Web browser.

- The text with the font styles applied appears.

Set Font and Background Color

You can change the color of the text on your Web pages, making the text easier to read or simply more aesthetically pleasing to you and those who view your page. You can use the style sheet property `color` to change the background color of an element on a Web page. When applying this property to a textual element, the actual color of the text itself changes. For example, you can create a sidebar effect by changing the background of a one-cell table with text in it by changing the background color of the table and then changing the font color to contrast against the background.

You can also specify the background color of characters, words, sentences, or complete paragraphs of text. When changing the background color of elements such as headers, the background color of the complete line from one side of the display to the other is changed.

Typically, the foreground and background colors most often used are the popular standard colors, but you can also use system colors. Your computer uses system colors to display applications. For example, the `activeborder` is the color of the border of the Web browser used to view the Web page.

When selecting foreground and background colors, make sure that adequate contrast remains so that the text can still be read easily. For example, placing a light font over a light background makes your text difficult to read, and any text that is difficult to read will not be read. Likewise, the use of colors that are difficult to read, such as fuchsia, may prevent people from reading your Web pages. You can ask friends, coworkers, or family their opinions on a color scheme to get their feedback before going live with your site if you are not sure.

Set Font and Background Color

① Open or create a Web page that contains an inline style sheet.

② Type **color: ;**.

③ Type the color of the font.

④ Type **background: ;**.

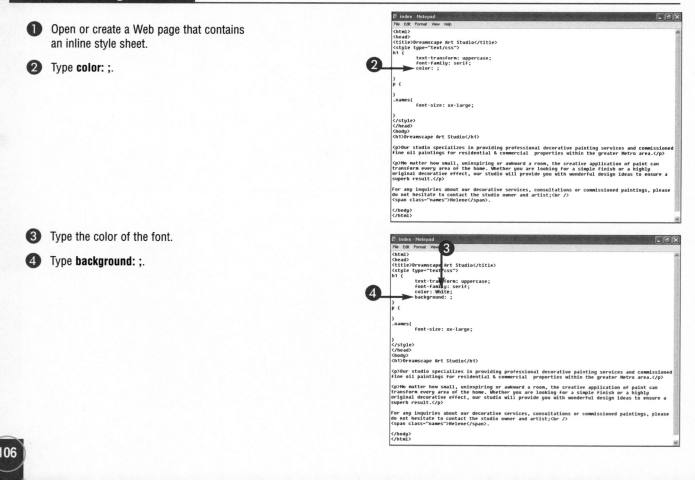

5. Type the background color.

6. Repeat steps **4** to **5** for each background color to be applied.

7. Save the Web page.

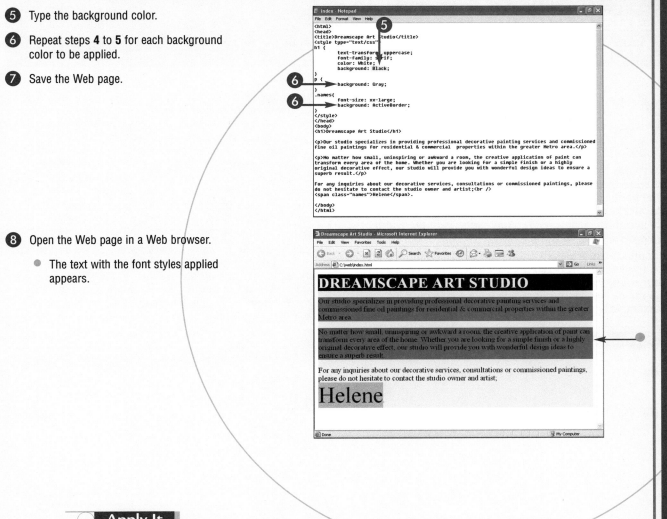

8. Open the Web page in a Web browser.

- The text with the font styles applied appears.

Create Borders Around Your Text

You can surround the text of your Web page with borders to help emphasize important messages, or to help separate different sections of your Web page from each other. You can also use small tables with borders, different background colors for the table cell, and a properly contrasting font color to create sidebars to your text.

The `border` style sheet property specifies the characteristics of the border to be drawn around your type. You can specify a dashed border with the value `dashed`, or a continuous border with the value `solid`. You can specify the width of the border as thin or thick.

Not only can you specify a complete border around your text, but you can also determine if you want a border on just the top, the bottom, or at the sides of an element. Using these single lines between news items on your page, for example, can help offset each news item from the one

above and/or below it. The `border-top-style` specifies the border style at the top of your element. If you specify only the `border-top-style` property, the border appears as a single line above your text. Similarly, the `border-bottom-style` determines what type of border to display underneath your text. For each style of border, either `left`, `right`, `top`, or `bottom`, a color may also be specified. For example, the `border-bottom-color` specifies the color of the border drawn underneath your element. You can specify a different color for all four borders of your element.

Although you can use a variety of border styles and widths to create quite complex effects for your text, not all Web browsers support the border properties. For this reason, you should make certain not to rely to heavily on borders; if your site becomes illegible without them, you might reconsider how you have chosen to use them.

Create Borders Around Your Text

① Open or create a Web page that contains an inline style sheet.

② Type **border: ;**.

③ Type the border property values.

④ Repeat steps **2** to **3** for each complete border to apply.

⑤ Type **border-bottom-color:** followed by a color and then **;**.

⑥ Type **border-bottom-style: ;**.

7 Type the bottom border style.

8 Type **border-top-style:** followed by a value and ;.

9 Save the Web page.

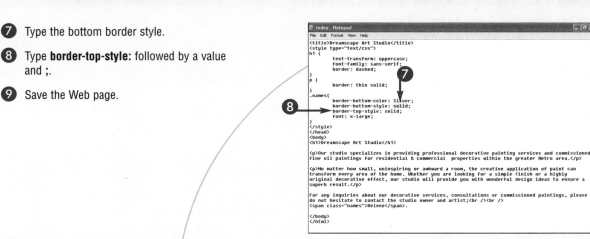

10 Open the Web page in a Web browser.

● The text with the border styles applied appears.

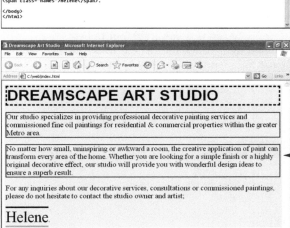

Apply Italics and Bold Face

You can use style sheets to apply bold and italics to your text. Bold and italic text helps you to make certain text stand out from surrounding text. Italic text, for example, is used a great deal to place emphasis on certain words in a sentence, while bold text is typically used to call out keywords that you want to highlight to help the user identify them as important terms.

The font-weight style sheet property, given a value of bold, forces the Web browser to bold any text to which the rule is applied. Not only can you specify a font to be bold, but you can also specify if you want the text to be bolder than the preceding text. This enables you to use different levels of boldness, providing the required fonts are available to the Web browser.

The font-style property with the italic value displays text as italicized. An italicized font is slanted slightly to the

right. Italicized fonts are usually used to add emphasis to a phrase a word, or sometimes to indicate that a phrase or word is a quotation.

When specifying values for the font-weight and font-style style sheet properties, it may also be useful to adjust the spacing of characters in the text. For example, fonts that are bolded may be slightly easier to read if the spacing between the characters increases. The letter-spacing property defines the spacing between characters on a Web page: the higher the value, the greater the distance between the characters. The value for the letter-spacing property is a numerical value that represents the spacing in pixels between the start of one character and the start of the next character. The numerical value must be followed by the letters px to indicate that the value being specified is in pixels.

Apply Italics and Bold Face

1. Open or create a Web page that contains an inline style sheet.

2. Type **font-style: ;**.

3. Type the font style value.

4. Type **font-weight: ;**.

5. Type **letter-spacing: ;**.

110

6 Type the font weight value.

7 Type the size of the letter spacing.

8 Repeat steps **2** to **6** for subsequent text properties.

9 Save the Web page.

10 Open the Web page in a Web browser.

● The text with font styles applied appears.

You can use different methods to specify the distance in style sheet properties such as `letter-spacing`. You can specify the distance in pixels, as indicated by `px`, or using the `em` unit of measurement. `1em` is the same as the current font size, so if the current font size is 10 pixels, `1em` is equivalent to 10 pixels.

You can use actual units of measurement to specify text size. The Web browser will attempt to draw the text at the specified size. You can specify sizes in inches, centimeters, millimeters, and points, using the characters `in`, `cm`, `mm`, and `pt` after a numerical value. You may also use negative values when specifying a value for the `letter-spacing` property to force text closer together.

You can also use the `font-weight` style sheet property to specify that the font to be more or less bold. The `lighter` and `bolder` values of the `font-weight` property instruct the Web browser to display the text in a slightly less bold or bolder font than the preceding text, respectively.

Example
```
p {font-weight:
lighter;}
```

Insert White Space and Control Indent

Y ou can change the way the Web browser handles the white space, spaces, and indents on your Web page. Changing the way the Web browser displays spaces and indents can make your Web pages easier to read, more functional, or simply more appealing to look at. White space and indenting can make the difference between your page looking clean and professional, or crammed and overwhelming.

You can indent text to make your paragraphs of text easier to read, or to indicate a new section. An indent occurs when the first word of a sentence or paragraph is preceded by some blank space. The `text-indent` property defines the amount of blank space before the text. The size of the blank text can be defined in pixels by appending `px` to a numerical value, or the size of the blank space can be

expressed as a percentage of the complete width of the Web browser display. For example, a value of `50%` creates an indent half the width of the current Web browser display. Indents only apply to the first word or character in a sentence or paragraph of text.

The `white-space` property enables you to force your text to scroll off the Web page. By default, Web browsers force the text to wrap to a new line when the right hand border of the display window is reached. When you specify the `nowrap` value for the `white-space` property, the Web browser does not insert any new lines into text to which the `white-space` property has been applied. If your text is wider than the Web browser window, the scroll bar at the bottom of the Web browser display appears and allows the user to scroll across to view the complete text.

Insert White Space and Control Indent

1 Open or create a Web page that contains an inline style sheet.

2 Type **text-indent: ;**.

3 Type the indent value.

4 Repeat steps **2** to **3** for any other text you want to indent.

5 Type **white-space: ;**.

6 Type the white-space value.

7 Save the Web page.

```
index - Notepad
File  Edit  Format  View  Help
<html>
<head>
<title>Dreamscape Art S    6    </title>
<style type="text/css">
h1 {
        font-style: italic;
        text-indent: 10px;
}
p {
        white-space: nowrap;
        text-indent: 40px;
}
.names{
        font-weight: bold;
        text-indent: 50%;
}
</style>
</head>
<body>
<h1>Dreamscape Art Studio</h1>

<p>Our studio specializes in providing professional decorative painting services and commissioned
fine oil paintings for residential & commercial  properties within the greater Metro area.</p>

<p>No matter how small, uninspiring or awkward a room, the creative application of paint can
transform every area of the home. Whether you are looking for a simple finish or a highly
original decorative effect, our studio will provide you with wonderful design ideas to ensure a
superb result.</p>

For any inquiries about our decorative services, consultations or commissioned paintings, please
do not hesitate to contact the studio owner and artist;<br /><br />
<div class="names">Helene, studio owner and artist</div>.


</body>
</html>
```

8 Open the Web page in a Web browser.

● The text with indent and white space styles applied appears.

```
Dreamscape Art Studio - Microsoft Internet Explorer
File  Edit  View  Favorites  Tools  Help
Back  -        -        Search  Favorites
Address  C:\web\index.html                                          Go  Links

Dreamscape Art Studio

    Our studio specializes in providing professional decorative painting services and commi

    No matter how small, uninspiring or awkward a room, the creative application of paint c

For any inquiries about our decorative services, consultations or commissioned paintings,
please do not hesitate to contact the studio owner and artist;

                          Helene, studio owner and artist
```

Apply It

Although not yet widely supported, the white-space property also enables you to specify a value of pre. The pre value, when implemented, displays text in a monospaced font. The result is similar to the effects achieved using the HTML tag <pre>.

Example
```
p
{
white-space: pre
}
```

You can specify a negative value for the text indent to move the first line of a paragraph closer to the left margin than the remaining lines of the paragraph. Be careful, though: if the text is already at the left-hand border, a negative value causes the text to move beyond the left margins and become unreadable.

Example
```
p{
    text-indent: -12px
    color: white;
}
```

Align Text to Fit Your Layout

Y ou can align text to better fit the layout of your Web page by specifying the distance between words in a paragraph of text. Depending on the font type and size used on the Web page, some text may be easier to read when the spacing between words is increased or decreased. A professional, easy-to-read layout is important if you want people visiting your page to keep coming back.

You can control the distance between words by using the word-spacing property. The value of the word-spacing property is the distance between the end of one word and the start of another. It is typical to specify the distance between words in pixels, which you indicate by appending the letters px to a numerical value.

You can align text on a Web page in a similar fashion to the way text is aligned in the document of a word processing program. A Web page aligns text to the left by default. You can align text to the right by specifying the value right for the property text-align. Right-aligned text is lined up on the right hand side of the Web page. The center value of the text-align property causes the text to display in the middle of the Web page. This is most often used for headers or other section indicators.

Text may also be justified, so that both the left- and right-hand sides of the paragraph are aligned to the left and right. The Web browser adjusts the spacing between words to align the text correctly. To justify text, specify justify as the value of the text-align property.

Align Text to Fit Your Layout

① Open or create a Web page that contains an inline style sheet.

② Type **text-align: ;**.

③ Type the align value.

④ Type **word-spacing: ;**.

⑤ Type the word-spacing value.

⑥ Repeat steps **2** to **3** for each text-align rule you want to create.

⑦ Save the Web page.

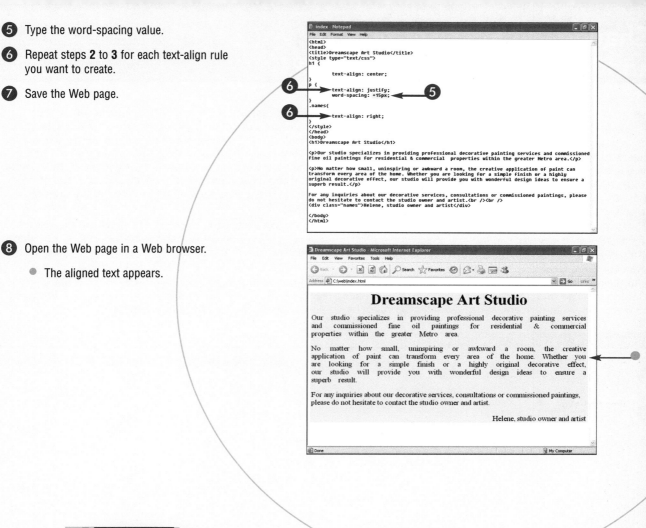

⑧ Open the Web page in a Web browser.

● The aligned text appears.

Change the First Letter and Line of Text

Y ou can use style sheets to change the appearance of the first letter of a sentence and the first line of a paragraph of text, which can make your pages more aesthetically appealing. For example, if you open any book to the beginning of a chapter, you are likely to see that the first letter of the first paragraph is larger and more stylized than the rest of the text. You can use this same type of letter, called a *drop cap*, or even apply a similar effect to a whole line of text or more. However, using the drop cap effect on more than one letter can look tacky, so be careful when you use it.

Style sheets use a technique called *pseudo elements* to apply rules to these text elements. Pseudo elements use special selectors to indicate that a style sheet rule should be applied to the first letter of an element. When defining the rule, the

selector should be the name of the element followed by a colon (:) and then the keyword first-letter. The element can be any element that contains text, such as a header or paragraph. Any style sheet rules that are then defined will only apply to the very first letter of the element. One of the most common uses of the pseudo element first-letter is to make the first letter of a paragraph a drop cap.

The pseudo element first-line is similar to the element first-letter, except that the style sheet rules will apply to the first line of the paragraph of text and not just the first letter.

Pseudo elements were not widely supported in older Web browsers, but it is safe to assume that most Web browsers now support the use of pseudo elements.

Change the First Letter and Line of Text

① Open or create a Web page that contains an inline style sheet.

② Type **p:first-letter** followed by { }.

③ Type the properties for the paragraph's first letter.

④ Type **p:first-line** followed by { }.

5 Type the properties to be applied to the first line of the paragraph.

6 Save the Web page.

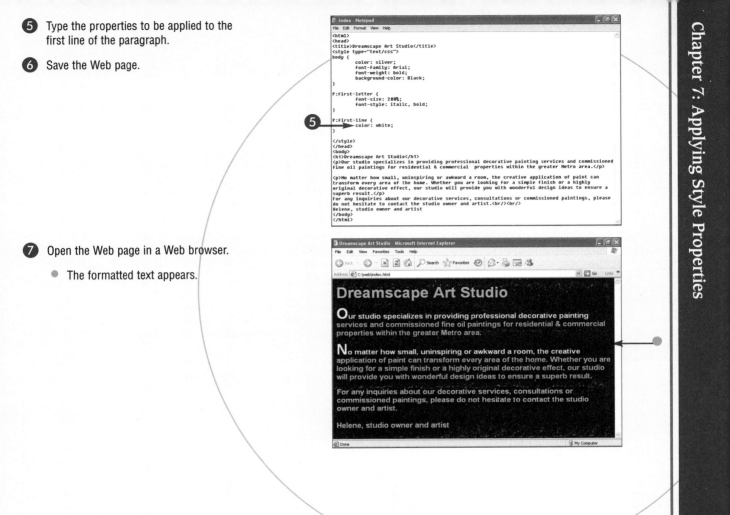

7 Open the Web page in a Web browser.

● The formatted text appears.

Apply It

Remember that the `first-line` pseudo element applies only to the first line and not the first sentence of a paragraph of text. You can apply style sheet rules directly to the first sentence using `<span>`, although this means specifying `<span>` for each sentence to which you want to apply this rule.

Example

```
<h2>CD Rewritable Drive:</h2>

<span style="color: Blue;">The best of
both worlds and now faster than ever!
</span>

This CD drive combines a CD-RW Drive
with a DVD-ROM Drive.
```

The `first-letter` and `first-line` pseudo elements can be used only with block-level elements such as headers or paragraphs. You cannot use the `first-letter` and `first-line` pseudo elements with links or on a word or phrase within a paragraph. If you want to alter the text in these cases or others, you will need to use other techniques to apply rules directly to those elements. For example, with a link you could use the `<span>` tag in conjunction with inline style sheets to achieve the desired effect.

Add a Background Image to Text

You can enhance the visual appearance of text on a Web page by applying a background image to the text. Many sites have background textures to achieve the effect of a background texture that is more interesting to look at than a solid color. Other sites use actual photographs or drawings as a background image that often relates to the content of the site in some way. For example, a site for a business that sells flowers over the Internet might use a background image of flowers.

The background-image style sheet property defines the name of the image that appears placed behind an element. The value of the background-image property is the address of the image to be used as the background. The address of the image is defined by url(), with the name of the image placed between the parentheses.

You can indicate that the background image is stored on the Web server locally by prefixing file:/// to the name of

the image. Specify a drive name by using the drive letter followed by an upright-line character. For example, d| indicates the local hard drive D:\.

If the size of the background image is smaller than the element, then the image will be repeatedly drawn, or *tiled*, to completely cover the background of the element. If the background image is larger than the element, then the background image will be automatically cropped to dimensions determined by the Web browser.

The background-image property can be applied to all elements, including headers, paragraphs of text, tables, individual characters, and even the whole Web page.

Although many different image formats are supported for the use of backgrounds, you should use GIF and JPG images to ensure compatibility with most Web browsers. Make sure adequate contrast exists between the element and the background image so that the text can be read over the image easily.

Add a Background Image to Text

1 Open or create a Web page that contains an inline style sheet.

2 Type **background-image: ;**.

3 Type **url(file:///)**.

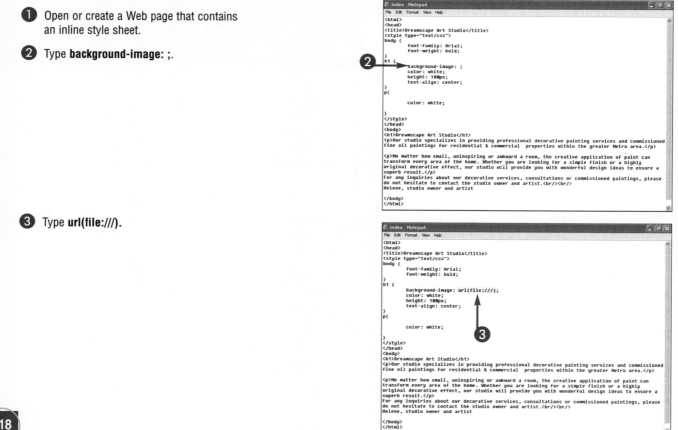

④ Type the name and location of the file.

⑤ Repeat steps **2** to **4** for each image to assign as a background.

⑥ Save the Web page.

⑦ Open the Web page in a Web browser.

- The text with background images appears.

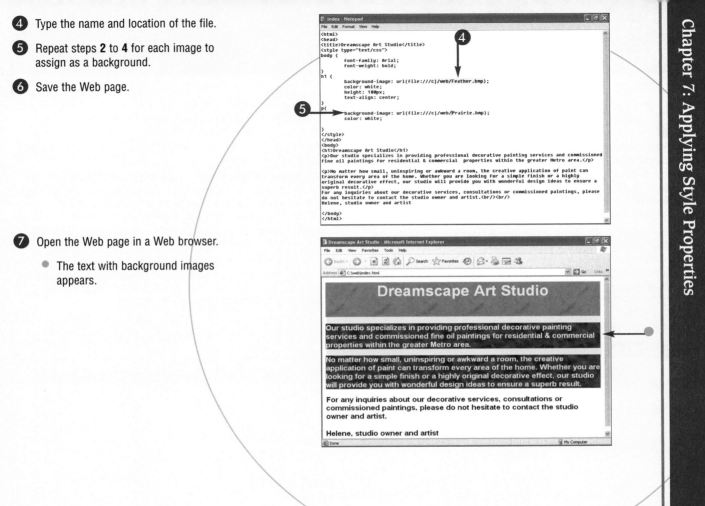

Apply It

If you apply a local style sheet rule that sets the `background-image` property value to `none`, no image will be used as a background for that element regardless of the rules defined in any other internal or external style sheet. This can be useful in particular when multiple style sheets are applied to a Web page, enabling you to instruct the browser to ignore any style sheet in the page that specifies that the text of the element in question should have a background image.

Example
```
<head>
    <title>Nature</title>
<style>
body {
    background-image: url(file:///c|/Web/orcas.jpg);
}
</style>
</head>
<body  style="background-image: none;">
```

Position Elements Absolutely

Y ou can use the `position` style sheet property to precisely specify the location of Web page elements such as images, paragraphs of text, and tables. Savvy Web designers know that just a pixel or two in placement of an element can make the difference between a page that looks perfectly proportioned and one that looks just slightly off. One of the benefits of CSS is this very ability to have greater control over the positioning of elements on your page than HTML tags alone provide.

The location of the element on the Web page is determined using an offset distance. For example, you can specify how far the top of an image is placed from the top of the Web browser window. Likewise, you can specify the distance between the right-hand side of an image and the right side of the Web browser window. It is important to remember that you are specifying the offset distance and not necessarily the exact coordinates of where you want to place the element.

The `absolute` value of the `position` property instructs the Web browser to position the element absolutely with no regard to the rest of the contents of the Web page. The properties `top`, `right`, `bottom`, and `left` specify the offset distance of the element.

You can specify the distance as a percentage of the Web browser display width or height by appending a percentage sign to numerical value. For example, a value of `50%` creates an offset at the center of the Web browser window. You can also specify the offset in pixels by appending the letters `px` to the numeral. For example, the value `10px` creates an offset 10 pixels wide.

Most Web browsers position elements absolutely in relation to the Web browser window; that is, offset distances are calculated from the margins of the Web browser.

Position Elements Absolutely

① Open or create a Web page.

② Type **style=""** in the tag of the element you want to position.

③ Type **position:**.

```
index - Notepad
File  Edit  Format  View  Help
<html>
<head>
        <title>Painting Auction</title>
</head>

<body>
<img src="bunnies.jpg" style="position:">

<p>
Oil on canvas.
Title: Rabbits
</p>

<h3>Bidding starts at $350</h3>


</body>
</html>
```

④ Type **absolute;** and a space.

⑤ Type **top:;** and a space.

⑥ Type **left:;** and a space.

```
index - Notepad
File  Edit  Format  View  Help
<html>
<head>
        <title>Painting Auction</title>
</head>

<body>
<img src="bunnies.jpg" style="position: absolute; top:; left:;">

<p>
Oil on canvas.
Title: Rabbits
</p>

<h3>Bidding starts at $350</h3>


</body>
</html>
```

7 Type the distance from the top margin.

8 Type the distance from the left margin.

9 Repeat steps **2** to **8** for each element you want to position.

10 Save the Web page.

11 Open the Web page in a Web browser.

The elements are positioned as specified.

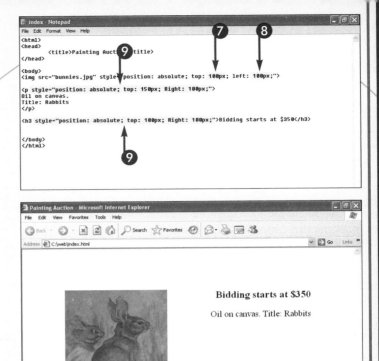

```
index - Notepad
File  Edit  Format  View  Help

<html>
<head>
        <title>Painting Auction</title>
</head>

<body>
<img src="bunnies.jpg" style="position: absolute; top: 100px; left: 100px;">

<p style="position: absolute; top: 150px; Right: 100px;">
Oil on canvas.
Title: Rabbits
</p>

<h3 style="position: absolute; top: 100px; Right: 100px;">Bidding starts at $350</h3>


</body>
</html>
```

Painting Auction - Microsoft Internet Explorer

Address C:\web\index.html

Bidding starts at $350

Oil on canvas. Title: Rabbits

Extra

If you specify an element's position absolutely, the remainder of the Web page may display in a manner that conflicts with the positioned element. For example, an image that you have positioned absolutely may partially cover a paragraph of text. When positioning elements absolutely, you must take great care to avoid conflicts and thoroughly test your Web pages in a variety of browsers. Also, specify absolute positioning using local style sheet rules as opposed to internal or external style sheets. Reuse the same rule to specify positioning for multiple elements causes overlap.

You cannot control the many sizes of Web browser display windows used to view your Web pages. You should therefore use offsets specified in percentages as opposed to pixels, as these offset distances will then change to match the size of the Web browser display window.

If a Web page containing absolutely positioned elements is rendered within a frame, the offset distances are computed from the surrounding frame border and not the Web browser display window. Keep this in mind to avoid extra space between the element and edge of the browser display window.

Specify Width and Height of Elements

Y ou can specify the width and height of elements such as images precisely, giving you more control over the layout of your Web pages. Specifying the width and height of images can also allow you to reuse the same image on your page multiple times at multiple sizes, which would help reduce the amount of loading time for your Web page. For example, say an image was 200 pixels tall by 100 pixels wide at full size. You wanted to use the image at that size — once on your page and once again at half size. You could specify that in the second case, the width should be 100 pixels and the height should be 50 pixels, which would force the image to display at that size on the Web page and give the appearance of a smaller image.

The `width` and `height` values for an element are specified using pixels or percentages. As with other style sheet

specifications that involve measure, pixels are specified by appending the letters `px` to a numerical value, and percentages are formed by adding a `%` to the value. When specifying a percentage, the value will be a percentage of the Web browser window's width or height, which may change depending on the user's preferences.

Typically, the width and height specifications will be values smaller than the Web browser display window. This is not required, however. You can create some interesting effects by using elements that do not fit within the Web browser display window; these elements can be accessed using scrollbars. However, in most cases, you do not want the combined width of the elements on your Web page to exceed the total width of the Web browser window. This is easily managed by specifying percentages for the width of your elements.

Specify Width and Height of Elements

① Open or create a Web page.

② In the tag of the element to be resized, type **style=""**.

```
<html>
<head>
          <title>Painting Auction</title>
</head>

<body>
<br />

<img src="bunnies.jpg" border="4" style="" />
<img src="orcas.jpg" border="4" />
<img src="daisies.jpg" border="4" />

<h3 style="position: absolute; top: 10px; Right: 10px;">Bidding starts at $350</h3>

</body>
</html>
```

③ Type **width:;** and a space.

④ Type **height:;** and a space.

```
<html>
<head>
          <title>Painting Auction</title>
</head>

<body>
<br />

<img src="bunnies.jpg" border="4" style="width:; height:;" />
<img src="orcas.jpg" border="4" />
<img src="daisies.jpg" border="4" />

<h3 style="position: absolute; top: 10px; Right: 10px;">Bidding starts at $350</h3>

</body>
</html>
```

5 Type the width of the element.

6 Type the height of the element.

7 Repeat steps **2** to **6** for each element to be sized.

8 Save the Web page.

9 Open the Web page in a Web browser.

The elements are resized.

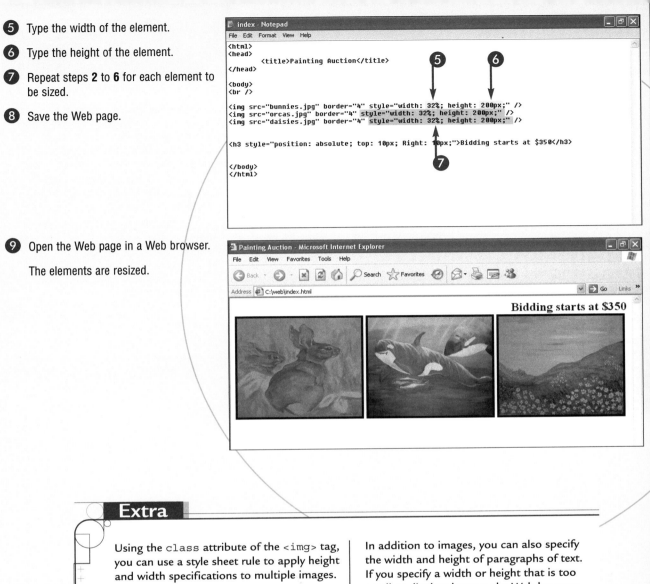

Extra

Using the `class` attribute of the `<img>` tag, you can use a style sheet rule to apply height and width specifications to multiple images.

Style Section
```
<style>
icon{
    width: 32px;
    height: 32px;
}
</style>
```

Usage
```
<img src="logo.gif" class="icon" />
```

In addition to images, you can also specify the width and height of paragraphs of text. If you specify a width or height that is too small to display the text, the Web browser ignores your specifications and displays the text according to the browser defaults.

If you specify the margins that surround an element, specifying the width and height may not be necessary. For more information on specifying margins, see the section "Adjust Padding and Margins" in this chapter.

Y ou can position elements on a Web page in relation to the surrounding elements and not just the Web browser display window. Relative positioning enables you to move certain elements without having to specify the positioning for all the elements on a Web page.

The position style sheet property specifies where an element will appear. Relative positioning places an element in relation to the original default location of the element on the Web page. The default location of the element is the place on a Web page where the element would appear if no style sheet positioning rules were applied. For example, if the first line of code within the body of an HTML document places an image on the Web page, the image appears in the top left-hand corner of the page, which is the default location. Relative positioning specifies where the element will appear in relation to that default location.

The Web browser uses a wide variety of parameters such as screen resolution, width of the Web browser window, and browser type to calculate the default location of an element. Users can also affect the normal flow of elements on a Web page by changing the settings of the Web browser.

The top, bottom, right, and left properties specify in pixels or as a percentage value the offset distance of the element you want to position.

Many old Web browsers do not support the positioning of elements either absolutely or relatively and thus ignore any style sheet rules that affect the positioning of elements. However, these browsers are now in such low usage that it is safe to assume that most users now have Web browsers that interpret style sheet rules correctly.

Position an Element Relatively

1 Open or create a Web page.

2 In the tag of the element you want to position, type **style="position:"**.

3 Type **relative;** and a space.

4 Type **left:;** and a space.

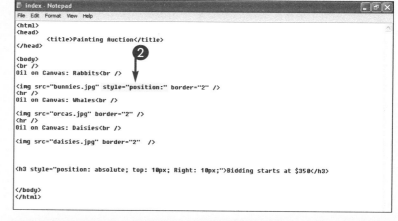

5 Type the distance to move the element from its original position.

6 Repeat steps **2** to **5** for each element you want to position.

7 Save the Web page.

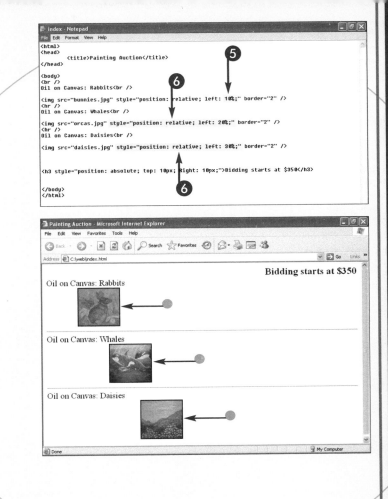

8 Open the Web page in a Web browser.

● The elements are shown positioned left of the margin.

Extra

You can also use negative values for the top, bottom, left, and right properties. For example, to slightly offset a main header from the content underneath, use a negative value for the left property.

Create a Negative Margin
```
<h1 style="position: relative; left: -
10px;">Table of Contents</h1>
<h2>Math</h2>
<h2>Reading</h2>
<h2>Writing</h2>
```

If you are not careful, you can craft your code in such a way as to instruct the user's browser to pile elements on top of each other, which will make your Web site at the least ugly and at worst illegible. To avoid this, make sure that you do not specify positioning that creates conflicts with other items. The following code displays the first header directly on top of the second header.

Incorrectly Positioned Elements
```
<h1 style="position: relative; top:
50px;">Table of Contents</h1>
<h2>Math</h2>
```

Overlap Elements

You can overlap elements on a Web page, which initially may not seem worthwhile; but careful overlapping of elements can sometimes create interesting and useful visual effects. For example, if you use transparency with some of the images that you want to use on your site, you can overlap an image that is partially transparent over other text elements so that you can see elements that are underneath through the transparent portion of the image on top. You can even use multiple transparent images over one another to create effects that are more complex.

All elements on a Web page that overlap are positioned using absolute positioning style sheet rules. The simplest way to overlap elements is to specify the absolute positioning for the elements that go on top later in the code. For example, if a small image overlaps a large image on a Web page, the code creating the smaller image comes later in the HTML document than the code that creates the larger image. If the code creating the large image came after the code for the smaller image, then the larger image would obscure the smaller image (unless the larger image was partially transparent).

The second method of overlapping elements involves using the z-index style sheet property. The z-index property contains a numerical value (which must be a whole number) indicating how elements should be stacked on top of each other. Elements with higher z-index values are placed on top of elements with lower z-index values. When specifying values for the z-index property, it may help to visualize the elements as being stuck to your display in layers, with the elements closest to you having the highest z-index value.

Overlap Elements

① Open or create a Web page.

② In the tag of the element you want to position, type **style=""**.

③ Type **position: absolute; bottom:; right:;**.

④ Type the distance from the bottom.

⑤ Type the distance from the right margin.

⑥ Repeat steps **2** to **3** for each element you want to position.

7 In the style value of the element to be placed on top, type **z-index: 1;**.

8 Save the Web page.

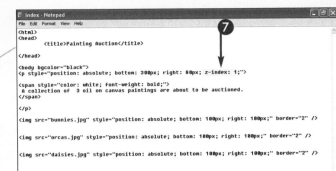

```
index - Notepad
File  Edit  Format  View  Help

<html>
<head>
        <title>Painting Auction</title>

</head>

<body bgcolor="black">
<p style="position: absolute; bottom: 300px; right: 80px; z-index: 1;">

<span style="color: white; font-weight: bold;">
 A collection of  3 oil on canvas paintings are about to be auctioned.
</span>

</p>

<img src="bunnies.jpg" style="position: absolute; bottom: 100px; right: 100px;" border="2" />

<img src="orcas.jpg" style="position: absolute; bottom: 100px; right: 100px;" border="2" />

<img src="daisies.jpg" style="position: absolute; bottom: 100px; right: 100px;" border="2" />


</body>
</html>
```

9 Open the Web page in a Web browser.

The elements are overlapped.

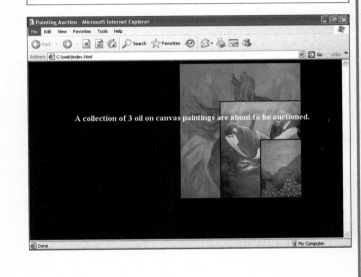

A collection of 3 oil on canvas paintings are about to be auctioned.

Extra

You can use either positive or negative whole number values for the z-index property. An element's default z-index value is zero. A z-index value of -1 places an element behind another element that does not have a z-index value implicitly defined, should the elements occur at the same location on the Web page.

When specifying z-index values for your Web page elements, space the numbers (such as by using multiples of five) so that you can easily add or modify them later. If all the numbers are sequential in increments of 1, you would have to renumber all of the elements whenever a single element is added to the Web page.

Overlapped elements on a Web page can become quite complex and confusing. Sketching out your Web page on paper before creating the code may make your work easier to maintain and troubleshoot. In this way, some of the conflicts you may run into may present themselves and you can work out those issues before you even start coding.

Adjust Padding and Margins

You can create white space around elements on your Web page by using padding and margin size specifications. Adding white space can make your Web pages more visually appealing and easier to read by providing appropriate spacing between elements to set them apart from one another. Not providing enough white space can make your page look too busy, hamper the user's ability to find the information they are looking for easily, and make your site look overall very unprofessional.

You can specify margin sizes for most HTML elements, including the body, which comprises the entire contents of the Web page. Applying margin settings to the `<body>` tag creates a margin around the entire Web page display window. Margin values are specified using the style sheet properties `margin-top`, `margin-right`, `margin-bottom`, and `margin-left`. You can save yourself typing when specifying the same values for all four margin properties by specifying only the `margin` property followed by just the margin values.

Padding is the space that surrounds an element. Padding is like a buffer that keeps an element separate from other elements on the Web page. The style sheet properties `padding-top`, `padding-right`, `padding-bottom`, and `padding-left` specify the amount of white space that appears on each corresponding side of an element. Two elements placed side by side will at least be separated by the amount of padding specified for the element in addition to the padding specified for the closest adjacent element.

Specify both padding and margin property values in pixels or as a percentage of the Web browser display window. You can use the `inherit` element to enable the element to inherit its `padding` or `margin` properties from the element containing it (such as a box).

Adjust Padding and Margins

① Open or create a Web page.

② In the body tag, type **style=""**.

③ Type **margin:;** and a space.

④ Type the top, right, left, and bottom margin size of the Web page.

⑤ In the tag of the element to apply padding to, type **style=""**.

⑥ Type **padding-right:;** and a space.

⑦ Type **padding-left:;** and a space.

8 Type the amount of right padding.

9 Type the amount of left padding.

10 Save the Web page.

11 Open the Web page in a Web browser.

- The Web page appears with the specified margins and padding.

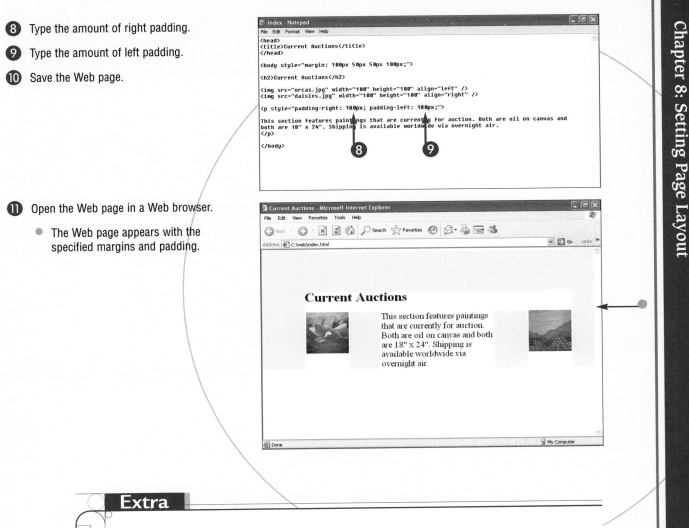

Extra

The browser may disregard values for margin and padding properties if some elements on a Web page utilize absolute or relative positioning. Elements that are positioned absolutely or relatively, although they may have their own margin and padding settings, do not take into account the margin or padding settings of other elements on the Web page.

You can use either positive or negative numbers to adjust the default size of the margins. Most Web browsers use a default margin of 1 pixel. If you reduce the margins around the Web page body by 1 pixel, any gaps that exist between the content and the side of the Web browser window are eliminated.

Eliminate Web Page Margins

```
<style>
        body{
            margin: -1px;
            margin: -1px;
            margin: -1px;
            margin: -1px;
        }
</style>
```

Float an Element

Y ou can flow elements like paragraphs of text around images and other similar elements. You can do this no matter where an image appears on a Web page. Paragraphs of text are usually positioned in a specific way around the images on a Web page, but *floating* an element can be used to embed images anywhere in a paragraph of text.

In HTML, floating images was accomplished by using the align attribute of the `<img>` tag. With style sheets, the float property is used instead. Use the float style sheet property to indicate where an element should be placed before floating the other elements around it. The valid values for the float property are left and right. Specifying the value left moves an element to the left-hand side of its default location. Any surrounding elements move out of the way and flow around the

positioned element. Likewise, a value of right floats an element to the right-hand side of its default location. The none value is useful if you want to negate a style sheet property that would otherwise float the element, and the inherit value will enable the element to inherit its float property from the containing element (such as a surrounding box).

The float style sheet property can be used to position elements other than images, such as tables containing paragraphs of text. You can also use multiple floated elements within the same Web page, even on the same line.

You can even use the float property with the `<span>` element. If you assign the `<span>` element a class that specifies the float property, the element that you include in `<span>` will be taken out of the paragraph and floated to wherever the class specifies.

Float an Element

1 Open or create a Web page.

2 In the tag of the element to be floated, type **style=""**.

```
index - Notepad
File  Edit  Format  View  Help
<head>
<title>Current Auctions</    e>

</head>
<body>
<h2>Current Auctions</h2>

<img src="orcas.jpg" style="" />

<img src="daisies.jpg" />


<h3>Bidding starts at $350</h3>

This section features paintings that are currently for auction. Both are oil on canvas
and both are 18" x 24". Shipping is available worldwide via overnight air.


</body>
```

3 Type **float:;** and a space.

```
index - Notepad
File  Edit  Format  View  Help
<head>
<title>Current Auctions</title>

</head>
<body>
<h2>Current Auctions</h2>

<img src="orcas.jpg" style="float:;" />

<img src="daisies.jpg" />


<h3>Bidding starts at $350</h3>

This section features paintings that are currently for auction. Both are oil on canvas
and both are 18" x 24". Shipping is available worldwide via overnight air.


</body>
```

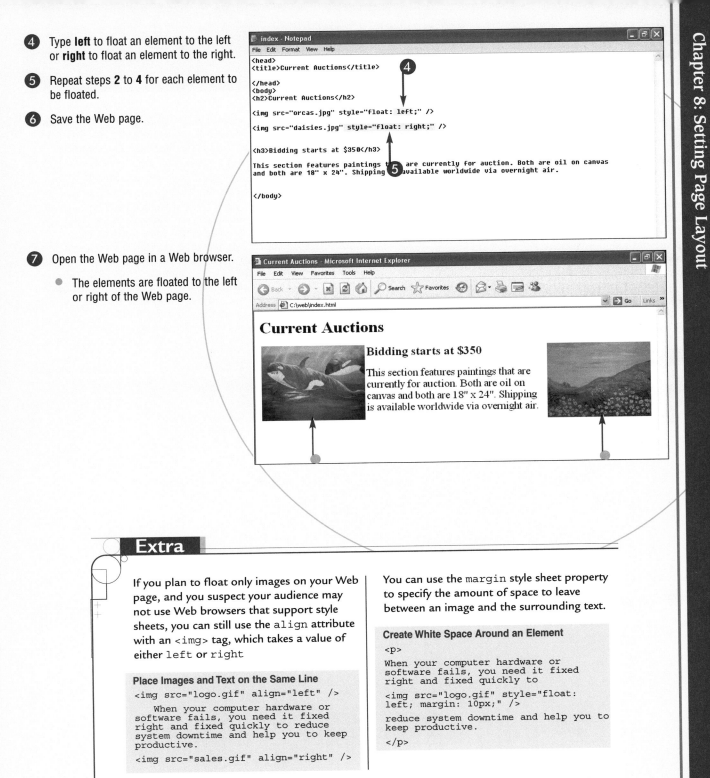

④ Type **left** to float an element to the left or **right** to float an element to the right.

⑤ Repeat steps **2** to **4** for each element to be floated.

⑥ Save the Web page.

⑦ Open the Web page in a Web browser.

● The elements are floated to the left or right of the Web page.

Extra

If you plan to float only images on your Web page, and you suspect your audience may not use Web browsers that support style sheets, you can still use the `align` attribute with an `<img>` tag, which takes a value of either `left` or `right`

Place Images and Text on the Same Line

```
<img src="logo.gif" align="left" />
    When your computer hardware or
software fails, you need it fixed
right and fixed quickly to reduce
system downtime and help you to keep
productive.
<img src="sales.gif" align="right" />
```

You can use the `margin` style sheet property to specify the amount of space to leave between an image and the surrounding text.

Create White Space Around an Element

```
<p>
When your computer hardware or
software fails, you need it fixed
right and fixed quickly to

<img src="logo.gif" style="float:
left; margin: 10px;" />

reduce system downtime and help you to
keep productive.
</p>
```

Show or Hide Elements

You can hide or unhide specific elements on your Web page, which enables you to easily modify the page simply by turning on or off the visibility of its elements. Programming languages such as JavaScript often use this technique to create interesting effects on a Web page.

The visibility style sheet property determines whether an element will display. Elements that are not displayed are referred to as invisible elements. Use the value visible for the visibility property to make Web page elements appear, and use the value hidden for the visibility property to make Web page elements invisible.

It is important to remember that invisible elements still take up space on the Web page. For example, if you make a large paragraph of text invisible, there will be a large area of blank space on your Web page where the paragraph of text would be, if it were still visible. Invisible elements can

still have margins, borders, and padding. The Web browser allocates space on the Web page not only for the invisible element, but also for any of the element's surrounding characteristics.

You can use the visibility style sheet property on any element that can appear on a Web page, including paragraphs of text, lists, tables, and images. The visibility style sheet property was not widely supported on many older Web browsers, but most current Web browsers do support its usage. Although it may seem redundant to use the visibility property to indicate that an element is visible, an external style sheet may indicate that a certain image is invisible under some circumstances. Using a local style sheet rule to indicate that the image should remain visible ensures that the image is always displayed, regardless of any previous style sheets.

Show or Hide Elements

① Open or create a Web page.

② Type **style=""** in the tag of the element to be hidden or made visible.

③ Type **visibility:;** and then a space.

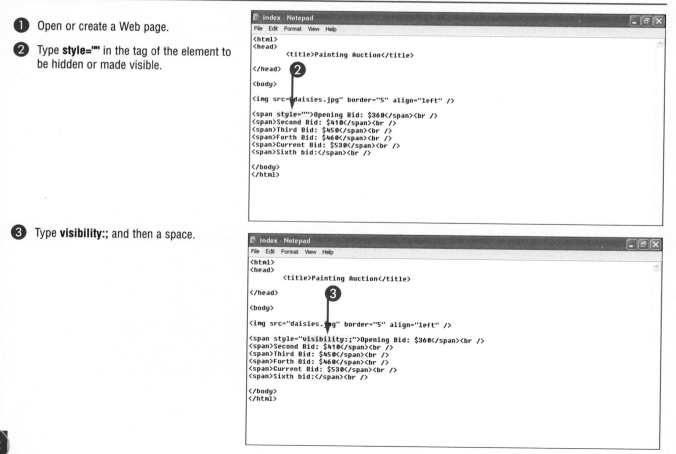

④ To hide an element, type **hidden**. To make it seen, type **visible**.

⑤ Repeat steps **2** to **4** for each element to be made hidden or visible.

⑥ Save the Web page.

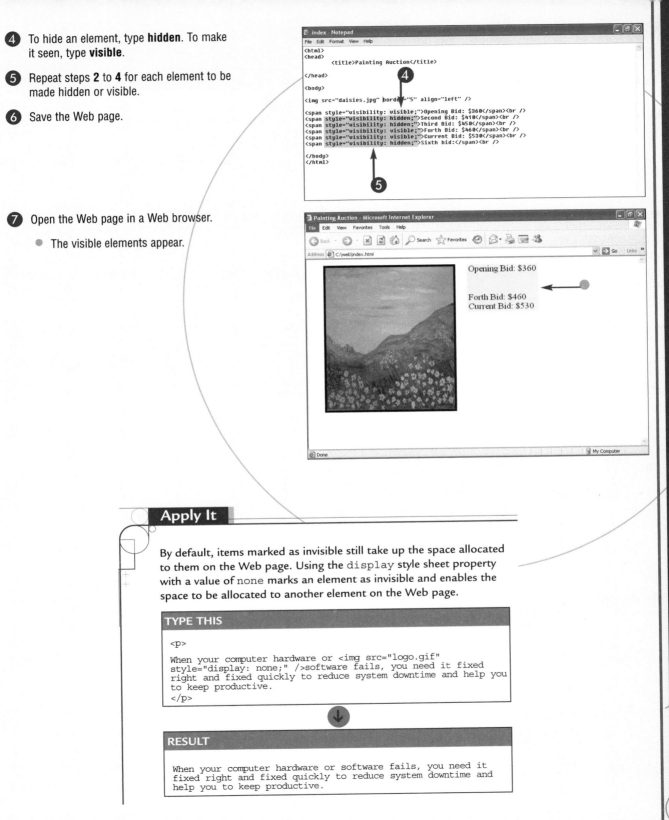

⑦ Open the Web page in a Web browser.

● The visible elements appear.

Apply It

By default, items marked as invisible still take up the space allocated to them on the Web page. Using the display style sheet property with a value of none marks an element as invisible and enables the space to be allocated to another element on the Web page.

TYPE THIS

```
<p>

When your computer hardware or <img src="logo.gif"
style="display: none;" />software fails, you need it fixed
right and fixed quickly to reduce system downtime and help you
to keep productive.
</p>
```

RESULT

```
When your computer hardware or software fails, you need it
fixed right and fixed quickly to reduce system downtime and
help you to keep productive.
```

Change the Mouse Pointer

The mouse pointer is the small graphical icon used to select items on a Web page. The movement of the mouse pointer corresponds to the movement of the mouse. You can change the appearance of the mouse pointer to provide better visual clues about the contents of your Web page, or you can change it for purely aesthetic reasons. For example, you can change the mouse pointer when it is placed over an image used as an image map to a mouse pointer consisting of a small crosshair to indicate to the user that they may click the image. This provides useful visual information to the user about the purpose of the image.

Many operating systems now allow users to customize their mouse pointers. You can use the cursor style sheet property to change the appearance of the mouse pointer.

The value of the cursor style sheet property indicates the type of mouse pointer used. The mouse pointer that results from changing the style sheet properties also depends on the user's customized configuration of their operating system. Regardless of the customizations, the resulting icons should still relate to the cursor type specified with the style sheet property. For example, if the value help is specified, the cursor may display a question mark or an image of a help manual. The mouse pointer reverts to its default state after being moved away from elements that are set to change its appearance.

You can apply the cursor style sheet property to individual elements using local style sheet rules, or to multiple similar elements on a Web page using an internal or external style sheet.

Change the Mouse Pointer

① Open or create a Web page.

② Type the opening and closing `<style>` tags.

③ Type the opening and closing { } on separate lines.

④ Type **cursor:;**.

⑤ Type the cursor type.

⑥ Save the Web page.

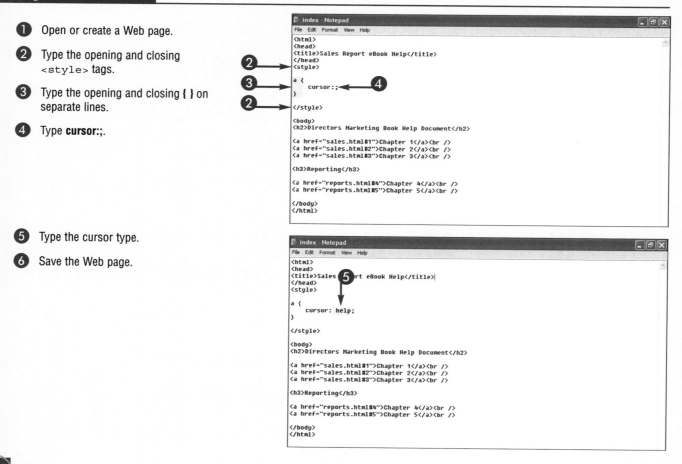

7 Open the Web page in a Web browser.

- The pointer is the default system pointer.

8 Position the mouse pointer over a link.

- The pointer type changes.

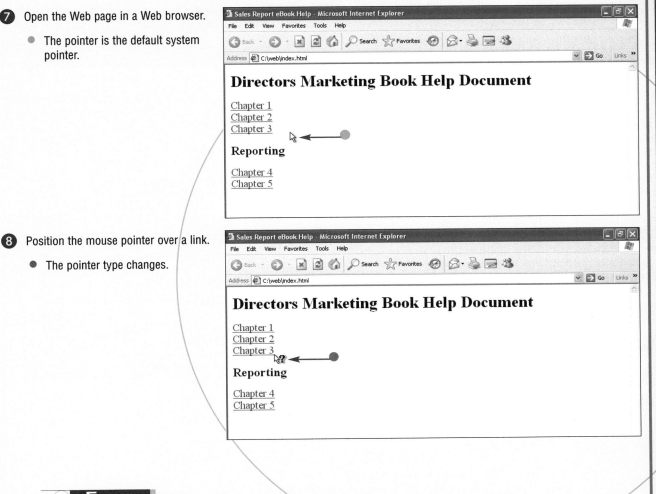

You can change the mouse pointer for each element on a Web page, although this may become annoying to some users. Because determining the purpose of all the different mouse pointers may become difficult, you should use only one or two mouse pointers for each Web page.

Different styles of mouse pointers are available, depending on the value of the cursor property. Not all mouse pointers are supported by all operating systems.

VALUE	TYPICAL POINTER APPEARANCE
crosshair	A very thin plus symbol.
default	The original mouse pointer as determined by the operating system.
pointer	A small hand, pointing.
help	A question mark next to a mouse pointer.
text	An upright line, used to indicate that text is expected.
move	A plus symbol with arrowheads indicating that an item may be dragged.
wait	An hourglass, indicating that the user must wait.

Draw an Outline

Y ou can use an outline to draw attention to important elements on your Web page. An outline is similar in appearance to a border; however, unlike a border, an outline takes up no space on the Web page. Although a thick border may displace the elements that surround it on the page, an outline does not affect the flow of any elements. An outline may also be irregular, unlike a border, which is always rectangular. This may also mean that an outline, when specified incorrectly, could be drawn on top of adjacent elements, obscuring them.

Specify the width of the outline using the `outline-width` property. You can specify the width of the outline in pixels by appending the letters `px` to a number. The width of an outline can also be specified as `thin`, `thick`, or `medium`.

Instead of using the shorthand `outline` property, you can use individual properties to specify the precise characteristics of an outline. Individual outline properties

are `outline-color`, `outline-style`, and `outline-width`. These properties will change the color, appearance, and thickness of the outline.

```
<style>
h1 {
    outline-color:blue;
    outline-style:dashed;
    outline-width:3px;
}
</style>
```

Many Web browsers do not currently support the `outline` style sheet property. Therefore, you should not depend on its usage unless you can ensure that Web browsers capable of displaying outlines are being used.

You can apply an outline to elements such as tables, images, and paragraphs of text. Outlines can be applied to individual words or sentences using the `<span>` tag.

Draw an Outline

1 Open or create a Web page.

2 In the tag of the element to which an outline is applied, type **style=""**.

3 Type **outline :;** and a space.

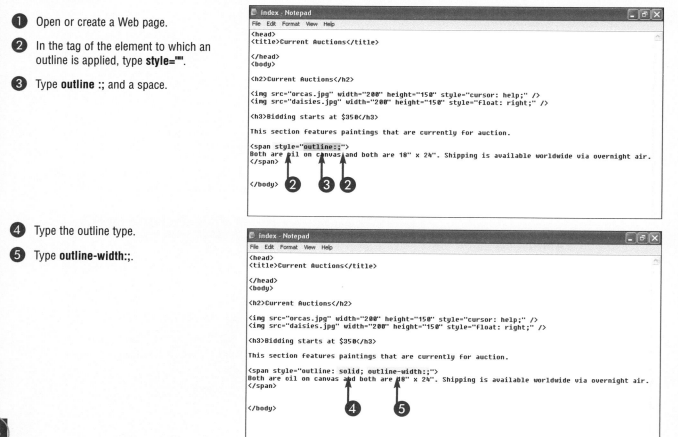

4 Type the outline type.

5 Type **outline-width:;**.

6 Type the width of the outline

7 Save the Web page.

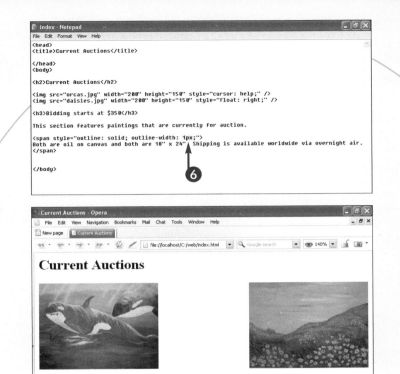

8 Open the Web page in a Web browser that supports outlines.

● The element appears with an outline.

You can change the appearance of the outline to better suit your Web page. The value of the `outline-style` property changes the appearance of the outline.

VALUE	APPEARANCE
none	No outline.
dotted	A series of small dots.
dashed	A dashed line.
solid	A solid line.
double	Two lines close together.
groove	A three-dimensional grooved appearance.
ridge	A three-dimensional ridged appearance.
inset	A three-dimensional outline which appears inset.
outset	A three-dimensional outline which appears outset.

Work with Element Overflow

You can inadvertently create elements on your Web page that are larger than expected. In these cases, the element is usually dynamically generated from a script or some other source outside of your control.

Some Web page elements that use absolute positioning can be difficult to lay out correctly if they are extremely large. You can use the overflow property to better control what happens to Web page elements that are larger or smaller than expected.

In the case of large elements, especially those that contain text, assign a scroll bar to enable users to see the full content of an element without changing the element's size. You can use the scroll value of the overflow property to create a set of scroll bars within an element. Use the scroll bars to view the complete contents of the element by moving the content up or down or from side to side as required.

When the scroll value of the overflow property is assigned, scroll bars are displayed within the element

regardless of whether the element's contents are completely visible or not. The overflow property can be used as a replacement for some types of frames.

Use the hidden value of the overflow property to prevent the content of an element from overflowing, but also to prevent access to the content that does via scroll bars. In practice, this means that any element's content larger than the specified size allocated for the element is not visible.

```
<style>
    p {
    position: absolute;
    top: 25;
    left: 5;
    width: 15%;
    height: 120px;
    overflow: hidden;
    }
</style>
```

Work with Element Overflow

① Open or create a Web page.

② Type the code that creates a local style specifying the width and height of an element.

③ Type **overflow:;** and a space.

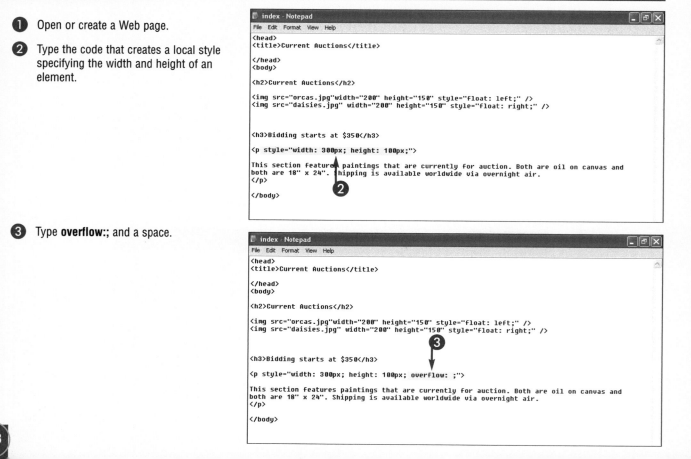

④ Type **scroll**.

⑤ Save the Web page.

```
index - Notepad
File  Edit  Format  View  Help
<head>
<title>Current Auctions</title>

</head>
<body>

<h2>Current Auctions</h2>

<img src="orcas.jpg"width="200" height="150" style="float: left;" />
<img src="daisies.jpg" width="200" height="150" style="float: right;" />
                                            ④
<h3>Bidding starts at $350</h3>

<p style="width: 300px; height: 100px; overflow: scroll;">

This section features paintings that are currently for auction. Both are oil on canvas and
both are 18" x 24". Shipping is available worldwide via overnight air.
</p>

</body>
```

⑥ Open the Web page in a Web browser.

● The element appears accompanied by scrollbars.

```
Current Auctions - Microsoft Internet Explorer
File  Edit  View  Favorites  Tools  Help
Back       Search    Favorites
Address  C:\web\index.html                              Go   Links
```

Current Auctions

Bidding starts at $350

This section features paintings
that are currently for auction.
Both are oil on canvas and both
are 18" x 24". Shipping is

Extra

Use the `auto` value of the `overflow` property to let the Web browser automatically determine if the content is too large for the element. If it is, the browser places a set of scroll bars within the element so that users can access the element's content.

Automatically Add Scrollbars
```
<p style="width: 200px; overflow: auto; height: 15%;">
    When your computer hardware or software fails, you need it
    fixed right and fixed quickly to reduce system downtime
    and help you to keep productive. But in your complex,
    multi-vendor computing environment, it is not always easy
    to find the level of expertise you need, much less a
    solution that also gives you flexible options designed
    to meet your unique needs.
</p>
```

Use System Fonts and Colors

You can create Web pages that utilize the colors that users have specified for their own computing environments. Users typically specify colors and font schemes that are most pleasing to them and that best suit their current environment. For example, a user with a small laptop screen may use a color scheme that has a high contrast between the text and the background, and that utilizes larger size fonts. Web pages created to utilize the color and font preferences chosen by that user will have the same high contrast and large font sizes, making the Web page easier to read on that user's screen.

The `color` property can be used to set the foreground color of an element to the same color used by the operating system. The `windowtext` value is a color of text used by the operating system in applications. The color value

`window` is the same background color of the application window. The font value `caption` changes an element's font to the same font that appears on buttons generated by the operating system and applications.

When utilizing system fonts and colors, the appearance of your Web page will change each time the user changes the system colors and fonts that you use in your Web page.

By using one of six popular computer font styles for specific items, such as dialog boxes or buttons, you can change the font of the item to the font currently used by the operating system. The six include: `caption` (on buttons), `icon` (underneath desktop icons), `menu` (on drop-down menus), `message-box` (in dialog boxes), `small-caption` (on small items and icons), and `status-bar` (in information area at the bottom of a window).

Use System Fonts and Colors

① Open or create a Web page.

② Type **style=""** in the <body> tag.

③ Type **color:;** and a space.

④ Type the color of the text on the Web page.

⑤ Type **background:;** and a space.

⑥ Type **font:;**.

7 Type the color of the Web page background.

8 Type the style of font.

9 Save the Web page.

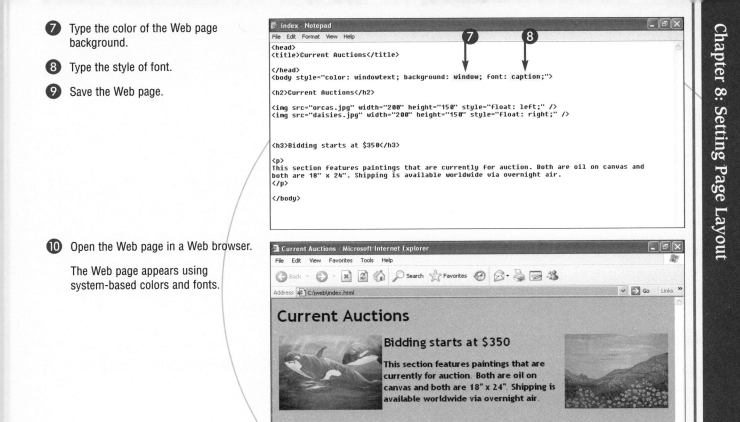

10 Open the Web page in a Web browser.

The Web page appears using system-based colors and fonts.

Extra

When specifying colors to be used on your Web page, you can specify a number of colors that reflect the colors of the user's computing environment.

COLOR	MEANING
Background	The background color of the user's desktop.
ButtonFace	The color used on the front of a button.
ButtonShadow	The shadow created by three-dimensional objects such as buttons.
GrayText	The system color of an item that has become disabled.
HighlightText	Items that are selected appear this color.
InfoBackground	The background color of ToolTips and help bubbles.
InfoText	The font color of ToolTips and help bubbles.
Scrollbar	The background color of the scroll bar.
Window	The background color of a window.
WindowFrame	The color of the window's frame.
WindowText	The color of the font in a window.

Create a Basic Table

Tables can format data into columns and rows on a Web page. Columns and rows can make data better organized and easier to read. Tables place information into cells, which are formed by the intersection of a column and a row.

You can create a table using the `<table>` tag. The `<table>` tag contains `<tr>` tags, which denote rows, and `<td>` tags, which specify individual cells. For example, within the table, three sets of `<td>` tags enclosed by a set of `<tr>` tags creates a row containing three cells of data. After one row has been created, additional rows can be added with the same or a different amount of cells if required. Although the initial setup may seem complex, tables are actually very simple to construct. To make the task of creating tables easier, you can indent your code to better indicate the various components of the table. For example, you can indent each `<tr>` tag once to indicate that the rows are within a `<table>` tag above them, and then indent each `<td>` tag twice to indicate that they are within the `<tr>` tag above them.

The Web browser automatically resizes the columns of table data to better fit the overall width of the table. Sometimes, when table cells are empty, the table may not appear the way you originally intended. The Web browser attempts to adjust the column width based upon the cell that contains the largest amount of data in that column.

You can format text information contained within the cells of the table just like text on any other part of the Web page. Although tables primarily contain text, you can also place elements such as images within the cells of a table.

Create a Basic Table

① Open or create a Web page.

② Type the opening and closing **<table>** tags.

③ Type the opening and closing **<tr>** tags.

④ Type **<td>**.

⑤ Type the contents of the first cell in the first row.

⑥ Type **</td>**.

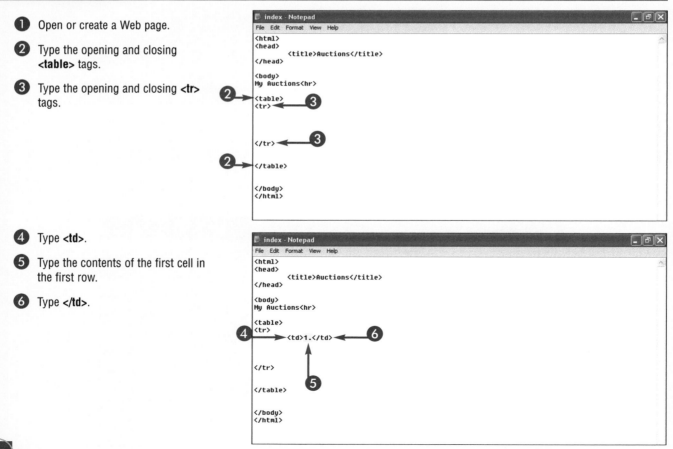

7. Repeat steps **4** to **6** for each remaining cell in the first row.

8. Repeat steps **3** to **7** for each remaining row in the table.

9. Save the Web page.

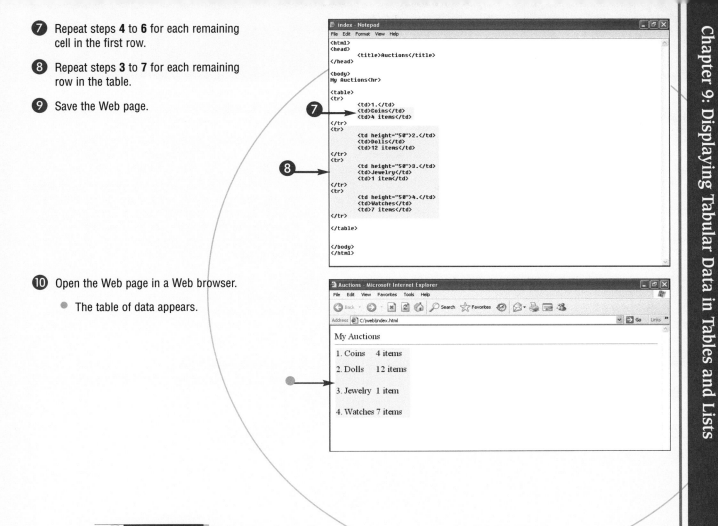

10. Open the Web page in a Web browser.

- The table of data appears.

Define the Table Border

Y ou can create a border around your table and around the cells contained within it. You can customize various aspects of the border, including its width and color. You can set the width to 0 so that your table is invisible to the user; this technique is used constantly by Web developers when tables are used to define a Web page's layout.

The width of the border is specified using the `border` attribute of the `<table>` tag. The value of the border attribute will be the width, in pixels, of the border. As with all XHTML tag attributes, the value should be enclosed within quotations.

You can specify the border color of a table, a row, or even an individual cell within the table. You can choose any valid color for the border. If you select the same border color as the background of the Web page, the cell will appear to have no border. This is another technique you

can use to make your tables invisible to visitors to your Web site.

The table border is rendered using a 3-D effect, using two colors to simulate the border itself and its cast shadow. You can select both the light and dark colors of the border.

The `bordercolor` attribute is used to specify the solid color of a border. Using just the `bordercolor` attribute renders the complete border in the specified color. The value of the `bordercolor` attribute can be any valid color. The `bordercolor` attributes are not fully supported by all Web browsers, although they are well supported by Internet Explorer.

The `bordercolordark` attribute determines the dark color, or "shadow," assigned to the border. The `bordercolordark` attribute is typically used with the `bordercolor` attribute to create a 3-D effect for the border. Both attributes use any valid color for their values.

Define the Table Border

① Open or create a Web page that contains a table.

② Type **border="7"** to set the border's width.

③ Type **bordercolor="white"** to set the table's main border color.

④ Type **bordercolorlight="silver"** to set the light border color.

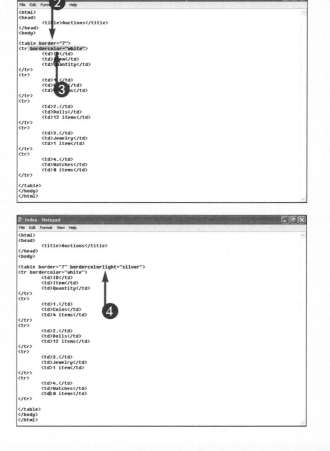

⑤ Type **bordercolordark="black"** to set the dark border color.

⑥ Type **bordercolor="red"** to set the cell's border color to red.

⑦ Save the Web page.

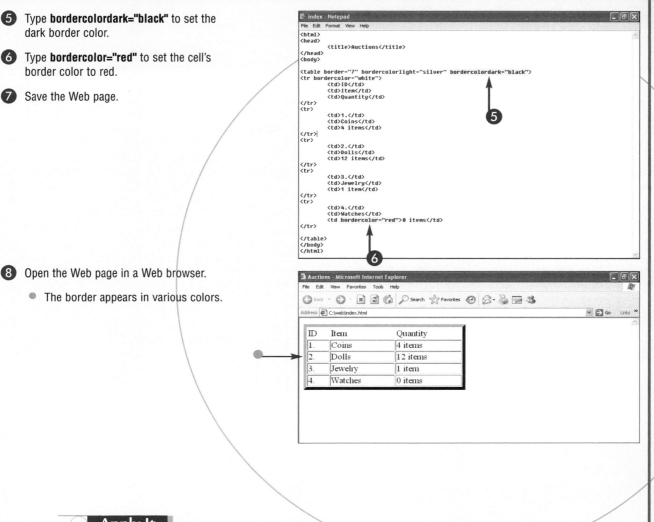

⑧ Open the Web page in a Web browser.

● The border appears in various colors.

You can use a local style sheet with the border property and a value of dashed to create a dashed line for the table border.

Example
```
<table border="7" bordercolor="black"
style="border: dashed;">
<tr>
    <td>Items for Sale</td>
</tr>
</table>
```

You can use style sheets to set the color of the borders of your table. You can apply formatting using external, internal, or local style sheets. The border-color style sheet property controls the color of the border.

Example
```
<tr>
    <td>1.</td>
    <td style="border-color:
Fuchsia;">Coins</td>
    <td style="border-color: blue;">4
items</td>
</tr>
```

Set Width and Height Properties

You can use the `width` attribute of the `<table>` tag to adjust the width of a table. The value of the `width` attribute can be a number, which specifies the number of pixels wide the table will be; or the value can be specified as a percentage of the Web browser window width. For example, you can create a table that is half the width of the Web browser window by specifying a value of `50%`. When the percentage symbol is included in the value, the Web browser resizes the table as a percentage as opposed to an exact pixel width.

Setting the height or width of a table as a percentage allows you to make your page more flexible as to how the page flows in different display resolutions or in windows that are not maximized to the entire screen. Setting the height or

width of a table by comparison allows you to hard code a table's size so that it is the same size regardless of resolution or window size. Depending on the layout of your site, you may prefer one of these techniques over the other at different times or even between table to table on your page.

Use the `height` attribute of the `<table>` tag to specify the actual height of the table. As with the `width` attribute, you can specify the height of the table as an absolute size or as a percentage of the Web browser window height.

You can also specify the width of a column by including the `width` attribute within a `<td>` tag. If a `<td>` tag also includes the `height` attribute, the height of the complete row of cells adjusts as well. Typically, the height of a row of cells is adjusted by specifying the height of the first cell in the row.

Set Width and Height Properties

① Open or create a Web page that contains a table.

② Type **width=""**.

③ Type the width of the table.

④ Type **height=""**.

146

5 Type the height of the table.

6 Repeat steps **4** to **5** in the first `<td>` tag of each row you want to change.

7 Save the Web page.

```
index - Notepad
File  Edit  Format  View  Help
<html>
<head>
        <title>Auctions</title>
</head>
<body>

<table width="50%" height="300" border="7">
<tr>
        <td width="10%" height="100"><strong>ID</strong></td>
        <td width="20%"><strong>Item</strong></td>
        <td><strong>Quantity</strong></td>
</tr>
<tr>
        <td>1.</td>
        <td>Coins</td>
        <td>4 items</td>
</tr>
<tr>
        <td>2.</td>
        <td>Dolls</td>
        <td>12 items</td>
</tr>
<tr>
        <td>3.</td>
        <td>Jewelry</td>
        <td>1 item</td>
</tr>
<tr>
        <td>4.</td>
        <td>Watches</td>
        <td>0 items</td>
</tr>

</table>
</body>
</html>
```

8 Open the Web page in a Web browser.

● The table appears with the cells in different sizes.

```
Auctions - Microsoft Internet Explorer
File  Edit  View  Favorites  Tools  Help
Back    Search  Favorites
Address  C:\web\index.html                         Go   Links
```

ID	Item	Quantity
1.	Coins	4 items
2.	Dolls	12 items
3.	Jewelry	1 item
4.	Watches	0 items

```
Done                                        My Computer
```

Extra

Sometimes the width and height specifications for a table or cell are smaller than required to display the data within the table. The Web browser always tries to display all the data in the table. If the width and height values are too small to display the available data, the Web browser ignores those values and enlarges the table to accommodate the data.

Do not forget to take into account the screen resolutions that most people may use to view the Web page. If you specify a table width of more than 1,000 pixels, users with low- or medium-resolution displays may not see the full table on their screens. Whenever possible, specify the height and width as a percentage of the Web browser display size.

When expressing the table as a percentage of the Web browser display, you are not limited to sizes of 100% or less. If a table wider than the browser window provides the desired result, scroll bars will appear at the bottom of the window to enable users to view the complete table.

Example
```
<table width="230%"
border="7"
cellspacing="5"
cellpadding="5">
```

Create Cells Spanning Multiple Columns and Rows

You can combine neighboring cells in a table to create larger cells. This is useful for displaying large amounts of data, combining data from multiple cells, or simply for aesthetic reasons, such as adding a banner to the top of the table.

When combining cells, you must pay attention to the structure of the table, particularly the cells surrounding the cells to be combined. Use the rowspan attribute of the <td> tag to span a cell across a row. When combining cells in the same row, the cells must be adjacent. The rowspan attribute is added to the first cell's <td> tag, and the second cell's <td> tag is removed. Of course, if you are creating a new table, there is no need to create the second cell.

Combining cells in different rows and different columns within the same table can be somewhat confusing. For more

complex tables, it is often easier to sketch out the table on paper before creating the code. Troubleshooting a table that contains incorrect rowspan and colspan attribute values can be very time-consuming.

Use the colspan attribute to merge cells that are adjacent to each other in the same column. The colspan attribute is added to the topmost <td> tag. Due to the complexity of tables with cells that span across rows and columns, initially creating these tables with borders turned on is a good idea, even if your finished table will not have a border. This makes seeing the outcome of your colspan and rowspan attributes much easier.

You can insert data into a spanned cell just like any other cell by placing the data between the start and end <td> tags.

Create Cells Spanning Multiple Columns and Rows

① Open or create a Web page that contains a table.

② Type **colspan=""**.

```
<html>
<head>
        <title>Auctions</title>
</head>
<body>
On Line Auctions
<hr>

<table width="500" border="7">
<tr>
        <td colspan="">Items For Sale</td>
</tr>
<tr>
        <td>1.</td>
        <td>Coins</td>
        <td>4 items</td>
</tr>
<tr>
        <td>2.</td>
        <td>Dolls</td>
        <td>12 items</td>
</tr>
<tr>
        <td>3.</td>
        <td>Jewelry</td>
        <td>Sold Out</td>
</tr>
<tr>
        <td>4.</td>
        <td>Watches</td>

</tr>

</table>
</body>
</html>
```

③ Type the number of columns to span.

④ Type **rowspan=""**.

```
<html>
<head>
        <title>Auctions</title>
</head>
<body>
On Line Auctions
<hr>

<table width="500" border="7">
<tr>
        <td colspan="3">Items For Sale</td>
</tr>
<tr>
        <td>1.</td>
        <td>Coins</td>
        <td>4 items</td>
</tr>
<tr>
        <td>2.</td>
        <td>Dolls</td>
        <td>12 items</td>
</tr>
<tr>
        <td>3.</td>
        <td>Jewelry</td>
        <td rowspan="">Sold Out</td>
</tr>
<tr>
        <td>4.</td>
        <td>Watches</td>

</tr>

</table>
</body>
</html>
```

⑤ Type the number of rows to span.

⑥ Save the Web page.

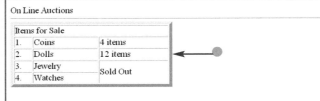

```
index - Notepad
File  Edit  Format  View  Help
<html>
<head>
        <title>Auctions</title>
</head>
<body>
On Line Auctions
<hr>

<table width="50%" border="7">
<tr>
        <td colspan="3">Items for Sale</td>
</tr>
<tr>
        <td>1.</td>
        <td>Coins</td>
        <td>4 items</td>
</tr>
<tr>
        <td>2.</td>
        <td>Dolls</td>
        <td>12 items</td>
</tr>
<tr>
        <td>3.</td>
        <td>Jewelry</td>
        <td rowspan="2">Sold Out</td>
</tr>
<tr>
        <td>4.</td>
        <td>Watches</td>

</tr>

</table>
</body>
</html>
```

⑦ Open the Web page in a Web browser.

● The table containing the spanned cells appears.

Auctions - Microsoft Internet Explorer
File Edit View Favorites Tools Help
Back · · · Search · Favorites
Address C:\web\index.html · Go Links »

On Line Auctions

Items for Sale		
1.	Coins	4 items
2.	Dolls	12 items
3.	Jewelry	Sold Out
4.	Watches	

Apply It

Sometimes the grid-like structure of a normal table does not allow you the flexibility you need to properly display the content of your Web page in the way you would like to. You can use the `colspan` and `rowspan` attributes within the same `<td>` tag to create a cell that spans both across the row and down the column.

Example
```
<tr>
    <td>2.</td>
    <td>Dolls</td>
    <td align="center">12 items</td>
</tr>
<tr>
    <td>3.</td>
    <td colspan="2" rowspan="2" align="center" valign="bottom">Sold Out</td>
</tr>
<tr>
    <td>4.</td>
</tr>
```

Adjust Cell Properties

You can adjust the properties of a cell to better present the data within the cell. The flexibility to adjust each cell's properties in a table is one of the reasons that tables are so popular today as a tool for laying out Web pages. For example, the space between cells can be adjusted, as well as the space between the cell data and the cell border.

Cell spacing and cell padding are useful when you want to adjust the amount of space between table elements. The distance between cells is called *cell spacing* and can be specified in pixels using the `cellspacing` attribute of the `<table>` tag. Specifying a small number value forces the cells closer together, and a large number forces the cells farther apart. The distance between the data in a cell and

the sides or the top and bottom of the cell is called *cell padding*. Use the `cellpadding` attribute of the `<table>` tag to specify the minimum distance in pixels the data will be from the sides of a cell.

You can specify both horizontal and vertical alignment attributes for each cell. Data within a cell can be aligned horizontally to the right, left, or center, similar in manner to text that is aligned within a word processing document. You can also align cell data vertically to the top, bottom, or middle of the cell. The `align` attribute of the `<td>` tag is used to specify the horizontal alignment of the cell. The values of the `align` attribute are `left`, `right`, and `center`. The `valign` attribute specifies the vertical alignment of data in a cell, and its values are `top`, `bottom`, and `middle`.

Adjust Cell Properties

1 Open or create a Web page that contains a table.

2 Type **cellspacing=""**.

3 Type **cellpadding=""**.

4 Type the amount of spacing between cells.

5 Type the size of the margins within the cells.

6 Type **align=""**.

7 Type the alignment type for the cell.

8 Type **valign=""**.

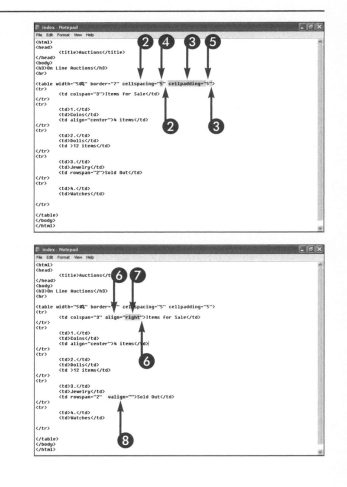

9 Type the vertical alignment type.

10 Repeat steps **6** to **7** for each cell you want to align.

11 Save the Web page.

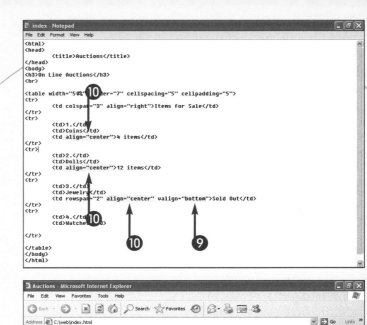

12 Open the Web page in a Web browser.

● The aligned cells appear.

Extra

To place data in adjoining cells right next to each other with no space between them, set the `cellpadding` and `cellspacing` attributes, as well as the border size, to 0. This is very useful when adjoining cells contain different parts of the same image and you do not want gaps between the different parts of the image.

Most Web browsers assign default values for the `cellpadding` and `cellspacing` attributes of a table unless you specify otherwise. Cell spacing is typically set to 1 pixel, and cell padding is usually 1 pixel wide.

When adjusting cell padding, text may start to wrap within a cell to accommodate the change. Most Web browsers display table text without wrapping when you add the `nowrap` attribute to the <td> tag of the cell.

Example

```
<td nowrap>Dolls and
Clocks</td>
```

Combine Tables

Y{.dropcap}ou can create one table inside of another table, resulting in *nested*, or combined, tables. Nested tables enable you to present more complex data and sophisticated layouts for your Web pages. A nested table is simply a separate table placed within the cell of an existing table. All the characteristics and appearances of a table and its related elements, including border color and width, apply to nested tables. One example of how this would be useful would be when you are using a table for defining your Web page's layout and you want to add an informational table to the page; in that case, you would add the informational table (or nest it) within the layout table.

In most cases, the nested table should be the full width and height of the cell that contains the table. You must set the width and height attributes of the nested table to a value of 100% to ensure that the table completely fits in the cell.

If you notice a gap around the nested table within a cell of the parent table, the cellpadding value of the parent table may be too high. To ensure that no gaps exist between the nested table and the table cell that contains it, you should set the cellpadding value of the parent table to 0.

Because of the numerous start and end tags associated with nested tables, making mistakes becomes very easy. Troubleshooting complex tables when a problem arises can be time-consuming. As with any complex table structure, sketching the table layout on paper before creating the code is a good idea.

Combine Tables

① Open or create a Web page that contains a table.

② Type the opening table tag.

③ Type the closing table tag.

④ Type **width="100%"**.

⑤ Type **height="100%"**.

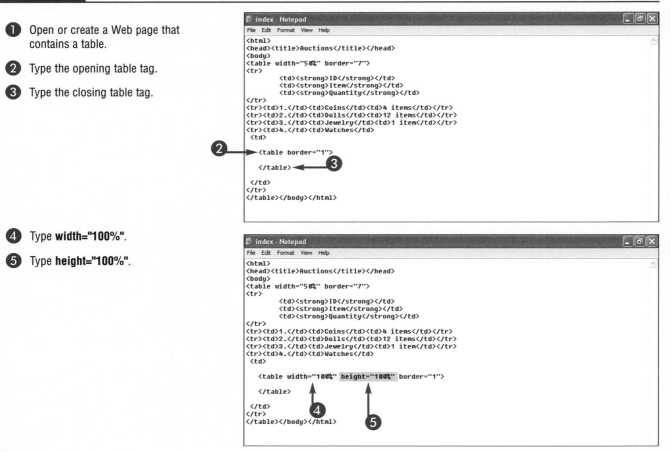

6 Type the code that creates the rows and columns of the table.

7 Save the Web page.

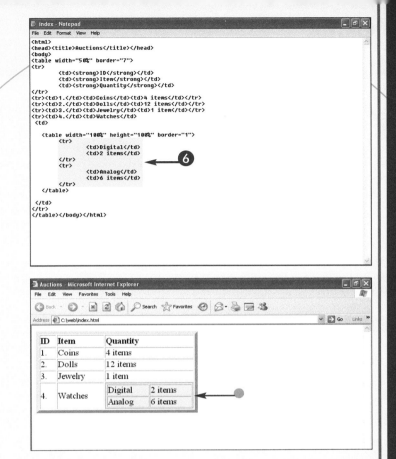

```
index - Notepad
File  Edit  Format  View  Help

<html>
<head><title>Auctions</title></head>
<body>
<table width="50%" border="7">
<tr>
        <td><strong>ID</strong></td>
        <td><strong>Item</strong></td>
        <td><strong>Quantity</strong></td>
</tr>
<tr><td>1.</td><td>Coins</td><td>4 items</td></tr>
<tr><td>2.</td><td>Dolls</td><td>12 items</td></tr>
<tr><td>3.</td><td>Jewelry</td><td>1 item</td></tr>
<tr><td>4.</td><td>Watches</td>
 <td>

    <table width="100%" height="100%" border="1">
        <tr>
                <td>Digital</td>
                <td>2 items</td>
        </tr>
        <tr>
                <td>Analog</td>
                <td>6 items</td>
        </tr>
    </table>

 </td>
</tr>
</table></body></html>
```

8 Open the Web page in a Web browser.

● The nested table appears.

```
Auctions - Microsoft Internet Explorer
File  Edit  View  Favorites  Tools  Help
Back ·  ·  ·    Search  Favorites     ·
Address  C:\web\index.html                          Go  Links
```

ID	Item	Quantity	
1.	Coins	4 items	
2.	Dolls	12 items	
3.	Jewelry	1 item	
4.	Watches	Digital 2 items	
		Analog 6 items	

Apply It

Sometimes undesirable gaps appear between the nested table's outside border and the border of the cell that contains the table. To avoid inserting spaces into a table cell along with a nested table, you should make sure that there is no space between the `<td>` tags of the table cell and the `<table>` tags of the nested table. The following code shows the proper format for ensuring that no errant spaces appear in your code (and thus between table borders).

Example
```
<tr>
    <td><table>
        <tr>
        <td>Digital</td>
        <td>2 items</td>
        </tr>
    </table></td>
</tr>
```

Display a Bulleted List

You can create bulleted lists to display series of items on a Web page. An unordered list arranges items in no particular order (as opposed to numbered lists, where there is an order to the items; numbered lists are discussed in the next task). Two tags are required to construct a list: the unordered list tag <ul>, which delimits all the items in a list; and the list item tag <li>, which denotes each individual item in a list. Unordered lists are good for listing items such as recipe ingredients, where there are multiple items required, but there is no certain order in which they need to be listed.

A bullet precedes each item displayed in a list. A bullet is a small graphical character, typically a solid circle. Your Web browser determines the graphical character used as the

bullet for a list of items. It is also possible that some users will have configured their Web browsers to use different characters than yours for bulleted lists.

Items displayed in a list on a Web page are also slightly indented to the right of the left margin. This helps to identify the items as belonging to a related list. Typically, a Web browser indents a list by two or three spaces.

It was once quite common to ignore the closing list item tag </li> on each item in a list. Although most Web browsers display items in a list that do not have the end tag, any HTML code you create is not XHTML compatible if you ignore the closing list item tag. You should always include both the start and end list item tag for each item in your list.

Display a Bulleted List

① Open or create a Web page.

② Create a list of items.

③ Type **<ul>** to indicate the beginning of an unordered list.

④ Type **</ul>** to indicate the end to your unordered list.

⑤ Type **<li>** to indicate the beginning of a list item.

⑥ Type **</li>** to indicate the end of a list item.

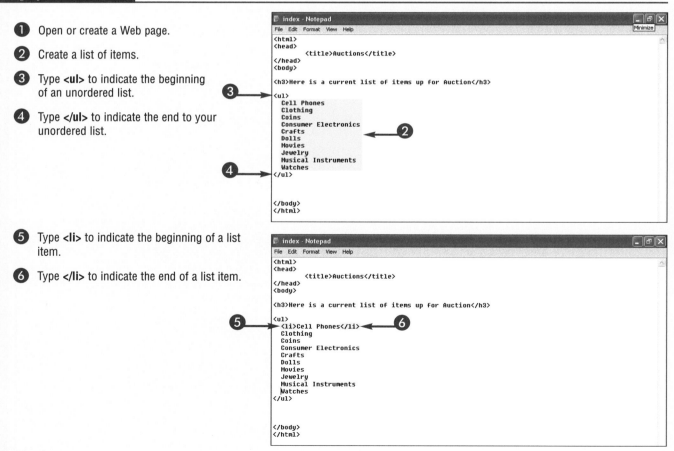

7 Repeat steps **5** to **6** for the remaining items in the list.

8 Save the Web page.

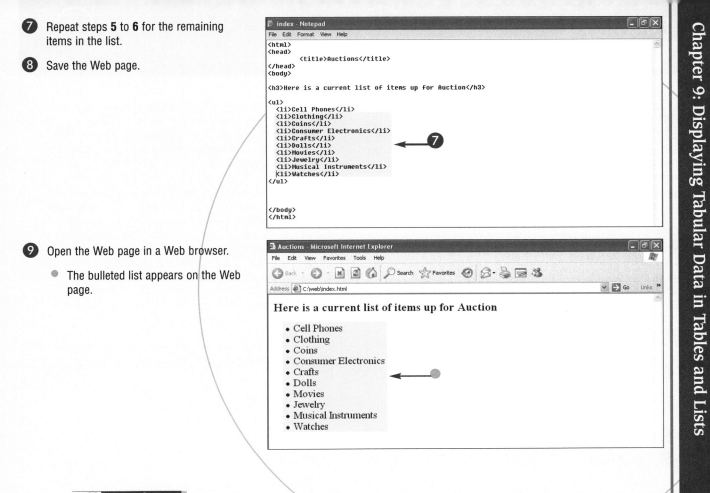

9 Open the Web page in a Web browser.

● The bulleted list appears on the Web page.

Apply It

The type attribute of the `<ul>` tag changes the type of bullet used in the list. You can choose from the values `disk`, `square`, and `circle`. The following code creates a bulleted list that uses a small square as the bullet, as opposed to the default circle.

Example
```
<ul type="square">
    <li>Create schedule</li>
    <li>Call meeting</li>
</ul>
```

You can use a list without bullets to indent items on your Web pages that are not list items.

TYPE THIS
```
Hello
<ul>
    <h3>
        Welcome to my Web page
    </h3>
</ul>
```

RESULT

Hello

Welcome to my Web page

Display a Numeric List

You can create a list in which the items are numbered to better organize a series of items. For example you may want to present the chapter titles of a book in a numeric list, with each chapter title preceded by the number of the chapter, or you could indicate the steps of a recipe that have to be followed in a certain order.

Numbered lists are similar to unordered lists except that the ordered list tag <ol> is used instead of the unordered list tag <ul>. Items in a numbered list are defined in the same way as those in a bulleted list, with each item enclosed in a starting and ending <li> list item tag.

By default, numbered lists start at the number 1, and each item in the list increases by increments of 1. In some cases, you may want the list to start at a different number. The start attribute of the <ol> tag defines the starting number

of the list. After defining the starting number, each item in the list is subsequently numbered in increments of 1. This is useful if you have one list containing the same data broken up in different locations on your Web page. For example, you might have a numbered list broken up by images.

Make sure that any items you place into an ordered list are in the order that you want them. The browser does not rearrange list items, but simply numbers them from first to last. After you create a numbered list on a Web page, you can quickly insert additional items into the list. The Web browser renumbers the list to accommodate the new items.

As with any list, there are no restrictions on the line length used for each item; although for ease of readability, you should keep each list item to less than a line long.

Display a Numeric List

① Open or create a Web page.

② Type the opening and closing ordered list tags.

③ Type the code that creates the list items.

④ Repeat steps **2** to **3** to create a second list.

⑤ Type **start=""**.

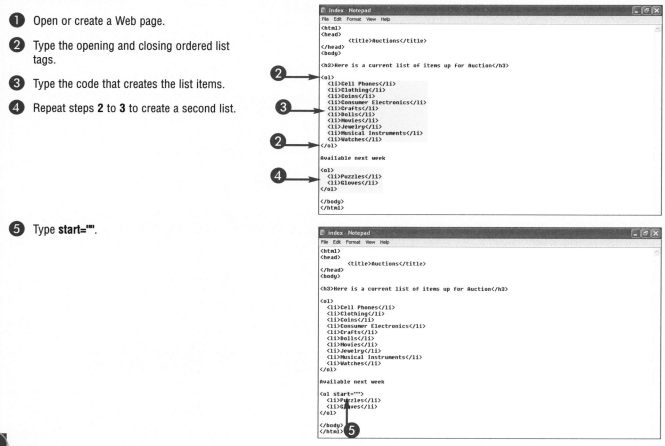

6 Type the number to start numbering the list items.

7 Save the Web page.

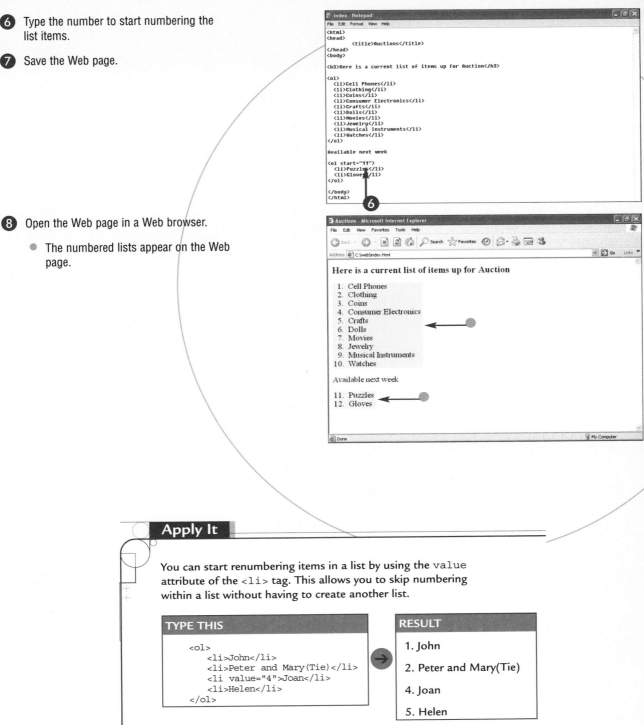

8 Open the Web page in a Web browser.

● The numbered lists appear on the Web page.

Apply It

You can start renumbering items in a list by using the `value` attribute of the `<li>` tag. This allows you to skip numbering within a list without having to create another list.

TYPE THIS

```
<ol>
    <li>John</li>
    <li>Peter and Mary(Tie)</li>
    <li value="4">Joan</li>
    <li>Helen</li>
</ol>
```

RESULT

1. John

2. Peter and Mary(Tie)

4. Joan

5. Helen

Nest a List

You can include lists within lists (a process called *nesting lists*) to create more complex lists than standard lists. Nesting lists enables you to include lists within lists, such as underneath list items. Some of the many uses for nested lists include creating outlines, a table of contents, or complex steps.

An outline is the definitive nested list: outlines are lists of topics with subtopic lists under each topic and sub-subtopics under subtopics, and so on. Outlines use numbers and letters in an alternating fashion to keep each level separate from the levels above and below it. You can define which type of numbers and/or letter you want for a given list by using the `type` attribute.

A table of contents is usually an outline without the variegated numbers that start each list item. Instead of list items being differentiated by the numbers and/or letters,

items in a table of contents are differentiated by indenting and style of headings alone.

Complex steps are numbered lists that require either bulleted lists or more numbered lists to be appended to individual list items. For example, in a recipe you might have a bulleted list detailing the ingredients necessary for an individual step. Alternatively, a step in a numbered list might itself be its own multi-step process that requires a sublist. Using the recipe example, if a step was to mix the ingredients for a sauce required by the recipe but mixing the sauce required several definite, individual steps, you might have a sublist for that step.

The following task shows you how to include a bulleted list under an item in a standard numbered list. As you can see, the sublist further described the items in the list item; in this case, the category Clothing is expounded upon to include the items Gloves, Hats, and Scarves.

Nest a List

① Open or create a Web page that contains a list.

② Type **<ol>** after a list item.

③ Type **</ol>** on another line before the next list item.

④ Type **type="".

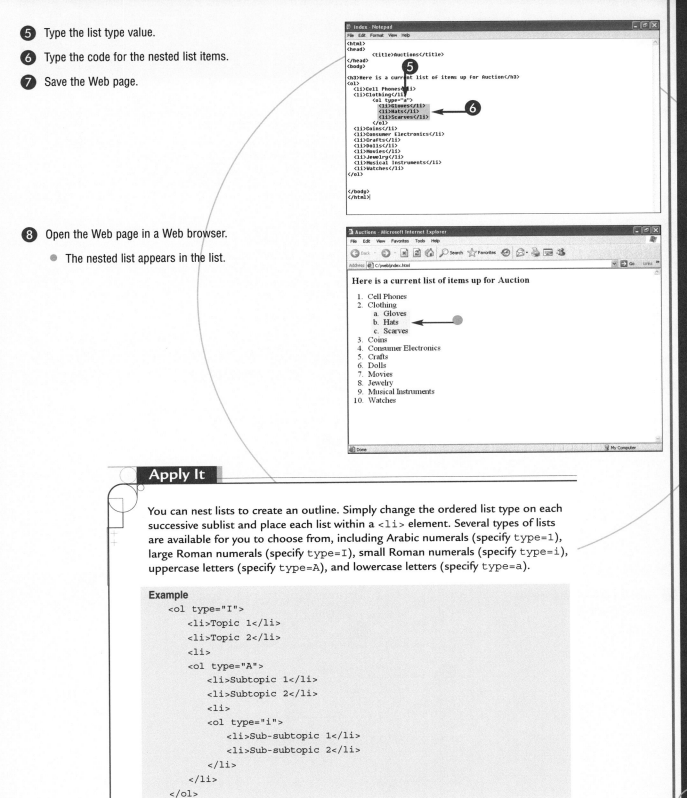

5 Type the list type value.

6 Type the code for the nested list items.

7 Save the Web page.

8 Open the Web page in a Web browser.

● The nested list appears in the list.

Apply It

You can nest lists to create an outline. Simply change the ordered list type on each successive sublist and place each list within a `<li>` element. Several types of lists are available for you to choose from, including Arabic numerals (specify `type=1`), large Roman numerals (specify `type=I`), small Roman numerals (specify `type=i`), uppercase letters (specify `type=A`), and lowercase letters (specify `type=a`).

Example

```
<ol type="I">
    <li>Topic 1</li>
    <li>Topic 2</li>
    <li>
    <ol type="A">
        <li>Subtopic 1</li>
        <li>Subtopic 2</li>
        <li>
        <ol type="i">
            <li>Sub-subtopic 1</li>
            <li>Sub-subtopic 2</li>
        </li>
    </li>
</ol>
```

Create a
Definition List

Definition lists enable you to present a list of items along with explanations of each item in an orderly manner. A definition list is the most flexible way of displaying complex list items such as glossaries and indexes. Definition lists are encompassed by an opening `<dl>` tag and a closing `</dl>` tag.

Definition lists are different from ordered and unordered lists in that each item in the list is comprised of two elements. The first element of the list item is often a word or phrase, which is enclosed with the `<dt>` tag. The second part of the list item is the definition, which is enclosed by the `<dd>` tag. The definition is an explanation of the first part of the list item. Although the definition itself can be any length, it is usually only a few lines long. Although

definition lists mainly present text information, you can also use images within a list.

The definition is placed underneath the list item and is typically indented. This allows the user to easily differentiate between a list item and its definition. Some Web browsers may differ in the way they present items in a definition list; for example, some browsers may not indent the definition at all.

Some Web browsers can still correctly display definition lists that do not use the closing `</dt>` or `</dd>` tags. However, in order to remain completely compatible with XHTML, as well as with Web browsers in the future, you should always include the closing `</dt>` or `</dd>` tags on your list items.

Create a Definition List

① Open or create a Web page.

② Type the opening and closing definition list tags.

③ Type the opening and closing definition term tags.

④ Type a list item.

⑤ Type the opening and closing definition tags.

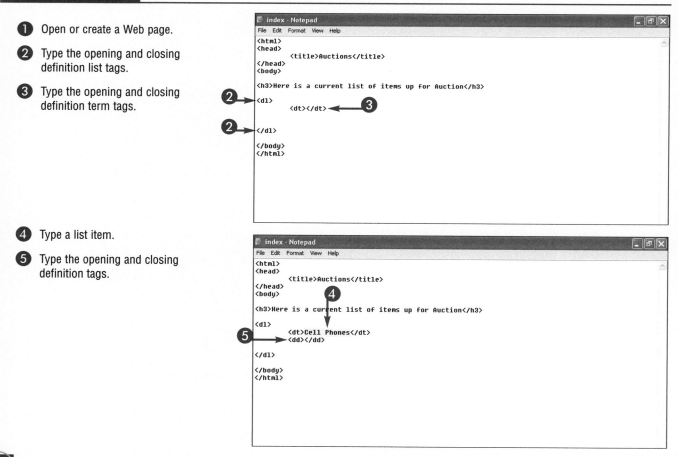

6 Type the definition of the list item.

7 Repeat steps **3** to **6** for each item in the list.

8 Save the Web page.

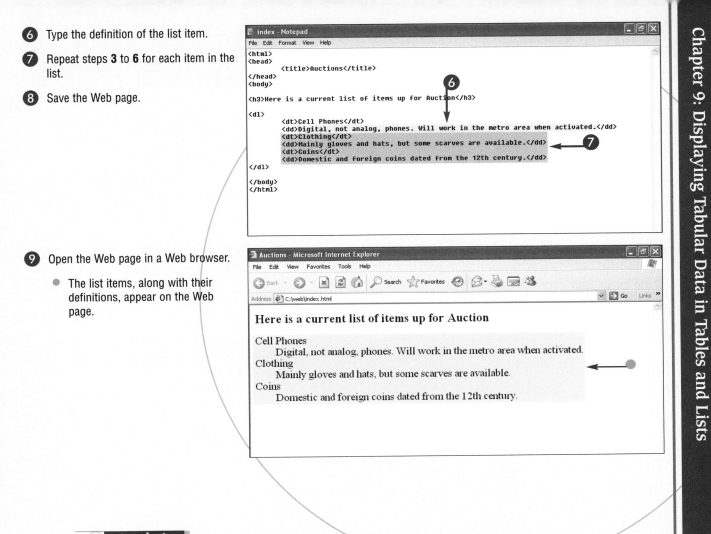

9 Open the Web page in a Web browser.

● The list items, along with their definitions, appear on the Web page.

To change the color of the definition description and create a multicolored list, add the style attribute to the `<dd>` tag and assign a value to the color property.

Example

```
<dl>
    <dt>Monday</dt>
    <dd style="color: gray;">Monday's
meeting is a</dd>
    <dt>Tuesday</dt>
    <dd style="color: gray;">This is
a wrap up meeting</dd>
</dl>
```

You can use the `<dt>` tag to display an image and the `<dd>` tag to display text that describes the image, like a caption.

Example

```
<dl>
  <dt>
    <img src="cat.gif" />
  </dt>
  <dd>
    Our first cat
  </dd>
</dl>
```

Create a Form

You can create a form to enable users of your Web pages to send information over the Internet to you or to applications that process the data; for example, the user might submit credit card data to purchase something from you. Unless your Web page is the most basic possible and least interactive of Web sites (and there are indeed a lot of these sites on the Internet that are perfectly useful), you probably will have use for a form. After creating the basic form, you can then add elements such as text boxes and buttons. The remainder of this chapter contains information about adding elements to a form.

The start and end `<form>` tags define a form on your Web page. Attributes of the `<form>` tag configure how the form data is handled. The `action` attribute contains the name of the script or program on the Web server that will process

the information submitted by the user in the form. Many Web service providers have scripts on their Web servers that you can use to process the form data. You should contact your Web service provider to determine the best method of processing data collected in forms on your Web pages. The value of the `action` attribute is the file name of the script, including the script's location on the Web server.

Information submitted in a form is transferred to the Web server that hosts the Web page containing the form. You should specify how the information transfers to the Web server using the `method` attribute of the `<form>` tag. There are two possible values for the `method` attribute: `get` and `post`, with `post` being the best method. The form's location on your Web page depends on where you have placed the `<form>` tags in the HTML code.

Create a Form

① Open or create a new Web page.

② Type **<form>**.

③ Type **</form>**.

④ Type **action =""**.

5 Type the name of the script that will process the form data.

6 Type **method =""**.

```
index - Notepad
File  Edit  Format  View  Help
<html>
<head>
        <title>My Auctions</title>
</head>

<body>
Sign up here to be notified of all new auctions.<br />
Enter you email address:<br />

<form action="ProcessData.php" method="">


</form>


</body>
</html>
```

5 **6**

7 Type the method value of the form.

8 Save your Web page.

Note: You have now created a form on a Web page. To add elements to the form, such as buttons and text boxes, please refer to the remainder of this chapter.

```
index - Notepad
File  Edit  Format  View  Help
<html>
<head>
        <title>My Auctions</title>
</head>

<body>
Sign up here to be notified of all new auctions.<br />
Enter you email address:<br />

<form action="ProcessData.php" method="post">


</form>


</body>
</html>
```

7

Extra

Scripts that process form data are available in many different programming languages. Scripts that process form data, although initially appearing complex, are relatively easy to create if you have any programming knowledge. Scripts may be created using easy-to-learn programming languages such as PHP and Perl, or much more complex programming languages such as C++.

If you do not want to create your own scripts, there are many sources of ready-made form processing scripts available on the Internet. To locate forms on the Internet, use your favorite search tool to search for "forms processing scripts."

PHP is one of the easiest programming languages you can use to create form processing scripts. Here is a sample PHP script that displays username and address information submitted in a form.

Example
```
<?php
     echo "The information in the form
is<br />";
     echo "Username: ";
     echo $_POST['username'];
     echo "<br />E-mail address: ";
     echo $_POST['address'];
?>
```

Add a
Text Box

Y ou can use text boxes on a form to allow users to enter a small amount of text. Text boxes are typically used for information such as names, e-mail addresses, and brief comments. A user can type directly into a text box, paste information into a text box, or edit any existing information in the text box. You might want to use text boxes to allow users to identify themselves to you or give you demographic information that you can use however you wish.

The `<input>` tag inserts a text box into a form. The `<input>` tag must be placed between the start and end `<form>` tags. The `type` attribute of the `<input>` tag must have a value of `text` to indicate that a text box will appear on the Web page.

Information typed into a text box on a form must be identified to the script that processes the form data. The

`name` attribute of the `<input>` tag is the name of the information contained in the text box. The script processing the form data needs to know the name you specify for the text box before determining how to handle the data in the text box.

A form needs a Submit button in order to send the information in the text box to the Web server. A Submit button is added to a form by using an `<input>` tag, with the value of `submit` for the `type` attribute. As with the `<input>` tag used to generate a text box, the `<input>` tag used to generate the Submit button must be placed within the `<form>` start and end tags. The Submit button is usually the last element in a form so that users are not tempted to submit their information before filling out all relevant fields.

Add a Text Box

① Open or create a new Web page.

② Type **<input />**.

③ Type **type=""**.

④ Type **text**.

⑤ Type **name=""**.

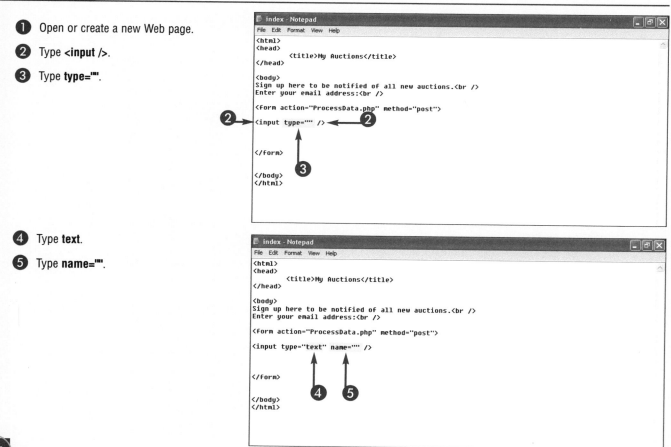

⑥ Type the form data name.

⑦ Type **<input type="submit" />**.

⑧ Save the Web page.

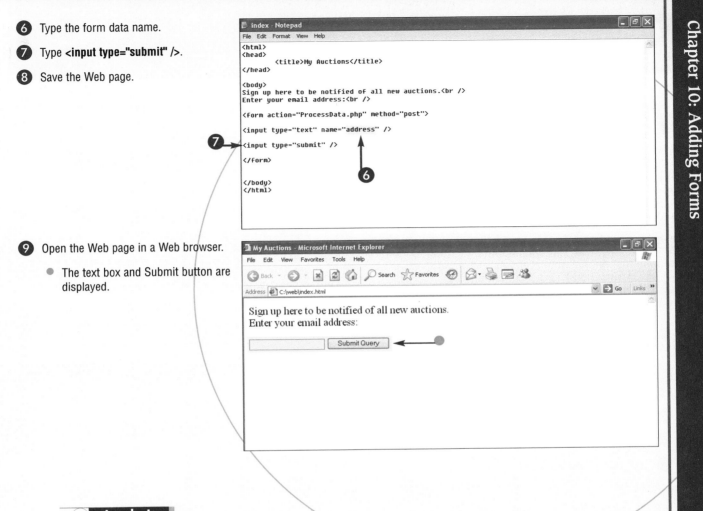

⑨ Open the Web page in a Web browser.

● The text box and Submit button are displayed.

Notepad window:
```
index - Notepad
File  Edit  Format  View  Help

<html>
<head>
        <title>My Auctions</title>
</head>

<body>
Sign up here to be notified of all new auctions.<br />
Enter your email address:<br />

<form action="ProcessData.php" method="post">

<input type="text" name="address" />

<input type="submit" />

</form>


</body>
</html>
```

Browser window:

My Auctions - Microsoft Internet Explorer

Address C:\web\index.html

Sign up here to be notified of all new auctions.
Enter your email address:

[   ] Submit Query

Apply It

You can change the size of the text box as it appears on the Web page by using the `size` attribute of the starting `<input>` tag. The value of the size and attribute is the number of characters that can fit into the text box.

Example
```
<input type="text"
name="email_address"
size=20>

<input type="text"
name="phone" size=12>
```

You can restrict the amount of characters that a user can type in a text box, and therefore the amount of information submitted, by specifying a number for the `maxlength` attribute of the starting `<input>` tag.

Example
```
<input type="text"
name="email_address"
maxlength=20>

<input type="text"
name="phone" maxlength=12
size=13>
```

You can populate text boxes with default values by using the `value` attribute. The value of the `value` attribute is the text that will appear in the text box when the form is initially displayed on the Web page.

Example
```
<form action="GetInfo.php"
method="post">

<input type="text"
name="email" value="Type
email address here" />

<br />

<input type="text"
name="phone" value="(000)
000-0000 " />

</form>
```

Insert a Text Area

Whereas a text box is useful for entering small amounts of text like e-mail addresses, a text area allows for much larger quantities of text. You might use a text area in combination with text boxes to allow users to submit notes or comments to you.

A text area is generated using a start and end `<textarea>` tag. As with most other form elements, the `name` attribute identifies the information in the element to the script that will process the data in the form.

The size of the text area can be specified in terms of characters. The `rows` attribute specifies the height of the text area in character rows. For example, a value of `10` for the `rows` attribute creates a text area that can contain ten lines of text. The `cols` attribute specifies the number of columns of text that can appear in the text area. For

example, a `cols` attribute value of `30` limits the number of characters per line of text to 30. Any typed characters exceeding 30 will appear on a new line.

Each user's Web browser settings, as well as the dimensions of the screen, determine the actual physical height of the text area as it appears on a Web page. So although you can specify the size of the text area in rows and columns, the size specification is more of a guideline as opposed to an absolute guarantee. A user cannot resize the text area on a Web page, so make sure that you have allocated adequate space in the text area for the information you have requested. Most Web browsers automatically insert a scroll bar on the right-hand side of the text area if a user types more text than can fit in the area you originally specified.

Insert a Text Area

1. Open or create a new Web page that contains a form.

2. Type **<textarea>**.

3. Type **</textarea>**.

4. Type **cols="" rows=""**.

5. Type the number of columns in the text area.

6. Type the number of rows in the text area.

7. Type **name=""**.

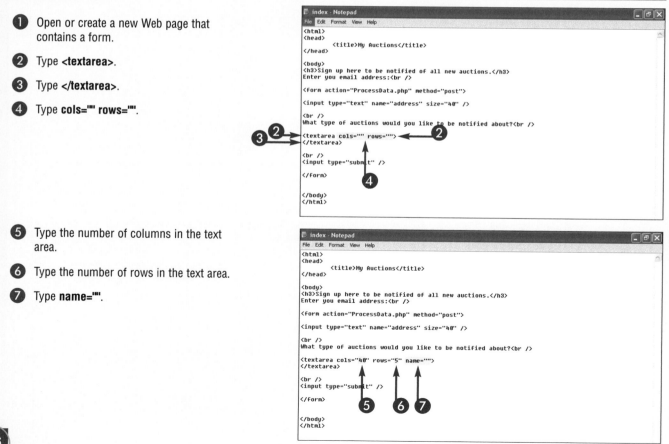

8 Type the text area name.

9 Save the Web page.

```
index - Notepad
File  Edit  Format  View  Help
<html>
<head>
        <title>My Auctions</title>
</head>

<body>
<h3>Sign up here to be notified of all new auctions.</h3>
Enter you email address:<br />

<form action="ProcessData.php" method="post">

<input type="text" name="address" size="40" />

<br />
What type of auctions would you like to be notified about?<br />

<textarea cols="40" rows="5" name="question">
</textarea>

<br />
<input type="submit" />

</form>


</body>
</html>
```

8

10 Open the Web page in a Web browser.

● The text area appears.

```
My Auctions - Microsoft Internet Explorer
File  Edit  View  Favorites  Tools  Help
Back          Search   Favorites
Address  C:\web\index.html                          Go   Links

Sign up here to be notified of all new auctions.

Enter you email address:

What type of auctions would you like to be notified about?

Submit Query
```

Apply It

The only line breaks in form text submitted to a form processing script occur when a user presses Enter within the text area. You can force each line in the text area to break by using the `wrap` attribute with a value of `physical`.

Example
```
<textarea cols="40" rows="16"
name="question" wrap="physical">
```

You can insert default text into the text area that initially appears on the Web page. Default text usually consists of instructions or directions on what type of information to place within the text area. If the user does not edit or replace the default text in this area, that text will be sent to the script processing the form data when the user clicks the Submit button.

Example
```
<textarea cols="40" rows="16"
name="question">

Enter your questions about our online
auctions here.

</textarea>
```

Build a
Drop-Down Box

Yet ou can add a drop-down box to your form to make it easier for a user to select from a range of options. Drop-down boxes give you more control over the information that a user can enter on a form. A drop-down box looks like a simple text box but with a small down-arrow icon on one side of it. When the user clicks the icon, a list of options appears. The user selects an option by clicking on the desired choice.

A drop-down box consists of two tags: the `<select>` tag and the `<option>` tag. The `<select>` tag sets up the element, and the `<option>` tag denotes the individual selections. The `<select>` tag assigns an identity to the data using the `name` attribute. All `<option>` tags are placed between the start and end `<select>` tags.

Each item that you want to appear in the drop-down menu must be enclosed by the start and end `<option>` tags. The `<option>` tag uses the `value` attribute to pass information to the script that processes the form data. Remember that the information passed to the form processing script is the value of the `value` attribute and not the information contained between the start and end `<option>` tags. The information contained between the start and end `<option>` tags primarily describe the selection to the user. The value of the `value` attribute is often some type of abbreviation of the data used to describe the selection. For example, a value of `air` may be described as "Next day shipping by air." There is no limit to `<option>` tags that you can place in a `<select>` form element, but if you have too many options, the user may have difficulty selecting the choice they want.

Build a Drop-Down Box

① Open or create a new Web page that contains a form.

② Type **<select>**.

③ Type **name=""**.

④ Type **</select>**.

⑤ Type the name of the select data.

⑥ Type **<option value="">**.

⑦ Type the value of the option.

⑧ Type **</option>**.

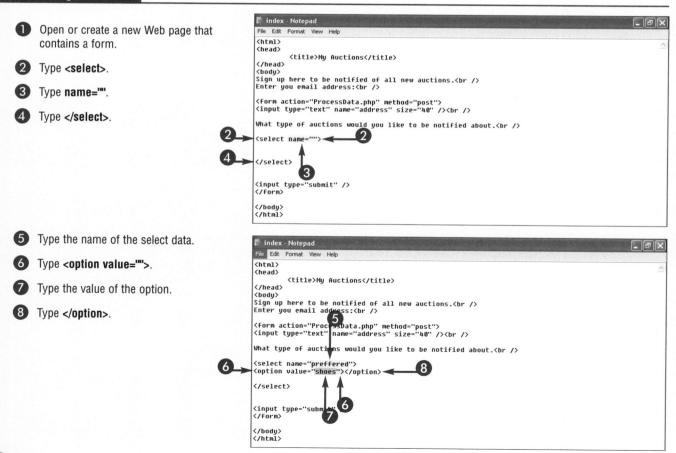

9 Type the description of the option.

10 Repeat steps **6** to **8** for each option.

11 Save the Web page.

```
index - Notepad
File  Edit  Format  View  Help
<html>
<head>
        <title>My Auctions</title>
</head>
<body>
Sign up here to be notified of all new auctions.<br />
Enter you email address:<br />

<form action="ProcessData.php" method="post">
<input type="text" name="address" size="40" /><br />

What type of auctions would you like to be notified about.<br />

<select name="preffered">
<option value="shoes">Boots and Shoes</option>
<option value="headwear">Hats and scarves</option>
<option value="toys">Dolls and teddy bears</option>
</select>


<input type="submit" />
</form>

</body>
</html>
```

12 Open the Web page in a Web browser.

13 Click the down arrow.

● The options appear in a drop-down list.

```
My Auctions - Microsoft Internet Explorer
File  Edit  View  Favorites  Tools  Help
Back           Search  Favorites
Address  C:\web\index.html                              Go   Links

Sign up here to be notified of all new auctions.
Enter you email address:

What type of auctions would you like to be notified about.
Boots and Shoes          Submit Query
Boots and Shoes
Hats and scarves
Dolls and teddy bears
```

Apply It

The first item in the option list will be the default item that appears in the text area of the drop-down box. To display a different selection as the default, add the selected attribute to the <option> tag.

Example
```
<select name="choice">
     <option value="yes"
>Yes</option>
     <option value="no"
selected>No</option>
</select>
```

By default, a drop-down menu displays only one item unless the user clicks the down-arrow icon. You can increase the number of items displayed by specifying a value for the size attribute of the <select> tag. After increasing the number of items displayed, a scroll bar replaces the drop-down arrow icon, enabling the user to scroll through the other selections.

Adding the multiple attribute to the <select> tag enables a user to choose more than one item from a drop-down list by holding down the control key while clicking on each desired item. If you allow multiple selections to be made in your drop-down lists, you should inform users that they have the option to do so.

Example
```
<select name="choice"
multiple>
```

169

Hide Data in a Form

Sometimes you may want to create a form that contains hidden data. Hidden data is typically data that you do not want users or administrators to have access to, and can be information that is embedded directly into the Web page or information like a password that you requested a user to type into the form.

Hidden data can be placed directly into a form using the `<input>` tag with a value of `hidden` for the `type` attribute. The `name` attribute of the `<input>` tag identifies the element to the form processing script, and the `value` attribute contains the data sent to the form processing script. For example, you may have hidden data called `author` that stores the name and e-mail address of the person that created the form. Although this is not data that you would want the user to enter, it may be very helpful to

the person creating or troubleshooting the form processing script.

In order to hide data that a user types, the `<input>` tag is used with the value `password` assigned to the `type` attribute. This type of `<input>` tag generates a text box in which each character that a user types is replaced by a symbol, typically a small circle. Regardless of the character used to represent the text that the user types, the information submitted to the form processing script is the text that the user types on the keyboard. Except for the fact that the characters are replaced on-screen as the user types them, the `password` element functions the same way as the text box form element. As with the text box form element, you can constrain the information that is entered into a password text box by specifying numerical values with the `size` and `maxlength` attributes.

Hide Data in a Form

① Open or create a new Web page that contains a form.

② Type **`<input type="hidden" />`**.

③ Type **`name=""`**.

```
index - Notepad
File  Edit  Format  View  Help
<html>
<head>
        <title>My Auctions</title>
</head>
<body>
Sign up here to be notified of all new auctions.<br />
Enter you email address:<br />

<form action="ProcessData.php" method="post">

<input type="hidden" name="" />

<input type="text" name="address" size="40" /><br />

Enter your Password.<br />


<input type="submit" />
</form>

</body>
</html>
```

④ Type the name of the hidden field.

⑤ Type **`value=""`**.

⑥ Type **`<input />`**.

⑦ Type **`type="" name=""`**.

```
index - Notepad
File  Edit  Format  View  Help
<html>
<head>
        <title>My Auctions</title>
</head>
<body>
Sign up here to be notified of all new auctions.<br />
Enter you email address:<br />

<form action="ProcessData.php" method="post">

<input type="hidden" name="member" value="" />

<input type="text" name="address" size="40" /><br />

Enter your Password.<br />
<input type="" name="" />

<input type="submit" />
</form>

</body>
</html>
```

8 Type the value of the hidden field.

9 Type **password**.

10 Type the name of the password field.

11 Save the Web page.

```
index - Notepad
File Edit Format View Help
<html>
<head>
        <title>My Auctions</title>
</head>
<body>
Sign up here to be notified of all new auctions.<br />
Enter you email address:<br />

<form action="ProcessData.php" method="post">

<input type="hidden" name="member" value="yes" />

<input type="text" name="address" size="40" /><br />

Enter your Password.<br />
<input type="password" name="pass" />

<input type="submit" />
</form>

</body>
</html>
```

12 Open the Web page in a Web browser.

● The hidden field data is not displayed, and the characters typed in the password box are hidden.

```
My Auctions - Microsoft Internet Explorer
File  Edit  View  Favorites  Tools  Help
Back        Search  Favorites
Address  C:\web\index.html                          Go   Links

Sign up here to be notified of all new auctions.
Enter you email address:

[                              ]

Enter your Password.
[••••••]            [Submit Query]
```

In most straightforward forms, there is very little need to embed hidden data fields directly into the HTML code using the <input> tag. Hidden data becomes useful when you are creating your own forms processing script, and you use a single script to process data from multiple forms. The hidden data can then contain information about the form, ensuring that the data is processed correctly.

The symbol that replaces the character data when the user enters a password is determined by the Web browser and operating system. You cannot specify which character will be used. In Internet Explorer each character will be replaced by a small circle, but in other browsers it may also be replaced by an asterisk or other similar character.

Although the password form element may appear to provide some degree of security, it is only to prevent others from viewing information that appears on-screen; the information is transferred to the Web server as plain text with no encryption applied. If you want to secure the data, you must use a security method other than the password form element.

Include Check Boxes and Radio Buttons

By adding check boxes and radio buttons, you can enable your users to quickly select items on a form. Check boxes allow users to select one or more items in a form. For example, a user may select multiple newsletters they would like to receive or delete by simply clicking on the check box next to the name of each newsletter. A check mark appears next to each selected item, enabling users to quickly verify which items they have clicked. The `<input>` tag generates a check box when the `checkbox` value is used with the `type` attribute.

A radio button is similar to a check box, except that only one item may be selected at a time. A radio button is created by specifying a value of `radio` for the `type` attribute of the `<input>` tag. As with the `checkbox` form element, you can display a radio button as already selected by adding the `checked` attribute to the `<input>` tag. When

using HTML, you can simply add the `checked` attribute; but to ensure that your Web page is compliant with XHTML, you must assign the value `checked` to the `checked` attribute. The `<input>` tag used to create both check boxes and radio buttons must also use the `value` attribute. The `value` attribute will contain the data submitted to the script processing the form data when the radio button or check box is selected. The `name` attribute identifies the form data to the form's processing script. Each check box may have a different `name` value, but the `name` values of the radio buttons must be the same.

Note that the Web browser only submits information from selected check boxes or radio buttons to the script processing the form data. If a radio button or check box is not selected, the form processing script has no way of knowing that the check box or radio button even existed.

Include Check Boxes and Radio Buttons

① Open or create a new Web page that contains a form.

② Type **<input type="checkbox" name=""
value="" />**.

③ Type the text you want to appear next to the check box.

④ Type the name of the check box.

⑤ Type the value of the check box.

⑥ Repeat steps **2** to **5** for each additional check box.

⑦ Type **<input type="radio" name=""
value="" />**.

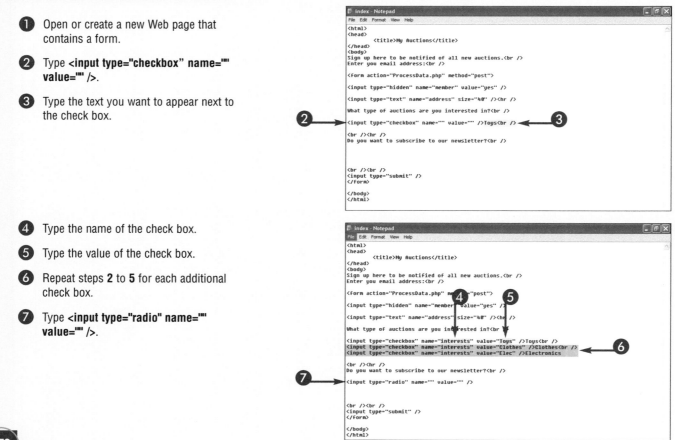

8 Type the name of the check box.

9 Type the value of the check box.

10 Repeat steps **2** to **5** for each additional check box.

11 Save the Web page.

```
index - Notepad
File Edit Format View Help
<html>
<head>
        <title>My Auctions</title>
</head>
<body>
Sign up here to be notified of all new auctions.<br />
Enter you email address:<br />

<form action="ProcessData.php" method="post">

<input type="hidden" name="member" value="yes" />

<input type="text" name="address" size="40" /><hr />

What type of auctions are you interested in?<br />

<input type="checkbox" name="interests" value="Toys" />Toys<br />
<input type="checkbox" name="interests" value="Clothes" />Clothes<br />
<input type="checkbox" name="interests" value="Elec" />Electronics

<br /><hr />
Do you want to subscribe to our newsletter?<br />

<input type="radio" name="news" value="yes" />
<input type="radio" name="news" value="no" />

<br /><br />
<input type="submit" />
</form>

</body>
</html>
```

12 Open the Web page in a Web browser.

● The check boxes and radio buttons are displayed and can be selected.

```
My Auctions - Microsoft Internet Explorer
File Edit View Favorites Tools Help
Address C:\web\index.html

Sign up here to be notified of all new auctions.
Enter you email address:

What type of auctions are you interested in?
☑Toys
☑Clothes
☐Electronics
Do you want to subscribe to our newsletter?
◉ ○

Submit Query
```

Apply It

You can define certain check boxes to be selected by default. This is most useful when you can safely assume that users will typically select one or more of the items next to a check box; you are in fact then saving them the time it would take them to manually check the box. To display a check box as already checked, add the `checked` attribute to the `<input>` tag and assign to it a value of `checked`.

Example
```
<input type="checkbox" name="jaz" value="on" checked="checked" /> Jazz<br />
<input type="checkbox" name="blu" value="on" /> Blues<br />

<input type="checkbox" name="pop" value="on" /> Pop<br />

<input type="checkbox" name="cla" value="on" checked="checked" />Classical<br />
```

Configure Submit and Reset Buttons

You can change the appearance of Submit buttons to better reflect the purpose of your forms. You can also add a Reset button that allows users to quickly clear any information they have entered on a form and start over again.

You can change the text that appears on the Submit button to text that is more descriptive if you wish. For example, if you have a form that sends a question, you can change the text on the Submit button to read "Send the Question," as opposed to the default text "Submit." Changing the text on the Submit button gives the user a better indication of how your forms and Web pages work. You should try to keep the text on a Submit button short and to the point. Regardless of the amount of text you place on a Submit button, the

Web browser automatically adjusts the size of the button to display the text; if you do not keep the text short and to the point you are likely to wind up with a very bulky looking button. The Submit button text is assigned using the value attribute of the `<input>` tag used to create the button.

Clicking the Reset button causes all data in a form to be deleted. This can be a useful security precaution for users who may be typing sensitive data on a form and need to clear it quickly. Typically, a Reset button clears incorrect data from a form before the entry of the correct information. When a Reset button is clicked, the user cannot display the information that has been cleared from the form; that data must be retyped into the form. As with the Submit button, you can easily assign text to a Reset button using the value attribute of the `<input>` tag.

Configure Submit and Reset Buttons

① Open or create a new Web page that contains a form.

② Type **<input type="submit" />**.

③ Type **value=""**.

④ Type **<input type="reset" />**.

⑤ Type the text you want to appear on the Submit button.

⑥ Save the Web page.

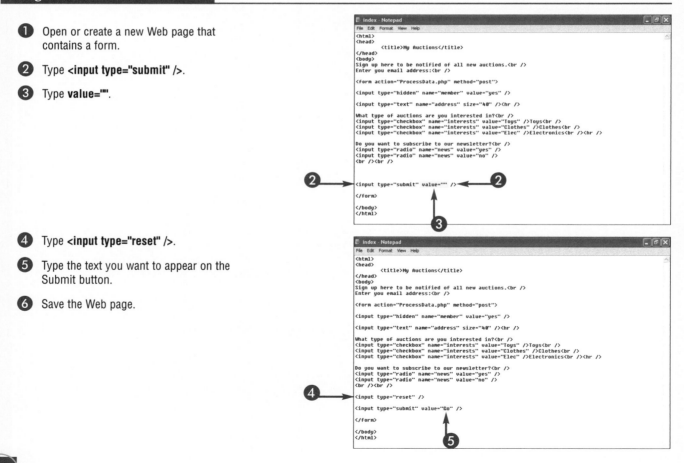

⑦ Open the Web page in a Web browser.

⑧ Enter data into the form to test.

⑨ Click the Reset button.

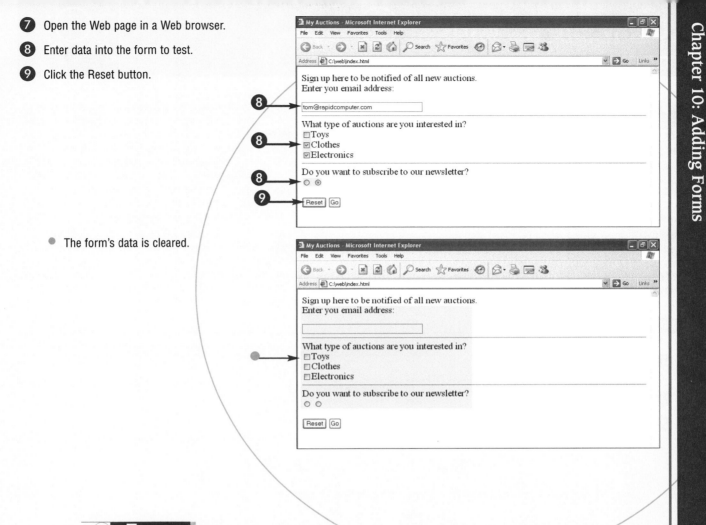

● The form's data is cleared.

Allow File Uploads to Your Site

You can allow users to upload files to your Web site. This is a great way of exchanging information other than plain text (which can simply be typed into a text form) such as spreadsheets, complex word processing files, and images. Some Web sites are exclusively devoted to file sharing; for example, many universities allow their students a certain amount of space to host files for a portfolio. Other sites rely on file uploading; for example, monster.com allows users to upload their resume documents instead of requiring them to enter the text of their resumes from scratch.

The `<input>` tag, with the value `file` assigned to the `type` attribute, facilitates the upload of files. The `name` value identifies the file to the Web server and to the script that will process the file.

The form element will appear as a text box with a Browse button beside it. Users can type the name of the file directly into the text box or click the Browse button to navigate to the file on their computer. The dialog box that appears enabling the user to browse their system depends on each computer's operating system. After the user selects the file from the dialog box, the name of the file appears in the text area of the element. At that point, the user can click a button that will upload the file from their system to the Web server.

Before you allow users to upload files to your Web server, make sure you have the proper permissions and authorization to accept the files. You must also have a forms processing script that can manage the transfer of files. For all of these needs you must consult with your Web service provider. Most Web service providers do facilitate the upload of files.

Allow File Uploads to Your Site

① Open or create a new Web page that contains a form.

② Type **<input type="file" />**.

③ Type **name=""**.

④ Type the name that will identify the file to the Web server.

⑤ Save the Web page.

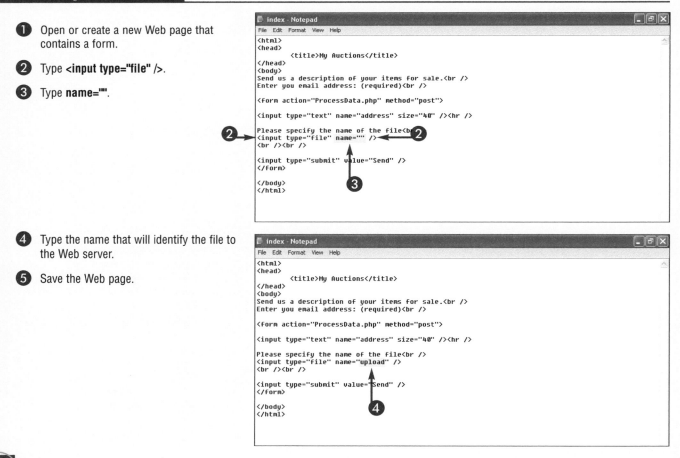

6 Open the Web page in a Web browser.

7 Click the Browse button.

The Choose file dialog box appears.

8 Select the file to upload and click Open.

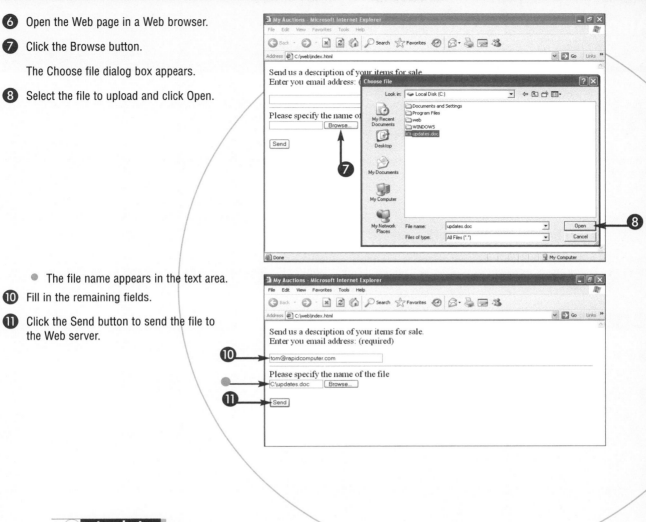

● The file name appears in the text area.

10 Fill in the remaining fields.

11 Click the Send button to send the file to the Web server.

Arrange Tab Order

When users display a Web page that contains a form, they can select each element in the form by clicking it and then entering the data. If a form has many fields, users may move to the next element in the form by pressing the Tab key. You can specify the sequence in which the form elements are selected by using the `tabindex` attribute of the tag used to create the form element.

When the Tab key is first pressed, the first element in the form will be selected. Each subsequent press of the Tab key selects the next element on the form. The tab sequence repeats itself after all form elements have been selected. For example, if the last element on a form is selected, pressing the Tab key selects the element indicated by the lowest `tabindex` attribute.

Most tabbing sequences start at the first element and proceed to the last element; but for some cases, such as forms that do not need to be filled out completely, you may want to change the tab sequence to include only required fields. This may be useful for forms that require extensive data entry.

The value of the `tabindex` attribute will be a number that specifies where in the tab sequence the element will fall. Lower numbers have highest priority, so elements with a `tabindex` value of 5 are selected before elements with a `tabindex` value of 10. All numbers assigned to the `tabindex` attribute must be positive whole numbers. If two elements contain the same `tabindex` value, the first element specified is selected first when the Tab key is pressed.

Arrange Tab Order

1. Open or create a new Web page that contains a form.

2. In the form element to be included in the tab index, type **tabindex=""**.

3. Type the number of the element in the tab sequence.

4. Repeat steps **2** to **3** for each form element in the tab index.

5. Save the Web page.

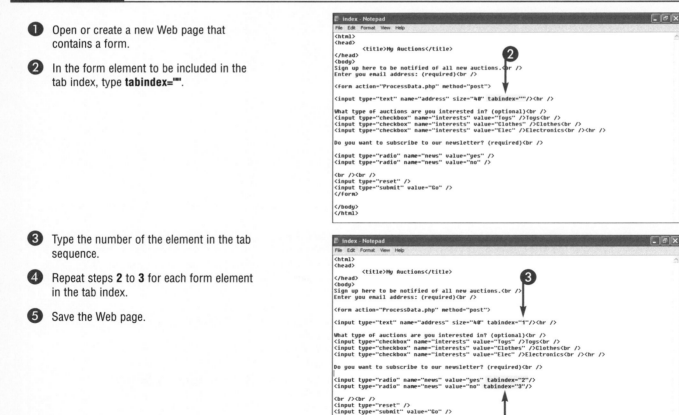

6 Open the Web page in a Web browser.

7 Press the Tab key.

- The first element in the tab index is selected.

8 Press the Tab key.

- The next element in the tab index is selected.

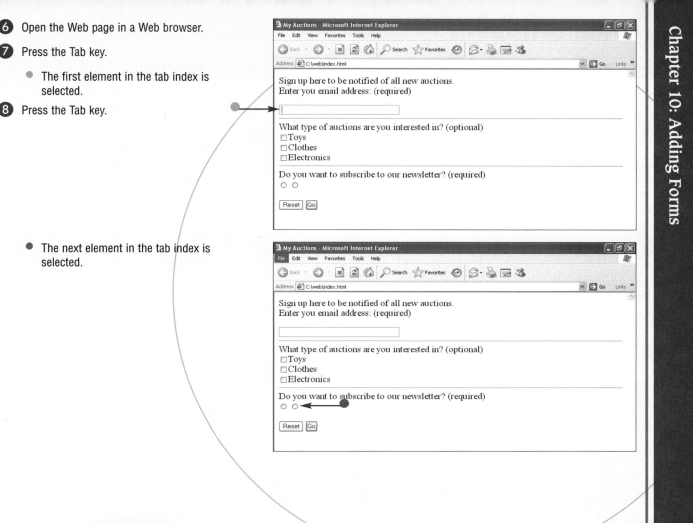

Extra

You should test the usability and efficiency of any changes you make to the tab sequence before going live with your Web site. The sequence should be logical; an incoherent and illogical tab sequence will only frustrate and annoy users, which you do not want to do if you want users to visit your site again in the future.

After all the form elements that contain the `tabindex` attribute have been selected in sequence via the Tab key, the elements are then selected from top to bottom, starting with the first element that does not contain the `tabindex` attribute. For this reason, if you are using the `tabindex` attribute, it is probably best to use it on all elements in the form.

The value assigned to the `tabindex` attribute indicates the priority of the element in the tab sequence. You should leave reasonable gaps between the numbers used for the `tabindex` attribute. This ensures that if you later want to rearrange or insert additional form elements that use the `tabindex` attribute, you will not have to renumber all other elements in the form.

Disable and Lock Form Elements

Y ou can lock elements by marking them as read-only or disabled. Users cannot change read-only elements. Incorporating read-only elements can be useful if a user has already completed part of a form on another page; for example, you can display the previously submitted data as read-only to remind users of what they have already submitted.

Disabled elements appear grayed out on a Web page. Disabled elements can contain default information that you want the user to see but not be able to change; for example, you might disable an option for a user to indicate that they are pregnant if they had previously indicated that they are male.

Although read-only elements may look like normal elements, nothing happens when the user selects the element to enter data. Any characters the user types do not appear, and any check box or radio button the user selects does not change

state. The data in a read-only element is still sent when the form's Submit button is clicked. A form element can be rendered read-only by including the `readonly` attribute in the start tag of the element. A read-only form element is similar to a hidden element, with the exception that a user can view a read-only element on the Web page.

A disabled element is an element that will appear unusable on the Web page. In most cases, a disabled element appears grayed out in the Web browser, indicating to the user that they may not select that element. Usually the values and information of a disabled element are not submitted to the script processing the form data.

You can use the `disabled`, and `readonly` attributes with any valid form element. The appearance of the `disabled` and `readonly` elements depends on the Web browser displaying the Web page.

Disable and Lock Form Elements

① Open or create a new Web page that contains a form.

② In a text element, type **value=""**.

③ Type a text value for the element.

④ Type **readonly**.

180

5 In the form element to be disabled, type **disabled**.

6 Save the Web page.

```
index - Notepad
File  Edit  Format  View  Help
<html>
<head>
        <title>My Auctions</title>
</head>
<body>
<h2>Auctions Administration Page:</h2>
<h3>Step 2: login</h3>
<Form action="ProcessData.php" method="post">

Enter your email address.<br />
<input type="text" name="address" value="admin@rapidcomputer.com" readonly />

<br /><br />
Enter your password.<br />
<input type="password" name="pass" />

<h3>Are you a user or an administrator?</h3>
<input type="radio" name="login" value="user" disabled />User
<input type="radio" name="login" value="user" checked disabled />Administrator

<hr />
<input type="submit" />
</Form>

</body>
</html>
```

7 Open the Web page in a Web browser.

● The read-only elements cannot be altered.

● The disabled elements are grayed out.

```
My Auctions - Microsoft Internet Explorer
File  Edit  View  Favorites  Tools  Help
 Back      X          Search    Favorites
Address   C:\web\index.html                           Go   Links

Auctions Administration Page:

Step 2: login

Enter your email address.
admin@rapidcomputer.com

Enter your password.

Are you a user or an administrator?

 User  ● Administrator

Submit Query
```

Apply It

To use valid XHTML code, the `readonly` and `disabled` attributes need the values `readonly` and `disabled` assigned to them, respectively.

Example
```
<input type="text" name="music"
readonly="readonly" />


<input type="checkbox"
name="classical" disabled="disabled"
/>


<textarea cols="9" rows="9"
disabled="disabled"
readonly="readonly">

</textarea>
```

The `readonly` and `disabled` attributes are quite useful when creating complex forms. If you have multiple forms spread across multiple Web pages, you can use the `readonly` or `disabled` attributes to display form items that have already been completed. For example, if a user has already entered a comment in a text area on a previous form, you could display the comment as disabled on the current Web page, providing the user with a visual clue that he or she has already entered the information.

Group Related Form Elements

You can group elements on a form so that related elements appear together on the Web page, making it easier for users to enter information in your forms. Grouping elements makes your page more logical to the user who is using your site. Tax sites such as turbotax.com, for example, group elements to make the process of doing your taxes more intuitive.

Form data can usually be divided into related items. For example, personal information such as a user's name, e-mail address, and home phone number may appear in one area of the form; and another section may contain more specific data such as what information the user would like to request, any user preferences, and how the user is to be contacted. Grouping similar elements together on a form makes those elements easier to identify on the Web page. The `<fieldset>` tag groups related form elements together;

all form elements that are related must be placed between the start and end `<fieldset>` tags.

Elements placed inside the `<fieldset>` tags are often contained within a border on the Web page. Each Web browser determines the size and type of border, but it is usually a thin border and very faint in color. You can add some interesting effects to the border that the `<fieldset>` tag generates by using local style sheets and some border altering rules.

You can attach a label to a group of related form items by using the `<legend>` tag. The `<legend>` tag specifies a description of the related items, which should be very short and to the point. The `<legend>` tag is enclosed within the start and end `<fieldset>` tags. A Web browser will normally draw a border around the related items, placing the text indicated by the `<legend>` tag on top of the border at the top-left corner of the box.

Group Related Form Elements

① Open or create a new Web page that contains a form.

② Type **<fieldset>**.

③ Type **</fieldset>**.

④ Type **<legend>**.

⑤ Type **</legend>**.

⑥ Type the description of the grouped information.

⑦ Save the Web page.

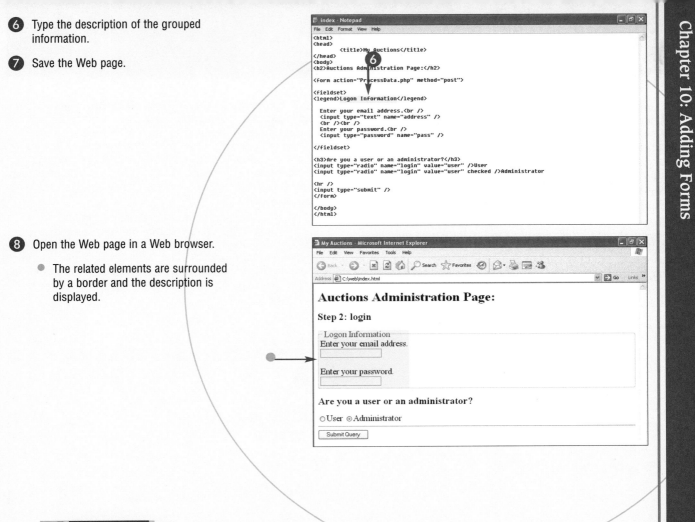

⑧ Open the Web page in a Web browser.

● The related elements are surrounded by a border and the description is displayed.

Some Web browsers still do not support the use of the `<fieldset>` and `<legend>` tags for grouping together related form elements. If a browser does not support the `<fieldset>` and `<legend>` tags, they will just be ignored so you can safely use these tags in any Web page; if the user's browser does not support them, they simply will not be visible.

Although the `<fieldset>` tag supports attributes that change the characteristics of the box drawn around related form items, you can use the `style` attribute to apply local style sheet rules to the area enclosed in the box generated by the `<fieldset>` tag. For example, to change the background of the related items to red, use

Example
```
<fieldset style="background-
color: red;">
```

By default, the text specified using the `<legend>` tag is placed at the top-left side of the box drawn by the `<fieldset>` tag. If you prefer to place the text at the top-right side of the box, you can do so using the `align` attribute with the value `right`.

Example
```
<legend
align="right">Personal
Information</legend>
```

Send Form Data Using E-mail

Instead of using a script to process form data, you can have the data that a user enters in a form submitted to you via e-mail. This can be useful if you want immediate notification of feedback to your site or its contents. For example, if your site is a public face for a business you are running, you may want to be able to field customer complaints or concerns in a timely manner by having an e-mail sent to a personal account that you check often.

The `action` attribute of the `<form>` tag indicates the program or script that will process the form data submitted by the user. You can change the value of the `action` attribute to send the data to an e-mail address instead of to a script or program. The value of the `action` attribute is `mailto:` followed by the e-mail address to where the data will be sent.

When a user clicks on the Submit button, his or her e-mail program opens and sends the form data. Most users will receive multiple warnings from their Web browser and operating system before the information is sent. The data is sent in the form of a plain text e-mail message. You can make sure this is the case by adding the `enctype` attribute with a value of `text/plain` to your `<form>` tag so that you receive only plain text.

Users who submit data to an e-mail address must have a properly configured e-mail program on their computer. It is safe to assume that most users will have an e-mail program capable of submitting data via a form; but as a precaution, you should provide a warning next to the Submit button on your Web page that clicking the button will require the use of an e-mail program.

Send Form Data Using E-mail

① Open or create a new Web page that contains a form.

② In the action value, type **mailto:**.

③ Type the e-mail address where the form data will be sent.

④ Save the Web page.

⑤ Open the Web page in a Web browser.

⑥ Enter some form data.

⑦ Click the Submit button.

● A dialog box appears, informing you that the data will be sent using e-mail.

8 Click OK.

● The e-mail program displays a confirmation message.

9 Click Send.

The form data is sent via e-mail.

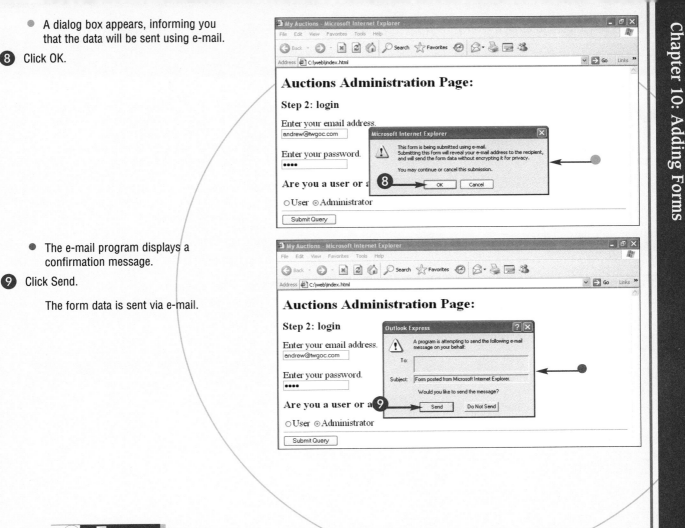

The `mailto:` action of the `<form>` tag is very useful if you have no other Web server or forms processing system available. However, the multiple warnings provided by most Web browsers before submitting e-mail can be somewhat inconvenient for users. Also, given the prevailing abundance of spam and viruses, users may be reluctant to open their e-mail programs as required to send form data.

If you have the ability to do so on your server, create a dedicated e-mail address that can receive form data instead of using your own e-mail address. This enables you to better manage information submitted via forms, and will prevent your personal e-mail address from being targeted by spammers.

Although using an e-mail address to receive form data may not be feasible on a Web site, it may be ideal for troubleshooting problems with forms and the related form processing script. You can also use e-mail as a quick alternative to using a script as you develop your forms and then replace the e-mail with a script when you have perfected it.

Create a Frame-Based Web Page

You can create a Web page that is comprised of frames. Frames enable you to include information from multiple sources on your Web page. They also allow you to combine static and dynamic content on a single Web page.

Frames are individual Web pages loaded into one page that is specifically designed only to specify where and how the frames are divided up. A page that includes two frames is really three pages. The first is a skeleton that specifies how the two frames are divided and the second two are pages loaded into each frame.

The skeleton Web page that defines the frames differs from other Web pages in that the `<body>` tag is replaced with a `<frameset>` tag. The `<frameset>` tag tells the Web browser that the page will consist of frames.

The `<frameset>` tag defines how many frames your Web page will have. The `rows` attribute of the `<frameset>` tag specifies the size of each horizontal frame as a percentage of the height of the Web browser window. For example, if you specify a size of 50% and 50%, a thin border is drawn across the middle of the Web page, creating two frames, one on top and one below. After you define the total number of frames with the `<frameset>` tag, use the `src` attribute value of the `<frame>` tag to specify the Web pages to load into the frames. You will need as many `<frame>` tags as there are frames in the Web page.

You do not need to specify the value for the size of the last frame. If you use an asterisk, the Web browser determines the correct size of the frame automatically. For example, `rows="20%, 80%"` produces frames the same size as if you had used `rows="20%, *"`.

Create a Frame-Based Web Page

① Open or create a Web page.

Note: You must have two other Web pages available to display in both frames.

② Type **<frameset>**.

③ Type **</frameset>**.

```
index - Notepad
File  Edit  Format  View  Help
<html>
      <head>
            <title>Dreamscape Art Studio</title>
      </head>
      <frameset>          ②

      </frameset>          ③
</html>
```

④ Type **rows="20%, 80%"**.

⑤ Type **<frame src="" />**.

```
index - Notepad
File  Edit  Format  View  Help       ④
<html>
      <head>
            <title>Dreamscape Art Studio</title>
      </head>
      <frameset rows="20%, 80%">
            <frame src="" />          ⑤

      </frameset>
</html>
```

6 Type the name of the Web page to place in the frame.

7 Repeat steps **5** to **6** to create the second frame.

8 Save the Web page.

9 Open the Web page in a Web browser.

The frames are displayed.

Apply It

In order to be completely XHTML compliant, the Web page that contains your `<frameset>` tags must have a specific document type declaration in the first line of HTML code. Insert the following code in all of your Web pages that contain `<frameset>` tags.

Example
```
<!DOCTYPE html PUBLIC "-
//W3C//DTD XHTML 1.0
Frameset//EN"
"http://www.w3.org/TR/xhtm
l1/DTD/xhtml1-
frameset.dtd">
```

As long as you have the required number of `<frame>` tags, you can create multiple frames by specifying additional sizes in the `rows` attribute. Each size will be represented by a frame on the page. For example, you can create three frames by specifying three values separated by commas for the frame sizes.

Example
```
<frameset rows="20%, 20%",
60%>
```

The `rows` attribute of the `<frameset>` tag enables you to create frames split horizontally across the Web page. To create frames that are divided vertically, use the `cols` attribute.

Example
```
<frameset cols="20%,
80%">

    <frame
src="title.html"/>

    <frame
src="body.html"/>

  </frameset>
```

Create Rows and Columns of Frames

Y ou can create Web pages that contain both rows and columns, enabling you to divide your pages into complex structures of frames. You should be careful, however, using complex frames pages, because your page can become unreadable on lower resolutions if you are not careful, or at the very least become a mess of scrollbars with only minimal amounts of information being displayed. Make sure to test your frames page at various resolutions, including 640 x 480, to ensure that it is functional on all major resolutions.

The `<frame>` tag specifies frames within the `<frameset>` tag. The `<frame>` tag is an empty element, which means that it does not require a closing `</frame>` tag. In order to make your code XHTML-compliant, you should include a space followed by a / at the end of the `<frame>` tag, as in `<frame src="index.html" />`.

Instead of a `<frame>` tag, you can use another `<frameset>` tag to indicate that you are creating multiple frames instead of a single frame. Within that `<frameset>` tag, use the appropriate number of `<frame>` tags to create the desired amount of frames. The Web page that creates your frames can consist of multiple `<frameset>` tags, but make sure that each `<frameset>` tag has the corresponding start and end tags.

The `rows` attribute determines the height of the frames that divide the Web browser window horizontally. The `cols` attribute creates and specifies the width of frames that divide the Web page vertically, or side by side.

Combining columns and rows of frames is sometimes referred to as *nesting* frames. Because of the complexity involved in creating frames that consist of multiple rows and columns, you should indent your code to make it easier to understand and less prone to errors.

Create Rows and Columns of Frames

① Open or create a Web page.

② Type the `<frameset>` tags that create two rows and the first frame.

③ Type **<frameset cols="">**.

④ Type **</frameset>**.

⑤ Type the sizes of the two frames.

⑥ Type **<frame src="" />**.

7 Type the name of the Web page to place in the frame.

8 Repeat steps **5** to **6** to create the second frame.

9 Save the Web page.

10 Open the Web page in a Web browser.

The frames are displayed.

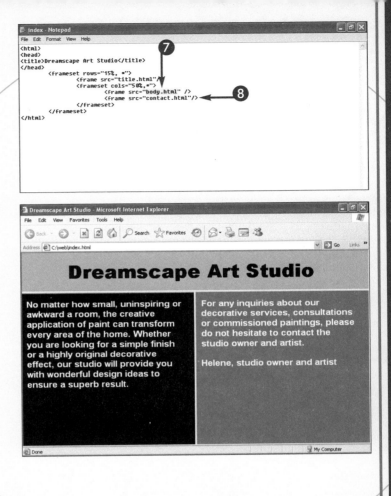

Extra

You can place any number of frames on a Web page, but remember that each frame increases the amount of time that it takes for the Web page to load. Also, frames pages look very different depending on the resolution and window size being used. The more frames that you have on a certain page, the more likely that your page will look bad or be even unusable on a small display setting. Test your frames pages in different resolutions, such as 640 x 480, to ensure that they still work properly in lower resolutions.

To ensure that all of your frames fit in the Web browser window, the combined value of all of the frame sizes must be 100%. Whenever possible, you should use the asterisk as a size specification. This allows the Web browser to determine the proper size of the frame, and insures that the total size of all frames does not exceed 100%.

Example

```
<frameset cols="10%, 20%, *, 20%, 5%">
<frameset rows="*, 12%, 24%">
```

189

Show or Hide Scroll Bars

Y ou can add scroll bars to the frames of your Web page, enabling your users to better navigate the pages that load into your frames. Scrollbars allow you to include more information in a frame than is immediately visible by allowing the user to scroll in the frame to access the rest of the information.

Web browsers automatically display scroll bars on a window or frame when the information does not fit in the frame. The user can scroll the Web page up or down or side to side to see all of the content in the frame. In some cases, you may not want a frame to use scroll bars. For example, you may not care if the bottom part of an image is cropped out of the frame, as long as the important top part of the image is always clearly displayed.

In other cases, you may want a scroll bar to appear if the information in the frame is dynamic (that is, if it changes

periodically). Sometimes it fits within the frame and no scrollbar is required, while at other times, the information is more sizeable and so a scrollbar is automatically added.

The `scrolling` attribute of the `<frame>` tag indicates if a scroll bar will be displayed. The `no` value suppresses scroll bars, and the `yes` value displays scroll bars regardless of whether the frame requires one or not. Although it is the default action, you can also use a value of `auto` for the `scrolling` attribute if you want the Web browser to determine whether or not to use a scroll bar. Many older Web browsers do not support the `scrolling` attribute of the `<frame>` tag. Those Web browsers automatically determine whether a scroll bar is required for pages that include the `scrolling` attribute.

Show or Hide Scroll Bars

① Open or create a Web page.

② Type the code that creates the frames on the Web page.

③ Type **scrolling =""**.

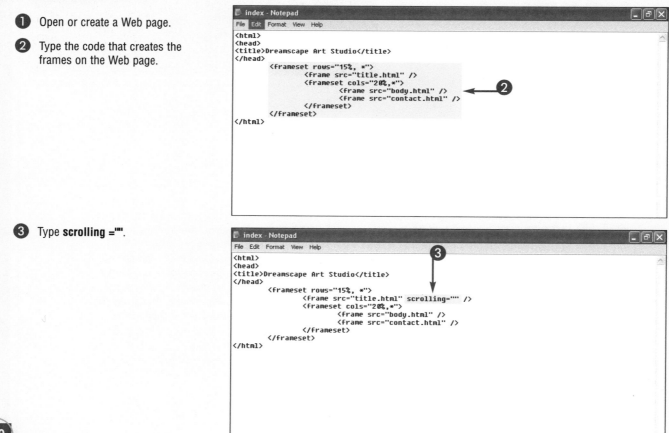

④ Type the value for the scrolling attribute.

⑤ Repeat steps **3** to **4** for each `<frame>` tag.

⑥ Save the Web page.

```
index - Notepad
File  Edit  Format  View  Help
<html>
<head>
<title>Dreamscape Art Studio</title>
</head>
        <frameset rows="15%, *">
                <frame src="title.html" scrolling="Auto" />
                <frameset cols="20%,*">
                        <frame src="body.html" scrolling="No" />
                        <frame src="contact.html" scrolling="Yes" />
                </frameset>
        </frameset>
</html>
```

⑦ Open the Web page in a Web browser.

The frames and the desired scroll bars are displayed.

Dreamscape Art Studio

No matter how small, uninspiring or awkward a room, the creative application of paint can transform every area of the home. Whether you are looking for a simple finish or a highly original decorative effect, our studio will provide you with wonderful design ideas to ensure a superb result.

For any inquiries about our decorative services, consultations or commissioned paintings, please do not hesitate to contact the studio owner and artist.

Helene, studio owner and artist

Extra

Several parameters affect whether the Web browser displays scroll bars. The size of the browser window, the size of the frame, the resolution of the screen, and the amount of information in a frame are all taken into account. You should view your Web pages at different resolutions and at different sizes and ensure that the pages display properly at all times.

The Web browser determines the appearance of the scroll bars, though many Web browsers have settings that allow the user to change the color of these and other browser components. You may even be able to use style sheets to change the color of scroll bars, although doing so is outside the scope of this book.

Scroll bars can be vertical or horizontal. If the content of the Web page is too long to fit into the frame horizontally, a scroll bar appears at the bottom of the frame, allowing the user to move the Web page left or right. Unlike the vertical scroll bar, there is no way to make the display of a horizontal scroll bar mandatory.

Work with Frame Borders

You can control the size, color, and width of the frame borders on your Web page. For example, you may want to set your frame borders to 0 to render them invisible if you want to try and make your page appear as though it does not have frames, or at least to minimize them visually on the page. In other cases, you might want to highlight the borders by making them stylistically appealing. By default, a frame border appears three-dimensional, and uses colors determined by the Web browser or operating system. You can specify a new border color with the `bordercolor` attribute of the `<frameset>` tag. You can use any valid color for a border by including the common color name or a hexadecimal color code.

You can totally suppress the display of borders using the `frameborder` attribute. A value of 0 for the `frameborder` attribute causes the Web page to display frames without borders.

The `framespacing` attribute controls the width of the frame border. Some browsers support the use of the `border` attribute instead of the `framespacing` attribute. Both attributes do the same thing. The value of the `framespacing` attribute is the width in pixels of the border. The spacing allocated using the `framespacing` attribute overrides the `frameborder` attribute setting. So even if the `frameborder` attribute is set to 0, the distance between frames will be the number specified with the `framespacing` attribute.

A value of 0 for the `framespacing` attribute displays frames right next to each other with no gap in between. This is useful if you are displaying different parts of the same image in different frames.

When two adjacent frames have different colored borders, the Web browser determines which color to use for the border between them. In many cases, the border will have no color.

Work with Frame Borders

① Open or create a Web page that contains frames.

② Type **bordercolor=""**.

③ Type the color of the border.

④ Type **framespacing=""**.

⑤ Type **frameborder=""**.

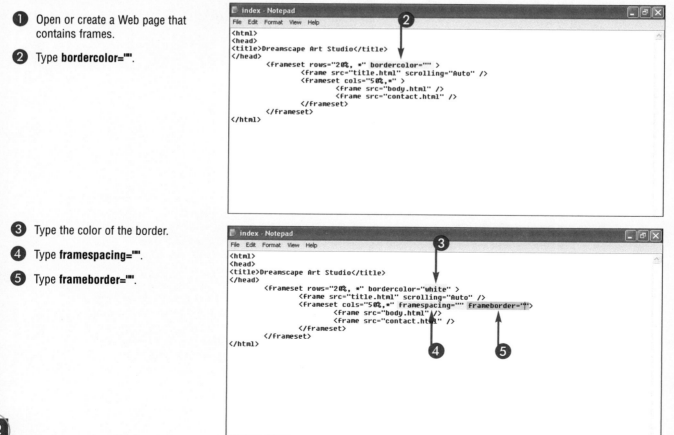

6 Type the spacing between frames.

7 Type the width of the frame border.

8 Save the Web page.

9 Open the Web page in a Web browser.

The frame borders are displayed.

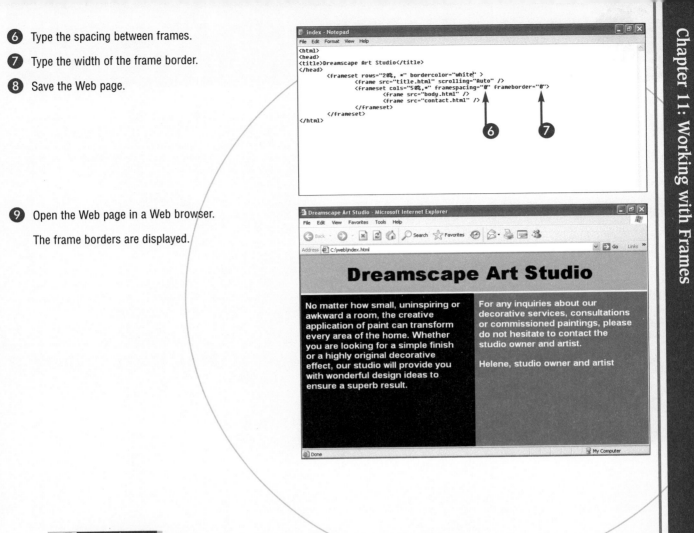

Force the Frame Size

You can specify exactly how far from your frame border you want information to appear, and at the same time prevent users from changing the size of your frames. This will ensure that your Web pages look exactly how you intended when you originally designed them.

In addition to specifying the size of a frame as a percentage of the Web browser window, you can also specify the exact width or height of the frame using either the rows or cols attribute of the <frameset> tag. This gives you greater control over the exact size of the frame, but also results in less flexibility for the browser to resize the frame according to the size of the window or the screen resolution. The size is represented by a number value in pixels.

Regardless of how the size is specified, the user can resize any frame by clicking on and dragging the frame border. This may totally disrupt your intended layout of the Web page. You can prevent users from resizing your frames by including the noresize attribute within the start <frameset> tag.

A margin of blank space usually separates the Web page content displayed within a frame from the border of the frame. Margins are placed on each side and at the top and bottom of the frame. You can control the size of the top and bottom margins with the marginheight attribute, and the size of the side margins with the marginwidth attribute. The size of the margin is specified in pixels. You do not want to specify a margin size that is too large or you will crop out the information on your Web page.

Force the Frame Size

1 Open or create a Web page that contains frames.

2 Type **noresize**.

3 Type **marginwidth=""**.

4 Type **marginheight=""**.

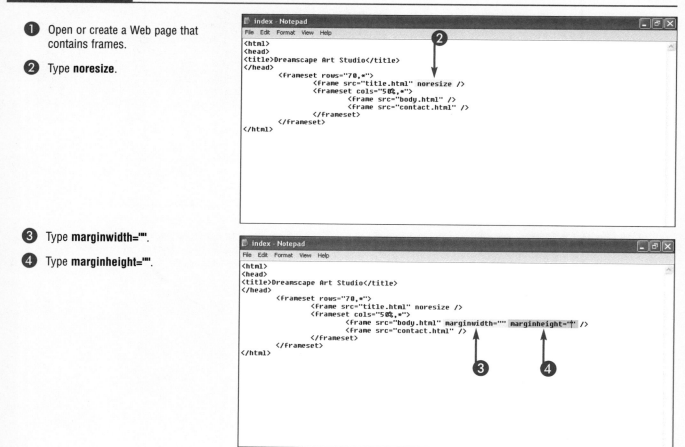

5. Type the value for the margin width.

6. Type the value for the margin height.

7. Save the Web page.

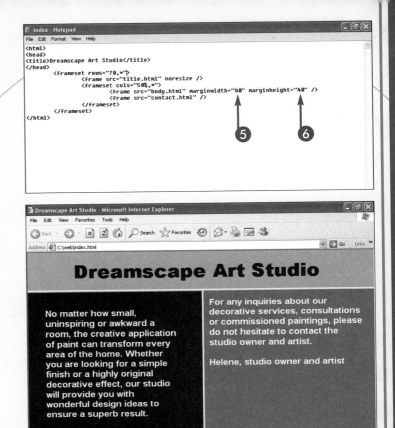

8. Open the Web page in a Web browser.

The immovable frame borders are displayed with the specified margins.

Extra

The noresize attribute is useful for frames that contain information that must remain visible, such as links, images, or advertising. You should use the noresize attribute on frames for which you know the exact amount of space required by its content.

If the margin sizes on your page are too large, the Web browser will most likely ignore the margin specifications and use its own default values to display the content of the frame, possibly causing some information to be cropped off your page.

Specifying a margin size of 0 in combination with proper frame border sizing can make the content of adjacent frames appear continuous. This is extremely useful when placing different parts of the same image side by side.

Example

```
<frameset rows="20%,*"
framespacing="0"
frameborder="0">

    <frame src="body.html"
marginwidth="0"
marginheight="0" />

    <frame src="tip.html"
marginwidth="0"
marginheight="0" />

</frameset>
```

Target Links to a Frame

You can target links to open in a specific frame, which allows a Web page to load in a frame other than the one that contained the page's link. This technique can be useful if you have a left frame that includes contents and a right frame where you want to display that content, which is one of the most typical uses for frames pages.

The first step in targeting links is to create the Web page that defines the frames, and then assign each frame a name. A frame name is assigned using the `name` attribute of the `<frame>` tag. The value chosen for the `name` attribute should be short and descriptive of the purpose of the frame. For example, a frame that contains a menu could be named `menu`.

A link's `<a>` tag uses the `target` attribute to specify the name of the frame into which the Web page will open.

Unless the `target` attribute is used, a Web page will open in the same frame containing the link used to access the page. The linked Web page is assigned to the `src` attribute of the `<a>` tag.

In most multiframe Web sites, one frame contains a Web page that displays the links, and another frame contains the Web pages that are being linked.

In some cases, you may want to load a Web page that completely replaces all of the frames on the current Web page. Setting the `target` value to `_top` in the `<a>` tag of the link opens the specified Web page in the entire browser window.

You should always thoroughly test your Web page links that target individual frames. It is quite easy to target links to the incorrect frames.

Target Links to a Frame

① Open or create a Web page that contains two frames.

② Type **name=""** in one of the `<frame>` tags.

③ Type a name for the frame.

④ Save the Web page.

⑤ Open or create a Web page that contains links.

⑥ Type **target=""**.

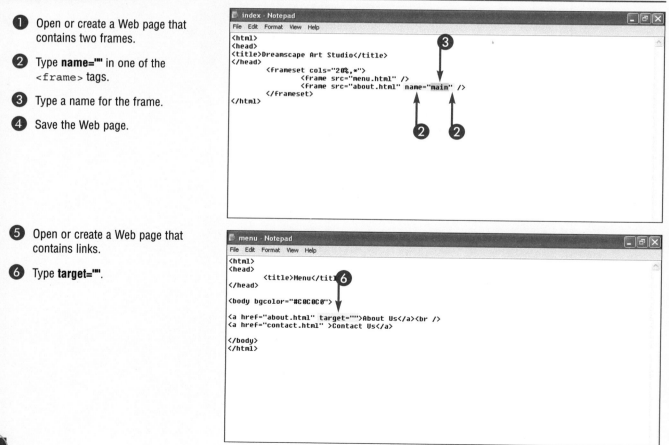

7 Type the name of the frame specified in step **3**.

8 Repeat steps **6** to **7** for each link on the page.

9 Save the Web page.

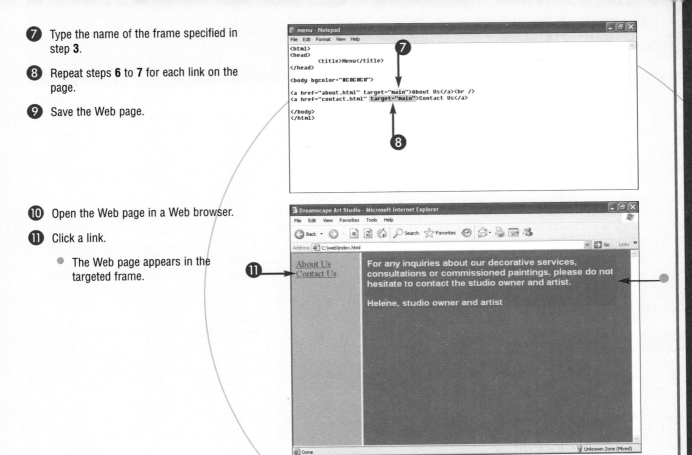

10 Open the Web page in a Web browser.

11 Click a link.

● The Web page appears in the targeted frame.

Apply It

Frames can be handy for creating a navigation bar that allows quick access to different parts of your Web site. You can use images instead of text links to create a sophisticated, efficient, and flexible navigation system for your Web site. For more information about using images as links, see Chapter 5.

Example
```
<a href="about.html" target="main"><img
src="about.gif"></a>

<a href="contact.html" target="main"><img
src="contact.gif"></a>

<a href="main.html" target="main"><img
src="products.gif"></a>

<a href="home.html" target="main"><img
src="home.gif"></a>
```

Example
```
<a href="home.html" target="_top">Back to
home page.</a>
```

If you want all of your links to open in a targeted frame, you can simply add the `target` attribute to the `<base>` tag in the `<head>` section of the Web page. Each link will then open in the frame specified in the `<base>` tag, and you will not have to specify the `target` attribute for each individual link.

Example
```
<head>
    <title>Dreamscape Art Studio</title>
    <base target="main">
</head>
```

Use a Hidden Frame to Preload Images

Y ou can decrease the amount of time a Web browser needs to display large images by preloading images, as discussed in Chapter 5. Unlike described in Chapter 5, however, you can also use a hidden frame to preload images.

Many Web sites contain large images. When a user clicks a link to a large image, the Web browser may take a period to retrieve the image from the Web server. After the image has been displayed on a Web page, reloading the page retrieves the image from the Web browser's cache as opposed to the Web server.

One way to help speed up the display of images on a Web site is to preload images. Preloading places images in the Web browser's cache, so that when a user clicks a link to see an image, the image is already on the computer and

does not need to be retrieved from the World Wide Web.

You can create a hidden frame that displays the preloaded images. The user never sees the hidden frame or the Web page it contains, but the image displayed within that hidden frame is placed in the Web browser cache. Whenever a user requests to see that image on any of the other pages of your Web site, the image is retrieved from the cache.

A hidden frame is created using two frames: one sized to 100% of the Web browser display's width, and the other sized to 0. Only the frame being used for your Web pages is seen.

You should also use the noresize attribute of the <frameset> tag so that a user does not accidentally locate and drag a border to reveal the hidden frame. Likewise, set the border width to 0 to allow for Web browsers that display the borders of hidden frames.

Use a Hidden Frame to Preload Images

① Open or create a Web page that contains two frames.

② Type **100%,0**.

③ Specify a Web page that contains the images to be preloaded.

④ Save the Web page.

```
index - Notepad
File Edit Format View Help
<html>
<head>
<title>Dreamscape Art Studio</title>
</head>

<frameset rows="100%,0" noresize border="0" frameborder="0" frameborder="NO" framespacing="0">
        <frame src="pictures.html">
        <frame src="preload.html">
</frameset>

</html>
```

⑤ Open or create a Web page that contains links to images in the Web page specified in step **3**.

⑥ Save the Web page.

```
pictures - Notepad
File Edit Format View Help
<html>
<head>
        <title>Dreamscape Art Studio</title>
</head>

<body>
<h3>Sample Images</h3>
<a href="horses.jpg">Horses</a><br />
<a href="ceiling.jpg">Ceiling</a><br />
<a href="bigcat.jpg">Jaguar</a>

</body>
</html>
```

7 Open the Web page specified in step **1** in a Web browser.

8 Click a link to open an image.

The image displays almost instantaneously.

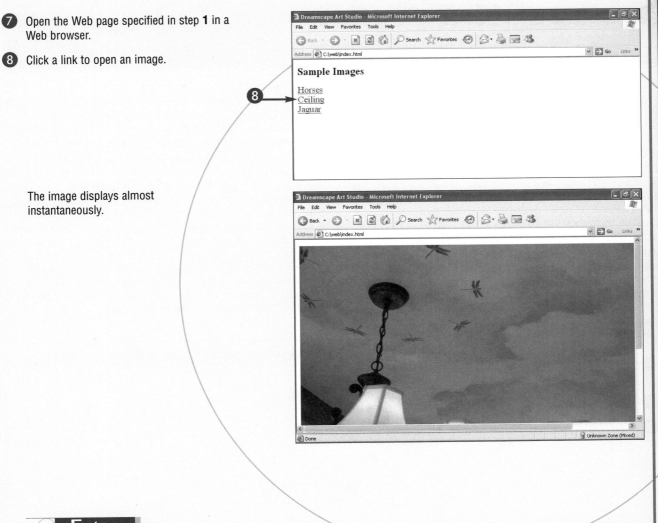

Extra

Using a hidden frame to preload images does not decrease the amount of information that is transferred from the Web server to the user; it only preloads the images when a user first visits your site.

You can preload any image into a hidden frame, not just large photographs. You can preload logos, letterheads, buttons, and menus. You can even preload images that will be used as imagemaps. For more information about imagemaps, see Chapter 5.

Sometimes users configure their Web browsers not to use the cache, in which case preloading images in a hidden frame will have absolutely no effect. Luckily, most users leave their Web browsers with the default settings and cache enabled.

If your images will take a long time to preload, the user may wonder why a page looks fully loaded but is still loading. To avoid confusing your users you may want to include a message in the nonhidden frame stating that images are currently preloading.

Display a Message for Non-Frame-Enabled Browsers

Y ou can display a warning message to users who may have older Web browsers that cannot render information in frames using the `<noframes>` tag. Besides displaying a warning message, the text contained within the `<noframes>` tags may also assist various search tools to better catalog your Web pages. Some search tools only catalog the first page of your Web site. If that page contains a `<frameset>` tag, no useful information can be gathered. Putting useful information within the `<noframes>` tags gives these types of cataloging and search tools better information with which to catalog your Web site.

The vast majority of users have Web browsers that fully support frames. Major browsers such as Netscape Navigator and Internet Explorer have supported frames for a decade now. However, some users may turn off the frames option or

may be viewing your Web page with a device such as a small handheld computer that cannot display frames. You can create a message warning users that they will not be able to access your site properly without a frames-enabled browser.

The `<noframes>` tag encloses information that will be displayed in Web browsers that do not support frames. The `<noframes>` tag should appear on the same Web page that includes the `<frameset>` tag used to create your frames structure. Typically, the `<noframes>` tag is placed just before the `<frameset>` tag. The `<noframe>` tag consists of a start and end tag, and the information placed between those tags will be displayed while the remaining content of the Web page is ignored by the browser. You should include text within the `<noframes>` tag to kindly inform the user that their browser does not support frames and suggest to them that they obtain a browser that does.

Display a Message for Non-Frame-Enabled Browsers

① Open or create a Web page that contains frames.

② Type **<noframes>**.

③ Type **</noframes>**.

```
index - Notepad
File  Edit  Format  View  Help
<html>
<head>
<title>Dreamscape Art Studio</title>
</head>

<noframes>          ←──── ②

</noframes>  ←──── ③

<frameset rows="70,*" >
        <frame src="title.html">
        <frameset cols="50%,*">
                <frame src="body.html">
                <frame src="contact.html" />
        </frameset>
</frameset>

</html>
```

④ Type the text to appear when frames are not enabled.

⑤ Save the Web page.

```
index - Notepad
File  Edit  Format  View  Help
<html>
<head>
<title>Dreamscape Art Studio</title>
</head>

<noframes>

For any inquiries about our decorative services, consultations or commissioned paintings, please
do not hesitate to contact the studio owner and artist.<br/><br/>
Helene, studio owner and artist

</noframes>

<frameset rows="70,*" >
        <frame src="title.html">
        <frameset cols="50%,*">           ④
                <frame src="body.html">
                <frame src="contact.html" />
        </frameset>
</frameset>

</html>
```

6️⃣ Open the Web page in a Web browser that supports frames.

The Web page appears as intended.

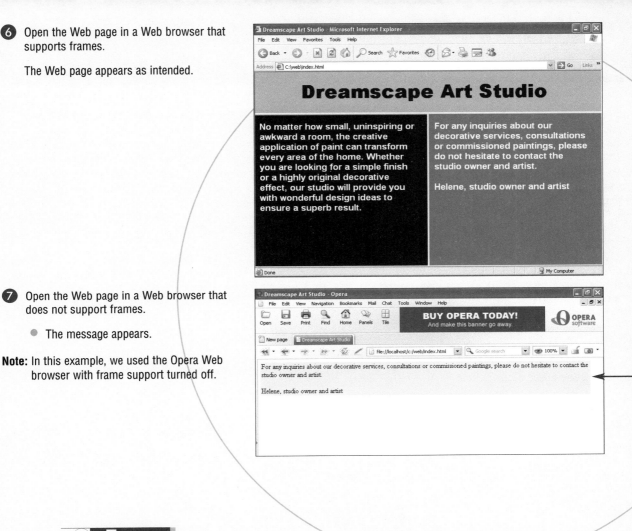

7️⃣ Open the Web page in a Web browser that does not support frames.

● The message appears.

Note: In this example, we used the Opera Web browser with frame support turned off.

Extra

The Web page that contains the `<frameset>` tag used to create your frames structure should not also contain a `<body>` tag. In most cases, you can use the `<body>` tag within the noframes attribute to create a Web page that does not utilize frames. However, XHTML does not support the inclusion of a `<body>` tag. So, if you want your code to be XHTML-compliant, do not use the `<body>` tag within the `<noframes>` tags. Simply display a message indicating to the user that a browser with frame support is required.

Including a method for users whose browsers do not support frames to obtain a frame-enabled browser can be extremely helpful.

Example

```
<noframes>
You need a frame-enabled Web browser
to view this site. The following
browsers are frame-enabled:<br />

<a
href="http://www.getfirefox.com">GetFir
efox.com</a><br />
<a
href="http://www.netscape.com">Netscape
Navigator</a><br />

</noframes>
```

Create a Floating Frame

Y ou can create a frame that looks like an element on your Web page instead of a part of the browser. This type of frame is referred to as an inline frame or a floating frame.

The <iframe> tag specifies the parameters of the floating frame. As with the <frame> tag, the src attribute indicates the Web page that will be loaded into the floating frame, as well as the frame's width and height. The frame size can be specified absolutely in pixels, or as a percentage of the Web browser display width.

The <iframe> tag can be placed within the text of your Web page. The placement considerations of a floating frame are similar to those of an image. You can place an inline frame in a paragraph, in the cell of the table, or you can let the frame stand on its own. Barring size constraints, there

is no limit to the number of floating frames you can have on a Web page.

Inline frames are not widely supported in older Web browsers; however, it is safe to assume that most users today utilize Web browsers that can display floating frames.

As with other types of frames, you can have a link open a Web page in a floating frame by assigning the floating frame a name with the name attribute. Then you can use the target attribute of the link to identify the floating frame.

In most cases, Web browsers automatically insert scroll bars into a floating frame if necessary. If you decide that you do not want scrollbars in your floating frames, you can suppress the display of scroll bars by setting the scrolling attribute of the <iframe> tag to the no value.

Create a Floating Frame

① Open or create a Web page.

② Type **<iframe src="">**.

③ Type **</iframe>**.

④ Type the name of the Web page to be displayed in the floating frame.

⑤ Type **width=""**.

⑥ Type **height=""**.

⑦ Type the width of the floating frame.

⑧ Type the height of the floating frame.

⑨ Save the Web page.

⑩ Open the Web page in a Web browser.

The floating frame appears in the Web page.

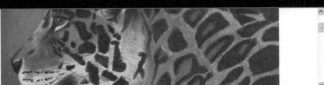

Apply It

You can place text information within the start and end `<iframe>` tags that will display to users whose Web browsers do not support floating frames. This text should firstly inform the user that their browser does not support frames and then indicate to the user sites where they can download a Web browser that does supports them.

Example

```
<iframe src="reference.html">
You need a frame-enabled Web browser to view this page. You can obtain one
from;<br />
<a href="http://www.microsoft.com">Microsoft Internet Explorer</a><br />
<a href="http://www.netscape.com">Netscape Navigator</a><br />
<a href="http://www.getfirefox.com">GetFirefox.com</a><br />
</iframe>
```

Center Elements on a Web Page

You can use XHTML and HTML code to center elements on a Web page. When centering Web page elements, the Web browser determines the mathematical center of an element and aligns that point with the center of the Web browser window. The element therefore moves as the Web browser window is resized but always remains centered regardless of the size of the window or the resolution of the display.

Enclose elements that you want to center on a Web page with `<div>` tags. A `<div>` tag is a *block-level element*, or an element that will be placed on a Web page after a new line has been inserted. The Web browser also adds a new line after the element, helping to divide your Web pages into distinct sections. Block-level elements include inline elements, but the reverse is not true. Inline elements must be included within a block-level element. Similarly, inline

elements cannot appear on their own. They have to be part of block-level elements. To center elements enclosed by the `<div>` tag, specify the value center for the align attribute of the `<div>` tag.

An alternative to the `<div>` tag is the `<center>` tag. Unlike the `<div>` tag, the `<center>` tag does not require an align attribute: it automatically centers, and places a new line before and after, any elements it encloses.

You can center any element, including headings, images, paragraphs of text, and horizontal rules, using either the `<div>` or the `<center>` tags.

Note that while centering elements is a convenient feature, sometimes it can make text more difficult because it can destroy the left-aligned justification that people are used to reading from books, magazines, and newspapers.

Center Elements on a Web Page

① Open or create a Web page.

② Position the cursor before the elements you want to center and type **<div align="">**.

③ Position the cursor between the quotes and type **center**.

④ Position the cursor after the elements you want to center and type **</div>**.

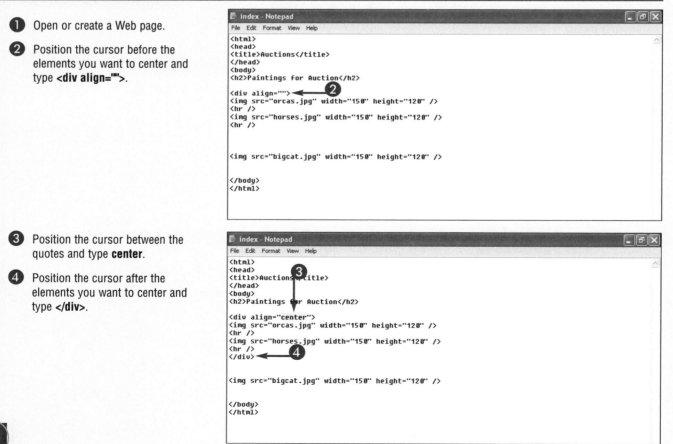

⑤ Position the cursor before the element you want to center and type **<center>**.

⑥ Position the cursor after the element you want to center and type **</center>**.

⑦ Save the Web page.

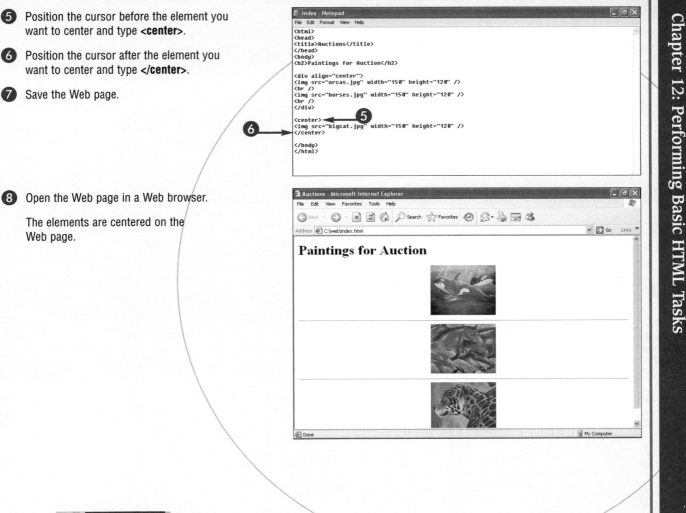

⑧ Open the Web page in a Web browser.

The elements are centered on the Web page.

Extra

Although the `<div>` and `<center>` tags are both commonly used methods of centering items on a Web page, both tags are deprecated in XHTML because they are formatting-related HTML tags. Even though you can be sure that Web browsers will support these older HTML-formatting methods for many years to come, you should use style sheets if you want your code to fully comply with the XHTML specification. For more information about aligning elements on a Web page using style sheets, refer to Chapter 6.

You can center an item within a table cell to allow you to center an element within a certain portion of a Web page. For example, say you have a navigation bar at left that is two inches or so wide and your page's content is to the right of the navigation bar. If you centered the element without enclosing it in a table, it will not appear centered in the content area. Simply enclose the content area in a simple table of one large table cell and center that element within the cell to achieve the desired effect.

Apply Background Color and Images

Yₒu can use XHTML or HTML code to change the background color of a Web page. Background color can be very important. If you use the wrong background color or do not specify a background color at all, some of your users who have non-standard browser settings may find it difficult or impossible to read the text on your Web page. You can also use a background image to improve the aesthetic appeal of your Web page.

The `<body>` tag, which encloses all of the content and specifies characteristics of a Web page, can also be used to define the background. You can use either a solid color or an image for the background.

Specify a solid color for the background with the `bgcolor` attribute of the `<body>` tag. The value of the `bgcolor` attribute may be the common name of a color, such as gray

or black, or a hexadecimal code that specifies a Web-safe color. A # symbol precedes the hexadecimal color codes.

To use an image as the background of a Web page, specify the name of the image with the `background` attribute of the `<body>` tag.

If the background image is not large enough to completely fill the Web browser window, then the image will *tile*. Tiling simply means that the image repeatedly displays until the window is filled. Complicating matters, an image that does not tile at 640 x 480 resolution may tile at higher resolutions, depending on the size of the image. Always view your page at multiple resolutions to ensure that your page looks good in all of them.

If you do not specify a color or image for the background of a Web page, the Web browser uses the default solid color (usually white, but the user can change this setting).

Apply Background Color and Images

USE A SOLID COLOR

1. Open or create a Web page.

2. Position the cursor in the `<body>` tag and type **bgcolor=""**.

3. Position the cursor between the quotes and type the background color.

4. Save the Web page.

5. Open the Web page in a Web browser.

   The Web page appears with the specified background color.

USE AN IMAGE

① Open or create a Web page.

② Position the cursor in the `<body>` tag and type **background=""**.

③ Position the cursor between the quotes and type the name of the image.

④ Save the Web page.

⑤ Open the Web page in a Web browser.

The Web page appears with the specified background image.

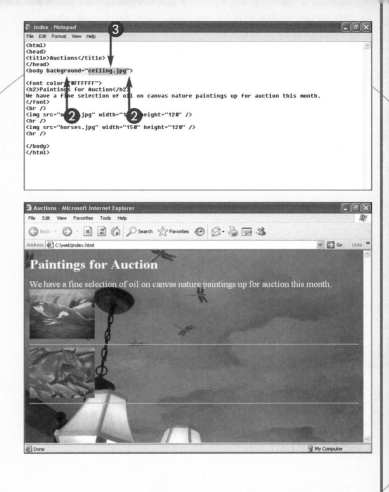

Extra

Background images often end with the file extension .gif or .jpg. Smaller images work best as GIF files, and larger, more complex images look better as JPEGs. In addition, the .png format was introduced to replace the .gif format, which is owned by a single company and not very capable of complex images. PNG files are typically larger in size than GIF files, but are roughly equivalent in size to JPEGs. Current browsers typically support PNG files. Remember that the larger the file size of the background image, the longer your Web page takes to load.

You should choose whether you want the background color or an image as your background. You cannot have both at the same time. If you use both the `bgcolor` and `background` attributes together in the `<body>` tag, the Web browser usually displays the background image and not the solid color. If you like, though, you can specify a background color that the user will only see if he or she has images turned off or if the image is missing.

Align
Elements

You can align elements on a Web page using just HTML code. Alignment attributes give you better control over the design and appearance of elements in your Web pages. For example, you might want to align the title of a page in the center of the page, or align page numbers to the right side of the page.

You can align elements to the left, right, or center of a Web page using the align attribute of the element tag. You can align most elements, such as paragraphs, images, tables, and horizontal rules, using the align attribute.

Specifying values of left or right for the align attribute aligns an element to the left or right. A value of center for the align attribute centers an element on the Web page.

Test your Web pages when using different values for the align attribute to make sure the elements display correctly. Web browsers sometimes rearrange Web page content in order to align elements in the locations you specify; however, this arrangement may be contrary to your initial expectations.

Elements enclosed in another element's tags are aligned in relation to the parent element. For example, if you center align an image within the cell of a table, the image is placed in the center of the table cell, not the center of the Web page. However, you can also choose to align elements in table cells individually by cell, allowing you quite a bit of freedom in the presentation of elements on your page.

Be careful aligning elements; some alignments do not suit certain elements. For example, aligning text to the right is not often done for good reason: it makes the text difficult to read (at least with languages that read left to right).

Align Elements

① Open or create a Web page.

② Position the cursor in the tag of the element you want to align and type **align=""**.

③ Position the cursor between the quotes and type the type of alignment.

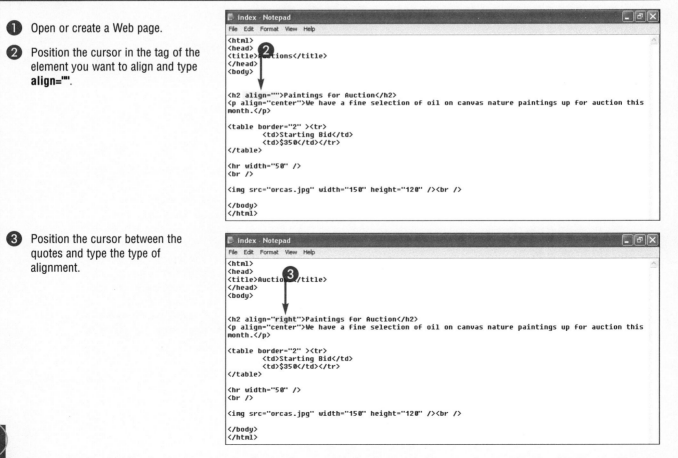

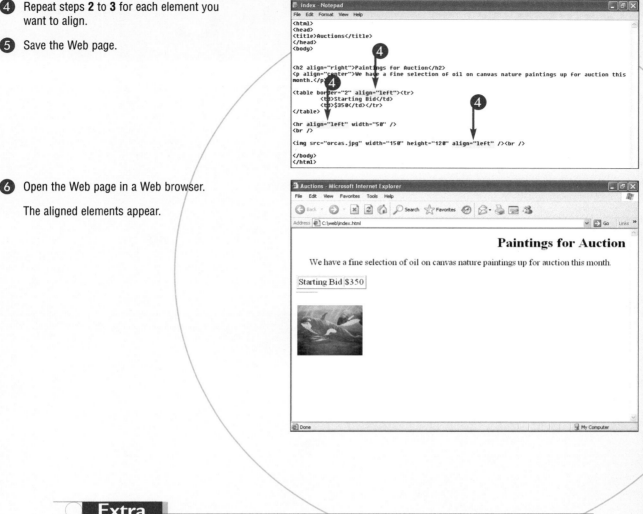

④ Repeat steps **2** to **3** for each element you want to align.

⑤ Save the Web page.

⑥ Open the Web page in a Web browser.

The aligned elements appear.

Extra

The use of the `align` attribute is not valid in the XHTML specification because, as mentioned elsewhere in the book, XHTML mandates that style sheets be used to format the presentation of Web page elements. Although Web browsers will support the `align` attribute for many years to come, you should use style sheets if you want your Web pages to be truly XHTML-compliant. For more information about using style sheets to position elements on a Web page, see Chapter 6.

You may have trouble when positioning multiple elements on the same line. For example, if you have five elements on one line and you want to align them with the same amount of spacing between each one, you are likely to become frustrated trying to accomplish this. To get around this, use a table to align each element appropriately within a table cell. The rest of this chapter deals with using tables to lay out your Web pages.

Lay Out a Web Page Using Tables

Y ou can use tables to help you arrange the elements on your Web page. The difficulty in arranging elements is one of the main problems of laying out Web pages. Although primarily used for organizing textual data, you can also use tables to specify how those elements are laid out on your page. Using size and alignment specifications for the table, you can easily place elements in locations such as the bottom right-hand corner of the Web page.

To lay out a Web page using a table, create a table that takes up the full width and height of the Web browser window, and then define table cells that divide the Web page into separate sections. For example, you could use a table with three cells with an element in the middle cell and

a certain number of spaces in the left and/or right cells to specify exactly how far from the margins of the page you want the element to appear. The complexity of your layout and the level of precision you require to position elements determine the number of cells you should add to your table. Indeed, you may wind up using multiple tables on your page to achieve different layouts in different sections of your page.

You can manipulate the position of elements on the Web page by changing the size specifications for the columns of cells in the table. The width attribute of the <td> tag resizes the width of a data cell. In the case of a simple table, this adjustment may affect the entire column to which the data cell belongs. Specify the width of a cell in pixels, or as a percentage of the width of the Web browser window.

Lay Out a Web Page Using Tables

① Open or create a Web page that contains a simple table.

② Position the cursor in the <table> tag and type **width="100%"**.

③ Type **height="100%"**.

```
index - Notepad
File  Edit  Format  View  Help
<html>
<head>
<title>Auctions</title>
</head>
<body>

<table width="100%" height="100%">
<tr>
        <td></td>
        <td></td>
</tr>
<tr>
        <td></td>
        <td></td>
</tr>
</table>

</body>
</html>
```

④ Position the cursor in the <td> tag of the cell you want to change the size of and type **width=""**.

```
index - Notepad
File  Edit  Format  View  Help
<html>
<head>
<title>Auctions</title>
</head>
<body>

<table width="100%" height="100%">
<tr>
        <td width=""></td>
        <td></td>
</tr>
<tr>
        <td align="center"></td>
        <td align="right" valign="bottom"></td>
</tr>
</table>

</body>
</html>
```

5 Type the width of the column.

6 Place the elements of the Web page in the table cells.

7 Save the Web page.

8 Open the Web page in a Web browser.

The Web page appears with the elements positioned.

```
index - Notepad
File  Edit  Format  View  Help
<html>
<head>
<title>Auctions</tit
</head>
<body>

<table width="100%" height="100%">
<tr>
        <td width="50%"><h2>Paintings For Auction</h2></td>
        <td>We have a fine selection of oil on canvas nature paintings up for auction this
            month.</td>
</tr>
<tr>
        <td align="center">Starting Bid: $350</td>
        <td align="right" valign="bottom"><img src="orcas.jpg" width="250" height="220" /></td>
</tr>
</table>

</body>
</html>
```

```
Auctions - Microsoft Internet Explorer
File  Edit  View  Favorites  Tools  Help
  Back          Search    Favorites
Address  C:\web\index.html                                Go  Links

Paintings for Auction              We have a fine selection of oil on canvas
                                   nature paintings up for auction this month.




          Starting Bid: $350

Done                                                      My Computer
```

Extra

Using tables to lay out your Web pages gives you an HTML solution to the problem of positioning items more accurately on your Web pages. XHTML by contrast specifies that style sheets be used to position elements on a Web page. If you want your page to comply with the XHTML specification, you should get away from using tables to lay out your page, but tables are useful if your Web pages will be viewed on older Web browsers incapable of processing style sheet information.

Table cells without elements or spaces in them are flexible on a Web page. They stretch and squeeze as necessary to take up the space in the browser display window. Specify the width and height of a table or cell as a percentage of the Web browser window instead of as an absolute pixel size. This helps your Web page maintain its layout when the browser window is resized, or when the page is viewed on displays of different sizes.

Insert Spacer Images

Spacer images enable you to precisely position items on a Web page without having to create style sheets. Spacer images are often used to position images on a Web page relative to the margins of the Web browser window.

A spacer image is usually only one pixel wide and one pixel high. By using multiple spacer images, you can effectively mandate that invisible pixels be placed in certain areas. For example, if you have an image under a paragraph of text and you want it to be indented exactly two spaces from the left edge of the browser display window, you could place two spacer images to the left of the image. By defining `height` and `width` attributes for the `<img>` tag, you can create a spacer image any size you want, separating Web page elements by at least the width or height you specify.

Regardless of the original size of the spacer image, the Web browser either shrinks or expands the image to fit the size defined by the `width` and `height` attributes.

Your spacer image should be either transparent or the exact color as the background of the Web page. A transparent image is an invisible image that does not display on a Web page. Almost all image-editing programs can easily create a transparent image that you can use as a spacer. Note, though, that a spacer image that is the same color as the Web page background may become visible if the user overrides the Web page settings and changes the background color of the Web page. Therefore, if you can use transparent spacer images instead of images the same color as the background you can be better assured that the user will not be able to see those images.

Insert Spacer Images

Note: These steps assume your spacer image is called clear.gif.

① Open or create a Web page.

② Position the cursor where you want to place a vertical space and type **<img src="*clear.gif*" width="1">**, replacing *clear.gif* with the name of your spacer image.

③ Position the cursor where you want to place a horizontal space and type **<img src="clear.gif" height="1">**.

④ Position the cursor in the vertical spacer image tag and type **height=""**.

⑤ Position the cursor between the quotes and type the height of the spacer.

⑥ Position the cursor in the horizontal spacer image tag and type **width=""**.

```
index - Notepad
File  Edit  Format  View  Help
<html>
<head>
<title>Auctions</title>
</head>
<body>

<img src="clear.gif" width="1" /><br />
<img src="clear.gif" height="1" />
<img src="orcas.jpg" width="250" height="220" />

<hr />
<h2>Paintings for Auction</h2>
We have a fine selection of oil on canvas nature paintings up for auction this month.<br />

Starting Bid: $350

</body>
</html>
```

```
index - Notepad
File  Edit  Format  View  Help
<html>
<head>
<title>Auctions</title>
</head>
<body>

<img src="clear.gif" width="1" height="55" /><br />
<img src="clear.gif" width="" height="1" />
<img src="orcas.jpg" width="250" height="220" />

<hr />
<h2>Paintings for Auction</h2>
We have a fine selection of oil on canvas nature paintings up for auction this month.<br />

Starting Bid: $350

</body>
</html>
```

7 Position the cursor between the quotes and type the width of the spacer.

8 Save the Web page.

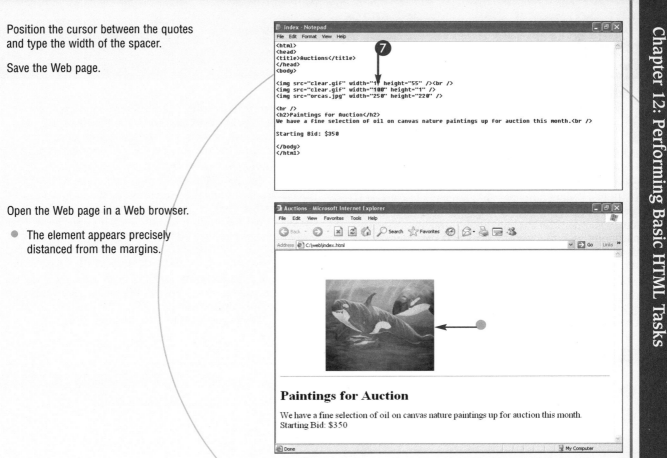

9 Open the Web page in a Web browser.

● The element appears precisely distanced from the margins.

Apply It

Determining the effect of transparent spacer images can be somewhat difficult. You can easily locate transparent spacer images on a Web page by adding the `border` attribute with a value of `1` to the `<img>` tag. This draws a very thin border around the spacer image, enabling you to locate it on the Web page. After you finish laying out your Web page, you can change the `border` value to `0`.

Enable border
```
<img src="clear.gif" width="250"
height="0" border="1"/>
```

Turn off border
```
<img src="clear.gif" width="250"
height="0" border="0"/>
```

Keep in mind as you design your Web pages how the decisions you make will affect non-visual browsers such as Web page readers for blind or visually-impaired users. For example, spacer images on your Web pages will appear as images to Web page readers and are likely to confuse or frustrate users of these alternative browsers when the reader tells the user that an image is on the page but neglects to describe it. To make your page better accessible to these alternative browsers, add empty `alt` attributes in your spacer image tags so that the Web reader will know to ignore the space.

Add an XHTML Declaration

You must add a declaration to your code to make your Web pages fully XHTML-compliant. This declaration specifies to the Web browser exactly which XHTML specification your page follows and allows the browser to know how to parse (or interpret) the page accordingly.

XHTML is a coding language that attempts to convert HTML to an XML-compliant coding language. XML is a universally accepted standard for exchanging information between applications such as Web browsers and Web servers. Converting HTML to XML will enable different applications to access and display Web pages more easily in the future.

The XHTML declaration is a single line of information placed at the beginning of your Web page code. A Web browser displaying your Web page reads the XHTML declaration and knows that the code that follows is XHTML. If you did not

include this declaration, the browser would assume that HTML was being used and would parse the page accordingly, which would likely cause your page to be displayed in a broken manner inconsistent with your design.

There are two types of XHTML declarations that you can place at the top of your Web page code. The XHTML Strict Declaration notifies the Web browser that you are using only XHTML code in your Web page. The XHTML Transitional Declaration lets the Web browser know that, although your code is XHTML-compliant, it also utilizes some HTML elements to format the data. For most Web pages, you can use the transitional XHTML declaration.

After you add an XHTML declaration, you can then validate your Web page to make sure that the code is XHTML-compliant. For more information about checking the validity of your XHTML Web pages, refer to the remainder of this chapter.

Add an XHTML Declaration

1 Open your text editor.

2 On the first line, type **<!DOCTYPE html PUBLIC>**.

3 Position the cursor in the declaration and type **"-//W3C//DTD XHTML 1.0 Transitional//EN"**.

4 Position the cursor in the declaration and type **"http://www.w3.org/TR/xhtml1/DTD/xhtml1-transitional.dtd"**.

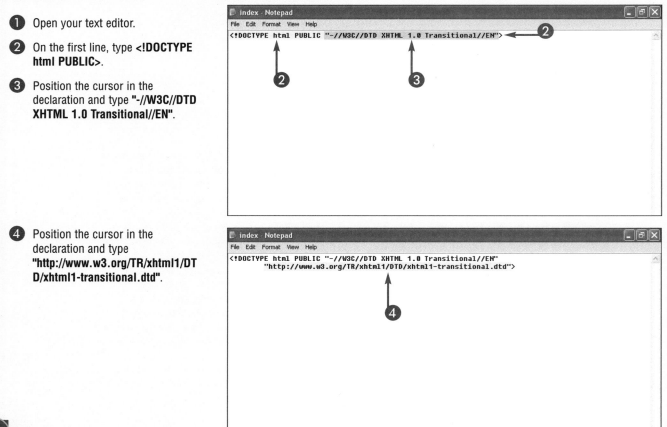

⑤ On a new line, type the XHTML-compliant code that creates the Web page.

⑥ Save the Web page.

⑦ Open the Web page in a Web browser.

The Web page appears.

Extra

As has been mentioned elsewhere in this book, all XHTML tags must come in sets: an opening and a closing tag. The XHTML declaration tag is no different: the XHTML declaration is a single tag placed at the beginning of your Web page code. Make sure you close the declaration tag by including a space and a forward slash (/) at the end of the tag. Failure to include this ending tag will result in the browser misinterpreting your code and displaying your Web page in a broken manner if at all.

You may recall from Chapter 11 that HTML pages that use frames require the use of the `<frameset>` tag in place of the `<body>` tag. XHTML pages that use frames also require special treatment. Firstly, XHTML frames pages require a DOCTYPE declaration that reflects the use of frames. Include the following XHTML declaration for Web pages that utilize frames:

Example
```
<!DOCTYPE html PUBLIC "-
//W3C//DTD XHTML 1.0
Frameset//EN"
"http://www.w3.org/TR/xhtml1/DTD/
xhtml1-frameset.dtd">
```

Secondly, you must insert a `<body>` tag in the `<noframes>` element on an XHTML page for the page to be compliant with the XHTML specification.

215

Verify Your XHTML Code

You can and should verify your XHTML code to make sure that it is valid and structured properly. The XHTML specification analyzes precisely how the code for Web pages should appear. Web pages created with invalid code may not display properly in Web browsers. The process of verifying your XHTML code for compliancy with the XHTML specification is called *validation*.

You may find that you still use HTML specifications when creating tags for your XHTML code. For example, in XHTML, all tag names must be lowercase. This is not the case with HTML. Although the <P> tag is valid in HTML, it would be considered invalid when used in an XHTML Web page. Validating your XHTML code helps you find these types of subtle errors.

The beginning of your code must contain the XHTML declaration before your Web page can be verified and

validated. The declaration that you use depends on what XHTML specification you are using; different declarations are used for XHTML Strict, XHTML Transitional, and XHTML Frameset specifications. See the section "Add an XHTML Declaration" earlier in this chapter for more information on the XHTML declaration. See Chapter 1 for more information on the different XHTML specifications.

You can use an online XHTML validation service to easily verify your XHTML Web pages. If your Web pages are not XHTML-compliant, the validation service will usually provide a list of errors in your Web page or simply declare the page to have failed validation. The World Wide Web Consortium (or W3C for short) hosts a validator you can use to validate your pages at http://validator.w3.org. See Chapter 16 for more information on this and other XHTML validators.

Verify Your XHTML Code

① Open or create an XHTML-compliant Web page.

② Publish the Web page to a Web server.

Note: To publish your Web page, see Chapter 2.

③ Open the Web browser, type **validator.w3.org** in the address bar, and press Enter.

● The validation service's Web page appears.

Note: The validation service's appearance and functionality may be different.

④ In the validation address area, type the name of the Web page published in step **2**.

⑤ Click Check.

● A message appears informing you of the page's validity.

Extra

Some validation services allow you to validate your XHTML code as a separate file without publishing your Web pages on the World Wide Web. This is useful for Web pages that are published on an intranet, protected by a firewall, or stored locally on your own computer. One example of this type of validator is the validator hosted by the World Wide Web Consortium (or W3C for short), which you can use to validate your pages. The W3C validator can be found at `http://validator.w3.org`.

Although online XHTML validation services are quick and free, you can also use a dedicated application installed on your computer if you are creating a large number of XHTML Web pages, or if you do not have access to the Internet. If the application you use to create your pages includes a validator, it will probably be most compatible with the code created by the application. On the other hand, you might want to use another validator to ensure that your code is as compliant as possible. See Chapter 16 for more information on the various validators you can use.

Enhance Site Promotion with HTML Tags

You can use simple HTML tags to increase the efficiency with which search engines on the Internet catalog your Web pages. Search engines are tools on the Internet that organize and catalog literally hundreds of millions of Web pages, and that make finding information easy. If you anticipate that users will search for your Web pages, then you should make sure the various search engines on the Internet properly catalog your Web site. For example, if you sell certain products at your site, you will want to ensure that your Web page comes up in user searches in major search engines if possible.

The `<meta>` tag in the `<head>` section of a Web page enables you to specify information such as keywords and a description of your Web page. Some search engines use this information when cataloging a Web page. The `<meta>` tag

does not display anywhere on a Web page. It is only used by search tools or other applications that analyze your Web site. The keywords that you use should reflect the most defining aspects of your site. For example, if your page is about Calico cats, you will want to include keywords such as "Calico" and "cats" and perhaps even "feline" to ensure that your site is properly categorized in search engines.

Almost all search engines will catalog the title of your Web page. Adding keywords to the title is a simple yet effective way of an improving the efficiency of the cataloging process. You should incorporate keywords into the title that still make sense to users viewing and bookmarking your Web page. In the previous example with Calico cats, you would probably want both the words "Calico" and "cats" in the title of your page.

Enhance Site Promotion with HTML Tags

① Open or create a Web page.

② In the <head> section of the Web page, type **<meta />**.

③ Position the cursor in the <meta> tag and type **name=""**.

④ Position the cursor between the quotes and type **keywords**.

⑤ Position the cursor in the <meta> tag and type **content=""**.

⑥ Position the cursor between the quotes and type the keywords that best describe the Web site.

⑦ On the following line, type **<meta name="description" content="" />**.

8 Position the cursor between the quotes and type a description of the Web page.

9 Position the cursor between the start and end <title> tags and add the title that includes keywords that best describe your site.

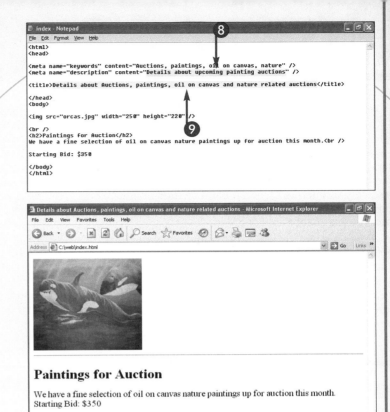

10 Publish the Web page to a Web server.

Note: To publish your Web page, see Chapter 2.

● The Web page is now ready to be cataloged by search tools.

When specifying keywords in the <title> and <meta> tags, choose words that a user would most likely type into a search engine when trying to locate pages like yours. In the preceding task, the keywords were "auctions," "paintings," "oil on canvas," and "nature."

Almost all search engines analyze the textual content of a Web site when cataloging the pages in their database. To help increase the efficiency of this process, use keywords in the headers and section titles of your Web page.

Some people think that using the same keyword multiple times in your <meta> tags might increase the relevance of their page to search engines. Using a specific keyword multiple times on your Web page has no effect; most search engines simply ignore repetitive words.

A quick way to prompt a search tool to catalog your Web page is to visit the search tool's site and search for your Web page address. Some search tools will automatically search for Web pages not yet cataloged if a user attempts a search.

Add a
Welcome Message

You can add a sound file to your Web page that will play a message when the page is initially loaded. You can use a sound file to welcome visitors to your site, clue them in to the purpose of your page, or just entertain them. The sound can play music, a spoken welcome message, or both. Note that the `<bgsound>` tag works only in Internet Explorer. For a method of embedding sound in your page that works on all browsers, see the next section in this chapter.

The `<bgsound>` tag generates the sound when the Web page loads. You can use the `src` attribute of the `<bgsound>` tag to specify the name of the audio file to be played.

You can use the `delay` attribute to delay the playing of the background sound. Specify the value of the `delay` attribute as the number of seconds you want the Web browser to

wait before playing the sound. Give the user's Web browser time to fully load the Web page before starting to play the background sound.

Use a WAV or MIDI file as the background sound file. WAV and MIDI are very common formats for the audio files that you can create on a computer or download from the Internet. WAV audio files, which have the file extension .wav, typically consist of music or spoken messages. WAV audio files can be very large. Because Web browsers have to download the entire audio file before playing it, you should try to keep a file's playing time short. MIDI audio files, which use either .mid or .midi for the file extension, are strictly instrumental and much smaller in size.

Make sure that you have permission to use any audio file that you download from the World Wide Web.

Add a Welcome Message

① Open or create a Web page.

② Position the cursor in the head area of the Web page and type **<bgsound src="">**.

③ Type the name of the sound file you want to use for a welcome message.

④ Type **delay =""**.

---

index - Notepad
File Edit Format View Help

```
<html>
<head>
<title>Airplane Spotters Group</title>

<bgsound src="">          ——②

</head>
<body>

<h3>Welcome</h3>
Welcome to the new issue of the Aircraft Spotters Club newsletter. First off, let me
say that we cannot mail this newsletter to all of our members so as of now we are
putting it on the Web. Starting with the January 3rd newsletter, Tom Smith will no
longer be mailing the newsletter to any members.
<hr>
<h3>Charter Bus</h3>
Alice will be in charge of signing up members for the charter bus to the Harbor Front
airport in February. Any members that are interested, please contact Alice at
555-234-6719
</body>
</html>
```

---

index - Notepad
File Edit Format View Help

```
<html>
<head>
<title>Airplane Spotters Group</title>

<bgsound src="airplane.wav" delay="">

</head>
<body>

<h3>Welcome</h3>
Welcome to the new issue of the Aircraft Spotters Club newsletter. First off, let me
say that we cannot mail this newsletter to all of our members so as of now we are
putting it on the Web. Starting with the January 3rd newsletter, Tom Smith will no
longer be mailing the newsletter to any members.
<hr>
<h3>Charter Bus</h3>
Alice will be in charge of signing up members for the charter bus to the Harbor Front
airport in February. Any members that are interested, please contact Alice at
555-234-6719
</body>
</html>
```

⑤ Position the cursor between the quotes and type the number of seconds to wait after the Web page loads before playing the sound.

⑥ Save the Web page.

```
index - Notepad
File  Edit  Format  View  Help

<html>
<head>
<title>Airplane Spotters Group</title>

<bgsound src="airplane.wav" delay="10">

</head>
<body>

<h3>Welcome</h3>
Welcome to the new issue of the Aircraft Spotters Club newsletter. First off, let me
say that we cannot mail this newsletter to all of our members so as of now we are
putting it on the Web. Starting with the January 3rd newsletter, Tom Smith will no
longer be mailing the newsletter to any members.
<hr>
<h3>Charter Bus</h3>
Alice will be in charge of signing up members for the charter bus to the Harbor Front
airport in February. Any members that are interested, please contact Alice at
555-234-6719
</body>
</html>
```

⑤

⑦ Open the Web page in a Web browser.

After the time specified in step **5**, the welcome message plays.

```
Airplane Spotters Group - Microsoft Internet Explorer
File  Edit  View  Favorites  Tools  Help
Back       Search   Favorites
Address  C:\web\index.html                              Go   Links
```

Welcome

Welcome to the new issue of the Aircraft Spotters Club newsletter. First off, let me say that we cannot mail this newsletter to all of our members so as of now we are putting it on the Web. Starting with the January 3rd newsletter, Tom Smith will no longer be mailing the newsletter to any members.

Charter Bus

Alice will be in charge of signing up members for the charter bus to the Harbor Front airport in February. Any members that are interested, please contact Alice at 555-234-6719

Extra

Microsoft's Internet Explorer is currently the only Web browser that recognizes the <bgsound> tag, and so it is likely that if a visitor to your site is not using IE they may not hear the sound you intended. Fortunately, Internet Explorer is the most popular Web browser used today, but to be safe make sure not to rely on the background sound to convey any important information that is not otherwise obvious on the site itself. This way, if a user surfs your site using another browser, they will still be able to successfully navigate your site.

Many users browse the World Wide Web at the workplace or in other locations where sound may not be appropriate. If you are creating a Web site that will be viewed primarily in a place of business, you may want to avoid using background sounds. For personal Web pages or pages for local community groups, background sounds may be less objectionable. Keep in mind also that these users may not have their speakers hooked up or their volume might be very low or muted. Do not rely on background sounds to convey important information to the user.

Embed a Background Sound

You can insert a background sound into a Web page that will work with any major current Web browser used on a computer that has an audio application capable of playing that sound. You can use background sounds to play music, a voice welcome message, or both.

Use the `<embed>` tag to add an audio file to your Web page. The `<embed>` tag, which places both audio and video files in a Web page, is supported by most current Web browsers and some older Web browsers.

Use the `src` attribute of the `<embed>` tag to specify the name of the audio file to play when the Web page loads. Specify a value of `true` for the `autostart` attribute of the `<embed>` tag to ensure that the sound plays as soon as the Web page loads.

Because the `<embed>` tag is also used to place items such as videos on Web pages, if you use the default settings the tag will cause the file to take up space on a Web page. Utilize the `hidden` attribute of the `<embed>` tag, with a value of `true`, so that the `<embed>` tag does not disrupt the flow of information on your Web page.

To replay the background sound continuously, specify a value of `true` for the `loop` attribute. Set the value of the `volume` attribute to `10` so that the volume of the background sound will be loud enough for the user to hear. Be careful, though, many users can become annoyed very quickly with a sound that loops continuously and chances are you are not aiming to annoy people who visit your site.

As with any audio file, the user must have a functional sound system and operational speakers or headphones to hear the background sound.

Embed a Background Sound

1 Open or create a Web page.

2 Position the cursor in the Web page code and type **<embed src="">**.

3 Type **hidden="">**.

4 Position the cursor between the quotes after `src=` and type the name of the audio file.

5 Position the cursor between the quotes after `hidden=` and type **true**.

6 Position the cursor in the `<embed>` tag and type **autostart="true"**.

7 Type **loop=""**.

⑧ Position the cursor between the quotes and type **true**.

⑨ Position the cursor in the `<embed>` tag and type **volume="10"**.

⑩ Save the Web page.

```
index - Notepad
File  Edit  Format  View  Help
<html>
<head>
<title>Airplane Spotters Group</title>
</head>

<body>

<embed src="airport.mid" hidden="true" autostart="true" loop="true" volume="10">

<h3>Welcome</h3>
Welcome to the new issue of the Aircraft Spotters Club newsletter. First off, let me say that we
cannot mail this newsletter to all of our members so as of now we are putting it on the Web.
Starting with the January 3rd newsletter, Tom Smith will no longer be mailing the newsletter to
any members.
<hr>
<h3>Charter Bus</h3>
Alice will be in charge of signing up members for the charter bus to the Harbor Front airport in
February. Any members that are interested, please contact Alice at 555-234-6719
</body>
</html>
```

⑪ Open the Web page in a Web browser.

The Web page appears and the audio file starts playing.

```
Airplane Spotters Group - Microsoft Internet Explorer
File  Edit  View  Favorites  Tools  Help
Back        Search   Favorites
Address  C:\web\index.html                          Go   Links

Welcome

Welcome to the new issue of the Aircraft Spotters Club newsletter. First off, let me say that
we cannot mail this newsletter to all of our members so as of now we are putting it on the
Web. Starting with the January 3rd newsletter, Tom Smith will no longer be mailing the
newsletter to any members.

Charter Bus

Alice will be in charge of signing up members for the charter bus to the Harbor Front
airport in February. Any members that are interested, please contact Alice at 555-234-6719
```

Extra

A user must have an audio playback application properly installed and configured on his or her computer to properly hear the sounds embedded in your Web page. If the user does not have an audio application capable of playing the audio file, if the user's speakers are not hooked up, or if the user's sound is turned all the way down or muted, the sound will not be heard. Knowing this, make sure not to rely on the background sound to convey any important information to the user.

If you decide that your sound is so important that you cannot bear the thought of a user not hearing it upon visiting your page, you can display a message to users letting them know if their browser does not support playback of your sound file. You can use the `<noembed>` tag to display a message in older Web browsers that do not support the `<embed>` tag.

Example
```
<embed src="hello.wav"
autostart="true" hidden="true">

<noembed> This web page contains
sounds that you cannot hear
because you are using an
incompatible Web browser
</noembed>
```

Include a Media Player in a Web Page

Y ou can include Windows Media Player controls along with your sound file to allow users to decide whether or not to play the file, the volume at which they want to listen to it, and controls to fast forward or rewind the file at will. Windows Media Player is a multimedia playback application included with recent versions of the Microsoft Windows operating system.

Use the `src` attribute of the `<embed>` tag to specify the name of the audio file to play. The format of the sound file can be any type that Windows Media Player is capable of playing. When the media player is embedded into a Web page, the controls of the media player are displayed on the page. The media player controls allow the user to adjust the volume, start and stop playback, and fast-forward or rewind the audio file.

You must specify the size of the audio player controls that are displayed on the Web page. Current media player controls are best displayed with a height of 45 pixels. Specify the height and width of the media player controls with the `height` and `width` attributes of the `<embed>` tag.

In order for the media player controls to display on a Web page, the user must have Windows Media Player installed and properly configured. It is safe to assume that most people who use recent versions of the Microsoft Windows operating system (such as Windows XP) will already have a correctly installed and configured version of Windows Media Player. Unfortunately, any Mac users, Linux users, or users of versions of Windows without Windows Media Player set up and configured will not be able to see or use the controls.

Add a Media Player to a Web Page

1 Open or create a Web page.

2 Position the cursor where you want the media player to appear on your Web page and type **\<embed src="">**.

```
index - Notepad
File  Edit  Format  View  Help
<html>
<head>
<title>Speech</title>
</head>
<body>

Listen to the chairman's message concerning last year's performance.
<hr />


<embed src="">          ← 2

</body>
</html>
```

3 Position the cursor between the quotes and type the name of the audio file.

4 Position the cursor within the `<embed>` tag and type **width="".**

```
index - Notepad
File  Edit  Format  View  Help
<html>
<head>
<title>Speech</title>
</head>
<body>

Listen to the chairman's message concerning last year's performance.
<hr />


<embed src="message.mp3" width="">

</body>
</html>
              3           4
```

⑤ Position the cursor between the quotes and type the width of the media player controls.

⑥ Position the cursor within the `<embed>` tag and type **height="45"**.

⑦ Save the Web page.

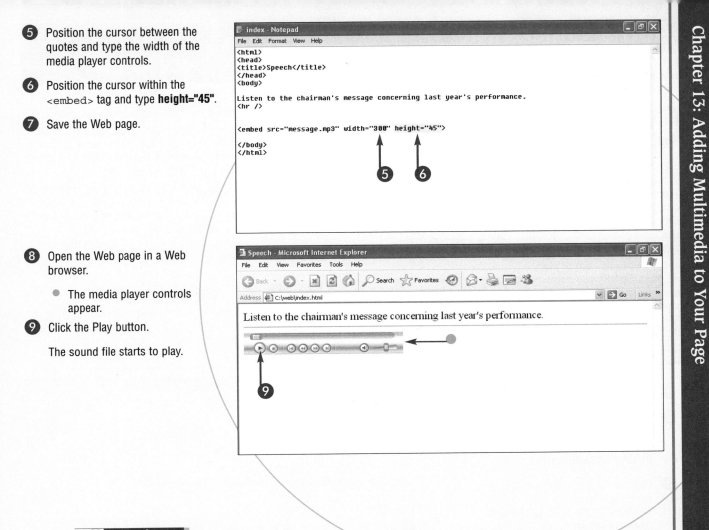

⑧ Open the Web page in a Web browser.

● The media player controls appear.

⑨ Click the Play button.

The sound file starts to play.

Apply It

Use the `align` attribute of the `<embed>` tag to control the flow of text around the media player controls. This is useful when the media player controls are surrounded by other content on the Web page and you want the controls to stay in one consistent location on the page. If you use `align`, the text or other content will then flow around the controls and reflow dynamically if the user resizes the page.

Example
```
<embed src="hello.mp3"
height="45" width="300"
align="right">
```

While it would be ideal for page load speed if the audio files that you use were in the same directory on the same server as the rest of your Web page files, audio files that are played using the `<embed>` tag do not have to be stored on the same Web server as the Web page. You can specify the location of the remote audio file as well as the name of the file using the `src` attribute.

Example
```
<embed
src="www.rapidcomputer.com/audio/
hello.mp3" height="45"
width="300"  >
```

Add a QuickTime Video to a Web Page

QuickTime is a popular video format that was designed by Apple Computer. You can easily incorporate QuickTime videos into your Web page. QuickTime is a media player much like Windows Media Player with the added benefit that it runs on Windows and Mac computers (Windows Media Player runs only on Windows). Users must have QuickTime Player installed and properly configured before they can display QuickTime videos embedded within a Web page. For more information about QuickTime videos and QuickTime Player, visit Apple's QuickTime Web site at www.apple.com/quicktime.

Use the `<object>` tag to place a QuickTime video on your Web page. Specify the value `clsid:02BF25D5-8C17-4B23-BC80-D3488ABDDC6B` for the `classid` attribute of the `<object>` tag to identify the movie clip as a QuickTime video. This value for the `classid` attribute is unique and identifies different types of objects that can be embedded in a Web page

(audio files, for example, have a different `classid` value).

Specify the size of the video in pixels using the `width` and `height` attributes of the `<object>` tag. Make sure that the size you choose matches the size of the video or the video will appear distorted on your Web page.

QuickTime uses `<param>` (param as in "parameter") tags to configure video file playback. Three `<param>` tags within the `<object>` tag specify the configuration of the player used for the QuickTime video. Use the tag `<PARAM name="SRC" VALUE="message.mov">` to specify the name of a video called `message.mov`.

Use `<PARAM name="CONTROLLER" VALUE="false">` to hide QuickTime Player controls from the user if you do not want them to be able to stop, rewind and fast forward, or adjust the volume of the file. The video will start to play automatically after the Web page loads by including the `<PARAM name="AUTOPLAY" VALUE="true">` tag.

Add a QuickTime Video to a Web Page

1 Open or create a Web page.

2 Position the cursor where you want the QuickTime movie to appear on your Web page and type **<OBJECT CLASSID="">**</OBJECT>**.

3 Position the cursor between the quotes and type **clsid:02BF25D5-8C17-4B23-BC80-D3488ABDDC6B**.

4 Position the cursor within the `<object>` tag, type **width=""**, entering the width of the video between the quotation marks.

5 Type **height=""**, entering the height of the video between the quotation marks.

6 Position the cursor in the `<object>` tag and type **<PARAM name="SRC" VALUE="message.mov">**.

7 Type **<PARAM name="AUTOPLAY" VALUE="true">**.

8 Type **<PARAM name="CONTROLLER" VALUE="false">**.

9 Save the Web page.

10 Open the Web page in a Web browser.

● The video file message.mov plays.

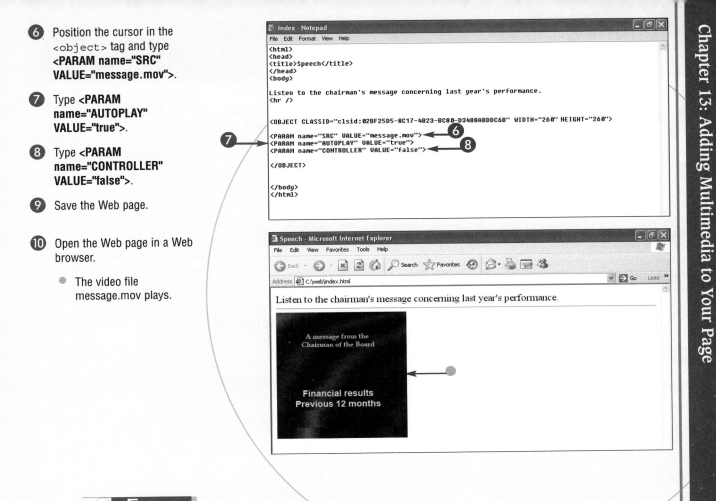

Extra

You can adjust the values of the `<param>` tags to allow users to stop and play the video whenever they want. Users will also be able to adjust the volume and fast forward or rewind the video at will. To display the player controls and to stop the video from playing automatically when the Web page loads, omit the `<param>` tags containing the `autoplay` and `controller` attributes.

If you add the controls for the user and do not adjust the height value of the video, some of the video will be lost. When including the player controls with the QuickTime video, you can add an additional 16 pixels to the height of the video to allocate space for the controls. Specify the height of the video using the `height` attribute of the `<object>` tag.

The value `classid` attribute of the `<object>` tag defines the class, or type, of the file and media player that the file is designed to play on. This value is unique to each type of multimedia player incorporated on a Web page. If you need to find a certain `classid` value, you can obtain it from the manufacturer of the media player.

Enable Users to Download a Media Player

Many media players exist on the Web today, and typically, only one of them is installed by default on any user's computer. Each multimedia file format has its own strengths and weaknesses. You can enable users to automatically download and install the required application needed to play the audio and video files on your Web page if they do not already have this player on their computer. This allows your users to choose the type of audio or video files you want to include without being restricted by the player applications available on each user's computer. If you allow users to download the required applications necessary to play the different multimedia file formats, you will have greater flexibility in choosing the correct format for your information and at the same time you will be helping your users to have greater choice of media players.

The codebase attribute of the <object> tag specifies the location where users can obtain the necessary application required to play your multimedia file. In many cases, this will be the Web site of the multimedia player's manufacturer. The Web site will contain instructions on how to download and install the necessary application files. The download and installation process is usually automated and requires very little intervention from the user.

The value of the codebase attribute will be provided by the manufacturer of the multimedia player.

The process of downloading and installing the multimedia application only takes place once. After that, the multimedia player will be available whenever the Web browser encounters the same type of content. The next time a user views your Web page after downloading and installing the player, the multimedia files will be accessible immediately.

Allow Users to Download a Media Player

Note: In this example, we are downloading QuickTime Player from Apple.

1. Open or create a Web page that uses the <object> tag to display a video.

2. Position the cursor within the <object> tag and type **CODEBASE=""**.

3. Position the cursor between the quotes and type the location where the user can get the player.

4. Save the Web page.

5. Open the Web page in a Web browser.

   - A message appears asking if you would like to install the player.

6. Click Yes.

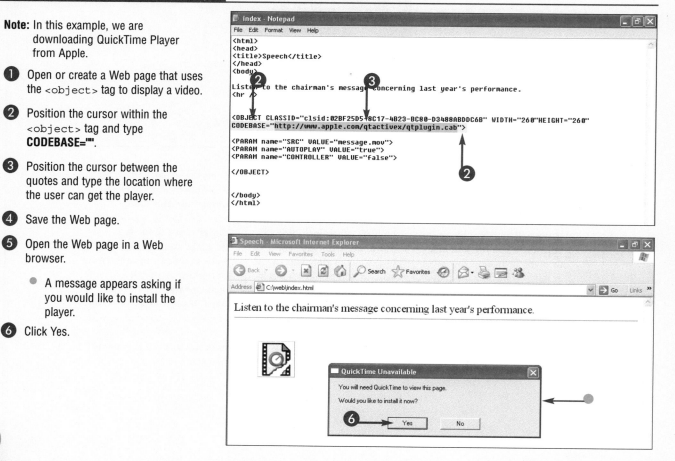

A Web page appears that allows the user to download the player.

⑦ Follow the instructions on the Web page to download and install the player.

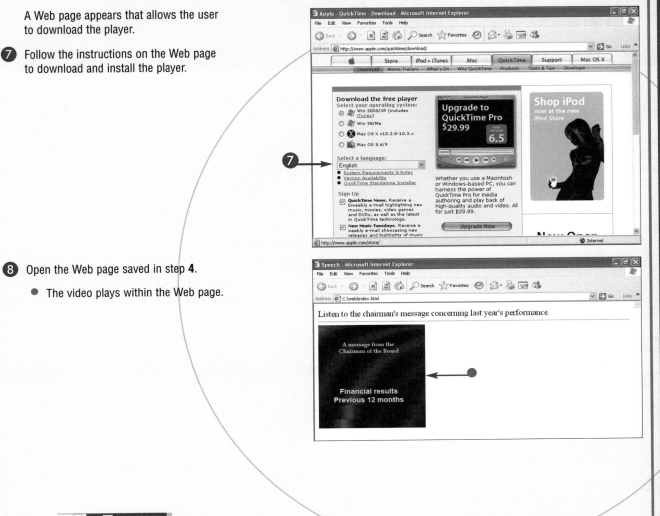

⑧ Open the Web page saved in step **4**.

● The video plays within the Web page.

Extra

The fact that many media players exist allows you a lot of freedom as to which player you decide to create content for, but users need to know that they need a certain player if you expect them to use it to view your content. You should create a message informing users that you require a separate application to view the multimedia files contained on your Web page. If you do not include such a message, your users may not install the multimedia application at all and may therefore miss content you worked hard to create.

Each type of multimedia player will have a different method of installation, and each player will have a unique location from which to download the player. The location from which the user should download the player is specified in the codebase attribute of the <object> tag, which should be provided by the manufacturer of the multimedia player. Before specifying the value of the codebase attribute, be sure to confirm the validity of the address by visiting the Web site and installing the application yourself.

Add a Flash Presentation

A Flash presentation is a multimedia file displayed using the Macromedia Flash Player within a Web page. Macromedia's Flash has been around for a decade or so and has proven to be extraordinarily popular on the Web. Because of Flash's popularity, the vast majority of current and even older Web browsers come with a Flash player installed by default.

Flash files are often saved with the extension .swf. Flash presentations can contain audio and video. Because many Flash presentations use animated graphics instead of video, the quality of the presentations is usually very high while the file size is typically fairly low. For more information about Flash Player and Flash files, visit the Macromedia Web site at www.macromedia.com.

Use the <object> tag to place a Flash presentation on your Web page. Identify the movie clip as a Flash presentation by

specifying the value clsid:D27CDB6E-AE6D-11cf-96B8-444553540000 for the classid attribute of the <object> tag. This value is unique to the Flash Player.

Include the codebase attribute of the <object> tag to ensure that the Flash Player can be accessed if it is not already installed on a user's computer. Specify the value http://active.macromedia.com/flash4/cabs/swflash.cab#version=4,0,0,0 for the codebase attribute to direct users to the Web site where they can download and install the Flash Player application.

A <param> tag with a value of movie assigned to the name attribute must be specified within the <object> tag. Specify the name of the Flash file to display on the Web page with the value attribute of the same <param> tag.

Specify the size of the Flash presentation in pixels using the width and height attributes of the <object> tag.

Add a Flash Presentation

1 Open or create a Web page.

2 Position the cursor where you want the Flash presentation to appear and type **<object classid= "clsid:D27CDB6E-AE6D-11cf-96B8-444553540000"**.

3 Type **codebase="">** placing the value for the attribute between the set of double primes to direct users to the Website.

4 Type **</object>**.

5 Position the cursor within the <object> tag and type the code that specifies the width and height of the Flash presentation.

6 Position the cursor within the <object> tag and type **<param name="movie" value="">**.

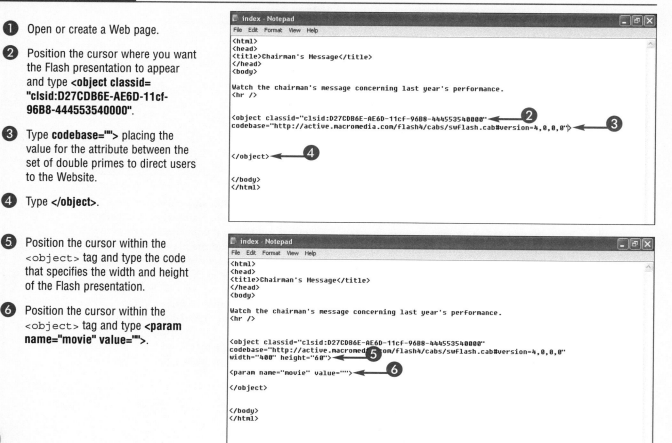

7 Position the cursor between the quotes and type the name of the Flash presentation file.

8 Save the Web page.

```
index - Notepad
File  Edit  Format  View  Help

<html>
<head>
<title>Chairman's Message</title>
</head>
<body>

Watch the chairman's message concerning last year's performance.
<hr />


<object classid="clsid:D27CDB6E-AE6D-11cf-96B8-444553540000"
codebase="http://active.macromedia.com/flash4/cabs/swflash.cab#version=4,0,0,0"
width="400" height="60">

<param name="movie" value="welcomecurl.swf">

</object>


</body>
</html>
```

9 Open the Web page in a Web browser.

● The Flash presentation begins to play.

```
Speech - Microsoft Internet Explorer
File  Edit  View  Favorites  Tools  Help

Back        Search   Favorites

Address  C:\web\index.html               Go   Links

Watch the chairman's message concerning last year's performance.
```

Extra

Flash presentations are platform independent. That means a Flash file can be viewed on any computer using any operating system on which Flash Player is installed. All major operating systems are capable of viewing Flash presentations. A Flash movie will look almost identical regardless of the computer or operating system used to run the file.

Creating Flash presentations is not an intuitive or straightforward project, and dedicated development tools are required to create a Flash file. You can use Macromedia's Flash Professional software to create a Flash presentation. Creating files with Macromedia Flash Professional involves piecing together multiple image, sound, and other files, such as video, into one cohesive file that plays them all together based on a specified timeline. For more information about the tools needed to create Flash files, visit the Macromedia Web site at www.macromedia.com.

Most graphics firms now provide Flash file creation services, making it easier than ever to quickly obtain customized Flash presentations even if you do not want to invest the time and/or money in obtaining and learning how to use Macromedia Flash Professional. Many Web sites also offer free Flash presentations for files such as welcome messages that you can use on your own Web site. To locate providers of these services, use your favorite Internet search engine to look for free Flash presentations.

Create
Moving Text

Y ou can use the `<marquee>` tag to create a text message that scrolls from the right to the left of the display. The `<marquee>` tag was created by Microsoft during the late 1990s when Microsoft and Netscape were still competing in what is now called the "Browser War." Like most HTML tags, the `<marquee>` tag consists of an opening and closing tag. Place the message you want to scroll across your Web page between the opening and closing `<marquee>` tags.

Internet Explorer is currently the only browser that supports the `<marquee>` tag, and it is not likely that other browsers will ever support the tag. So, if your Web pages will be viewed over the Internet or in any setting where you cannot assume that users are using IE 4 or higher, you should not use the `<marquee>` tag to display important information.

Most Web browsers that do not support the `<marquee>` tag will simply display the message as plain text, however, so at least the text will be visible even if it does not scroll.

The `<marquee>` tag is not part of HTML or XHTML, but you can safely implement it if you know that your users will be viewing Web pages with Internet Explorer, as on an internal company network.

You can format the information that you want to display within the `<marquee>` tag using standard HTML or XHTML formatting. For example, insert header tags around the message contained within the `<marquee>` tag to scroll a header across the Web page.

The moving text comes from the right-hand side margin, proceeds across the Web page to the left-hand side margin, and then disappears. This process continually repeats. Some users may find scrolling text messages somewhat annoying, so avoid overusing the `<marquee>` tag.

Create Moving Text

① Open or create a Web page.

② Position the cursor where you want the moving text to appear and type **<marquee>**.

③ Type **</marquee>**.

④ Position the cursor between the opening and closing `<marquee>` tags and type the text that you want to animate.

⑤ Save the Web page.

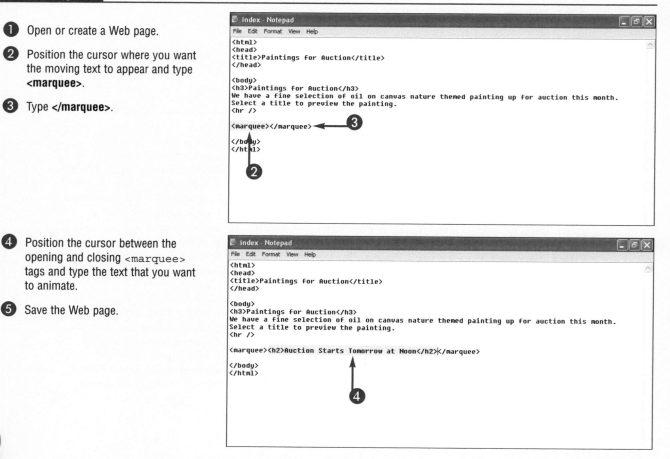

6 Open the Web page in a Web browser.

- The text appears at the right of the display

- The text scrolls to the left and off the display.

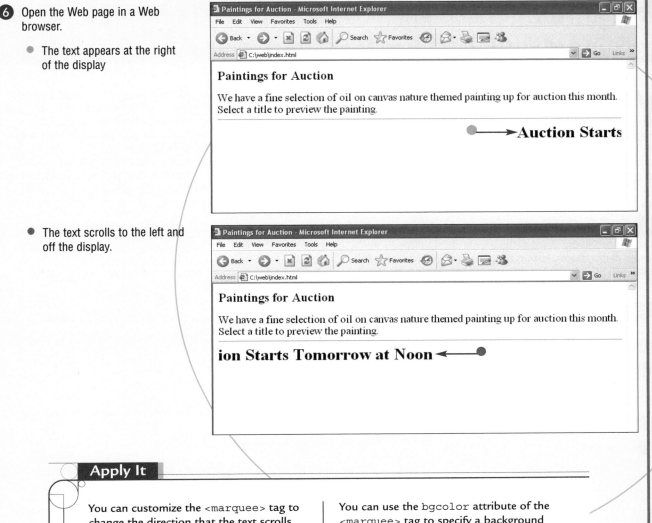

Apply It

You can customize the `<marquee>` tag to change the direction that the text scrolls using the tag's `direction` attribute and specifying the direction (either `left` or `right`) that you wish the text to scroll. To make the text scroll from the left to the right side of the Web page, specify a value of `right` for the `direction` attribute.

Example
```
<marquee direction="right">
    Welcome
</marquee>
```

You can use the `bgcolor` attribute of the `<marquee>` tag to specify a background color for the text. The area behind the text as it scrolls across the Web page will have the background color applied to it. Make sure to choose a background color that contrasts with the text color or you will render your text either invisible or nearly so.

Example
```
<marquee bgcolor="red">
    <font color="yellow">Alert!</font>
</marquee>
```

Stream Video Using RealPlayer

You can include streaming video in your Web page using the RealVideo format, which plays in RealPlayer. RealPlayer is a multimedia application specially suited to the playback of video files that stream over the Internet. A streaming video file is a video clip that plays at the same time as it is downloaded from the Internet to a computer, typically a Web server. The big advantage to streaming video is that users do not have to download a large video file before being able to view it. The video player starts to play the video as the rest of the video downloads in the background. Streaming video data has become more popular with the advent of high-speed Internet connections, making it now possible to view high-quality video over the Internet with little or no wait time.

Video files that can be streamed using RealPlayer end with the extension .ram. You can store these video files on your Web server and make them available to your users by creating a link to the video file as you would for any other type of file. If the user has RealPlayer installed, the video files will start playing almost immediately after they click the link, regardless of the size of the video. The player will tell the user that it is buffering (meaning that the player is synching the file for play) and, after a brief delay, will start playing the video.

Before users can view streaming video files, they must have RealPlayer installed on their computers. You may want to create a message on your Web page indicating that RealPlayer is required before viewing streaming videos.

Stream Video Using RealPlayer

① Open or create a Web page.

② Position the cursor where you want the link to the video file to appear and type **<a href="">**.

③ Type the text to use as the link.

④ Type **</a>**.

```
index - Notepad
File  Edit  Format  View  Help
<html>
<head>
<title>Paintings for Auction</title>
</head>

<body>
<h3>Paintings for Auction</h3>
We have a fine selection of oil on canvas nature themed painting up for auction this month.
Select a title to preview the painting.
<hr />

<a href="">Video Presentation</a>          ④

</body>
</html>
```

⑤ Position the cursor between the quotes and type the name of the streaming video file.

⑥ Save the Web page.

```
index - Notepad
File  Edit  Format  View  Help
<html>
<head>
<title>Paintings for Auction</title>
</head>

<body>
<h3>Paintings for Auction</h3>
We have a fine selection of oil on canvas nature themed painting up for auction this month.
Select a title to preview the painting.
<hr />

<a href="video.ram">Video Presentation</a>

</body>
</html>
```

7 Open the Web page in a Web browser.

8 Click the link to the video file.

● The player starts and displays the video file.

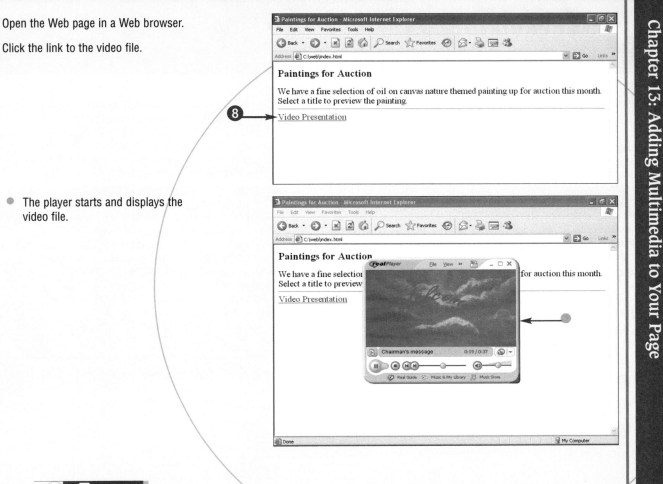

Extra

Not only can you make video files available for streaming on the Internet, you can also use RealPlayer to broadcast live events, such as auctions or presentations. Special applications are required to create these more complex types of streaming video. For more information about creating streaming video files for RealPlayer, visit the Web site of Real Networks at www.real.com.

There are utilities available from the World Wide Web that can convert existing video files into the format required for streaming over the Internet, which can save you a lot of time. For more information on how to convert these video files into the RealVideo format, use your favorite search engine to look for "convert to Real video."

You may not want to rely on users to download RealPlayer to view your files. Many sites accommodate users of different media players by offering multiple versions of their video files. For example, you could offer three versions of your video file: one for QuickTime, one for RealPlayer, and one for Windows Media Player, so that the user can choose which they want to view.

Add JavaScript to a Page

JavaScript is a computer programming language originally developed by the folks at Netscape Communications Corp. (now a subsidiary of America Online) that enables you to enhance your Web pages with dynamically generated text and effects such as pop-up messages. There is no need to configure a Web browser to be able to view Web pages that contain JavaScript code. All but the very oldest Web browsers are capable of viewing Web pages that contain JavaScript. Note that other than the word "java" JavaScript has nothing whatsoever to do with Sun Microsystems' Java programming language: Java and JavaScript are two completely different languages and even are dissimilar types of languages.

Use the `<script>` tag to insert JavaScript into the code of the Web page. The `language` attribute with a value of `JavaScript` denotes that the code within the `<script>` tag is JavaScript. The `type` attribute of the `<script>` tag is `text/javascript`.

JavaScript uses simple commands to generate text. Any textual information generated by JavaScript is inserted directly into the Web page at the place where the `<script>` tags appear in the code. When a user views the source code of a Web page that contains JavaScript, they will see the actual JavaScript code in the Web page's source code.

JavaScript commands that only generate text are quite simple to create. The command `document.write()` generates text information by placing the text, enclosed in quotation marks, within the parenthesis. `document.write()` can also display information such as the type of Web browser being used to view the Web page. The `navigator.appName` property stores the name of the Web browser, which can be displayed by placing `navigator.appName` within the parentheses of `document.write()`.

Add JavaScript to a Page

① Open or create a Web page.

② Type **<script language ="">**.

③ Type **</script>**.

④ Type **JavaScript**.

⑤ Type **type=""**.

⑥ Type **text/javascript**.

⑦ Type the JavaScript code that generates some textual output.

⑧ Save the Web page.

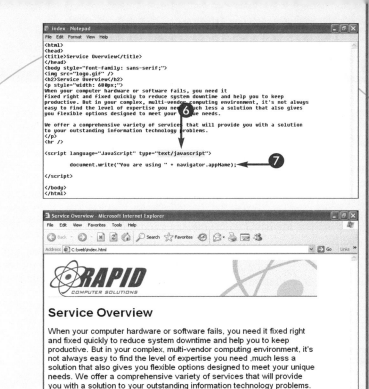

⑨ Open the Web page in a Web browser.

● The JavaScript-generated text appears.

Extra

There are programming languages other than JavaScript that you may use within the `<script>` tag of a Web page, and each has its own strengths and weaknesses. JavaScript is an ideal programming language for learning and is more than suitable for producing the most popular kinds of Web page enhancements.

You can use traditional XHTML tags to change the appearance of the text generated by JavaScript. For example, both of the following items of code will generate the same result.

Example 1
```
<div style="font-family: Arial;">
<script language="JavaScript"
type="text/javascript">
document.write("You are using" +
navigator.appName);
</script>
</div>
```

Example 2
```
<script language="JavaScript"
type="text/javascript">
document.write("<div style='font-family:
Arial;'>");
document.write("You are using" +
navigator.appName);
document.write("</div>");
</script>
```

237

Get Up to Speed with JavaScript Basics

Before you make use of JavaScript in your Web page, you need to be comfortable with JavaScript basics. One of the key concepts that you need to know to work with JavaScript (and with most major programming languages) is what variables and arrays are and how to use each.

Variables are names that you can assign to values. Variables make changing data that you use in a Web page much easier. The keyword `var` indicates a variable. `var` is followed by the name of the variable, an equal sign, and the value that will be initially assigned to the variable. You can assign different types of data, such as text or numbers, to a variable. Text information must be enclosed within quotation marks.

You can make variables easier to work with by combining them into an index called an *array*. Items within an array

share the same name, but each has a unique index number enclosed in square brackets. For example, `age[1]` and `age[2]` are two items of an array called `age`. Using index numbers makes manipulating large amounts of related data easier. You can create an array in a similar manner as a variable; however, after the `=`, use `new array()` to specify the number of items in the array, with the number of items enclosed in parentheses: for example, `new array(2)`. Indexing in an array starts with the number `0`, so an array declared with `new array(2)` contains three items.

You can display the value that has been assigned to a variable by using `document.write()`. You must not enclose a variable name in quotes within the `document.write()` statement, otherwise, the name of the variable will be displayed, not the value.

Use JavaScript Basics

1. Open or create a Web page.

2. Type the opening and closing `<script>` tags.

3. Type **var** and the name of the variable to create.

4. Type = and the value to assign to the variable, followed by ;.

5. Type **var** and the name of the array to create.

6. Type = **new Array()** ;.

7. Type the number of items in the array.

8. Type the code that assigns values to the items in the array.

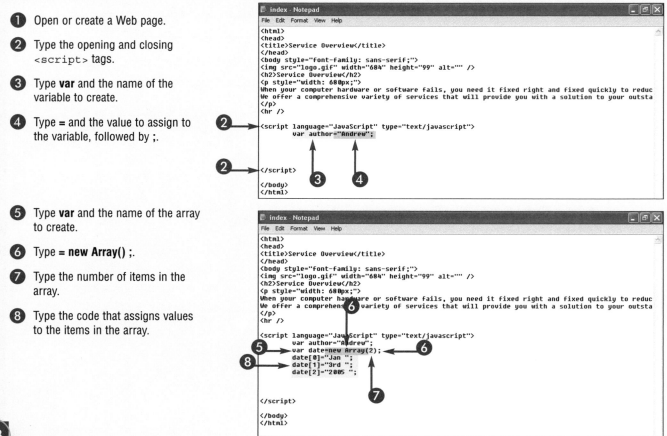

9 Type the code that displays the values assigned to the variables.

10 Save the Web page.

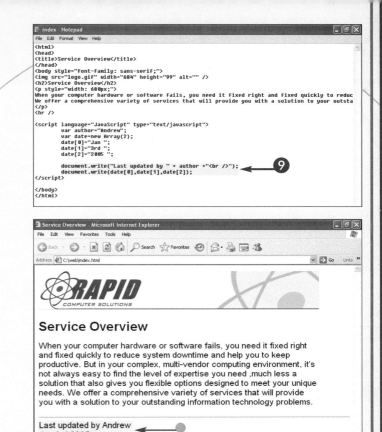

11 Open the Web page in a Web browser.

● The values assigned to the variables appear.

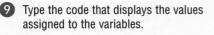

Apply It

You can also create an array by declaring variables as the array is being initialized. This ensures that the array will have the exact number of items needed to store the data that has been assigned to the array. The following example creates an array that contains the days of the week, and then displays the first and the last item in the array.

TYPE THIS

```
<script language="JavaScript" type="text/javascript">
var days=new Array("Monday","Tuesday","Wednesday",
"Thursday","Friday")
document.write(day[0] + " to ");
document.write(day[4]);
</script>
```

RESULT

Monday to Friday

Multiple items may be generated using a single `document.write` statement, with the multiple items separated by a plus symbol (+). You can use the `document.write` statement to display variables, text, and numbers.

TYPE THIS

```
<script language="JavaScript" type="text/javascript">
var today="Monday";
document.write("Today is " + today + " March " +
3 + ".");
</script>
```

RESULT

Today is Monday March 3.

Utilize if Statements

You can use your JavaScript code to make decisions depending on if a condition is true or false. This enables you to dynamically adjust the content of your Web pages to suit different environments. For example, you can display a different Web page banner for different times of the year based on the current date. The JavaScript code you write will then make the necessary determinations and decide based on the information you have given which is the proper action to take.

The if statement takes as its argument a statement that can be evaluated as being true or false. The most common type of statement is one that determines if a value is equal to another. Because JavaScript uses the equal sign (=) to assign values to variables, two equal signs together are used to create a statement comparing two values. For example, the statement age == 38 can be described as, "Is the variable age 38?" Conditional statements are evaluated as either true or false. If the conditional statement evaluates as true, then the portion of JavaScript code contained within curly brackets of the if statement executes. If the condition evaluates as false, then the next line of code that follows the if statement executes.

A typical if statement may perform a task depending on the type of Web browser being used to view a Web page. The navigator.appName property is ideal for this purpose. You can easily incorporate the navigator.appName property into the conditional part of your if statement. The script then looks to find which browser is being used to access the file and makes a decision based on what it finds.

Utilize if Statements

① Open or create a Web page.

② Type the opening and closing JavaScript `<script>` tags.

③ Position the mouse pointer within the `<script>` tags and type if ().

④ Type { }.

⑤ Position the pointer between the parentheses and type the condition to evaluate.

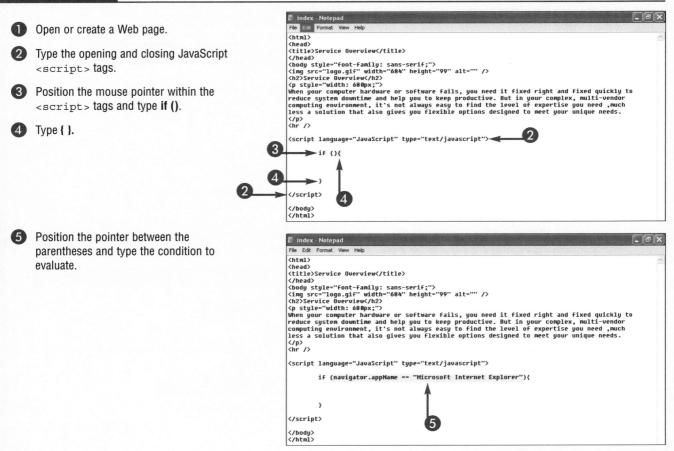

6 Position the pointer between the curly brackets and type **document.write("");**.

7 Position the pointer between the quotes and type the text to be displayed if the condition created in step **5** is `true`.

8 Save the Web page.

9 Open the Web page in a Web browser.

● If the condition is true, the text specified in step **7** is displayed.

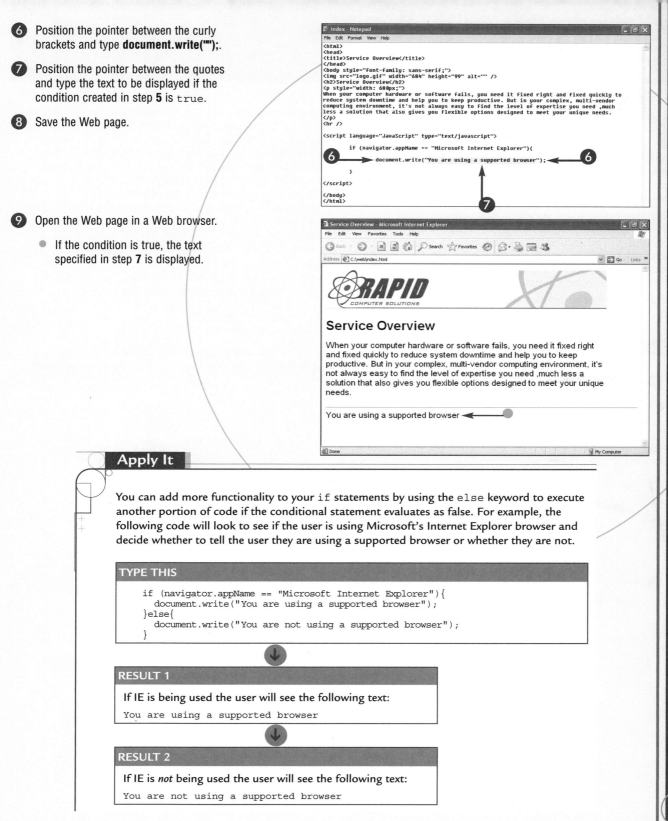

You can add more functionality to your `if` statements by using the `else` keyword to execute another portion of code if the conditional statement evaluates as false. For example, the following code will look to see if the user is using Microsoft's Internet Explorer browser and decide whether to tell the user they are using a supported browser or whether they are not.

TYPE THIS

```
if (navigator.appName == "Microsoft Internet Explorer"){
  document.write("You are using a supported browser");
}else{
  document.write("You are not using a supported browser");
}
```

RESULT 1

If IE is being used the user will see the following text:

```
You are using a supported browser
```

RESULT 2

If IE is *not* being used the user will see the following text:

```
You are not using a supported browser
```

Create for Loops

You can repeat the processing of specific JavaScript statements by using a `for` loop, allowing you to create code that runs a certain amount of times until a specific goal has been achieved. For example, you can use a `for` loop to display all the items in an array that contains the names of the months until the code has been processed 12 times and therefore displayed the names of all twelve months.

The statement that creates a `for` loop consists of the `for` keyword followed by a number of arguments enclosed in parentheses. The arguments are used to create and increment a variable within the JavaScript code that will be repeatedly processed. The code to be repeatedly processed is enclosed in a set of curly brackets.

The arguments of a `for` loop have three parts, with each part separated by a semicolon (;). The first part initializes

the counter variable, usually by creating a variable with a value of `0`. The second part generally instructs the `for` loop to execute until the counter variable reaches a specific number. The last part changes the counter variable each time the loop is executed. Appending two plus symbols (++) to a variable name indicates that the variable will be increased by `1`. For example, the argument `age=20;age<50;age++` creates a variable called `age` that has a value of `20`. Each time the code in the loop runs, the variable `age` increases by `1` until the value of `age` reaches `50`. Therefore, the code in the loop will be processed 29 times.

After the loop has finished processing, code execution continues with the line immediately following the `for` loop.

Create for Loops

① Open or create a Web page.

② Type the opening and closing JavaScript `<script>` tags.

③ Position the mouse pointer within the script tags and type **for ()**.

④ Type **{ }**.

⑤ Position the pointer before the for statement and type the code that creates one or more arrays.

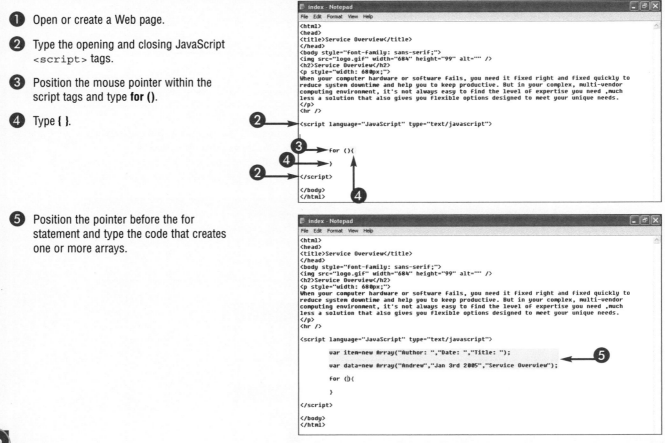

6 Position the pointer between the parentheses and type the argument of the for loop.

7 Position the pointer between the curly brackets and type the code to be executed.

8 Save the Web page.

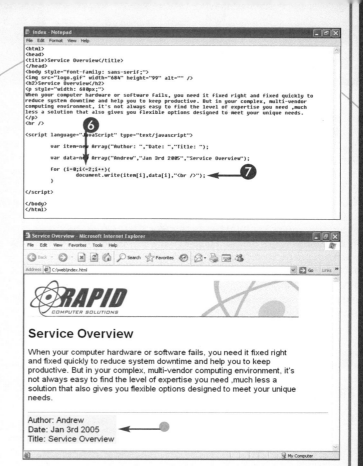

9 Open the Web page in a Web browser.

● The text generated by the for loop appears.

Extra

When the code to be processed within a `for` loop consists of only one line, you do not need to enclose the code that will be executed within curly brackets. You can simply add that code onto the end of the line containing the `for` statement. Using this technique can save you time and typing and also has the added benefit of making your code cleaner and more professional to read through, which can make it much easier to maintain your code later.

Example
```
for (i=1;i<=13;i++)
document.write("Item:" + i + "<hr
/>");
```

While it is common to see JavaScript code that increments by one, the code that increments the counter each time the loop runs does not have to increment by only one. You can also code your script to increase the counter by a number other than 1. For example, you might want code that increments by multiples of two, five, or ten, depending on what you want the script to do. The following code displays all the even numbers from 1 to 10.

Example
```
for (i=2;i<=10;i=i+2)
document.write( i + "<br />");
```

Use Event Handlers

U se event handlers to add enhancements such as menu rollovers and dynamic text messages to your Web pages. An event is a specific action that takes place with elements on your Web page, as when a mouse pointer is positioned over a certain image, or when the user presses the mouse button while the mouse pointer is positioned over an element. An event handler is the code that executes (or "handles") the event. For example, adding the onmouseover attribute to an element's tag can trigger the processing of JavaScript code when the mouse is hovered over the element. The value of the onmouseover attribute is the JavaScript code that will be executed.

Various types of events can trigger JavaScript scripts. These events can be categorized into two major categories: window events and user events. Window events include such events as a page opening or closing, focusing

changing from one part of the page to another, or a certain amount of time elapsing. User events include events triggered by a user moving the mouse over or away from certain elements or interacting with their keyboard.

You can use any valid JavaScript code with an event handler. For example, JavaScript can be used to display text messages in the status bar located at the bottom of the Web browser window. Displaying messages in the status bar is useful not only for providing information to your users, but also to help you display messages while you are developing your JavaScript code to assist you in stepping through (executing your code line by line) and debugging your code. To display text messages in the status bar, assign a value to the window.status property. For example, the code window.status='Hello' displays the text message Hello in the status bar of the Web browser.

Use Event Handlers

① Open or create a Web page.

② Position the pointer in an element tag and type **onmouseover=""**.

③ Position the pointer between the quotes and type **window.status=" ;**.

④ Position the pointer between the quotes and type the text to appear in the status bar.

⑤ Save the Web page.

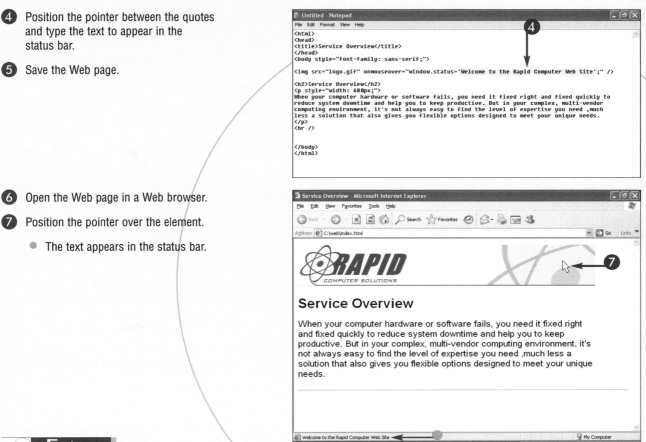

⑥ Open the Web page in a Web browser.

⑦ Position the pointer over the element.

● The text appears in the status bar.

You can assign JavaScript code to many events on a Web page. The following table describes the most commonly used events.

EVENT NAME	WHEN USED
onMouseDown	When the button on the mouse has been pressed but not released.
onMouseUp	When the button on the mouse has been released.
onMouseOver	When the mouse pointer is positioned over an element.
onMouseMove	When a button on a mouse has been moved while hovering over an element.
onMouseOut	When the mouse pointer is positioned off an element.
onClick	When the mouse pointer is positioned over an element and the primary mouse button is clicked.
onLoad	When the Web page is fully loaded in the Web browser.
onUnload	When the user views another Web page.

EVENT NAME	WHEN USED
onDblClick	When the user double-clicks an element.
onKeyDown	When the user presses a key while an element is selected.
onKeyPress	When a key is pressed and released.
onKeyUp	When a key is released.
onFocus	When an element receives focus, for example, from being clicked in or tabbed to.
onBlur	When an element loses focus, for example, from being clicked or tabbed.
onSubmit	When a form is submitted.
onReset	When a form is reset.
onSelect	When a user selects text in a text field.

Generate Dynamic Content

You can add information to your Web page that changes automatically over time. Information on your Web page that changes depending on the time or because an event takes place is called *dynamic content*. Dynamic content keeps your Web page looking current and up-to-date.

Users may see different information each time they view your Web page depending on the dynamic content being generated. Dynamic content can be as simple as a clock stating the current time or a thermometer displaying the current temperature in a given location. On the other hand, it could be as complex as an auction site that automatically displays auctions that a user is hosting and/or following, as well as the status, current top bids, and current top bidders of each auction.

You can quickly and easily add dynamic content to your Web page by including the current date and time, which is automatically generated by the JavaScript function `Date()`. The `Date()` function generates the date and time in text format, which leaves you free to apply your own styles and formatting to the text.

The `document.write()` function can generate text from within the JavaScript code that is inserted into your Web page. When `Date()` is the argument of the `document.write()` function, the current date and time appears on your Web page. The date and time information generated by the `Date()` function is the date and time of the user's computer, not the Web server.

The JavaScript code used to generate the dynamic content should be enclosed within the `<script>` tags of your Web page code. Where you place the `<script>` tags determines where on the Web page the dynamic content will appear.

Generate Dynamic Content

1 Open or create a Web page.

2 Type the opening and closing JavaScript `<script>` tags.

3 Position the mouse pointer within the `<script>` tags and type any additional code required.

4 Position the pointer within the `<script>` tags and type **document.write();**.

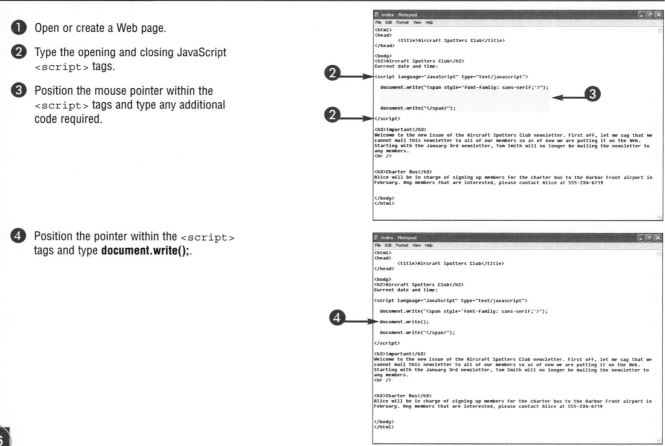

⑤ Position the pointer between the parentheses and type the code that generates the dynamic content.

⑥ Save the Web page.

```
index - Notepad
File  Edit  Format  View  Help
<html>
<head>
        <title>Aircraft Spotters Club</title>
</head>

<body>
<h2>Aircraft Spotters Club</h2>
Current date and time:

<script language="JavaScript" type="text/javascript">

  document.write("<span style='font-family: sans-serif;'>");

  document.write(Date());

  document.write("</span>");

</script>

<h3>Important</h3>
Welcome to the new issue of the Aircraft Spotters Club newsletter. First off, let me say that we
cannot mail this newsletter to all of our members so as of now we are putting it on the Web.
Starting with the January 3rd newsletter, Tom Smith will no longer be mailing the newsletter to
any members.
<hr />

<h3>Charter Bus</h3>
Alice will be in charge of signing up members for the charter bus to the Harbor Front airport in
February. Any members that are interested, please contact Alice at 555-234-6719


</body>
</html>
```

⑦ Open the Web page in a Web browser.

● The dynamic content appears on the Web page.

Aircraft Spotters Club - Microsoft Internet Explorer

Address C:\web\index.html

Aircraft Spotters Club

Current date and time: Wed Jan 05 08:47:42 2005 ◄

Important

Welcome to the new issue of the Aircraft Spotters Club newsletter. First off, let me say that we cannot mail this newsletter to all of our members so as of now we are putting it on the Web. Starting with the January 3rd newsletter, Tom Smith will no longer be mailing the newsletter to any members.

Charter Bus

Alice will be in charge of signing up members for the charter bus to the Harbor Front airport in February. Any members that are interested, please contact Alice at 555-234-6719

Done   My Computer

Apply It

Use the `document.lastModified` property to dynamically generate the date and time that the Web page was last changed.

TYPE THIS

```
<script language="JavaScript">
document.write("This page was updated
on ");
document.write(document.lastModified);
</script>
```

RESULT

This page was updated on 1/12/2005 18:10:20

In addition to being able to create your own scripts for dynamic content, you can find thousands of scripts that are available to you free on the Web. Certainly you would not want to spend time "inventing" a script that you could just copy and paste from a Web page into your code. Even if you do want to build your own code, you can benefit from looking at code others have built. Try searching at your favorite search engine for "free JavaScript scripts" to find some free scripts to use.

Display a Message

Y ou can display a pop-up box that contains important information for users to read. A pop-up message is accompanied by a button. The user must click the button to discard the message. This forces users to stop what they are doing and read the message before continuing. For example, you could include a script in your page that would trigger when a user clicks a link that would take them away from your page. A box could pop up and alert the user to the fact that they are about to leave your page.

The onclick event handler can be used to display the message box when a user clicks on a Web page element. As with all event handlers, the code that will be executed will be the value of the event handler attribute, in this case onclick.

Use the JavaScript function alert() to display a message box with a button that must be clicked before the message

disappears. The argument for the alert() function is the text that you want the message box to display. Enclose the text of the message within single quotes. You can also use other JavaScript functions to create the message that will appear in the box. For example, the JavaScript function Date() generates the current date and time, which can then be displayed within the message box.

Each user's Web browser and operating system will determine the appearance of the message box. Most Web browsers generate a message box that contains a button labeled "OK." The button must be clicked before the user can continue viewing your Web page. The message box will also typically display a message or an informational type of icon or graphic.

Display a Message

① Open or create a Web page.

② Position the pointer in an element tag and type **onclick=""**.

③ Position the pointer between the quotes and type **alert();**.

248

④ Position the pointer between the parentheses and type the code that will appear on the message box.

⑤ Save the Web page.

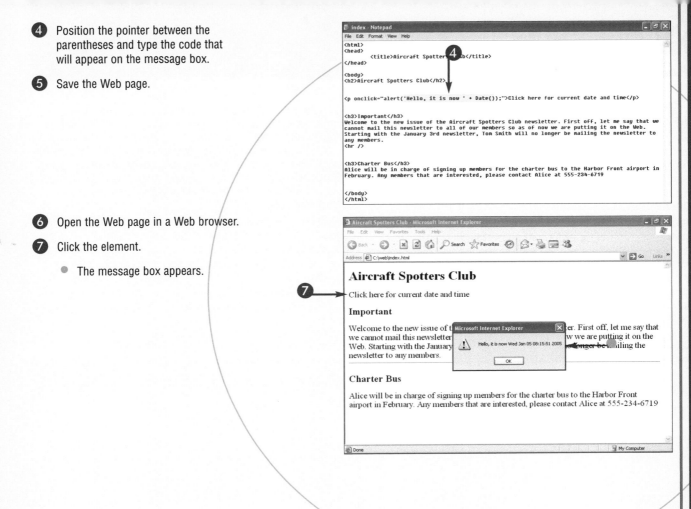

⑥ Open the Web page in a Web browser.

⑦ Click the element.

● The message box appears.

Extra

Use message boxes sparingly throughout your Web site. Message boxes require the user to stop reading the Web page and physically click the message box, so too many message boxes can be distracting and annoying. The earlier example in which a box alerts the user that they are about to leave your page is a good example: many users would be seriously annoyed by this tactic. There is a trade-off between what you want and what will exasperate your user. Keep this in mind and decide what is most important to you.

You do not have to wait for your user to interact with your page before using a pop-up JavaScript box. Use the onload event handler within the <body> tag to display a message box as soon as the browser loads your Web page. Again, keep in mind the trade-off between what you want and how annoyed your user will be. The following example code will load a welcome box as soon as the Web page loads.

Example
```
<body onload="alert('Welcome to my Web
page');">
```

Create a Pop-Up Window

Y

ou can create windows that open if a user performs a certain task, such as clicking on an image. This allows you to present additional information about items on your Web page without requiring the user to open an entirely new page. This process is similar to that in the last section, but in that case the pop-up was merely a message with a single button, in this case the window can be more versatile.

The `window.open` function, which creates a pop-up window, takes three parameters as its argument. The first parameter is the name of the image or Web page that will be displayed in the pop-up window. The second parameter is the name of the pop-up window. This is an arbitrary name to identify your pop-up window to the JavaScript code, and will not be displayed to the user. The last parameter contains the size specifications of the window. You can specify the size of the

window in pixels by assigning `height` and `width` values. All three parameters of the `window.open` function must be enclosed with quotes. Make sure that the size of the window you specify can adequately display the content of the pop-up window. Pop-up windows are typically used to present small amounts of information. If you must display a large amount of data, you may be better off placing the content on a separate Web page.

Some older Web browsers may have difficulty interpreting the JavaScript code that creates the pop-up window. You can prefix the word `JavaScript` and a `:` to the beginning of your code to specifically identify the code that follows as JavaScript.

Users can close the pop-up window by clicking the Close icon, located in the top right-hand corner of the window frame.

Create a Pop-Up Window

1 Open or create a Web page.

2 Position the pointer in an element tag and type **onmouseover="javascript:window. open(,,);"**.

```
index - Notepad
File Edit Format View Help
<html>
<head>
<title>Paintings for Auction</title>
</head>

<body>
<h3>Paintings for Auction</h3>
We have a fine selection of oil on canvas nature themed painting up for aution this month. Select
a title to preview the painting.

<hr />
<div onmouseover="javascript:window.open(,,);">
   Jaguar
</div>


</body>
</html>
```

3 Position the pointer after the first parenthesis and type the name of an image or Web page, enclosed within single quotes.

4 Position the pointer between the commas and type **"**.

```
index - Notepad
File Edit Format View Help
<html>
<head>
<title>Paintings for Auction</title>
</head>

<body>
<h3>Paintings for Auction</h3>
We have a fine selection of oil on canvas nature themed painting up for aution this month. Select
a title to preview the painting.

<hr />
<div onmouseover="javascript:window.open('bigcat.jpg','',);">
   Jaguar
</div>


</body>
</html>
```

5 Position the pointer between the quotes and type the name of the pop-up window.

6 Position the pointer before the closing parenthesis and type the size specification of the pop-up window, enclosed within single quotes.

7 Repeat steps **2** to **6** for any other elements to which you want to assign pop-up windows.

8 Save the Web page.

9 Open the Web page in a Web browser.

10 Position the pointer over the element.

● The pop-up window appears.

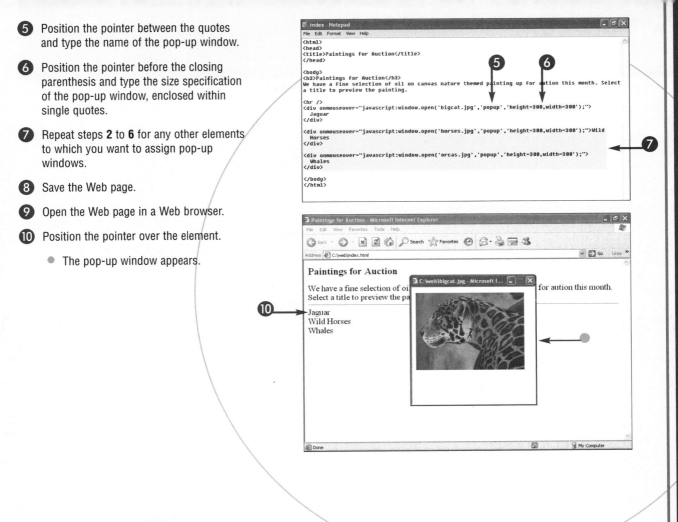

Apply It

Add the Web browser toolbar to your pop-up window by adding the word `toolbar` to the last parameter of the `window.open` function. This will give the user access to the standard features that are available to them on the toolbar, such as the Back, Forward, Reload, and Stop buttons.

Example
```
<p onClick=" window.open
('information.html', 'message',
'toolbar,width=150,height=100')">
click here for more information
</p>
```

Add vertical and horizontal scroll bars to your pop-up window by including `scrollbars=yes` in the last parameter of the `window.open` function. These scroll bars will allow the user to scroll back and forth and up and down on the new window in case the content of the page is larger than the window that pops up.

Example
```
<p onClick=" window.open
('information.html', 'message',
'scrollbars=yes,width=150,height
=100')">
Click here for more information
</p>
```

Create an XML Declaration

You can create your own XML documents and view them in a Web browser. XML documents are used to store data. XML documents typically describe data and information, and XHTML and Cascading Style Sheets function to present the information stored in the XML document. As an example of how you could use XML data, you could store names and addresses in an XML database and then view that data through a Web browser, or you could create an XHTML page that uses the name and address data to allow you to view that information in address book or spreadsheet-style format through a Web browser.

You can easily create an XML document with a simple text editor. Specifying a file extension of .xml enables a Web browser to recognize the document as XML and not a Web page.

The first step in creating an XML document is to write an XML declaration. Every XML document must include an XML declaration as the first line of the document. The XML declaration, contained within `<?xml` and `?>`, is the first line of code in an XML document. The XML declaration consists of two parts: the *version declaration* and the *encoding declaration*. The version declaration tells the program processing the XML document what version of XML to use. The current version of XML is `1.0`. The encoding declaration helps the processing application determine what language was used to create the XML document. `utf-8` is the value of the encoding declaration for English language documents.

Create an XML Declaration

① Open a text editor program.

② Type **<?xml?>**.

③ Type **version="1.0"**.

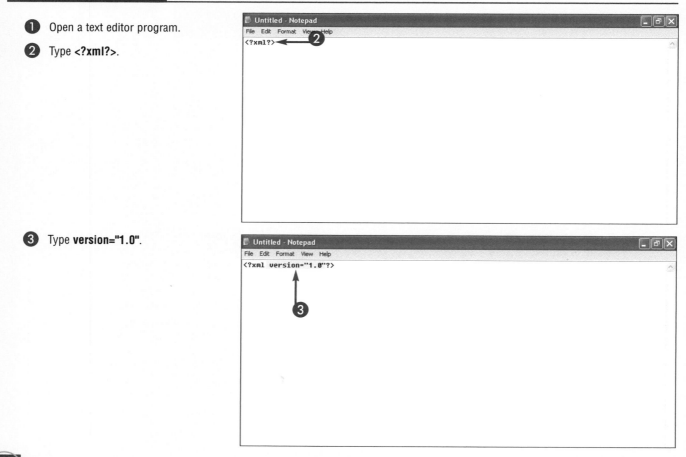

4️⃣ Type **encoding="UTF-8"**.

5️⃣ Click File.

6️⃣ Click Save.

7️⃣ In the Save As dialog box, type the name of the XML file and the extension .xml.

8️⃣ Click Save.

The XML file is saved.

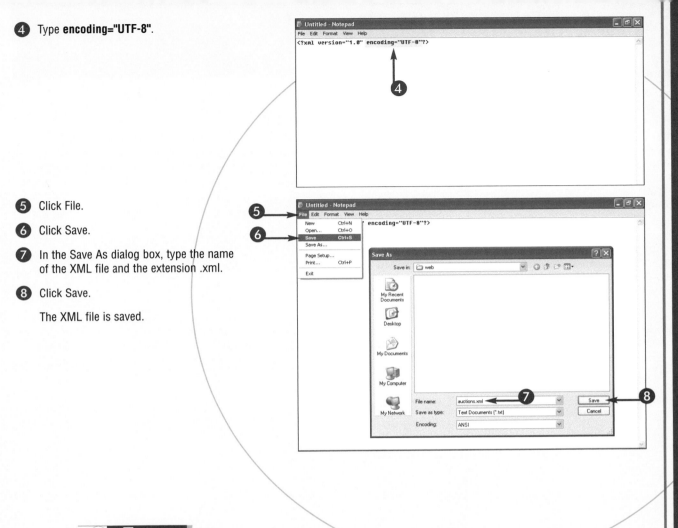

Extra

Although you can create simple XML documents using a text editor, using a text editor to create more complex documents is not recommended: text editors force you to type everything in manually, which is not easy and can be a very error-prone process. Dedicated XML applications are available if you need to write more complex XML documents and can simplify your life with features such as error-checking and the ability to write some of your code for you. You can download a free trial of XMLSpy, an XML editor, from the World Wide Web at www.xmlspy.com.

Unlike elements within an XHTML document, the XML declaration is not a tag and therefore does not require a closing tag. Furthermore, the XML declaration technically is not considered part of the XML document. Remember the distinction between XML and XHTML so that you do not get confused: XML is a markup language akin to HTML, whereas XHTML is HTML rewritten in XML-compliant code. The two languages are similar, but not identical, and so it makes sense that the declaration statements in XHTML and XML do not follow the same rules.

Add XML Elements

Y ou can create XML documents where you can store text data of any kind. You store data within an XML document by inserting the data into an element. Elements are similar to tags in XHTML or HTML documents. The < and > symbols delimit an element name, as in `<data>`. Knowing this you might be able to see how XHTML and XML are related in this way: both languages define elements by opening and closing tags.

When creating your own XML documents, you can decide what name to assign to each element. That is part of the beauty of XML. You can create entire languages (just as XHTML was created) using elements that make sense to you. The name that you choose for an element depends on the type of data stored in the XML document. For example, you can name an element `<price>`, `<cost>`, or `<amount>`

to store information about the current retail price of an inventory item.

All XML documents should have a *root* element. A root element encloses all the other elements in an XML document with start and end tags. In that respect, the root element is very similar to the `<HTML>` tag found in XHTML documents.

Use individual elements to store information, other elements, or in some cases a combination of the two. Part of the benefit of XML is that you can create your own ways of storing and using data: it is all up to you to define.

After creating an XML document that contains information, you can view the XML document with a number of different Web browsers. The data should appear in pretty much the same format regardless of which Web browser you choose to view it in.

Add XML Elements

① Type the XML declaration.

② Type the opening and closing tags of the root element.

③ Type the opening and closing tags of the elements.

④ Type the textual content of the elements.

⑤ Type the opening and closing tags of any sub elements.

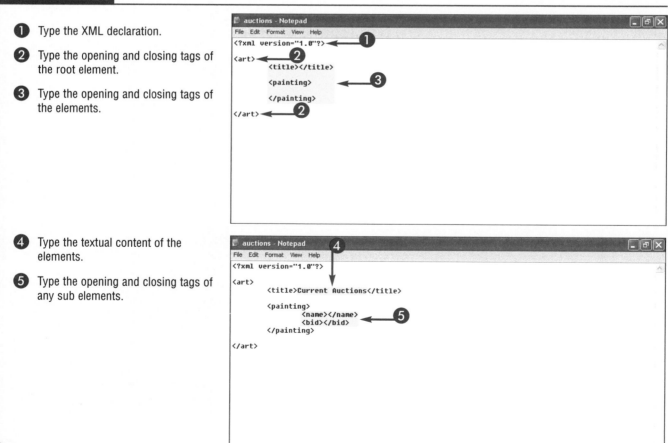

6 Type the textual content of any remaining elements.

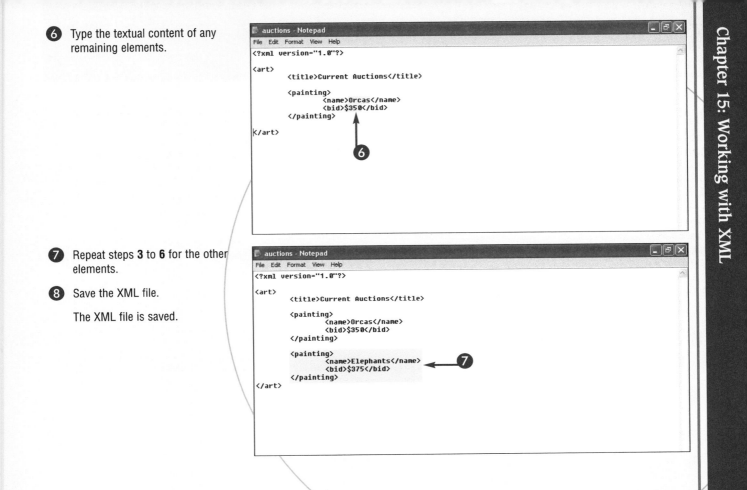

7 Repeat steps **3** to **6** for the other elements.

8 Save the XML file.

The XML file is saved.

Extra

Many of the rules that you learned in dealing with HTML and XHTML also apply to XML, and you can use this knowledge to your benefit when creating XML documents. For example, just as has been done with XHTML tags, you can save yourself typing by combining the start and end tags of an element that do not currently hold any data into one single tag that contains the forward slash character.

Example

```
<title></title>
```

can be written as

```
<title />
```

When creating names for elements, you should use names that accurately describe the content of the element. For example, if you wanted to store gender information on people, you would do well to create a `<gender>` element for this purpose. Element names can contain letters, numbers, and punctuation characters, although element names must not start with punctuation characters. Element names can also contain spaces, but it is more common to use the underscore character instead of the space, as in `<birth_month>`, to avoid confusion on the part of people who look at your code later.

Verify an XML Document

You can make your life easier if you create your XML documents with proper syntax and with proper formatting. XML documents must adhere to certain rules to ensure that the applications that process the documents can do so properly. XML documents that have been properly created are referred to as *well-formed* documents. You should always check the XML documents you create to make sure that they are well formed to not only ensure that they work as you intend them to but also to make life easier for you or someone else if they have to look through the code at some future point.

Web browsers typically display an error message or outright refuse to load the page at all when attempting to load an XML document that is not well formed.

You can use an XML application like XMLSpy to check whether your XML documents are well formed. You can download a free trial of XMLSpy at www.xmlspy.com.

The most common errors in an XML document include simple typing errors, or forgetting to give each element a start and end tag. Applications that check your XML documents usually indicate the location and type of error if the document is not well formed.

You should also make sure that you use comments when necessary in your file and that those comments are well formed. As mentioned in Chapter 2, comments can be used to explain your conventions to yourself (should you forget later) or others who have to maintain your code at some point after you publish your site. Comments fall outside of page elements, except in very specific locations that they are allowed within the declaration, start with `<!–`, and end with `–>`. Comments cannot contain double hyphens (`--`) within them.

Verify an XML Document

① Open the XML editor.

Note: In this example we use XMLSpy, available at www.xmlspy.com.

② Type the XML declaration.

③ Type the remaining content of the XML file.

④ Click the button that checks whether the file is well formed.

● An icon appears indicating that the XML file is well formed.

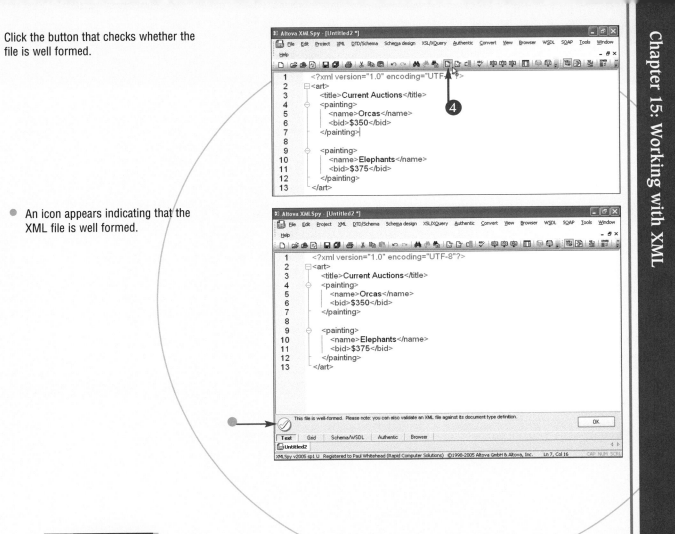

Extra

Just as in XHTML and unlike HTML, element names and values in XML documents are case-sensitive. Using a `<LIST>` starting tag with a `</List>` closing tag will cause an error when your XML document is evaluated. You would do well to simply lowercase all of your element names, as mandated in XHTML, although you always have the freedom to use uppercase element names should you need to. For example, you could create an element named `<frontpage>` to define your Web site's front page contents and later add a `<FrontPage>` element for content created with Microsoft's FrontPage.

Use attributes to provide additional information about the contents of an element. You can place attributes within the opening tag of an element and assign values in the same manner as you would with XHTML tags. In this way, you can better describe the various elements that you create for your XML document.

Example
```
<painting artist="helene">
    <name>Orcas</name>
    <bid open_bid="200">$350</bid>
</painting>
```

View an XML Document

You can use a Web browser to view the structure of any XML document that you create. In some cases, you can even view the information stored within the XML document.

The type of Web browser you use largely determines the appearance of the XML documents. Some Web browsers display your XML document character for character. Other Web browsers may only display an outline of your XML document, showing the elements and data contained within the document. Then still other Web browsers may simply display the information within the XML document without applying any formatting.

Save all XML documents with the file extension xml so that the Web browser correctly interprets the data within the document. If your Web browser does not automatically display XML documents, refer to the documentation for your Web browser or operating system for information on how to associate XML documents with your Web browser.

To view the formatted information of an XML document in most Web browsers, you can apply a style sheet to the XML document that will instruct the Web browser how to display the document correctly. For more information about applying Cascading Style Sheets to XML documents, see the "Apply a Style Sheet" section in this chapter.

Although viewing XML documents in a Web browser is useful while developing and learning how to create XML documents, most XML documents will ultimately be processed by applications such as spreadsheets, databases, or programs running on Web servers. Therefore, you will not know how well your XML documents really work until you use them with the application of your choice. If you find that the document opens just fine in a browser but crashes the application you intended it to work with, you will have to verify your document and use trial and error to ferret out the problems.

View an XML Document

① Open or create an XML document in a text editor.

② Save the XML document with a .xml extension.

③ Open the XML document in a Web browser.

Note: In this example, we open the XML document in Internet Explorer.

● The XML code is displayed.

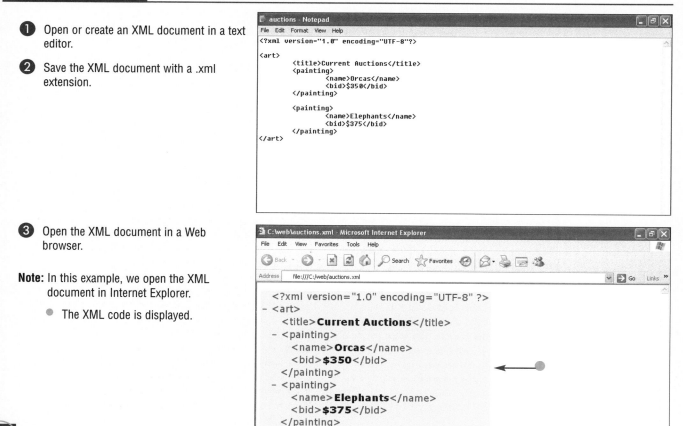

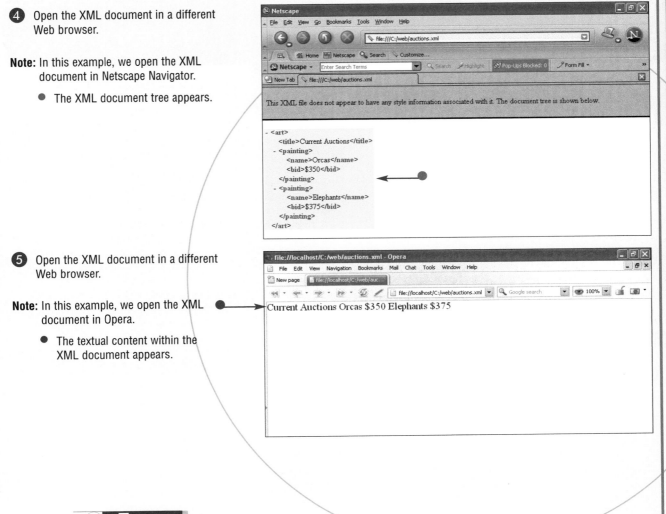

④ Open the XML document in a different Web browser.

Note: In this example, we open the XML document in Netscape Navigator.

● The XML document tree appears.

⑤ Open the XML document in a different Web browser.

Note: In this example, we open the XML document in Opera.

● The textual content within the XML document appears.

Extra

Although it is not an end-all check on your document's validity, you can quickly verify whether your XML document is well formed by opening the document in a Web browser. Most Web browsers will display an error message if your XML document is not well formed. If you do not get an error message and the document opens okay, you can assume that you at least got the basic structure of the document correct. To be sure your code is well formed, though, use an XML verifier such as XMLSpy (you can download a free trial from www.xmlspy.com).

Storing information in an XML document separates content from its formatting instructions. Although this may initially seem awkward, separating content and formatting information makes working with and maintaining the information easier. You can change the appearance of information without altering the content, and different people can work with the data without being concerned about how the changes may affect the appearance of the displayed information. Separating the content and formatting also enables a single set of information to be displayed in multiple ways, such as within a Web browser and a spreadsheet, without having to re-create the data.

Apply a Style Sheet

You can use Cascading Style Sheets to format the information in an XML document, thereby improving the appearance of that information in a Web browser. The same style sheet rules that apply to elements within an XHTML page also apply to elements of an XML document. For example, if your document includes information about retail items you have for sale such as jewelry, you might have subtypes under a `<jewelry>` tag such as `<costume>`, `<silver>`, and `<gold>`. You might then choose to highlight higher-price items in more visible colors, and so you could choose to highlight gold items in bold red text, and so on.

The XML document must include a processing instruction to indicate that a style sheet should be used when displaying the information. The processing instruction for an XML document is not all that different from one created for an XHTML document. A good example of a basic XML style sheet processing instruction is:

```
<?xml-stylesheet type="text/css"
href="css/xml-stylesheet_all.css"
media="all"?>
```

As you can see, the processing instruction also indicates the name of the external style sheet that the Web browser should use to display the XML document, in this case `css/xml-stylesheet_all.css`. The `href` attribute of the processing instruction specifies the name of the external style sheet. External style sheets typically end with the .css file name extension. Place the processing instruction immediately after the XML declaration on the second line of the XML document.

When creating the XML style sheet, use the element names from the XML document as the selector names for the style sheet rules. Any rules that are defined for a selector will then apply to the content of the XML element when the Web browser displays the document.

Apply a Style Sheet

① Open or create an XML document.

② Type **<?xml-stylesheet href=""?>**.

③ Type the name of an external style sheet.

④ Type **type="text/css"**.

⑤ Save the XML document.

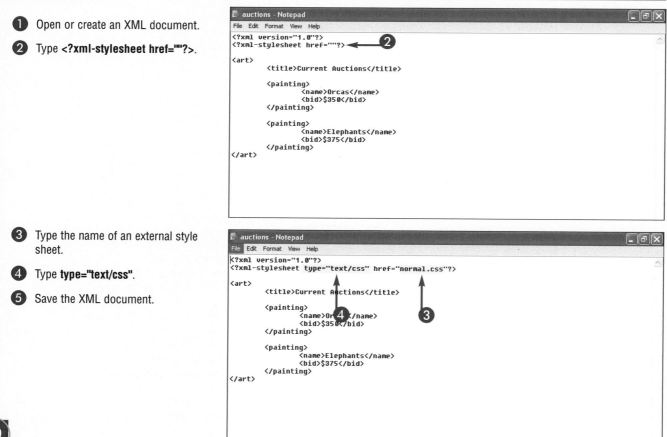

⑥ Open or create an external style sheet that creates rules for the XML document tags.

⑦ Save the style sheet with the file name specified in step **3**.

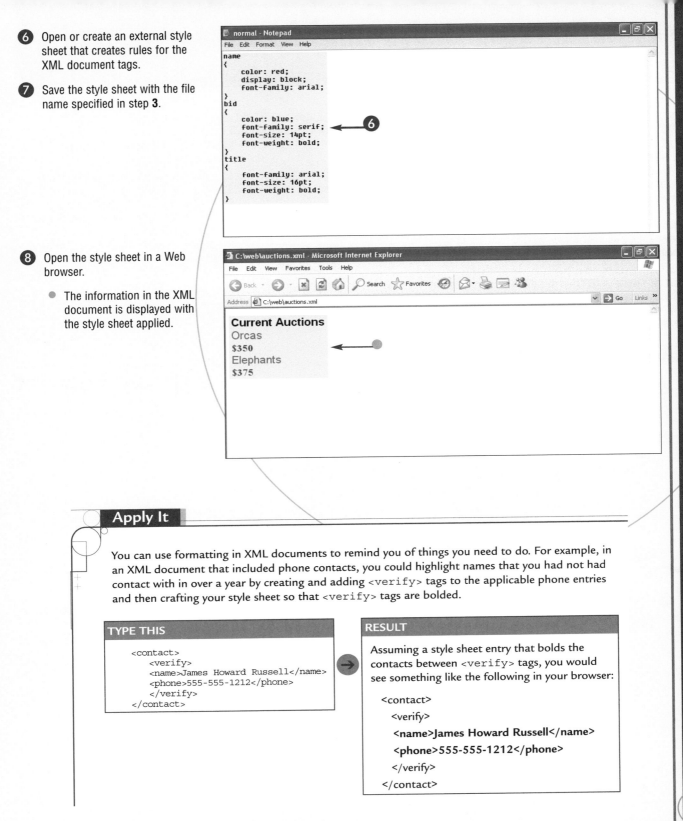

⑧ Open the style sheet in a Web browser.

● The information in the XML document is displayed with the style sheet applied.

Apply It

You can use formatting in XML documents to remind you of things you need to do. For example, in an XML document that included phone contacts, you could highlight names that you had not had contact with in over a year by creating and adding `<verify>` tags to the applicable phone entries and then crafting your style sheet so that `<verify>` tags are bolded.

TYPE THIS

```
<contact>
   <verify>
   <name>James Howard Russell</name>
   <phone>555-555-1212</phone>
   </verify>
</contact>
```

RESULT

Assuming a style sheet entry that bolds the contacts between `<verify>` tags, you would see something like the following in your browser:

```
<contact>
  <verify>
  <name>James Howard Russell</name>
  <phone>555-555-1212</phone>
  </verify>
</contact>
```

Create and Validate Document Type Definitions

You can create document type definitions (DTDs) that specify the makeup of the elements within your XML documents. A DTD gives you unlimited freedom to create your own XML "language" in a way. That is, you can use DTDs to define XML elements as well as dictate what those elements should contain and at the same time how they behave. A DTD thereby ensures that any changes made to your XML documents do not inadvertently add unintended data to the document. You can create as many DTDs as you have need for different types of documents — this is why XML is called "extensible": you can extend it to suit whatever your needs require.

You can insert a DTD into an XML document by using the <!DOCTYPE> tag. This tag contains the name of the root element followed by a set of square brackets that contain the DTD rules. The root element is the first element in an

XML document and surrounds all other elements in the document. In XHTML, the <body> element is similar in concept to a root element; everything within the <body> tags is part of the body of the page.

The <!ELEMENT> tag creates an element declaration that contains rules for individual elements. The declaration specifies the name of the element for which the rule is being defined, along with the type of contents that the element will store. The element declaration specifies the name of any other elements that an element may contain. If an element will contain textual data, the keyword #PCDATA indicates that the information stored in the element is text.

Each element in an XML document must have its own element declaration in the DTD or the document will not be valid.

Create and Validate Document Type Definitions

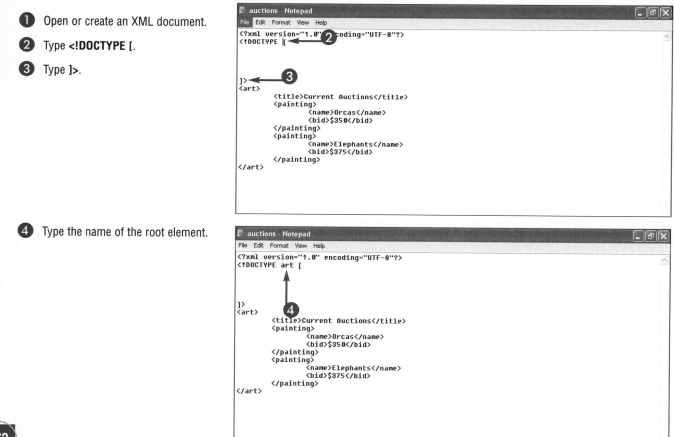

① Open or create an XML document.

② Type **<!DOCTYPE [**.

③ Type **]>**.

④ Type the name of the root element.

⑤ Type **<!ELEMENT**.

⑥ Type the name of the element.

⑦ Type **()>**.

⑧ Type the name of the tags between the parentheses you typed in step **7**.

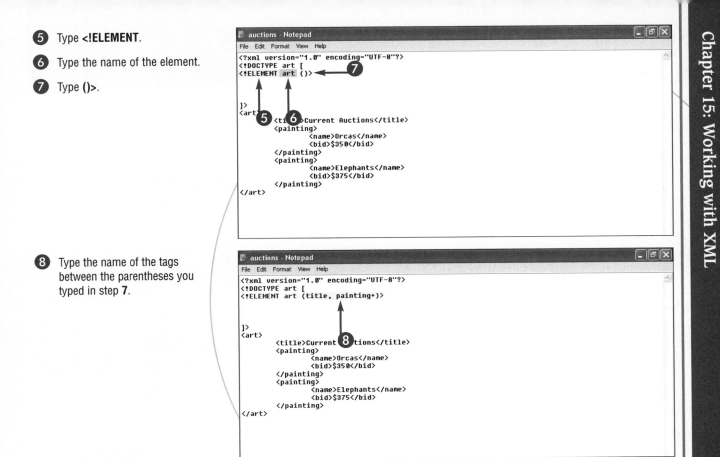

continued ➝

Extra

The beauty of DTDs is that they can change as the needs of your documents change. For example, say that you run a business and your XML document contains contact information for your employees. One day you decide that your employees need to be more easily accessible to you and mandate that your employees have beepers. If the DTD for your document specifies contact elements as containing phone, address, and/or e-mail contacts, changing your DTD to accommodate the beeper numbers is as simple as adding "beeper" to the list of elements that the contact element may contain.

The following table defines symbols that you can use within your element declarations.

SYMBOL	PURPOSE
*	Indicates that no elements exist or that multiple elements may exist.
,	Indicates in which order the elements will appear.
+	Mandates that at least one element exists.
|	Indicates one of a list of elements.

You can add symbols to the element declarations to further refine the element rules. For example, the | symbol allows an element to contain one out of a series of possible elements. The following element declaration defines an element called `bid` that contains another element called either `open`, `current`, or `closed`.

Example
```
<!ELEMENT bid (open | current | closed)>
```

You must validate any document type definitions that you create. Validation consists of comparing the rules in the DTD to the XML document to ensure that all the elements and information within the XML document conform to the rules outlined within the DTD. For example, if an element called "metals" was defined to potentially include gold, silver, copper, or bronze, and the validator discovered a `<metal>` element contained a `<flour>` subelement, the validation of the document would fail because the DTD had not specified `<flour>` as being a metal. Alternatively, if an element was stated in the DTD to contain PC data and instead contained an element, the document would again fail validation.

The easiest way to validate a DTD against an XML document is to use a specialized application designed to validate XML documents. This type of application will usually indicate if the document is valid. If the document is invalid, the application indicates the cause of the problem, such as an error in the DTD or in the XML document itself. To get a feel for what XML validation programs you can find, try searching for "XML validators" with your favorite search engine and see what results you get.

Well-formed XML documents that adhere to the rules as outlined in a DTD will be processed successfully by applications or services, such as Web cataloging utilities, which may access your XML documents.

Create and Validate Document Type Definitions *(continued)*

⑨ Repeat steps **5** to **8** for any other element that contains other elements.

⑩ Type **<!ELEMENT >**.

⑪ Type the name of an element that contains textual data followed by a set of parentheses **( )**.

⑫ Type **#PCDATA** within the set of parentheses.

⑬ Repeat steps **10** to **12** for each element that contains textual data.

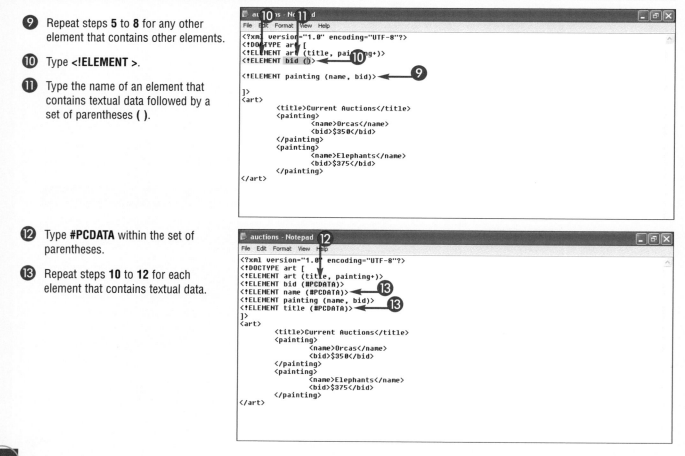

14 Open the document in, or copy the XML code to, an application that can validate XML code.

Note: In this example we use XMLSpy, available at www.xmlspy.com.

15 Click the button that validates the XML document.

● A message appears indicating that the XML document and DTD are valid.

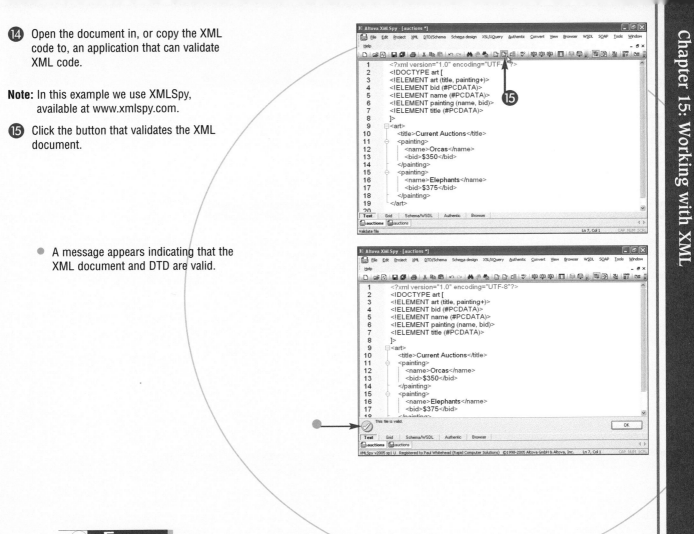

Extra

The World Wide Web Consortium (or W3C) offers a free validator for XML and other types of files at http://validator.w3.org. To validate an XML file on your hard drive, simply surf to the site and scroll down to where you see the Validate By File Upload heading. Next, click the Browse button and use the File Upload window to browse to and select your file, and then click Open. On the Web page, click the Check button. The site checks your XML file and tells you whether it is a valid XML file.

XML validation applications allow you to quickly and easily validate your XML documents. You might want to invest in an XML validation application that includes some bells and whistles beyond what you can get from free online validators such as the free validator provided by the W3C. Many XML validation applications are available over the Internet, and some online validation services even allow you to validate your XML documents over the Internet. XMLSpy is an application that contains an XML validation feature. You can download a free trial of XMLSpy at www.xmlspy.com.

Watch for Common HTML Mistakes

There are a number of common mistakes that you should look for when creating Web pages using HTML. Doing so takes some effort, but after you have done it a few times, it will start to become second nature to you. The time involved is also well worth the effort in that it helps you avoid major headaches down the road.

Inappropriate Title

You specify the title of your Web page within the `<title>` tag located in the head section of your Web page. The title identifies a Web page when a user adds the Web page to his or her bookmarks. Always specify a title for your Web page, and use a title that best describes your Web page. Using a more descriptive title for the home page will help users locate that page within their bookmarks. For example, do not use the title "Our Home Page" for the first page of a Web site for a local sports club. Use something more descriptive such as "Hometown's Web Site." Descriptive titles for Web pages are also useful if an Internet search tool will eventually catalog the pages.

Missing <meta> Tags

Search engines use `<meta>` tags, and the descriptive keywords within them, to catalog your site in search listings. If your Web page does not have `<meta>` tags, it may appear invisible to major search engines. If you want people to find your site through major search engines such as Google, Yahoo!, and Netscape Search, make sure your `<meta>` tags include keywords that are properly descriptive of your site.

Missing End Tags

One of the easiest mistakes to make when creating Web pages with HTML is forgetting to add the correct closing tags. As mentioned in Chapter 1, HTML is more forgiving than XHTML. If you forget some closing tags, your site may still look fine in your Web browser. However, just because the site looks good in your browser does not mean it will look good in all browsers. It is a good idea to review your HTML and make sure all of your tags are closed properly so that your site does not break in less-forgiving Web browsers. The most common tags that people forget to close seem to be `<font>` and `<table>`. One technique that can help when checking for missing end tags is to use proper indentation and spacing when creating your Web page code. This not only helps you avoid omitting the closing tags, but it also makes your code easier to read.

Failing to Test Your Web Pages

When creating Web pages, you should always keep in mind the various types of Web browsers and computers on which users may be viewing your Web pages. When you have finished designing your Web pages, you should view them in three or four of the most popular Web browsers. Subtle differences in how you code your Web pages can make a big difference to how the Web page displays in the different Web browsers. Good browsers to test your page on include Internet Explorer 6, Firefox 1.*x*, and both Netscape 7.2 and Netscape Communicator 4.8. (There are huge differences between Netscape 7.*x* and 4.*x*, and unfortunately, some people still use 4.*x*.)

Not Viewing Your Pages over Different Connections

There are many connection speeds that people use to connect to the Internet. You should test your Web pages over a variety of different speeds if you intend your Web pages to be placed on the World Wide Web. Although high-speed connections are becoming more popular each year, many people still connect to the Internet using telephone lines and modems. The Web pages you create and develop may display perfectly and quickly when stored on your own computer, or when transferred over a high-speed Internet connection, but the pages may be unbearably slow for users who are connected to the Internet via a telephone modem.

Not Viewing Your Pages after They Are Uploaded

Always view your Web pages after uploading them to the Web server. Just because your Web pages look fine and are functioning on your own computer, do not assume that they will be fine when transferred to the Web server. Some Web providers have restrictions on the type of files and images that users can access on the Web server, and on how you name or organize your Web pages. Some of these types of restrictions you may be able to verify only by viewing your Web pages after uploading them to the Web server.

Forgetting to Spellcheck Your Web Pages

Always spell check your Web pages. Many HTML editors now include spell checkers that check the spelling of the text elements in your Web page as you create them. It is also easy to copy the text elements of your Web page into a word processor and spell check them there. Not only should you use these tools for spell checking, but when you're finished creating your Web pages, you should also consider printing the Web pages and checking them for spelling errors visually. Pay close attention to buttons and icons that contain text, as these elements will not be spell checked in any other manner. A simple spelling error on one of your Web pages can make your whole Web site appear unprofessional.

Using Obsolete Tags

Many HTML tags are now obsolete. Using obsolete HTML tags in your code may prevent your Web pages from displaying properly in current and future Web browsers. Obsolete HTML tags were generally only supported by a specific Web browser. For example, the `<blink>` tag was used only by Netscape Navigator when that browser was first introduced a number of years ago. Its purpose was to make text blink to draw the user's attention to important information. Although the `<blink>` tag may still work on some Web browsers, there is no guarantee it will work on a future version of the same browser. You should use only HTML tags included in the latest HTML or XHTML specifications.

Check for Common XHTML Mistakes

As the Internet continues to become increasingly a part of the world's economy, transitioning from HTML to the more professional, consistent XHTML only makes sense. XHTML rules — which may seem strict in comparison to HTML rules — help ensure consistency in Web page design across the Internet, making both designers' and users' lives easier. However, this transition is certainly not devoid of bumps in the road: mistakes made

when creating XHTML Web pages typically result from a Web developer who is very familiar with HTML forgetting the differences between XHTML and HTML. Although the process of creating Web pages with XHTML is susceptible to the same mistakes as creating Web pages with HTML, it is the transition from HTML to XHTML that causes most problems with XHTML pages.

Not Closing All Tags

Unlike HTML, XHTML requires that all tags have both the start and end tags. It was quite common in HTML to see tags such as the break tag (`<br>`), the horizontal rule tag (`<hr>`), and the list item tag (`<li>`) with only the starting tag and no closing tag. If an XHTML element is empty — that is, if no content is placed between the start and end tag — you can add a forward slash (/) to the start tag instead of using a separate closing tag. For example, the break tag can be written as `<br />`, and the horizontal rule tag can be written as `<hr />`.

Improper Tag Nesting

A tag placed within another tag is called a *nested* tag. XHTML has stricter rules than HTML for determining how these tags may be nested. The parent tag must fully enclose each nested tag. For example, in HTML you could use `<b><i>Welcome</b></i>` to bold and italicize text. In XHTML, either the bold or italicized tag must be completely enclosed by the other, as in `<b><i>Welcome</i></b>`. Notice how the two tags have been rearranged: the two italic tags are now both enclosed within the bold tags.

Using Uppercase Tag Names

Because XHTML documents adhere to the rules set out in XML, all XHTML code is case-sensitive. You can no longer use uppercase letters for tag names in XHTML. For example, both `<Table>` and `<TABLE>` are both incorrect when creating XHTML documents. This also applies to ending tags, so a paragraph of text with the starting tag `<p>` and the ending tag `</P>` is invalid. Many HTML editors enable you to set a preference that will create all tag names in lowercase.

Forgetting the Document Type Declaration

All XHTML documents should use the `<DOCTYPE>` declaration. The `<DOCTYPE>` declaration is not an element of the Web page, but should instead always be the first line of code. The `<DOCTYPE>` declaration informs any application that processes the Web page, such as a Web browser, that the Web page is an XHTML document. The application will then know how to properly process the XHTML Web page. Most true XHTML Web pages can use the following `<DOCTYPE>` declaration:

```
<!DOCTYPE html PUBLIC "-//W3C//DTD
XHTML 1.0 Strict//EN" "http://www.w3.
org/TR/xhtml1/DTD/xhtml1-strict.dtd">
```

Not Placing Quotes Around Attribute Values

In HTML, it was not uncommon to see attribute values assigned without quotes, as in `border=10`. In valid XHTML, all attribute values must be enclosed in quotation marks. For example, `height="45"` is valid; however, `height=45`, which is valid in HTML, is not valid in XHTML. If quotation marks are required within the value of an attribute, single quotes should be used, as in `alt="a reading from 'great speeches from the past' by John Smith"`. Note that, as with tag names, attribute names are also required to be in lowercase when using XHTML.

Not Assigning Attribute Values

One area where XHTML differs from HTML — and this mistake catches a lot of Web developers — is when specifying an attribute that does not have a value assigned to it. For example, in HTML the `noresize` attribute of the `<frame>` tag is simply placed within the tag, as in `<frame noresize>`. In XHTML, all attributes must have a value assigned to them, even if those attributes do not require a value. The value that you should assign to attributes that traditionally do not have values is the name of the attribute itself. For example, the `noresize` attribute should have a value of `noresize` assigned to it, as in `<frame noresize="noresize">`.

Not Validating Your Web Pages

You can never be sure that the code within your XHTML Web pages complies with the XHTML specification unless you validate the Web page code. Validating your Web pages is a quick and easy method of locating any errors in your documents. Validating Web pages not only helps you locate typographical errors, but it also detects any problems with the structure of your Web pages. Validating your Web pages is the only method of ensuring that your Web pages will be compatible with current and future Web browsers. The World Wide Web Consortium (or W3C for short) hosts a validator with which you can validate your pages at http://validator.w3.org.

Not Checking Your Links

Most Web pages contain links to other Web pages. If you have links to other pages on your Web page, you should consider using a tool such as the W3C's link checker to validate those links. The tool will let you know if any of the links on your page are broken, at which point you can choose to remove the link or find an updated link to replace it. The W3C hosts a link checker that you can use to check the links on your page at http://validator.w3.org/checklink/. The results you get from the validator can be fairly verbose, but sorting through them to ensure that your page's links are valid is well worth the effort.

Look at Common CSS Problems

Web designers used to HTML are likely to face a learning curve when transitioning to using CSS for formatting. Even designers that have experience with CSS can still make some common mistakes when using CSS.

Not Specifying a Background Color

Even though the default color of most Web browser backgrounds is white, many users can and do change the default background color of the Web browser. This can result in your page looking quite different than you had intended, and can even impair your site's functionality. This is particularly important if you use spacer images that are the same color as the background color in order to remain hidden. To avoid this potential pitfall, use style sheets to specify the background color for your Web page.

Using Incorrect Measurement Units

There are a wide range of style sheet properties that require you to specify the value of the measurement. When specifying the measurement of values for style sheet properties, you must specify the correct numeric value followed by an abbreviation that indicates the unit of measurement. For example, specifying a font size value of `14pt` indicates a size of 14 points. Most measurements of length for style sheet properties are specified in pixels. Forgetting to add the abbreviation `px` to indicate that the value is in pixels is a common error. For example, `width: 20` is incorrect, but `width: 20px` is correct.

Creating Conflicting Rules

One of the great benefits of style sheets is that you can apply multiple rules in different ways. For example, rules determining the overall size and color of a Web page can be placed in an external style sheet and applied to all the pages of a Web site. Individual Web pages can have their own colors and sizes specified within an internal style sheet (located within the head section of the Web page). Elements such as paragraphs can have local style sheet rules applied within the elements' tags. If you do not keep track of the style sheet rules that are applied to your Web pages, you may inadvertently create rules that conflict with each other. Local style sheets take precedence over inline or external style sheets, and inline style sheets take precedence over external style sheets. Therefore, if your Web page breaks a rule in your external or inline style sheet, chances are that a conflicting inline or local style sheet is counteracting it somewhere.

Using Too Many Local Styles

You should avoid using local style sheet rules whenever possible. If you use a lot of local style sheet rules and have to change the formatting instructions for your Web page at some point, you will have to locate and alter each local style sheet individually, which can be a very time-consuming process. Instead, you should apply all style sheet rules using either an external style sheet, which is saved as a separate file, or an internal style sheet located within the head section of the Web page. Although this may not be as fast or as convenient as using local style sheet rules, external and internal style sheets make maintaining your style sheet rules much easier, especially across complex or multiple Web pages.

Using Fixed Font Sizes

Style sheet rules enable you to specify precise sizes of fonts. For example, you can define a heading's font size as 18 points by specifying the value `18pt` for the `size` property. Unfortunately, not all users have the same type, style, and size of fonts installed on their computer. If you specify precise font sizes and the computer being used to view your Web page does not have those font sizes installed, the Web browser substitutes for the font you specified a font it thinks is most appropriate, which may result in your page displaying differently from how you intended. You should only specify the precise point size of fonts on a Web page when you are sure that all users will have the appropriate fonts installed on their computers, such as on a company intranet.

Using HTML Instead of CSS for Formatting

Style sheets were created to enable users to separate the content from the formatting information of a Web page, making it easier to change the information on a Web page without affecting the formatting, and vice versa. Changing and maintaining the appearance of your Web pages is easier when you use style sheets instead of HTML or XHTML to format the information.

Forgetting to Include Semicolons

When applying style sheet rules locally using the `style` attribute of an element tag, each style sheet rule must be separated by a semicolon, as in `Style="width: 20px ; height: 10px"`. Failure to separate style sheet properties from their values with a semicolon can result in the Web browser interpreting the style sheet rule incorrectly. In some cases, the Web browser will simply fail to implement the style sheet rule and, worse, may not indicate that an error has occurred.

Creating Conflicting Shorthand Notation

You can condense related style sheet properties into a single property to make specifying values for those properties easier. For example, you can use the `font` property to specify values for the `font-family`, `font-size`, `font-style`, `font-weight`, and `font-variant` properties. Although this reduces the amount of time required to create style sheets, it can cause problems if the shorthand notation is used as well as one or more of the style sheet properties represented by the shorthand notation property. When creating style sheets, you should decide whether or not to use shorthand notation and remain consistent with your choice. Locating and changing style sheet property values that conflict with shorthand notation can be a time-consuming and frustrating endeavor.

Not Inserting Comments

Most style sheet selectors are abbreviations such as `bhdr` for a bold header or `lhm` for left-hand margin. Although these abbreviations may make perfect sense to the person who created the style sheets, they are probably meaningless for others, and can even be confusing to the original creator who may eventually forget what the abbreviations stand for. Always use comments within your style sheets to explain style sheet rules that are not obvious. To insert a comment into a style sheet, simply enclose the comment within `/*` and `*/`. Including appropriate comments alongside style sheet rules as you create them can save you and others time spent troubleshooting the style sheets in the future.

Avoid Common Design Mistakes

Some design mistakes can be made regardless of the technology used to create the Web page. Avoiding these simple design mistakes will help give your Web pages a more professional look.

Using the Wrong Resolution and/or Color Depth

Unfortunately, many Web page designers create Web pages that look good only on their own monitors. Always take into account the different types of displays and video adapters that may be used to view your Web pages. In a perfect world, all users would own 19-inch flat panel monitors and 32-bit video adapters, but unfortunately, many users still do not have this ideal configuration. It is always a good idea to test your site at various resolutions, such as 640 x 480, 800 x 600, and 1024 x 768, as well as various color depths, such as 32-bit, 16-bit, and even lower. If your site looks good (or is at least functional) on all resolutions and color depths, then you can be sure most users will be able to properly see and use your site. If your site does not look good — or is not even functional — at lower resolutions and color depths, you should reevaluate your layout, images, or color choices (depending on the nature of the problem) accordingly.

Not Allowing Users to Skip Presentations

Many Web sites can now incorporate multimedia presentations such as Flash movies, video, and audio features. Web designers commonly utilize these types of media to introduce users to the main content of the Web site, particularly when users first visit the site. For example, a site for a movie could include a preview trailer of the film. Although the presentations themselves may be appealing and informative, users can get frustrated if they are forced to view a presentation that they do not wish to see, especially if the presentation delays them from getting to the main site and accessing the information they need. Whenever you create a presentation for your Web site, always give the user the choice to skip the presentation. If you do not, you may find that users simply give up and surf to another site.

Creating Too Many Pop-Up Windows

Pop-up windows are a great, easy way of displaying very important or timely information that the user may require. However, you would be wise not to use pop-up windows to display information that may otherwise be placed on the actual Web page. For example, do not use a pop-up window just to welcome visitors to your Web site — incorporate your welcome message into the home page. For many users, pop-up windows are a source of annoyance. Web browser manufacturers are now incorporating technology into their Web browsers that suppresses the display of pop-up messages. Firefox and Internet Explorer (with service pack 2 installed) include pop-up blocking by default, and Google, Yahoo!, and Netscape all offer add-on toolbars to Internet Explorer to enable pop-up blocking. So, if you want to avoid annoying your site's users and the risk that your pop-up windows may never appear, try avoiding the use of pop-up windows altogether.

Using "Under Construction" Messages

It is not uncommon to come across Web pages that simply display the message "Web page under construction" because the Web page has not yet been completed and/or uploaded to the Web server by the Web site's developer. Try not to use "Under Construction" messages on your Web site. It can be very frustrating for users to take the time and effort to load a Web page only to find out it contains no information. If there are Web pages on your Web site that have yet to be finalized, do not display them at all, and omit references to them from your Web site structure completely. Only when a Web page has been finalized should you add it — and links or references to it — to your Web site.

Not Properly Reading Your Web Page

Many Web developers create their own content for their Web pages. Unfortunately, because the developers created and thus are so familiar with the content for their Web page, they may tend to overlook their own simple grammar or spelling errors. Although tools such as spell checkers are important for reducing errors, you should always have others read your Web page content to locate errors. Not only should the Web pages be reviewed on a computer display, but also you may find it more effective to print the pages and review the content one line at a time on paper. For commercial Web sites, you should employ the services of a professional proofreader, as errors on commercial sites may adversely affect a user's image of the company and any services or products being sold or advertised on the Web site.

Adding a Date-Modified Message

Adding a text message to a Web page containing the date that the Web page was last modified is now quite easy to do. This information may potentially interest users who are viewing Web pages that contain information that may change over time, such as results of sporting events or local news. However, placing the last-modified date on a Web page that contains static information, such as the mission statement of a company or the home page of your Web site, is not useful. In addition to the last-modified date, you can also include information that is automatically generated, such as the current time and date, and information about the user, such as which Web browser he or she is using.

Check for
Image Problems

Images are an important part of many Web pages. They can make pages more interesting to look at, convey information in ways that are not practical using only text, and help give your Web page its own unique style.

However, images can also have adverse effects on pages if not used properly. Knowing how and when to use images is an important part of creating well-balanced and effective Web pages.

Not Providing Enough Contrast for Backgrounds

Incorporating an image into the background of a Web page is quite easy to do. The text displayed on a Web page is placed over this image. A common mistake in Web design is to use images for a background that have little or no contrast with the text on the Web page, making the text difficult or even impossible to read. The contrast between a background image and the text of a Web page may differ from display to display, so it is important when using background images that you view the page on a number of different displays to ensure that the text stays readable. When using images as backgrounds, you should always specify the color of the text on the Web page, and always specify a background color that does not contrast with the background image.

Not Including the Proper Images for Printing

Users can easily print Web pages directly from their Web browsers using a single mouse click. When a Web page is printed, all of the page's content, including the images, are sent to the printer. If you intend the Web page you are designing to be printed, make sure that any images on the Web page are of the appropriate resolution to appear legible when printed. The resolution of printers is much higher than the resolution of most displays. Images that have been created to look good on a monitor may not necessarily appear as intended when printed, so always test the legibility of the images by printing the Web page on a number of different printers.

Using Incorrect Images When Tiling

The background images of a Web page are automatically tiled when the size of the image is less than the size of the Web browser display window. (Tiling simply repeats the display of the image by placing copies of the image adjacent to each other until the image completely fills the Web browser display window.) For example, one large image is commonly used as a background for a Web page. Although lower resolutions display the image only once within the Web browser window, at higher resolutions the Web browser window may be so large that the background image tiles. A Web page containing improperly created images may appear to have lines running across or from the top to bottom of the display, which can look tacky and also make the contents of the Web page harder to read. This not only applies to small images, but to larger images as well. You should test any images you have designed for tiled backgrounds to ensure that the images display correctly.

Using Images to Format Text

A common mistake that many Web developers make is using images that are too large. Images give a designer more control over the appearance of the Web page (with effects such as text shadows and animation), but you should not necessarily substitute images for text. Although you can create buttons and icons that contain text information, using images to display text increases the time it takes for your Web page to load, especially over dial-up modem connections. It also means that text will not be seen by users that have images disabled in their browsers, or blind users who rely on audio readers to access the content of a Web page.

Using Too Many Animated Images

Many image-editing programs enable you to easily create basic animations. Animated images can draw attention to important information on your Web page, or may simply be used to add a novelty factor to the page. However, overuse of animated images can quickly make your Web page too distracting. Too much motion may cause users to skip over your Web page and move on. Because finding important information may require examining the complete Web page, you should use animated images sparingly, if at all. Although popular on less serious Web pages such as personal home pages, animated images are rarely seen on Web sites of professional organizations.

Not Using Height and Width Attributes

When a Web browser displays an image, it first loads the image, determines the size of the image, and then creates and displays the Web page. If the Web browser does not know the size of the images on the Web page, it may wait until all the images transfer from the Web server before displaying the page. If you specify the width and height of an image on a Web page, the Web browser can start displaying the Web page without having to wait to transfer the image from the Web server. Do not just specify the size of an image when changing the image size. Always specify the width and height of your images regardless of if you are changing the size of the image or not. This allows your users to view and read the text information on your Web page without having to wait for all the images on the Web page to load.

Search for Linking Problems

links are crucial parts of Web pages that link to other resources around the Internet. Given the vital importance of links, it is critical that you pay close attention to the quality and validity of your links when designing Web pages. Failing to do so can render your Web page confusing, annoying, or even totally useless. From

aesthetic concerns to more practical ones such as specifying alternate text for images for users who either cannot or have chosen not to view the images on your Web page, there are more than a few common pitfalls that you should avoid when creating Web pages.

Changing the Appearance of Links

You can use style sheets to apply multiple effects to link text. For example, you can easily change the color of link text to any color you want. Although changing the colors and appearance of text links may make your Web page more aesthetically pleasing, it may also confuse the user as to which text is a link and which is not. For example, by default, most Web browsers display link text with an underline. Because this has been the default

appearance of links for so many years, users expect all text links to be underlined. Text links that are not underlined may be harder to identify as links, if they are identifiable at all. The primary importance of text links is not the appearance of the text, but rather their functionality in enabling users to access other Web pages. Do not change the color or appearance of links to make them appear less like links.

Check Your Links after You Publish Your Web Page

In the process of developing a Web site, Web pages may incorporate hundreds of links to other Web pages and resources. Links to Web pages on the same Web site may have been changed or moved for development reasons, and links to Web pages located on external Web sites that you do not control can change over time. If the target of the link becomes invalid, the user will encounter an error when they click the link. When you finish creating a Web site, you should verify all of the links on

your Web site before you publish the Web pages, and periodically check all the links on your Web site to ensure that they do not change over time. If you are providing links to Web pages that contain important information such as news stories, you may even have to verify the links on your Web site on a daily basis. There are few things more frustrating for a user than clicking a link that does not work.

Specifying the Wrong Path to a File

A common mistake of many Web page developers is specifying links to files that are stored on their own computers and forgetting to change the path names before transferring the files to the Web server. The result is that the Web site links that appeared to function normally when tested on the Web developer's computer fail when transferred to the Web server. The links still point to the computer, which is not available from the Web server. Always test your links after transferring the Web pages to the Web server. To expedite this task, you can use a link checker to help you. See the sub-section "Not Checking Your Links" earlier in this chapter.

Placing Borders Around Images Used as Links

Images used as links can have a border that changes color in the same manner that text links change color, depending on whether the user has clicked on the link. In many cases the border around an image is unnecessary: most image links are obvious to the user as links. Placing a border that changes color around the image may also adversely affect the aesthetic appearance of your Web page. When including image links on your Web page, specify a width of o for the `border` attribute to suppress the display of a border around the image.

Not Specifying Alternative Text

You can use images as links when creating Web pages with either HTML or XHTML. The `alt` attribute of the `<img>` tag specifies text information that will be displayed if the image is unavailable. An image may be unavailable for display if the image has moved, if the user has suppressed the display of images, or if a visually impaired user is visiting your Web page with the assistance of a Web browser that reads the content aloud. If you do not specify alternate text for an image, these users will have no idea what was meant to be displayed on your Web page when the image is missing or if they cannot see it. Always provide an alternative text value that describes the content of the image.

Consider Browser Differences

Many different types of Web browsers are in use across the Internet, as well as on many different types of operating systems and devices that can access Web pages. Although it is not possible to check your Web page on every browser available on the Internet, there are some precautions to keep in mind when developing your Web pages that will help ensure that your Web pages are compatible with, and supported by, the most popular Web browsers today.

Make Web Pages Accessible via Older Browsers

There are many Web browsers still in use across the Web that may be two or more years old. In most cases, older Web browsers do not fully support newer technologies such as XHTML, CSS, and possibly even the later versions of HTML. Your Web pages must be displayed by both new and old Web browsers in order to be accessible to the widest audience possible. You can choose among various methods to accomplish this goal, but mostly you just need to be careful when using technologies that may not be available in older Web browsers. You should set limits to this line of thinking, though, supporting Netscape 2.0 is probably more trouble than it is worth. However, it cannot hurt to test your Web page in Netscape 4.8 as a good example of how moderately old browsers can display your site.

Do Not Design for One Browser

Almost everyone who surfs the World Wide Web uses one particular Web browser. The same holds true for Web page developers, which often results in Web pages that can be viewed optimally only with their favorite Web browsers. Each Web browser displays Web pages slightly differently. When you are developing your Web pages, try to view them with as many Web browsers as possible. You may find a problem — either an aesthetic or a usability problem — that you would not have seen if you only viewed the page with your own Web browser. Keep in mind also that some Web development tools tend to design with one browser in mind. Microsoft's FrontPage, for example, has a habit of using code specific for Internet Explorer.

Do Not Indicate What Browser the Web Page Is Compatible With

In the early days of the Internet, it was not uncommon to see small buttons or icons at the bottom of Web pages with messages indicating that a Web page was fully compatible with a specific Web browser. Regardless of the Web browser you used to view and help develop your Web pages, you should not indicate that your Web pages were designed for a specific browser. Some users with Web browsers other than the ones indicated may think they are being deprived of content because of the Web browser they are using. At the very least, some users may feel you are slighting their favorite Web browser, so it may be best to avoid including this information altogether.

Do Not Use Browser-Specific Tags

In the past, Web browser manufacturers often created HTML tags that only their browsers could understand. If the HTML tag did not become popular, the other Web browser manufacturers would not include support for it in their browsers. For example, Netscape introduced the `<blink>` tag for use with the Navigator Web browser to cause text to flash on and off. Other Web browsers would not recognize

the tag. Microsoft's answer for Internet Explorer was the `<marquee>` tag, which had a similar purpose as `<blink>`, but was implemented differently. When developing Web pages, using only tags that are compliant with HTML, XHTML, and CSS specifications will ensure that your Web pages do not contain tags that only specific Web browsers recognize.

Do Not Give Instructions for Performing a Specific Task

Most Web browsers include methods that enable a user to perform tasks such as saving, or "bookmarking," a Web page. You should avoid giving specific instructions to users on how to perform certain tasks with their Web browsers. For example, you could give the instruction "Please click the Print button of your Web browser to print this Web page." Unfortunately, not all Web browsers have a Print button (at least not by default). Also, many users reconfigure their Web browsers to their own personal preferences, adding and removing buttons and features. Different browsers have different menus, buttons, and terms for certain things that

are not available in the same way in other browsers. Further, any references to specific functions in a given browser may change in later versions of the same Web browser, rendering your instructions invalid. If you want to include instructions on how to use a feature of a specific Web browser, place them in a separate pop-up window or a separate Web page, and include instructions on how to accomplish the task using the current versions of the most popular Web browsers. Adding a disclaimer that your instructions may not work if the user is not using the browser versions you have indicated is also a good idea.

Employ Debugging Resources

Many applications can make Web site creating infinitely easier. As with any project, using the right tool for the right job at the right time increases your productivity and improves the quality of your work. From validating your code and checking your links to properly formatting your code, you can save yourself and anyone else who ever looks at your code a lot of time and hassle by utilizing the debugging resources that are available to you.

Code Validation Applications

Regardless of whether you create code using HTML, XHTML, or CSS, you should always validate your code before transferring it to your Web server. This will verify that you are not posting broken code — and thus broken Web pages — to the Web. Ensuring that your code is valid will also help make your Web pages compatible with Web browsers both now and in the future. If you are creating a large number of Web pages, or if you will be maintaining the Web pages over a long period of time, you should consider investing in a dedicated code validation application. Code validation applications verify that

your HTML and XHTML code is structured properly and does not contain errors. There are also free online services with which you can validate your code, but applications that you pay money for tend to do multiple pages faster by automating the validation process. The World Wide Web Consortium (or W3C for short) hosts a validator you can use to validate your pages at http://validator.w3.org. A Real Validator is a dedicated HTML and XHTML syntax checker that you can run on your own computer. For more information, please see www.arealvalidator.com.

Link Verifiers

Some Web sites can contain hundreds if not thousands of links. Verifying that each link on your Web site functions properly can be very time-consuming if performed manually. Although one person can periodically maintain and verify the links on a few Web pages, much more than that is best maintained by an automatic link-verifying program. Link verifiers work by analyzing a Web page and checking that all the links still link to the appropriate resources. Link-verifying applications can easily validate hundreds of links in a matter of minutes. If you are maintaining a Web site that contains links to external Web sites

and Web resources, you may want to use one of these dedicated link-verifying applications. You can also find Web sites that offer free link-verifying tools, although you will likely find that the commercial applications that you pay for are faster and more automated than the free services. The W3C hosts a link checker that you can use to check the links on your page at http://validator.w3.org/checklink/. CyberSpyder Link Test is a link-verifier application that you can use with a single Web page or a large corporate Web site. For more information, see www.cyberspyder.com.

Code Beautifiers

One technique that many experienced programmers use to make their code easier to read is to keep the code properly spaced and indented. A *code beautifier* is an application that converts any HTML or XHTML code into an easy-to-read format, making your code easier to maintain and troubleshoot. You can even customize the application to reformat the code to suit your own personal preferences. You should use a code beautifier not only after you have created

the code for your Web page, but also while you are developing the code. Ideally, you should properly format your code as you create it and then use a code beautifier application to locate any inconsistencies in your formatting. Macromedia HomeSite offers a built-in code beautifier feature called CodeSweeper. For more information, see www.macromedia.com.

Syntax Highlighting

Many Web design applications make working with code easier by using a technique called *syntax highlighting*. Syntax highlighting helps differentiate between the different components of your Web page code by using different colors or different fonts. For example, an application that offers syntax highlighting may display HTML or XHTML tags in a different color from the textual content of your Web page. Other differences in color may include tags displaying in purple, numerical attributes in red, string (text) attributes in blue, and so forth. Syntax highlighting makes it easier to distinguish the HTML or XHTML tags used to create

elements and the actual content that will be displayed on the Web page. It also enables you to see the different parts of very long lines of code more easily. Together with properly formatted code (see the previous section), syntax highlighting makes your code easier to maintain and enables you to more easily spot errors such as missing closing tags. Many text editors used for programming include syntax highlighting specifically for XHTML or HTML documents. UltraEdit is a sophisticated text editor that includes syntax highlighting. For more information on UltraEdit, see www.ultraedit.com.

HTML Tag Summary

M any HTML tags have attributes that you can use to add additional information about the element or to increase the functionality of the tag. The following sections summarize the most used HTML element tags along with the most used attributes for those elements. Note that you should replace syntax in italics with whatever the italic text calls for; for example, `color=color` means that you should specify a color after the equal sign. Remember to add quotation marks on either side of the specified attribute; for example, to specify the color maroon, use `color="#800000"`.

<a>

The anchor tag is used to create a link to another Web page.

ATTRIBUTE	PURPOSE
accesskey=key_character	Create a keyboard shortcut.
href=URL	Specify the location of the Web page to link to.
name=string	Identify the anchor tag.
tabindex=number	Identify the location of the anchor tag in the tab index.
target=<window_name> (_parent | _blank | _top | _self)	Identify the frame or Web browser window in which to open the linked document.

<applet>

Embeds a Java applet.

ATTRIBUTE	PURPOSE
alt=text	The text displays when the applet is not available.
align=location	Align the applet on the Web page (absbottom | absmiddle | baseline | bottom | left | middle | right | top | texttop)
code=classname	The name of the applet.
codebase=URL	The location of the applet.
height=number	The height of the applet in pixels.
width=number	The width of the applet in pixels.

<area>

Designates an area of an image as a hotspot when creating an image map.

ATTRIBUTE	PURPOSE
shape=shape (circ [circle] | poly [polygon] | rect [rectangle])	Indicate the shape of an image map area.
cords=string	Specify the coordinates of a hotspot of an image map.
href=URL	Specify the Web page being linked to.
tabindex=number	Identify the location of the image map in the tab index.

<b>

Creates text with a bolded font.

<base>

Indicates the URL of the Web page.

ATTRIBUTE	PURPOSE
href=URL	The name of the Web page.
target=<window_name> (_parent | _blank | _top | _self)	The frame or Web browser window in which to open all links on the Web page.

\<basefont>

Specifies the font to use for the text on the Web page.

ATTRIBUTE	PURPOSE
`color=color`	Indicate the color of the default font.
`face=font_family_name`	Indicate the name of the default font.
`size=value`	Indicate the size of the font on the Web page.

\<bgsound>

Plays a sound when the Web page loads.

ATTRIBUTE	PURPOSE
`loop=number`	Indicate the number of times to play the sound.
`src=URL`	Specify the location of the sound to be played.

\<big>

Increases the size of the font.

\<blockquote>

Formats text as a quotation.

\<body>

Indicates the part of the Web page that the Web browser displays.

ATTRIBUTE	PURPOSE
`alink=color`	Specify the color of the link when the link is clicked.
`background=URL`	Specify the name of an image used as the background.
`bgcolor=color`	Specify a color for the background.
`bgproperties=fixed`	Fix the background of the Web page.
`link=color`	Specify the color of the link.
`text=color`	Specify the font and color of text on the Web page.
`vlink=color`	Specify the color of the link when the link has already been visited.

\

Inserts a new line.

ATTRIBUTE	PURPOSE
`clear=margin` (left | right | none | all)	Control the flow of text around an image.

\<caption>

Displays a caption for a table.

ATTRIBUTE	PURPOSE
`align=location` (top | bottom | right | left)	Place the caption at the top or bottom of a table.

\<center>

Centers an element.

\<cite>

Indicates that text comes from another source.

\<code>

Indicates that text is programming code.

\<colgroup>

Applies characteristics to one or more columns.

ATTRIBUTE	PURPOSE
`halign=location` (right | left)	Specify the horizontal alignment.
`span=number`	Specify the number of columns to span.
`valign=location` (bottom | top)	Specify the vertical alignment.
`width=number`	Specify the width of the column group.

\<comment>

Indicates that the following text is a comment.

continued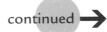

<dd>

Creates definition data for a definition list.

<dfn>

Creates a definition for a definition list.

<div>

The division tag. Used to group elements together.

ATTRIBUTE	PURPOSE
align=location (center | left | right)	Specify the alignment of the group elements.

<dl>

Creates a definition list.

ATTRIBUTE	PURPOSE
compact=compact	Reduce the space allocated to the list.

<dt>

Creates a definition term.

<em>

Emphasizes text, generally rendering it in italics.

<embed>

Places objects such as movies in a Web page.

ATTRIBUTE	PURPOSE
autostart=true_or_false	Determine whether the embedded object should start playing when the Web page is loaded.
align=location (absbottom | absmiddle | baseline | bottom | left | middle | right | top | texttop)	Align the embedded object.
controller=true_or_false	Specify whether the object's play controls are displayed.
height=number	Specify the height of the embedded object.
hidden=hidden	Prevent the object from being displayed on the Web page.
volume=number (number from 1 to 100 [50 is default])	Adjust the volume level of the embedded object.
width=number	Specify the width of the embedded object.

<font>

Specifies font characteristics.

ATTRIBUTE	PURPOSE
color=color	Set the color of the font.
face=font_family_name	Specify the font type used.
size=value	Specify the size of the font.

<form>

Creates a form that allows data to be submitted on a Web page.

ATTRIBUTE	PURPOSE
action=URL	Specify the URL to which form data should be sent.
method=action (get | post)	Determine the communication method used to submit data.
enctype=encoding	Describe the type of data being submitted.

<frame>

Creates a frame to contain a Web page.

ATTRIBUTE	PURPOSE
frameborder=*indicator* (no | yes | 1 | 0)	Specify the appearance of the frames border.
name=*string*	Specify the name of the frame.
noresize=noresize	Prevent the frame from being resized.
scrolling=*indicator* (auto | yes | no)	Determine whether scroll bars are present.
src=*URL*	Specify the name of the Web page to load in the frame.

<frameset>

Defines the structure of a Web page containing frames.

ATTRIBUTE	PURPOSE
cols=*number*	Determine the number of columns of frames in a frameset.
rows=*number*	Determine the number of rows of frames in a frameset.
frameborder= *indicator* (no | yes | 1 | 0)	Specify whether borders are placed around frames.
framespacing=*number*	Specify the space between frames.

<h1..h6>

Creates a heading. Heading tags range in value from h1 to h6.

ATTRIBUTE	PURPOSE
align=*location* (center | left | right)	Specify the alignment of the heading.

<head>

Denotes the head area of a Web page.

<hr>

Inserts a horizontal line.

ATTRIBUTE	PURPOSE
align=*location* (center | left | right)	Indicate the alignment of the horizontal line.
color=*color*	Specify the color of the horizontal line.
noshade=*noshade*	Remove the 3-D effect of the horizontal line.
size=*number*	Specify the size of the horizontal line.
width=*number*	Specify the width of the horizontal line.

<html>

Indicates that the following code is HTML.

<i>

Displays text in an italicized font.

<img>

Inserts an image into a Web page.

ATTRIBUTE	PURPOSE
align=*location* (absbottom | absmiddle | baseline | bottom | left | middle | right | top | texttop)	Determine the alignment of the image on the Web page.
alt=*text*	Specify the text to be displayed if the image is unavailable.
border=*number*	Specify the size of the border to draw around the image.
height=*number*	Specify the height of the image.
hspace=*number*	Specify the horizontal distance between the image and the surrounding elements.
src=*URL*	Specify the location of the image.
usemap=*URL*	Specify the name of the map to be used if the image is an imagemap.
vspace=*number*	Specify the vertical distance of the image from surrounding elements.
width=*number*	Specify the width of the image.

\<input>

Creates an object that allows users to input data into form.

ATTRIBUTE	PURPOSE
align=*location* (bottom | left | middle | right | top)	Determine the alignment of the object.
checked=checked	Indicate whether the object is to be checked on the form.
maxlength=*number*	Specify the maximum length of the data that may be entered.
size=*number*	Specify the size of the object on the Web page.
type=*type*	Indicate what type of form object is to be created.
tabindex=*number*	Indicate where in the tab index the form object is located.
value=*string*	Specify the default value for the object.

\<kbd>

Indicates that text is typed on the keyboard.

\<li>

Creates an item in a list.

ATTRIBUTE	PURPOSE
type	Specify the bullet type of the list item.
value	Set the count value in an ordered list.

\<link>

Defines a relationship between the Web page and another document.

ATTRIBUTE	PURPOSE
href=*URL*	Specify the location of the link.
rel=*relationship* (same | next | parent | previous | string)	Indicate that the link is a forward link.
rev=*relationship* (same | next | parent | previous | string)	Indicate that the link is a reverse link.
type=*type*	Specify the type of information being linked to.

\<listing>

Displays text in monofont, which makes it easier to display listings.

\<map>

Describes a hotspot on an image used as an imagemap.

ATTRIBUTE	PURPOSE
name=*string*	Specify the name of the imagemap.

\<marquee>

Creates text that can scroll across the screen.

ATTRIBUTE	PURPOSE
align=*location* (bottom | middle | top)	Specify the alignment of the scrolling text.
behavior=*behavior* (alternate | scroll | side)	Determine how the text should scroll.
bgcolor=*color*	Set the background color of the scrolling text.
direction=*direction* (down | left | right | up)	Specify which direction the text scrolls.
height=*number*	Specify the height of the scrolling message.
hspace=*number*	Specify the horizontal distance from other elements on the Web page.
loop=*number*	Specify the number of times a message scrolls.
scrollamount=*number*	Specify how far to scroll text each time it is moved.
scrolldelay=*number*	Specify how long to wait before scrolling the text.
vspace=*number*	Specify the vertical distance between other elements on the Web page and the scrolling text.
width=*number*	Specify the width of the marquee.

\<meta>

Provides hidden information about the Web page.

ATTRIBUTE	PURPOSE
name=*string*	Specify the name of the \<meta> tag.
content=*meta_content*	Specify the content of the \<meta> tag.
url=*URL*	Indicate the location specified in the \<meta> tag.

\<nobr>

Prevents the insertion of line breaks.

\<noframes>

Displays information to Web browsers incapable of displaying frames.

\<object>

Inserts an object, such as a multimedia player, into a Web page.

ATTRIBUTE	PURPOSE
align=*location* (absbottom | absmiddle | baseline | bottom | left | middle | right | top | texttop)	Specify the alignment of the object.
border=*number*	Determine whether a border will be placed around the object.
classid=*URL*	Specify the unique class identification number of the object.
codetype=*MIME_type*	Specify where the object can be found.
height=*number*	Specify the height of the object.
hspace=*number*	Specify the horizontal space to leave between the object and surrounding elements.
type=*MIME_type*	Specify the type of media.
vspace=*number*	Specify the vertical space to leave between the object and surrounding elements.
width=*number*	Specify the width of the object.

<ol>

Creates a list of ordered items.

ATTRIBUTE	PURPOSE
compact=compact	Reduce the amount of space the list takes on the Web page.
type=bullet_type	Specify the bullet type of the list.
value=value	Specify the starting value of the list.

<option>

Creates an item for a form list box.

ATTRIBUTE	PURPOSE
disabled=disabled	Disable a selection.
label=string	Specify the label to which the option belongs.
selected=selected	Determine whether the option is selected by default.
value=string	Specify the value for the option.

<p>

Indicates that text is in a paragraph.

ATTRIBUTE	PURPOSE
align=location (center | left | right)	Specify the alignment of the paragraph.

<param>

Specifies the properties for an object such as a multimedia player.

ATTRIBUTE	PURPOSE
name=string	Specify the name of the parameter.
value=value	Specify the value of the named parameter.

<plaintext>

Displays text in monofont.

<pre>

Displays text with no formatting.

ATTRIBUTE	PURPOSE
width=number	Specify the width of the text.

<s>

Draws a line through the center of text.

<samp>

Indicates that text is a sample, such as a sample of programming code.

<script>

Used to insert programming code, such as JavaScript, into a Web page.

<select>

Creates a formal drop-down list.

ATTRIBUTE	PURPOSE
disabled=disabled	Disable the object on the form.
multiple=multiple	Indicate whether multiple items may be selected.
name=name	Specify the name of the selection.
size=number	Specify the number of displayed items in the drop-down list.

<small>

Reduces the size of the font.

\<span\>

Group together items such as words or sentences.

\<strike\>

Uses strikethrough, which is a line through the center of text.

\<strong\>

Emphasizes text, typically by bolding it.

\<sub\>

Displays text as a subscript.

\<sup\>

Displays text as superscript.

\<table\>

Creates a table of information or items such as images.

ATTRIBUTE	PURPOSE
align=location (center | left | right)	Specify the alignment of the table on the Web page.
bgcolor=color	Set the background color of the table.
border=number	Specify the size of the border to draw around the table.
cellpadding=number	Specify the inside margins of table cells.
cellspacing=number	Specify the space between table cells.
width=number	Specify the width of the table.

\<tbody\>

Indicates the body of a table.

\<td\>

Creates a table cell.

ATTRIBUTE	PURPOSE
bgcolor=color	Specify the color of the cell.
colspan=number	Indicate a number of columns the row will span.
height=number	Specify the height of the table cell.
nowrap=nowrap	Determine whether text should wrap in the cell automatically.
rowspan=number	Specify the number of rows the table cell will span.
valign=location (bottom | top)	Specify the vertical alignment of the cell contents.
width=number	Specify the width of the cell.

\<textarea\>

Creates an area in a form where a user can enter text.

ATTRIBUTE	PURPOSE
disabled=disabled	Disable the use of the text area.
readonly=readonly	Prevent the text in the text area from being changed.

\<tfoot\>

Specifies the footer of a table.

ATTRIBUTE	PURPOSE
align=location (center | left | right)	Specify the alignment of the cell contents.
valign=location (bottom | top)	Specify the vertical alignment of the cell contents.

continued →

\<th\>

Creates headings in a table.

ATTRIBUTE	PURPOSE
bgcolor=*color*	Specify the color of the table header cell.
colspan=*number*	Indicate the number of columns the table header will span.
height=*number*	Specify the height of the table header cell.
nowrap=*nowrap*	Determine whether text should wrap in the table header cell automatically.
rowspan=*number*	Specify the number of rows the table header cell will span.
valign=*location* (bottom | top)	Specify the vertical alignment of the table header cell's contents.
width=*number*	Specify the width of the table header cells.

\<thead\>

Specifies the head of a table.

\<title\>

Specifies the title of a Web page, which will appear in the title bar of the Web browser.

\<tr\>

Creates a table row that will contain data cells.

\<tt\>

Displays text as teletype, which is typically monofont.

\<u\>

Underlines text.

Core HTML Attributes

Several attributes can be used with most HTML element tags. These core attributes further enhance or improve the functionality of existing HTML tags, as described in the following table.

ATTRIBUTE	PURPOSE
class=*name*	Indicate that the element is a member of a class. This attribute is most often used to associate elements with style sheet rules.
id=*name*	Identify different elements within a Web page. Elements that use the id attribute should have a unique value.
style=*style*	Assign style sheet rules to an element. The style sheet rules assigned by the style attribute are given preference over style sheet rules assigned using other style sheets, such as external and inline style sheets.
title=*string*	Display text assigned as a tooltip in most Web browsers. (A tooltip is the text that appears when the mouse pointer is placed over an element that includes the title attribute.)

HTML
Colors

When using HTML, XHTML, and CSS, there are many instances when you will have to specify the color of an item such as text, a border, or the background of the Web page. You can specify HTML colors using a hexadecimal number. The hexadecimal number represents a combination of red, green, and blue color values. Fortunately, you do not have to know hexadecimal notations in order to specify some of the more popular colors.

COMMON COLOR NAME	HEXADECIMAL NOTATION
Black	"#000000"
Silver	"#C0C0C0"
Gray	"#808080"
White	"#FFFFFF"
Maroon	"#800000"
Red	"#FF0000"
Purple	"#800080"
Fuchsia	"#FF00FF"
Green	"#008000"
Lime	"#00FF00"
Olive	"#808000"
Yellow	"#FFFF00"
Navy	"#000080"
Blue	"#0000FF"
Teal	"#008080"
Aqua	"#00FFFF"

Event Handlers

You can use a number of attributes with most HTML elements to enable the execution of code when a certain action takes place. For example, you can use the onload attribute to specify a section of code (called a *script*) that processes when the Web page initially loads into the Web browser. This type of action is called an *event*, and the attributes that are used to assign code to these events are called *event handlers*. Each event handler will have an attribute of the same name as the event handler.

ATTRIBUTE	PURPOSE
onblur=*script*	Occurs when the element that was previously selected becomes unselected because the insertion point has moved to another element, or the element has been selected with the mouse pointer. Typically used with form elements.
onchange=*script*	Occurs when changes have been made to an element on a form, and another element is subsequently selected.
onclick=*script*	Occurs when the mouse pointer is positioned over an element and the mouse button is pressed down.
ondblclick=*script*	Occurs when the mouse pointer is positioned over an element and the mouse button is clicked twice.
onfocus=*script*	Occurs when the mouse pointer selects, or the insertion point is moved to, an element. Typically used with form elements.
onkeydown=*script*	Occurs when an element is selected and a key on the keyboard is pressed.
onkeypress=*script*	Occurs when an element is selected and a key on the keyboard is pressed and then released.
onkeyup=*script*	Occurs when an element is selected and a key on the keyboard is released.
onload=*script*	Occurs when the Web browser initially displays a Web page. Generally used with the <body> tag.
onmousedown=*script*	Occurs when the mouse pointer is positioned over an element and the mouse button is pressed. The mouse button does not have to be released in order for the event to take place.
onmousemove=*script*	Occurs when the mouse pointer is positioned over an element and is moved.
onmouseout=*script*	Occurs when the mouse pointer is on top of an element and then moves away from the element.
onmouseover=*script*	Occurs when a mouse pointer is first positioned over an element.
onmouseup=*script*	Occurs when the mouse pointer is positioned over an element, the mouse button is pressed down, and then the mouse button is released.
onreset=*script*	Occurs when a form's Reset button is used.
onselect=*script*	Occurs when text is highlighted. Used with text fields in a form.
onsubmit=*script*	Occurs when the Submit button on a form is used.
onunload=*script*	Occurs when a user leaves a Web page. This event handler is generally used with the <body> tag.

Cascading Style Sheets Property Summary

You can use many style sheet properties with HTML and XHTML elements. Bear in mind that not all Web browsers support all style sheet properties. You should always thoroughly test any Web page that utilizes style sheets with a variety of browsers, particularly if you plan to make the Web page available on the Internet. The following table lists and describes the major CSS properties that are available.

CSS PROPERTY	PURPOSE
background	Shorthand notation enables you to combine many background properties into one. You can apply this property to many elements.
background-attachment	Determines whether a background image is fixed in place or scrolls with the Web page.
background-color	Specifies the background color of an element.
background-image	Specifies an image that can be used as the background of an element.
background-position	Specifies the position of a background image on the Web page.
background-repeat	Specifies whether a background image is repeatedly displayed adjacent to itself.
border	Shorthand notation for setting values for multiple border properties.
border-bottom	Shorthand notation for setting all of the properties that apply to bottom border of an element.
border-bottom-color	Specifies the color of the bottom border.
border-bottom-style	Specifies the type of border style to use for the bottom border.
border-bottom-width	Sets the width of the border at the bottom of the element.
border-collapse	Determines how adjacent cells should share their borders.
border-color	Specifies the color of the four borders.
border-left	Shorthand notation for setting all properties that apply to the left-hand side border of an element.
border-left-color	Specifies the color of the left-hand side border.
border-left-style	Specifies the type of border style to use for the left-hand side border.
border-left-width	Sets the width of the border on the left-hand side of the element.
border-right	Shorthand notation for setting all properties that apply to the right-hand side border of an element.
border-right-color	Specifies the color of the right-hand side border.
border-right-style	Specifies the type of border style to use for the right-hand side border.
border-right-width	Sets the width of the border on a right-hand side of the element.
border-spacing	Sets the spacing between borders of adjacent cells.
border-style	Shorthand notation to set the style of the border around the element.
border-top	Shorthand notation for setting all properties that apply to the top border.
border-top-color	Specifies the color of the top border.
border-top-style	Specifies the type of border style at the top of the element.

CSS PROPERTY	PURPOSE
border-top-width	Sets the width of the border at the top of the element.
border-width	Sets the width of the border to use around the element.
bottom	Specifies the distance from the bottom of the containing object to place the element.
caption-side	Specifies where to place the caption on a table.
clear	Specifies the placement of an element adjacent to a floated element.
clip	Specifies the area of an element that will remain visible.
color	Sets the foreground color of an element.
content	Specifies what kind of content can be placed adjacent to an element.
counter-increment	Increases the value of a counter variable.
counter-reset	Resets the value of the counter variable.
cursor	Specifies the appearance of the mouse pointer when it moves over an element.
direction	Indicates whether an item should be generated right to left or left to right.
display	Determines how and whether an element is displayed.
empty-cells	Determines whether cells with no content should be shown.
float	Specifies how an element should align with the surrounding elements.
font	Shorthand notation for setting the characteristics of a text font.
font-family	Sets the name of the font.
font-size	Specifies the size of the font.
font-style	Specifies in what style the font shall be rendered.
font-variant	Specifies whether small caps should be used.
font-weight	Specifies the weight of the font.
height	Specifies the height of an element.
left	Specifies the distance from the left-hand side of the container element to place the element.
letter-spacing	Sets the space between letters.
line-height	Specifies the height of a line.
list-style	Shorthand notation to specify the characteristics of a list.
list-style-image	Sets the image to use as a bullet in a list.
list-style-position	Specifies the position of a list item.
list-style-type	Specifies the type of bullet to use with a list.
margin	Shorthand notation for setting the properties of margins.
margin-bottom	Sets the bottom margin of an element.

continued →

CSS PROPERTY	PURPOSE
margin-left	Sets the left-hand margin of an element.
margin-right	Sets the right-hand margin of an element.
margin-top	Sets the top margin of an element.
max-height	Specifies the maximum height of an element.
max-width	Specifies the maximum width of an element.
min-height	Specifies the minimum height of an element.
min-width	Specifies the minimum width of an element.
orphans	Specifies the number of lines at the bottom of paged media.
outline-color	Specifies the color of an outline.
outline	Shorthand notation for specifying the properties of an element's outline.
outline-style	Specifies the style of an outline.
outline-width	Specifies the width of an outline.
overflow	Specifies what happens to content that does not fit within the element.
padding	Shorthand notation for the padding properties of an element.
padding-bottom	Specifies the amount of padding area at the bottom of an element.
padding-left	Specifies the amount of padding area at the left-hand side of an element.
padding-right	Specifies the amount of padding area at the right-hand side of an element.
padding-top	Specifies the amount of padding area at the top of an element.
page-break-after	Specifies a page break after an element in paged media.

CSS PROPERTY	PURPOSE
page-break-before	Specifies a page break before an element in paged media.
page-break-inside	Specifies a page break inside an element in paged media.
position	Specifies how an element should be positioned in relation to the surrounding elements.
quotes	Specifies how quotation marks should be rendered.
right	Specifies the distance from the right-hand side of the container element to place the element.
table-layout	Determines how some tables are displayed.
text-align	Sets the alignment of text in an element.
text-declaration	Specifies the declaration to apply to the text.
text-indent	Specifies how far to indent text.
text-transform	Sets the case of the text.
top	Specifies the distance from the top of an element to its container element.
vertical-align	Specifies the vertical alignment of an element.
visibility	Determines whether an element will be hidden.
white-space	Specifies how items such as spaces and new lines are handled inside an element.
width	Specifies the width of an element.
word-spacing	Specifies the spacing between words.
z-index	Specifies the order of the element along the z-axis.

INDEX

A

`<a>` tag, 282
`<abbr>` tag, 45
abbreviations, 45
`<acronym>` tag, 45
acronyms, 45
`<address>` tag, 44–45
aligning text, 16–17, 114–115
aligning Web page elements, 208–209
anchors, 48–49, 50–51, 282
animation, common problems, 275
`<applet>` tag, 282
`<area>` tag, 282
attributes, 3, 269, 291. *See also* tags

B

`<b>` tag, 282
background, 106–107, 206–207, 222–223, 270
banner. *See* marquee
`<base>` tag, 282
`<basefont>` tag, 283
`<bgsound>` tag, 283
`<big>` tag, 283. *See also* `<font>` tag; `<small>` tag
blank lines, 16–17
blank spaces, 112–113
block quotations, formatting, 40–41, 283
`<blockquote>` tag, 283
body, specifying, 283
`<body>` tag, 283
bold text, 34–35, 282, 284, 289
borders
  around image links, 277
  frames, 192–193
  images, 71
  outlines, 136–137
  tables, 144–145
  text, 108–109
`<br>` tag, 283
breaks, line, 283, 287
breaks, page, 94–95
browsers. *See* Web browsers
bulleted lists, 154–155
bumping heads, 19

C

caching images, 74–75
`<caption>` tag, 283
case sensitivity, common problems, 268
cells, 148–151, 289
`<center>` tag, 283
centering Web page elements, 204–205, 283
check boxes, 172–173
citations, 283
`<cite>` tag, 283
code beautifiers, 281
`<code>` tag, 283
code text, 44–45, 283, 288
code validation tools, 280
`<colgroup>` tag, 283
color
  common problems, 272
  fonts, 46–47, 106–107
  hexadecimal values for, 47, 107
  links, 62–63, 96–97
  summary of, 292
  system, 140–141
  Web page background, 106–107
columns, 148–149, 188–189, 283
comments
  `<!-...->` (less than...) indicator, 256
  — (hyphens), in XML comments, 256
  `<...>` (less than...) indicator, 20–21
  /*...*/ (slash asterisk...) indicator, 92–93
  adding to code, 20–21, 283
  `<comment>` tag, 283
  common problems, 271
  style sheets, 92–93
common problems. *See also* debugging
  CSS, 270–271
  design process, 272–273
  HTML, 266–267
  images, 274–275
  linking, 276–277
  Web browsers, 278–279
  XHTML, 268–269
components. *See* elements
connection speed, common problems, 267
contrast, common problems, 274
CSS (Cascading Style Sheets), 6–7, 260–261, 270–271, 294–297. *See also* style sheets

D

"date-modified" messages, 273

`<dd>` tag, 284

debugging, resources for, 280–281. *See also* common problems

declaration blocks, 6

declarations

  XHTML, 214–215

  XML, 252–253

definition lists, 160–161, 284

descendent selectors, 91

design process, common problems, 272–273

`<dfn>` tag, 284

directories *versus* folders, 31. *See also* folders

`<div>` tag, 284

`<dl>` tag, 284

drop caps, 116–117

drop-down boxes, 168–169

drop-down lists, 288

`<dt>` tag, 284

DTDs (Document Type Definitions), 262–265, 268

dynamic Web content, 246–247

E

elements of Web pages. *See also specific elements*

  block level, 15

  definition, 2

  floating, 130–131

  height and width, 122–123

  hiding, 132–133

  margins, 128–129

  overflow, 138–139

  overlapping, 126–127

  padding, 128–129

  positioning, 120–121, 124–125

  showing, 132–133

  white space, 128–129

`<em>` tag, 44, 284

e-mail, 58–59, 184–185

`<embed>` tag, 284

embedding

  objects in Web pages, 284, 287

  programming code in Web pages, 288

emphasizing text. *See* bold; `<em>` tag; italics; `<strong>` tag

encoding declarations, 252–253

event handlers, 244–245, 293

external style sheets, 6

F

file extensions, 11, 22, 29

files

  links to, 60–61

  organizing, 30–31

  uploading to Web sites, 176–177

Firefox, 8

Flash video, 230–231

floating elements, 130–131

floating frames, 202–203

folders, 30–31. *See also* directories

`<font>` tag, 284. *See also* `<big>` tag; `<small>` tag

fonts. *See also* text

  base, specifying, 283

  bold

    `<b>` tag, 34–35, 282

    `<em>` tag, 35, 44, 284

    `<strong>` tag, 35, 289

  characteristics, specifying, 284

  color, 46–47, 106–107

  emphasis. *See* bold; italics

  italic, 285

  names, 103

  size, common problems, 271

  size adjustment

    `<big>` tag, 283

    `<font>` tag, 284

    `<small>` tag, 288

    specifying, 104–105

  strikethrough, 289

  system, 140–141

  typeface, 46–47

`for` loops, 242–243

`<form>` tag, 284

forms

  check boxes, 172–173

  creating, 162–163, 284

  disabling elements, 180–181

  drop-down boxes, 168–169

  grouping elements, 182–183

  hiding data, 170–171

  locking elements, 180–181

  password protection, 171

  radio buttons, 172–173

  Reset buttons, 174–175

  sending data via e-mail, 184–185

  Submit buttons, 164–165, 174–175

  tab order, 178–179

INDEX

text areas, 164–167, 289
text boxes, 164–165
`<frame>` tag, 285
frame-based Web pages
  borders, 192–193
  columns of frames, 188–189
  creating, 186–187
  non-frame-enabled browsers, 200–201
  rows of frames, 188–189
  scroll bars, 190–191
  sizing frames, 194–195
frames
  alternate displays, 287
  creating, 285
  defining Web page structure, 285
  floating, 202–203
  hidden, 198–199
  linking to, 196–197
  preloading images, 198–199
  structure, defining, 285
`<frameset>` tag, 285
FTP (File Transfer Protocol), 28–29

G

GIF (Graphics Interchange Format), 22–23
.gif file extension, 22
global style sheets, 76–77
graphics. *See* images
grouping elements, 284, 289

H

`<h1...h6>` tags, 285
head area, specifying, 285
`<head>` tag, 285
headings
  tables, 290
  Web page, 18–19, 285
hexadecimal color values, 47, 107
hidden frames, 198–199
hiding elements, 132–133
horizontal lines, creating, 285
hotspots, 72–73, 282
`<hr>` tag, 285
HTML (Hypertext Markup Language)
  attributes. *See* attributes
  code, identifying, 285

common problems, 266–267
definition, 2
elements, 2
future of, 3
introduction, 2–3
obsolete tags, 267
standards, 2
tags. *See* tags
versus XHTML, 4
.html file extension, 29
`<html>` tag, 285
HTML tags. *See* tags
hypertext links, 48–49

I

`<i>` tag, 285
if statements, 240–241
images
  adding to Web pages, 22–23, 64–65
  `<area>` tag, 282
  borders, 71
  caching, 74–75
  common formats, 22–23
  common problems, 274–275
  displaying multiple versions of, 66–67
  flowing text around, 64–65
  hotspots, 72–73, 282, 286
  `<img>` tag, 285
  links from, 70–71
  `<map>` tag, 286
  mapping, 72–73, 282, 286
  preloading, 74–75, 198–199
  resizing, 66–67
  size, common problems, 275
  text alternatives to, 68–69
  text background, 118–119
  thumbnails, 70–71
  tiling, common problems, 274
  Web pages
    background, 206–207
    as spacers, 212–213
`<img>` tag, 285
indenting text, 16–17
indents, and Web browsers, 112–113
indexing Web pages, 287
inheritance, style sheets, 89
inline style sheets. *See* style sheets, local
`<input>` tag, 286

inserting. *See* embedding
internal style sheets, 6, 80–81
Internet Explorer, 8
italics
  applying, 34–35, 110–111
  <em> tag, 35, 44, 284
  <i> tag, 35, 285
  <strong> tag, 35, 289
  style sheets, 110–111

J

Java applets, embedding, 282
JavaScript, 236–245
.jpeg file extension, 22
JPEG (Joint Photographic Experts Group) format, 22–23
.jpg file extension, 22

K

<kbd> tag, 286
keyboard text, 45, 286

L

<li> tag, 286
line breaks, 167, 283, 287
<link> tag, 286
links
  <a> tag, 282
  anchors, 48–49, 50–51
  <area> tag, 282
  color, 96–97
  colors, 62–63
  common problems, 269, 276–277
  creating, 48–49, 50–51
  to e-mail, 58–59
  to files, 60–61
  to frames, 196–197
  hypertext, 48–49
  image hotspots, 282
  from images, 70–71, 282, 286
  <link> tag, 286
  mailto:, 58–59
  <map> tag, 286
  named anchors, 50
  style sheets, 96–97
  tab order, 54–55
  target, 52–53

  verification tools, 280
  visited and unvisited, 63, 96–97
list boxes, creating items for, 288
<listing> tag, 286
lists
  bulleted, 154–155
  definition, 160–161, 284
  nesting, 158–159
  numeric, 156–157, 288
  ordered, 156–157, 288
  unordered, 154–155
local style sheets. *See* style sheets, local

M

mailto: action, 185
mailto: links, 58–59
<map> tag, 286
mapping images, 72–73, 282, 286
margins, elements, 128–129
marquee, 232–233, 287
<marquee> tag, 287
media players
  adding, 224–225
  downloading, 228–229
  QuickTime, 226–227
  RealPlayer, 234–235
<meta> tag, 287
monospace fonts, 38–39, 44–45, 286
mouse pointer, changing, 134–135

N

named anchors, 50
 nonbreaking space, 16–17
nesting
  lists, 158–159
  tables, 152–153
  tags, 89, 268
Netscape Navigator, 8
<nobr> tag, 287
<noframes> tag, 287
numeric lists, 156–157, 286, 288

O

object properties, specifying, 288
<object> tag, 287
<ol> tag, 288
<option> tag, 288

INDEX

ordered lists. *See* numeric lists
outlines (borders), 136–137. *See also* borders
outlines (hierarchical), 158–159
overflow, elements, 138–139
overlapping elements, 126–127

P

`<p>` tag, 288
padding elements, 128–129
pages. *See* Web pages
paragraphs, 14–15, 16–17, 288
`<param>` tag, 288
password protection in forms, 171
pictures. *See* images
`<plaintext>` tag, 288
PNG (Portable Network Graphics) format, 22–23
pop-up messages, 248–249
pop-up windows, 250–251
pop-ups, common problems, 272
positioning elements, 120–121, 124–125
`<pre>` tag, 288
preformatted text, 38–39, 288
preloading images, 74–75, 198–199
printing pages, common problems, 274
properties, 6, 294–297
pseudo elements, 116–117
pseudo-class selectors, 97
publicizing Web pages, 218–219
publishing Web pages, 26–29

Q

QuickTime video, 226–227
quoted text, 40–41, 283

R

radio buttons, 172–173
RealPlayer, 234–235
RealVideo video, 234–235
reference names, 82–83
Reset buttons, 174–175
resolution, common problems, 272
root elements, 254–255
rows, 148–149, 290
rules (guidelines), for style sheets. *See* style sheets, rules
rules (lines). *See* horizontal lines

S

`<s>` tag, 288
`<samp>` tag, 288
saving Web pages, 10–11, 32–33
`<script>` tag, 288
scroll bars, frames, 190–191
search engines, cataloging Web pages, 218–219
search terms for Web pages, 287
`<select>` tag, 288
selectors, 6, 78–79
shorthand notation, common problems, 271
showing elements, 132–133
sidebars, 106–107
`<small>` tag, 288. *See also* `<big>` tag; `<font>` tag
sound files, 220–221
sounds, 222–223, 283
source code, viewing, 24–25
spaces, 16–17, 112–113
`<span>` tag, 289
spelling errors, 267
standards, 2, 4, 8
streaming video, 234–235
Strict Declaration, 214–215
`<strike>` tag, 289
`<strong>` tag, 289
style sheets. *See also* CSS (Cascading Style Sheets)
    applying to
        fonts, 100–101
        links, 96–97
        multiple elements, 90–91
        similar elements, 84–85
        single elements, 82–83
        text, 110–111
        Web page sections, 88–89
        XML documents, 260–261
    comments, 92–93
    definition, 76–77
    global, 76–77
    inheritance, 89
    internal, 80–81
    local
        common problems, 270
        definition, 6
        styling similar elements, 84–85
        using, 80–81
    pseudo elements, 116–117
    reference names, 82–83

rules
   classes, 84–85
   creating, 78–79
   descendent selectors, 91
   for multiple elements, 90–91
   for single elements, 82–83
   styling similar elements, 84–85
  selectors, 78–79
  user selectable, 98–99
`<style>` tag, 80–81
`<sub>` tag, 289
subfolders, 31
Submit buttons, 164–165, 174–175
subscripts, 42–43, 289
`<sup>` tag, 289
superscripts, 42–43
syntax highlighting, 281

T

tab order
  forms, 178–179
  links, 54–55
`<table>` tag, 289
tables
  body, specifying, 289
  borders, 144–145
  `<caption>` tag, 283
  captions, specifying, 283
  cells, 148–151, 289
  `<colgroup>` tag, 283
  columns, 148–149, 283
  combining, 152–153
  creating, 142–143, 289
  footers, creating, 289
  headers, specifying, 290
  headings, creating, 290
  height and width, 146–147
  nesting, 152–153
  rows, 148–149, 290
  `<table>` tag, 289
  `<tbody>` tag, 289
  `<td>` tag, 289
  `<tfoot>` tag, 289
  `<th>` tag, 290
  `<thead>` tag, 290
  `<tr>` tag, 290
  Web page layout, 210–211

tags. *See also* attributes; *specific tags*
  closing, 4
  definition, 3
  nesting, 89, 268
  summary of, 282–290
target links, 52–53
`<tbody>` tag, 289
`<td>` tag, 289
text. *See also* fonts
  aligning, 16–17, 114–115
  alternatives to images, 68–69
  background images, 118–119
  borders, 108–109
  drop caps, 116–117
  emphasizing. *See* bold; `<em>` tag; italics; `<strong>` tag
  first letter of sentence, 116–117
  first word of paragraph, 116–117
  flowing around images, 64–65
  formatting with headings, 19
  indenting, 16–17
  italics, 34–35
  keyboard font, 286
  monofont, 38–39, 286, 288
  paragraph format, 288
  preformatted, 38–39, 288
  programming code, 283, 288
  strikethrough, 288
  subscript, 289
  superscript, 289
  teletype format, 290
  title case, 101
  underlining, 290
text areas, forms, 164–167
text boxes, 164–165
`<textarea>` tag, 289
`<tfoot>` tag, 289
`<th>` tag, 290
`<thead>` tag, 290
thumbnail images, 70–71
tiling images, common problems, 274
title case, 101
`<title>` tag, 290
titles, Web pages, 266, 290
tools of the trade
  1st Page 2000, 9
  code beautifiers, 281
  code validators, 280
  HomeSite, 9

INDEX

HTML editors, 9
link verifiers, 280
summary of, 9
syntax highlighting, 281
text editors, 9
TopStyle, 9
UltraEdit, 9
WYSIWYG editors, 9
`<tr>` tag, 290
Transitional Declaration, 214–215
troubleshooting. *See* common problems; debugging
`<tt>` tag, 290
typefaces, selecting, 102–103

U

`<u>` tag, 290
`<ul>` tag, 154–155
"under construction" messages, 273
unformatted text. *See* preformatted text
unordered lists, 154–155
uploading
  files to Web sites, 176–177
  Web pages. *See* publishing Web pages
URLs
  common problems, 277
  specifying, 282
user input
  check boxes, 172–173
  drop-down boxes, 168–169
  drop-down lists, 288
  `<input>` tag, 286
  radio buttons, 172–173
  text areas, 164–167, 289

V

verifying XML documents, 256–257, 259, 265
version declarations, 252–253
video
  Flash, 230–231
  QuickTime, 226–227
  RealVideo, 234–235
  streaming, 234–235

W

W3C (World WideWebConsortium), 2
Web browsers
  blank spaces, 112–113
  common problems, 278–279
  compatibility, 8
  displaying Web pages, 12–13
  enhancements, 8
  file extensions, 29
  Firefox, 8
  indents, 112–113
  Internet Explorer, 8
  introduction, 8
  Netscape Navigator, 8
  non-frame-enabled, 200–201
  standards, 8
  versions, 8
  white space, 112–113
Web pages
  background, color and images, 106–107, 206–207, 270
  background, sounds, 222–223
  body, specifying, 283
  cataloging, 218–219, 266

common problems, 269
creating, 10–11
customizing appearance. *See* CSS (Cascading Style Sheets)
displaying in browsers, 12–13
dynamic content, 246–247
elements
 aligning, 208–209
 centering, 204–205
 multiple on same line, 209
file extensions, 11
frame structure, defining, 285
head area, specifying, 285
images
 background, 206–207
 inserting, 285
 as spacers, 212–213
indexing, 287
JavaScript, 240–241
 basics, 238–239
 event handlers, 244–245
 if statements, 240–241
 inserting, 236–237
 for loops, 242–243
layout, with tables, 210–211
marquee text, 232–233, 287
media players
 adding, 224–225
 downloading, 228–229
 QuickTime, 226–227
 RealPlayer, 234–235
objects, inserting, 287

opening, 32–33
playing sounds while loading, 283
pop-up messages, 248–249
pop-up windows, 250–251
pop-ups, common problems, 272
presenting to search engines, 218–219
programming code, inserting, 288
publicizing, 218–219
saving, 10–11, 32–33
search terms, 287
sound files, 220–221
titles, common problems, 266
titles, specifying, 290
URLs, specifying, 282
video
 Flash, 230–231
 QuickTime, 226–227
 RealVideo, 234–235
 streaming, 234–235
viewing on the Web. *See* publishing Web pages
welcome messages, 220–221
XHTML compliance, 214–215
welcome messages, 220–221
white space, 112–113, 128–129

X

XHTML (Extensible Hypertext Markup Language), 4–5, 214–217, 268–269
XML (eXtensible Markup Language), 4, 252–253
XML documents, 254–260, 262–265

There's a Visual™ book for every learning level . . .

Simplified®

The place to start if you're new to computers. Full color.

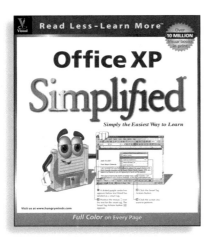

Also available:

- Windows XP Simplified, 2nd Edition
- Computers Simplified
- Microsoft Office 2000 Simplified
- Windows 98 Simplified
- Microsoft Word 2000 Simplified
- Excel 2002 Simplified
- Word 2002 Simplified
- PC Upgrade and Repair Simplified, 2nd Edition
- Creating Web Pages with HTML Simplified, 2nd Edition

Visual
An Imprint of ⊕WILEY
Now you know.

Teach Yourself VISUALLY™

Get beginning to intermediate level training in a variety of topics. Full color.

Also available:

- Teach Yourself VISUALLY Mac OS X v.10.3 Panther
- Teach Yourself VISUALLY Digital Photography, 2nd Edition
- Teach Yourself VISUALLY Office 2003
- Teach Yourself VISUALLY Photoshop Elements 3
- Teach Yourself VISUALLY Photoshop CS
- Teach Yourself VISUALLY Windows XP Special Media Edition
- Teach Yourself VISUALLY Weight Training
- Teach Yourself VISUALLY Guitar

Master VISUALLY®

Step up to intermediate to advanced technical knowledge. Two-color.

Also available:

- Master VISUALLY Windows XP
- Master VISUALLY Office 2003
- Master VISUALLY Office XP
- Master VISUALLY eBay Business Kit
- Master VISUALLY iPod and iTunes
- Master VISUALLY Project 2003
- Master VISUALLY Windows Mobile 2003
- Master VISUALLY Dreamweaver MX and Flash MX
- Master VISUALLY Windows 2000 Server
- Master VISUALLY Web Design